Re:ZERO -Starting Life in Another World-

SUBARU NATSUKI'S ELEGANT DOMESTIC LIFESTYLE

Tappei Nagatsuki

Illustration: Shinichirou Otsuka

Re:ZERO -Starting Life in Another World- Chapter 2: A Week at the Mansion ①
Short Story Extra

Subaru Natsuki's Elegant Domestic Lifestyle

1

"—Barusu, get up. It's morning."

He awakened to a cold voice and the sound of curtains being opened.

Dragged from dreamland to reality, Subaru Natsuki groaned and stirred. It was times like these that he hated being a quick riser.

As Subaru sat up in bed, the same voice tossed further invective his way.

"Useless as it is, it's a blessing that you need little time to wake up."

Before Subaru's still-sleepy eyes stood a pretty girl in a maid uniform. She had short pink hair and clear light-red eyes. Her lovely facial features were frozen in an expressionless look. Her name was Ram, and she was one of the two maids taking care of Subaru at the mansion.

"Come now, stop daydreaming and get dressed already. If you cause me too much trouble, I shall bear the responsibility of reporting it to Master Roswaal."

"Geez, not even a 'good morning' or anything... Ahhh."

Prodded by his senpai's stern words, Subaru restrained his yawn and somehow managed to crawl out of bed. When Subaru got to his feet, Ram tossed his change of clothes onto the bed beside him and headed toward the door.

"Change, then meet me as soon as possible. Do not do anything foolish like fall asleep again, yes?"

"What a thing to say to a passionately diligent worker like me. I'll be there, Sister."

"...Make it quick."

Subaru watched as Ram gave her parting words and left the room.

Tapering his lips at Ram's stiff demeanor, he stripped off the tracksuit he wore as pajamas and, down to his underwear, reached for the change of clothes.

It was his fourth day on the job as a servant at the mansion, Roswaal Manor. His body wasn't much accustomed to the particulars of the job, or to working for a living in general. His persistent weariness was proof of that.

He passed his hands through the sleeves of his clothes and did up the fairly numerous adornments. Subaru carefully put the last piece atop his head before walking into the corridor. The entry hall of the mansion was the customary rendezvous point. He wound his way toward it, stretching his back as he took in the cold morning air.

When he emerged from the corridor and arrived at the foyer, Ram stepped forward to greet him.

"So you came, Baru..."

But, when she looked at him, her expression stiffened, and she stopped mid-sentence. Subaru cocked his head a bit, puzzling over what warranted that reaction.

He wondered if, in his drowsiness, he'd somehow dressed oddly.

He heard another girl approaching behind him, opposite Ram.

"Subaru, is it? Good morning. Today's work is..."

He turned toward her. Rem was the younger of the twins and looked identical to her sister aside from her blue hair and eyes. Rem saw Subaru and froze just like her older sister had.

Though Rem's demeanor was gentler, she was stricter about work than Ram. Subaru looked down at his clothes, doing an impromptu fashion check to see if anything was off. There was nothing wrong with the white-over-black chic per se.

His long skirt extended well past his knees, and his black sleeves had a graceful flare. There was nothing off about the curvature of the apron, either. The trademark ribbon on the back was properly tied. He reached up to his head, wondering if the headpiece was crooked, when it finally struck him what was wrong.

"What the hell am I doing in a full-on maid outfit—?!!"

"Pfft—!"

Ram and Rem giggled as Subaru's wail shattered the morning calm.

2

After laughing themselves silly, Ram and Rem scolded Subaru repeatedly for his sluggishness. "Even half-asleep, one would think you'd have noticed in the middle of changing."

"To dress up and come all this way... I think this must be a hobby of yours."

Listening to their chiding, Maid Subaru crossed his arms as a vein bulged on his forehead.

"Is that all you have to say...?"

Ram replied, "I suppose not. In addition, it is exactly as I suspected. Frederica's clothes are a perfect fit for you."

Rem added, "As expected, Sister, I am astounded at the sharpness of your insight."

Subaru countered, "That's not the point!! It's not about whether the clothes fit right or not...! This is a social problem! Isn't this the senior maids bullying the maid under them?!"

The twins whispered to each other.

"I fear that Barusu already considers himself a maid."

"So he really does enjoy dressing like that...?"

Seeing no rational discussion that would come of this, Subaru threw in the towel, heading back to his room in the east wing to change.

Ram called after him, "Now, Barusu. Where do you think you're going? You have already dressed."

Subaru replied, "I thought I'd go cry in my room instead of where everybody can see me."

Ram countered, "We cannot have that. We have already lost precious time this morning. It would be very, very bad to squander any more."

Subaru countered. "Didn't the two of you waste a bunch of time laughing at me?"

Both feigned innocence. Their reaction drew a deep sigh out of Subaru. "Anyway, I'm changing clothes. I can still get through this only humiliating myself in front of you two. If Emilia-tan saw me like this, I'd never be able to live it down."

Even though she was the root of all his ills, Ram ruthlessly twisted the knife.

"He says that even though his first time in a skirt must be a sensation beyond compare—"

"Yeah, yeah, I'm a stupid screwup who might make a habit of this...!"

Subaru hastened for the stairs to escape to his room. He needed to rectify the situation as quickly as possible, imploring, "Got it? This is a secret—s-e-c-r-e-t. I'm begging you, don't even hint at it, please."

Ram replied, "It is just like Subaru to lose heart halfway through his request."

"I've got no time to argue against that venom right now. So, please, keep it secret."

A voice above him inquired:

"Keep what secret?"

Annoyed, Subaru glanced up and snapped:

"Listen when people speak, sheesh. I'm talking about the fact I'm walkin' around in the maid outfit I put on when I was half-asl..."

Midway through, this throat seized up as his gaze met those pure, violet eyes.

Subaru let out an "Eek!" A silver-haired girl was looking down at them from the great stairway above the entry hall. It was Emilia, a girl welcomed warmly by the lord of the manor and the person for whom Subaru reserved his fondest thoughts.

Emilia stroked her long, silver hair, tilting her head slightly as she looked at Subaru, who was frozen stiff.

"Err...ah, I'm sorry, I don't really know what I should say at a time like this."

Subaru replied dryly, "I think you can go ahead and laugh."

"I'm sorry. It's not really funny enough to laugh at."

A man could only endure being trampled so much. The situation made him wonder if God was indeed dead. Here she was, the girl who consumed his thoughts, looking at him decked out in a maid's uniform that didn't suit him at all, and it wasn't even funny? He wanted to die.

Behind him, the maid sisters clasped hands and quietly appraised Subaru's tragic scene.

"Sister, Sister. Could this be what they call a public execution?"

"Rem, Rem. I think this is a circumstance where one dies from completely losing the respect of others."

Subaru was too bowled over to rebut either of them.

In all likelihood, nothing Subaru could say that moment could alter her perception. If he moved, he'd die. If he spoke, he'd die. All he could do was minimize the damage to something less than fatal. Deep down, he wanted to do a little better than avoid permanent harm—to not have the memory haunt him forever.

Emilia spoke hesitantly, carefully choosing her words for Subaru's benefit.

"Subaru, I'm not really sure what to say here, but..."

In any other situation, he'd be overjoyed at her display of concern, but given the circumstances, it was cold comfort.

Watching Subaru's face go blank, Emilia's resolve seemed to harden. "I understand the desire to wear a cute outfit, but I don't think it's a good fit for you, Subaru!"

"...Yeah?"

"Ah, don't you think it's a little unfair? I'm just a little envious. I mean, if it was an outfit like Ram or Rem's it'd be embarrassing, but even I could wear something Frederica's size and not be embarrassed..."

As Emilia ventured into rapid-fire excuses, she veered further and further away from the core of the issue.

"So your only reaction to me wearing this is a low fashion score? You're not gonna call me a pervert or anything?"

It wasn't that he needed to drag things back on track, but what he was hearing was too far outside his expectations.

Emilia replied, "—? Isn't a pervert someone shady? Subaru, are you dangerous?"

"Not one bit! There's no safer man in this age than I! Oh, I get it! Emilia-tan likes the usual me more than how I am right now! Okay then, I'll go get changed!"

Subaru abruptly broke off the conversation before Emilia could object. He felt the irritated glares of the twins stabbing into his back, but that he could ignore.

"Emilia-tan's cute, head-in-the-clouds stuff helped, but I'm not out of the woods yet! Gotta get back to my room before Roswaal or, even worse, Beatrice sees me...!"

Just as he was about to make a break for it back to his room, though, there was a new arrival in the entry hall: a man dressed in an eccentric outfit wearing clown makeup. There was simply no mistaking Roswaal, lord of the manor. This was Subaru's first time seeing him earlier than at the breakfast table.

"Myyy, what is everyone doing gaaathered here?"

"Do you have some kinda grudge against me?! Today of all days, I bump into not just Emilia-tan but Rozchi, too...?!"

"As it so haaappens, I came here on a whim. I awoke early this morning, so I would have regretted not showing my face...and as a result, I am treated to quite an amuuusing scene."

As Roswaal walked over, he fixed Subaru with a buoyant, malevolent smile. Subaru unconsciously pushed down the hem of his skirt and retreated from his host's indecent gaze.

Roswaal commented, "It seems that I am interuuupting. This is the first time you have worn women's clothing, yes?"

"Actually for a bunch of reasons, back at my high school entrance ceremony, I... Wait, don't make me relive that stain on my past! Shit! I'll never become a bride now! Emilia-tan, lend me a hand here!"

"Eh? Subaru, you're a boy, so you wouldn't be a bride to begin with, would you?"

Subaru was already near tears when Emilia innocently smashed him to pieces, making him break down entirely.

He could only consider it an unmitigated disaster. Unwittingly exposed in drag, of course he'd get grief for it.

Ruefully, he bemoaned, "If I was gonna be seen in this thing, I should've just run with it and put on the makeup and underwear, too, just to see...!"

Emilia forced a strained smile at Subaru's half-sincere regret at how the circumstances had unfolded.

"That's your problem? Subaru, you really are an odd one."

Her reaction bringing him back to himself, Subaru folded his arms in what was now complete seriousness.

"So, four out of six people in the mansion! That's sixty-six percent that's already seen me, so the manly view is that it's not that bad! No, I should laugh that it wasn't a hundred percent!"

"It may be a manly view, but the outfit isn't manly at all..." Emilia countered.

A door to the entry hall opened, and a blond girl poked her face in, with a little cat parting the long, blond rolls of her hair.

"What are the lot of you doing, I wonder? You are all so very boisterous this morning."

"It's not like anyone called the two of you! Don't get full of yourselves!!"

"Wha—?! What is with that impertinence?! It is not as if I would show my face even if you did summon...me... What are you doing in those clothes, I wonder?! That is debased!"

"Shut up, drill loli! You've got no right to criticize what I'm wearing! Maybe this is a bit of a stretch, but your beloved Puckie runs around butt naked all the time, doesn't he?!"

Puck chimed in, "That's a rude thing to say. I'm wearing proper fur. Tsk, tsk."

"Puckie, don't! Is perversion contagious, I wonder?! We must escape!"

For some reason, the voices of all those assembled in the hall were boisterous that morning.

It goes without saying that breakfast was rather late that day.

3

With the day's work done, Subaru, now back in his bedroom and wearing his tracksuit, sighed and lamented, "For crying out loud... A whole helluva lot went down today. Was it cursed?"

In the end, he'd stubbornly plowed through his chores dressed as a maid. Though vaguely nursing a sense that he'd lost something precious as a person, he nevertheless felt he'd triumphed over an intangible obstacle.

Surely this was self-satisfaction. It surprised him how that trait of his was unchanged even after swapping worlds.

"I put too much energy into something ridiculous, huh? I should kinda seriously reflect on that."

He didn't want to be hated for going too far—in particular, by a certain lovely, silver-haired girl.

"Gotta say, I was surprised how tolerant Emilia-tan was about the whole maid outfit thing. Wait... Maybe she doesn't think I look the part in the usual butler uniform...? That kinda gets me down."

Subaru thought hard and pictured himself in the butler outfit, a look he'd had a fair bit of confidence about before.

"Then I wonder if I should play the part of the graceful servant to blow the whole maid outfit image away. Right, if the intimacy score's high enough, maybe I should ask her for a date finally?"

With work done, perhaps it was time to ask Emilia out once she freshened up after studying...

They'd go to the flower gardens of the village nearby where children ran around, playing with little animals. It'd be lots and lots of fun.

Subaru pictured fun scenes of the coming day in his head as he brought the current one to a close, knowing nothing about the days ahead or how the promised date, and the world itself, would cycle anew.

<END>

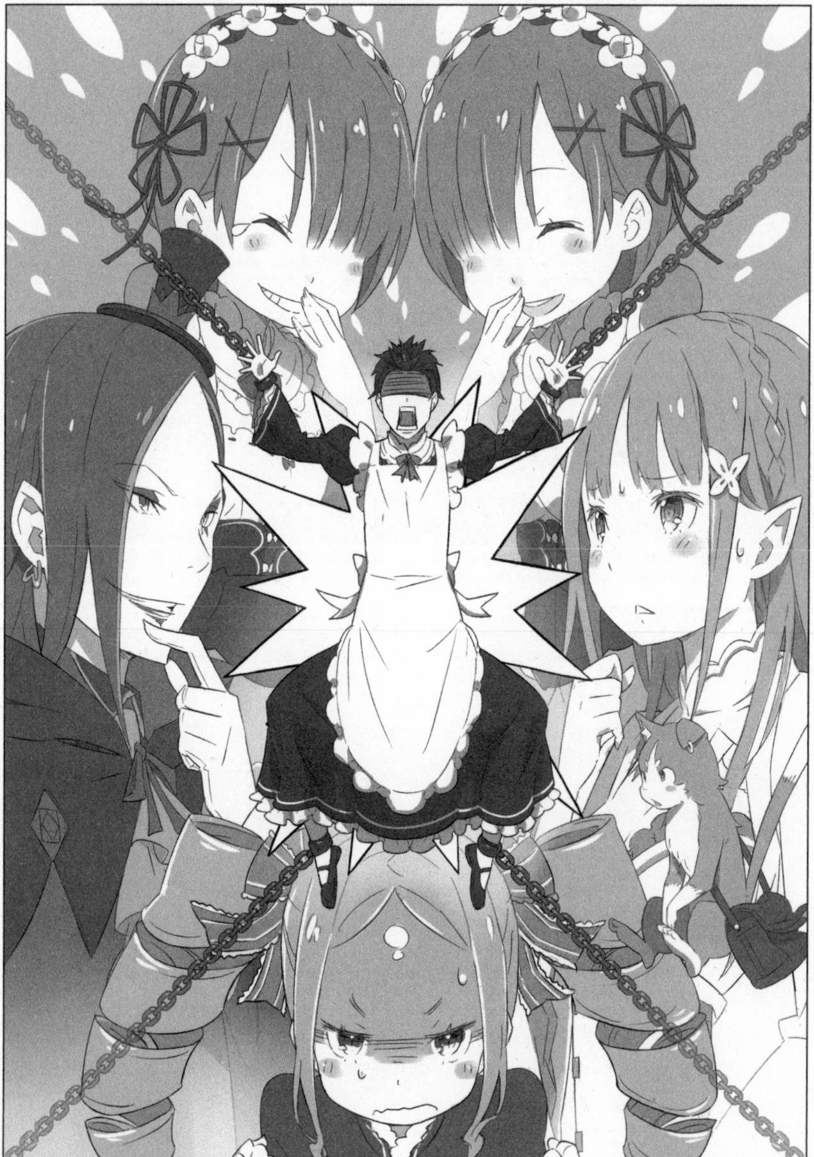

RE:ZERO -STARTING LIFE IN ANOTHER WORLD- ①
Chapter 2: A Week at the Mansion

Art: **Makoto Fugetsu**
Original Story: **Tappei Nagatsuki**
Character Design: **Shinichirou Otsuka**

Translation: ZephyrRZ
Lettering: Bianca Pistillo

RE:ZERO KARA HAJIMERU ISEKAI SEIKATSU DAINISHO YASHIKI NO ISSHUKAN-HEN Vol. 1
© Tappei Nagatsuki 2014
Licensed by KADOKAWA CORPORATION
© 2015 Makoto Fugetsu / SQUARE ENIX CO., LTD.
First published in Japan in 2015 by SQUARE ENIX CO., LTD. English translation rights arranged with SQUARE ENIX CO., LTD. and Yen Press, LLC through TUTTLE-MORI AGENCY, Inc.

English translation © 2017 by SQUARE ENIX CO., LTD.

Yen Press
1290 Avenue of the Americas
New York, NY 10104

Visit us at yenpress.com
facebook.com/yenpress
twitter.com/yenpress
yenpress.tumblr.com
instagram.com/yenpress

First Yen Press Edition: May 2017

Library of Congress Control Number: 2016936537

ISBNs: 978-0-316-47188-6 (paperback)
       978-0-316-51319-7 (ebook)

10 9 8 7 6 5 4 3 2 1

BVG

Printed in the United States of America

Re:ZERO

—Starting Life in Another World—

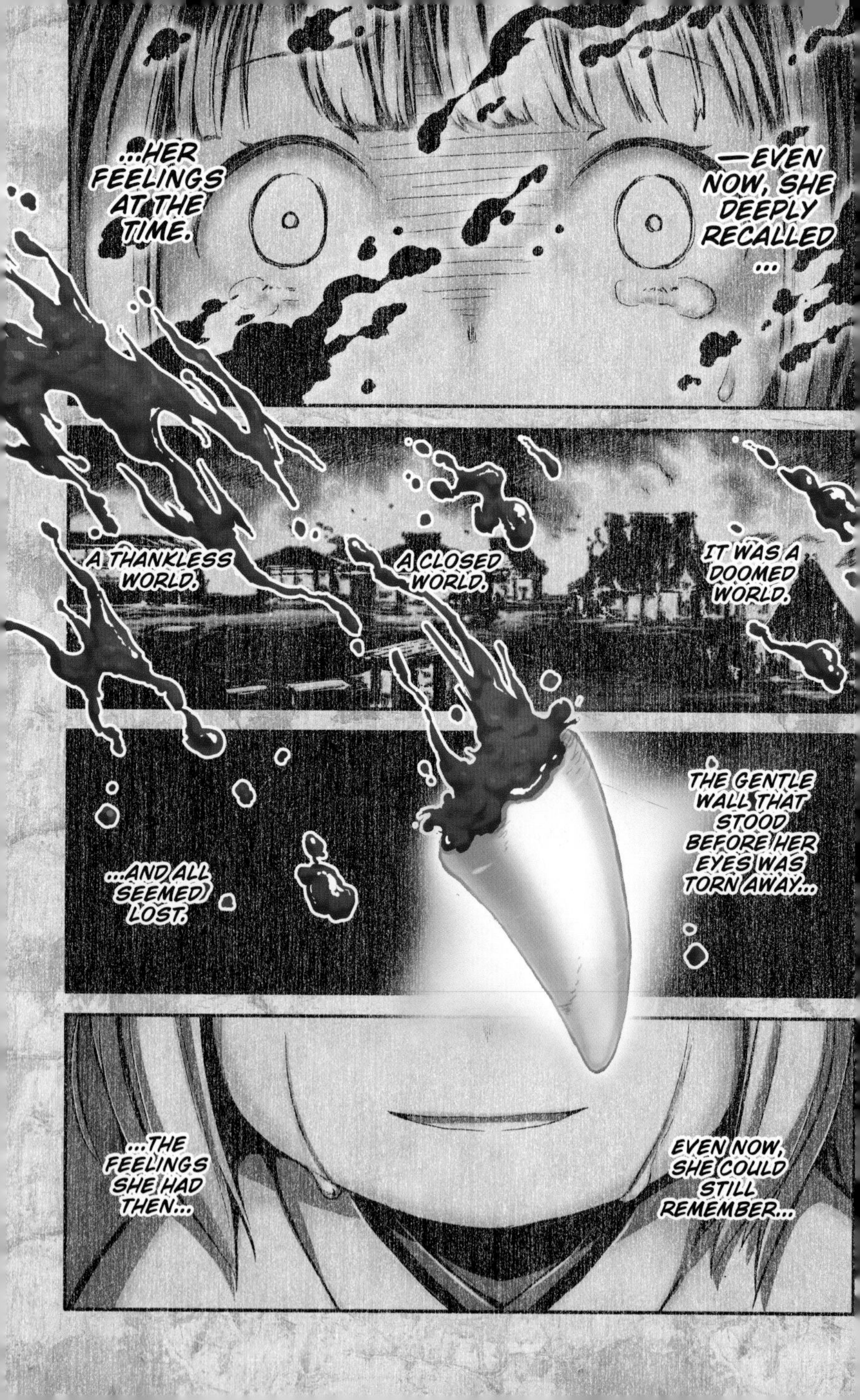
—EVEN NOW, SHE DEEPLY RECALLED...
...HER FEELINGS AT THE TIME.
IT WAS A DOOMED WORLD.
A CLOSED WORLD.
A THANKLESS WORLD.
THE GENTLE WALL THAT STOOD BEFORE HER EYES WAS TORN AWAY...
...AND ALL SEEMED LOST.
EVEN NOW, SHE COULD STILL REMEMBER...
...THE FEELINGS SHE HAD THEN...

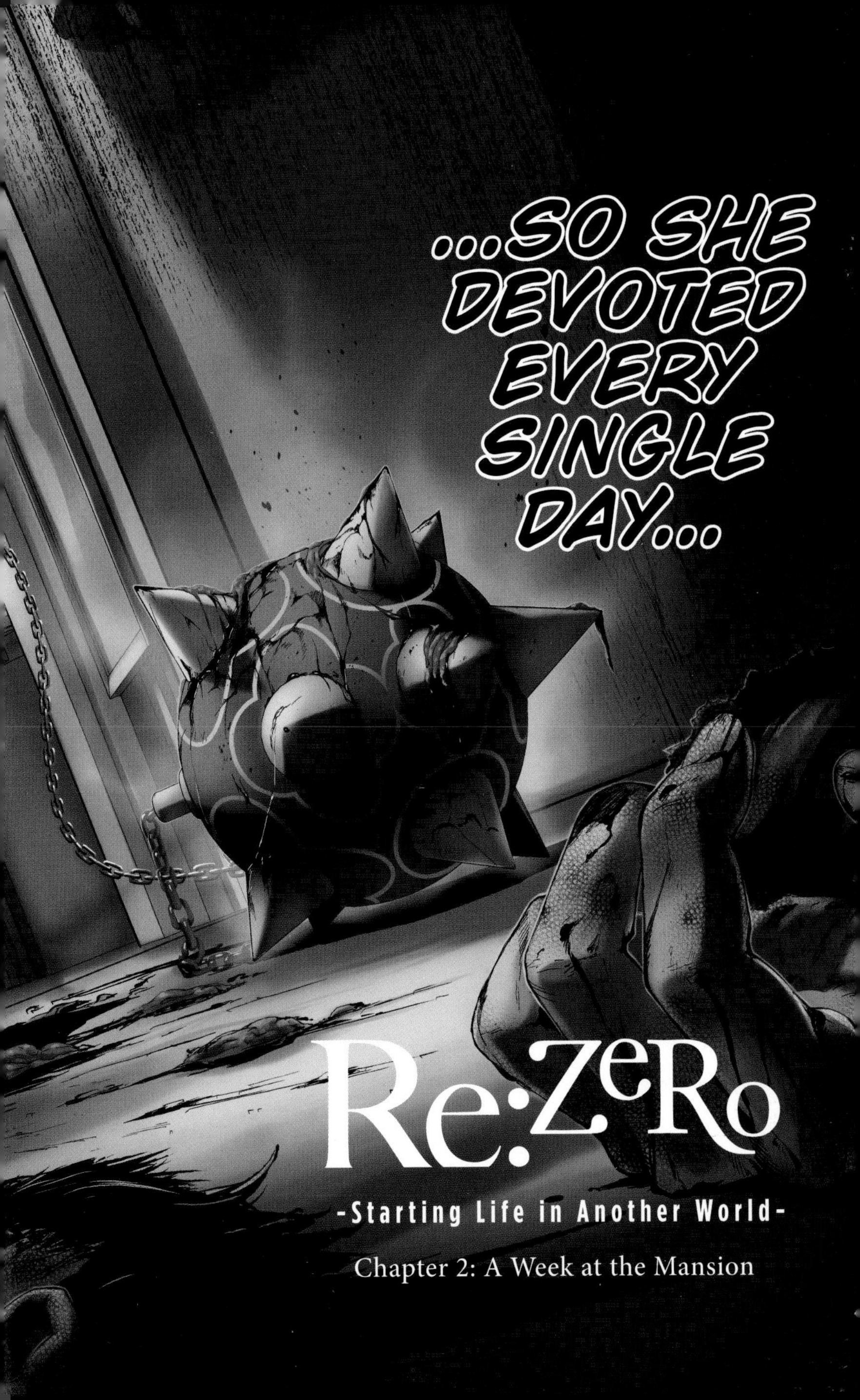
...SO SHE DEVOTED EVERY SINGLE DAY...
Re:ZeRo
-Starting Life in Another World-
Chapter 2: A Week at the Mansion

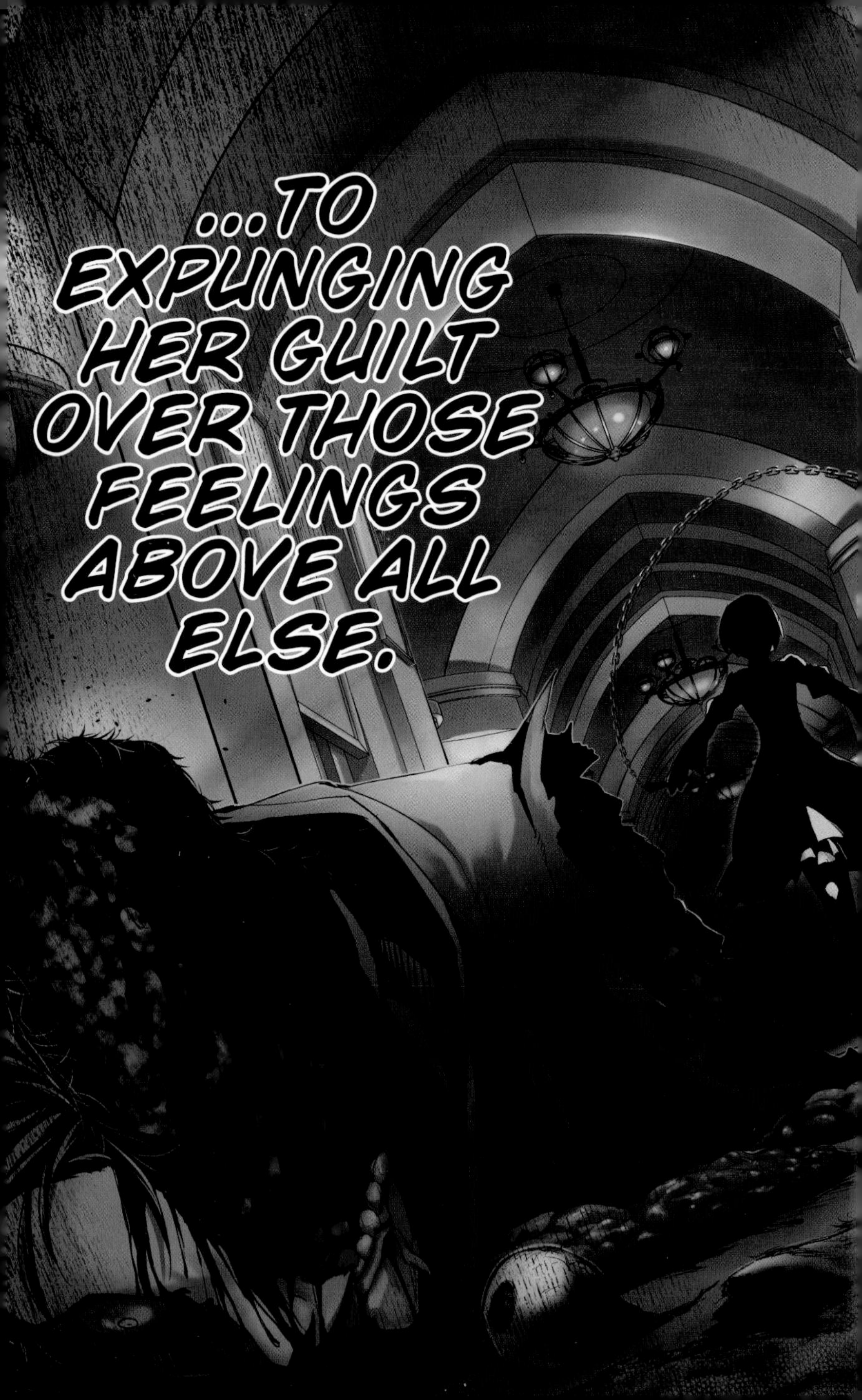
...TO EXPUNGING HER GUILT OVER THOSE FEELINGS ABOVE ALL ELSE.

Re:ZERO -Starting Life in Another World-

Chapter 2: A Week at the Mansion

The only ability Subaru Natsuki gets when he's summoned to
another world is time travel via his own death. But to save her,
he'll die as many times as it takes.

Contents

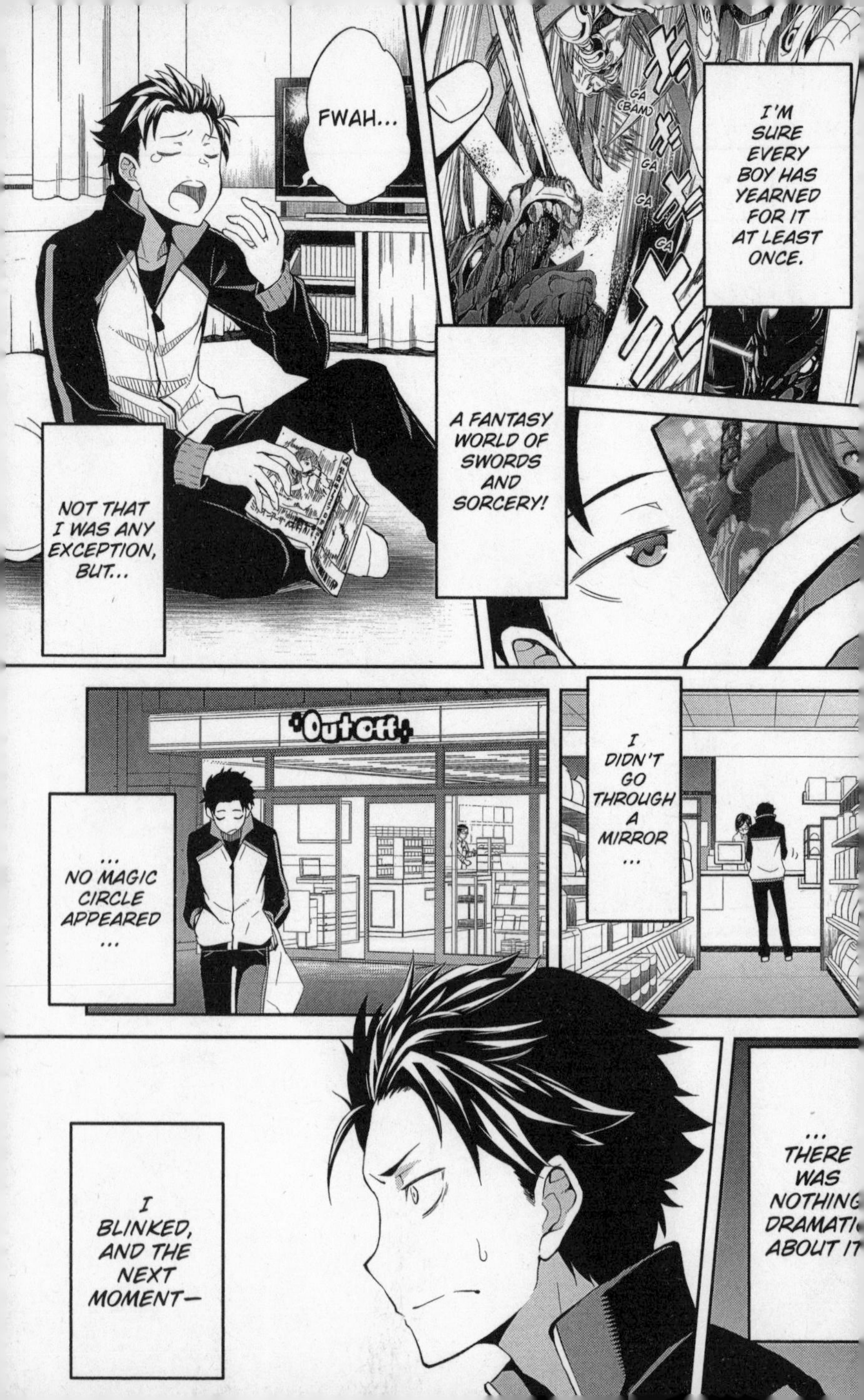
GA (BAM)
GA
GA
GA
I'M SURE EVERY BOY HAS YEARNED FOR IT AT LEAST ONCE.
A FANTASY WORLD OF SWORDS AND SORCERY!
FWAH...
NOT THAT I WAS ANY EXCEPTION, BUT...
I DIDN'T GO THROUGH A MIRROR ...
Out off
... NO MAGIC CIRCLE APPEARED ...
... THERE WAS NOTHING DRAMATI ABOUT IT
I BLINKED, AND THE NEXT MOMENT—

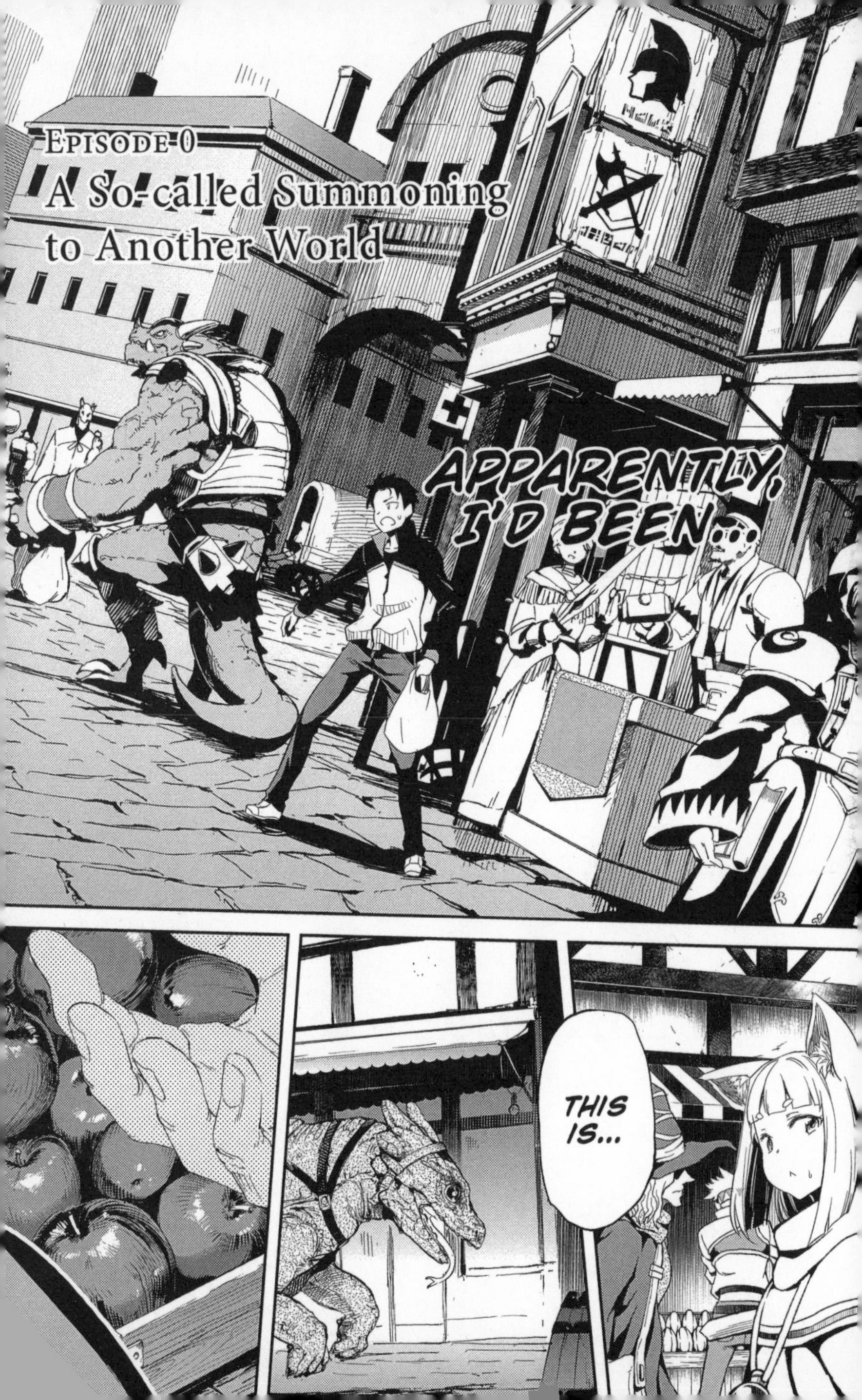
Episode 0
A So-called Summoning to Another World
APPARENTLY, I'D BEEN...
THIS IS...

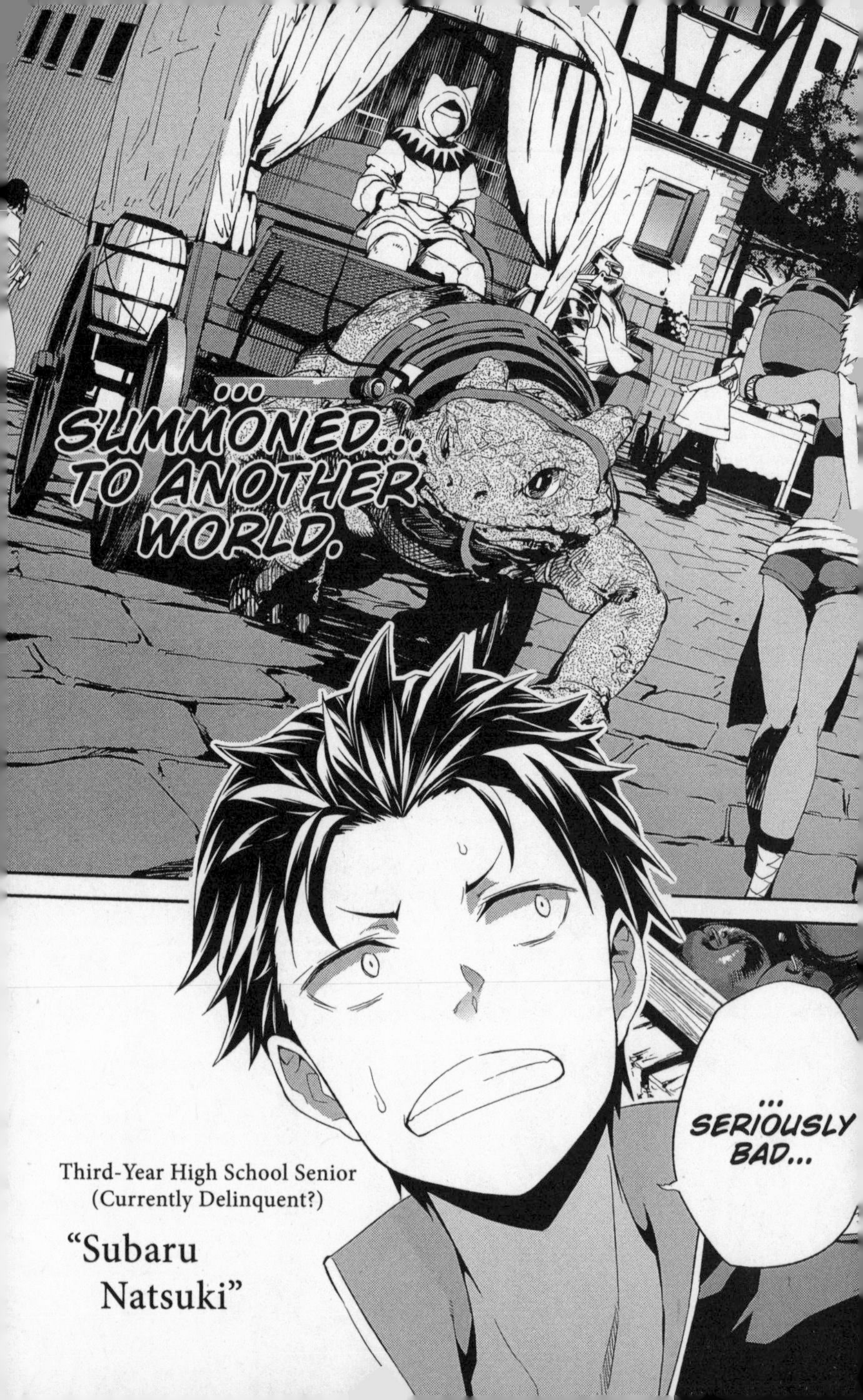
...SUMMONED... TO ANOTHER WORLD.
...SERIOUSLY BAD...
Third-Year High School Senior (Currently Delinquent?)
"Subaru Natsuki"

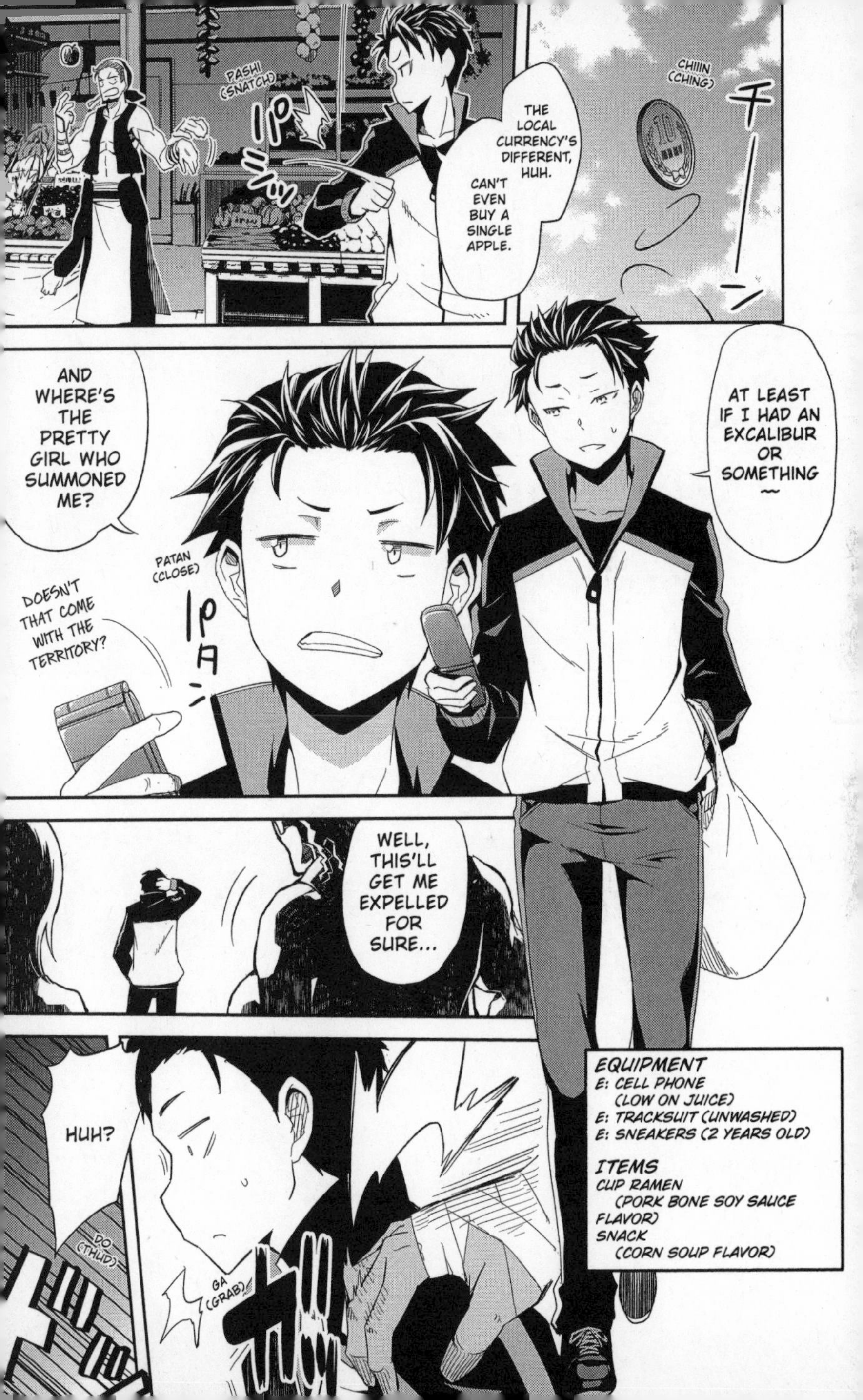
CHIIIN (CHING)
THE LOCAL CURRENCY'S DIFFERENT, HUH.
CAN'T EVEN BUY A SINGLE APPLE.
PASHI (SNATCH)
AT LEAST IF I HAD AN EXCALIBUR OR SOMETHING ~
EQUIPMENT
E: CELL PHONE (LOW ON JUICE)
E: TRACKSUIT (UNWASHED)
E: SNEAKERS (2 YEARS OLD)
ITEMS
CUP RAMEN (PORK BONE SOY SAUCE FLAVOR)
SNACK (CORN SOUP FLAVOR)
AND WHERE'S THE PRETTY GIRL WHO SUMMONED ME?
PATAN (CLOSE)
DOESN'T THAT COME WITH THE TERRITORY?
WELL, THIS'LL GET ME EXPELLED FOR SURE...
HUH?
DO (THUD)
GA (GRAB)

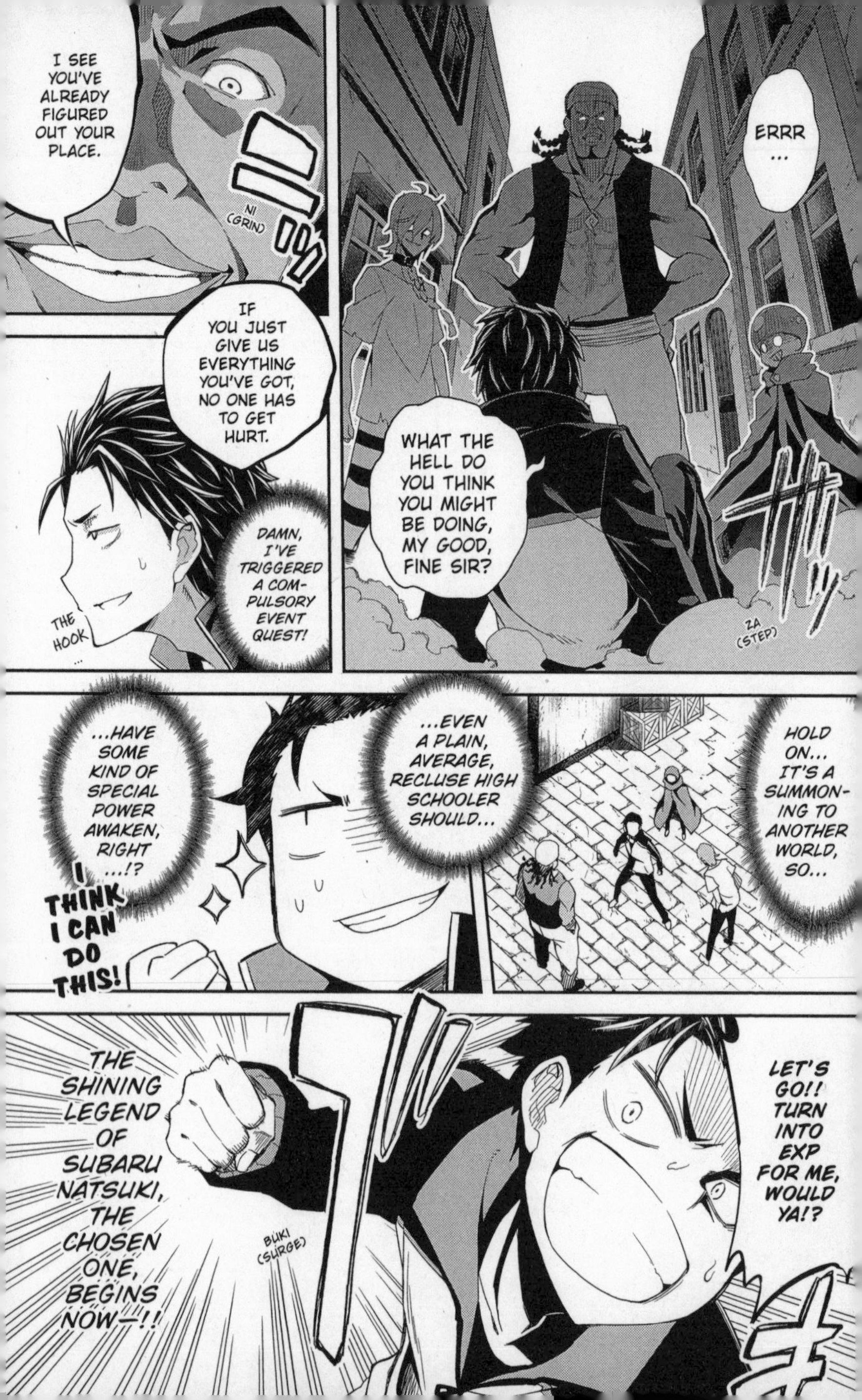
ERRR...
WHAT THE HELL DO YOU THINK YOU MIGHT BE DOING, MY GOOD, FINE SIR?
ZA (STEP)
I SEE YOU'VE ALREADY FIGURED OUT YOUR PLACE.
NI (GRIN)
IF YOU JUST GIVE US EVERYTHING YOU'VE GOT, NO ONE HAS TO GET HURT.
DAMN, I'VE TRIGGERED A COMPULSORY EVENT QUEST!
THE HOOK...
HOLD ON... IT'S A SUMMONING TO ANOTHER WORLD, SO...
...EVEN A PLAIN, AVERAGE, RECLUSE HIGH SCHOOLER SHOULD...
...HAVE SOME KIND OF SPECIAL POWER AWAKEN, RIGHT...!?
I THINK I CAN DO THIS!
LET'S GO!! TURN INTO EXP FOR ME, WOULD YA!?
BUKI (SURGE)
THE SHINING LEGEND OF SUBARU NATSUKI, THE CHOSEN ONE, BEGINS NOW—!!

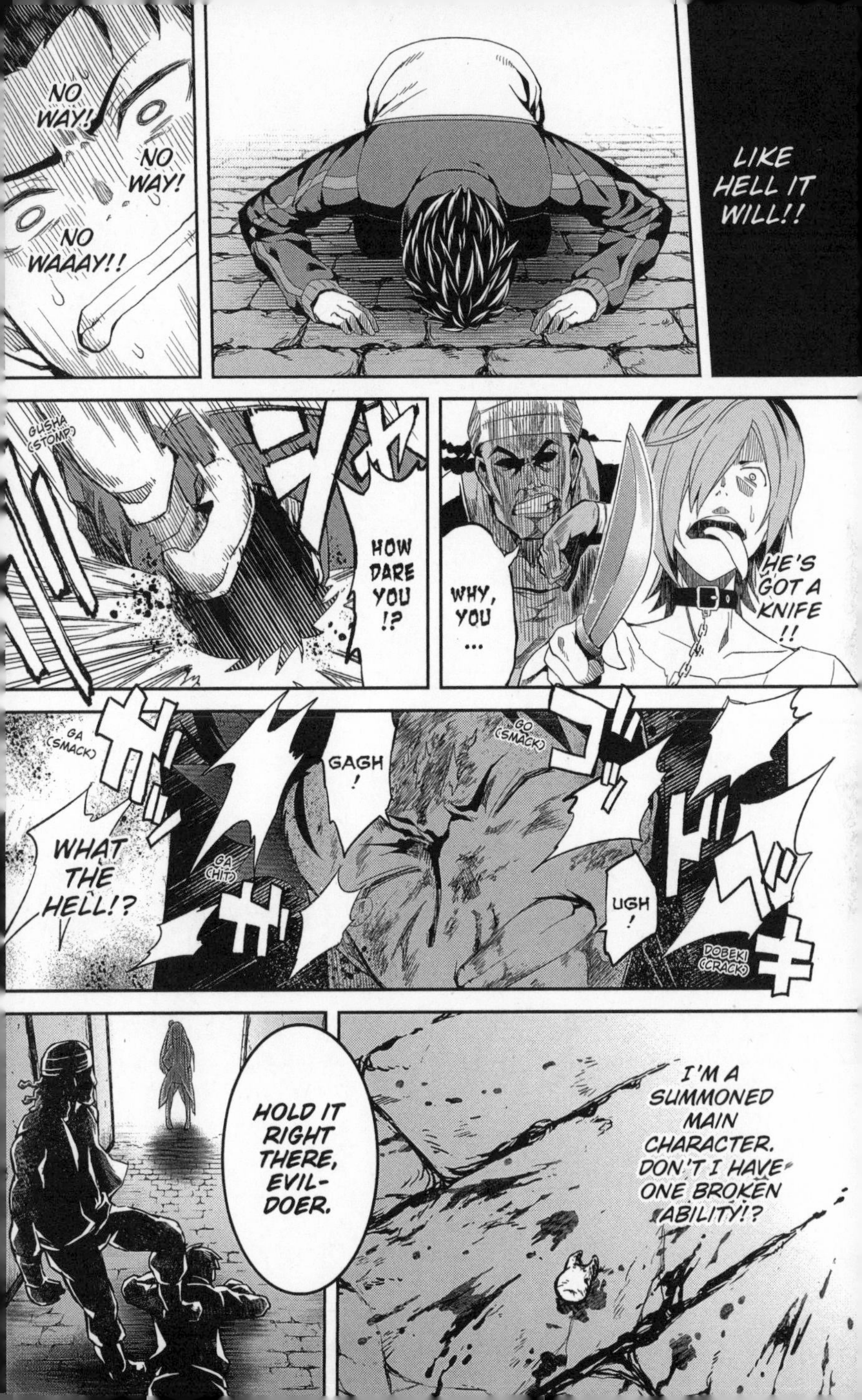
LIKE HELL IT WILL!!
NO WAY! NO WAY!
NO WAAAY!!
HE'S GOT A KNIFE!!
WHY, YOU...
HOW DARE YOU!?
GUSHA (STOMP)
DOBEKI (CRACK)
UGH!
GO (SMACK)
GAGH!
GA (HIT)
GA (SMACK)
WHAT THE HELL!?
I'M A SUMMONED MAIN CHARACTER. DON'T I HAVE ONE BROKEN ABILITY!?
HOLD IT RIGHT THERE, EVIL-DOER.

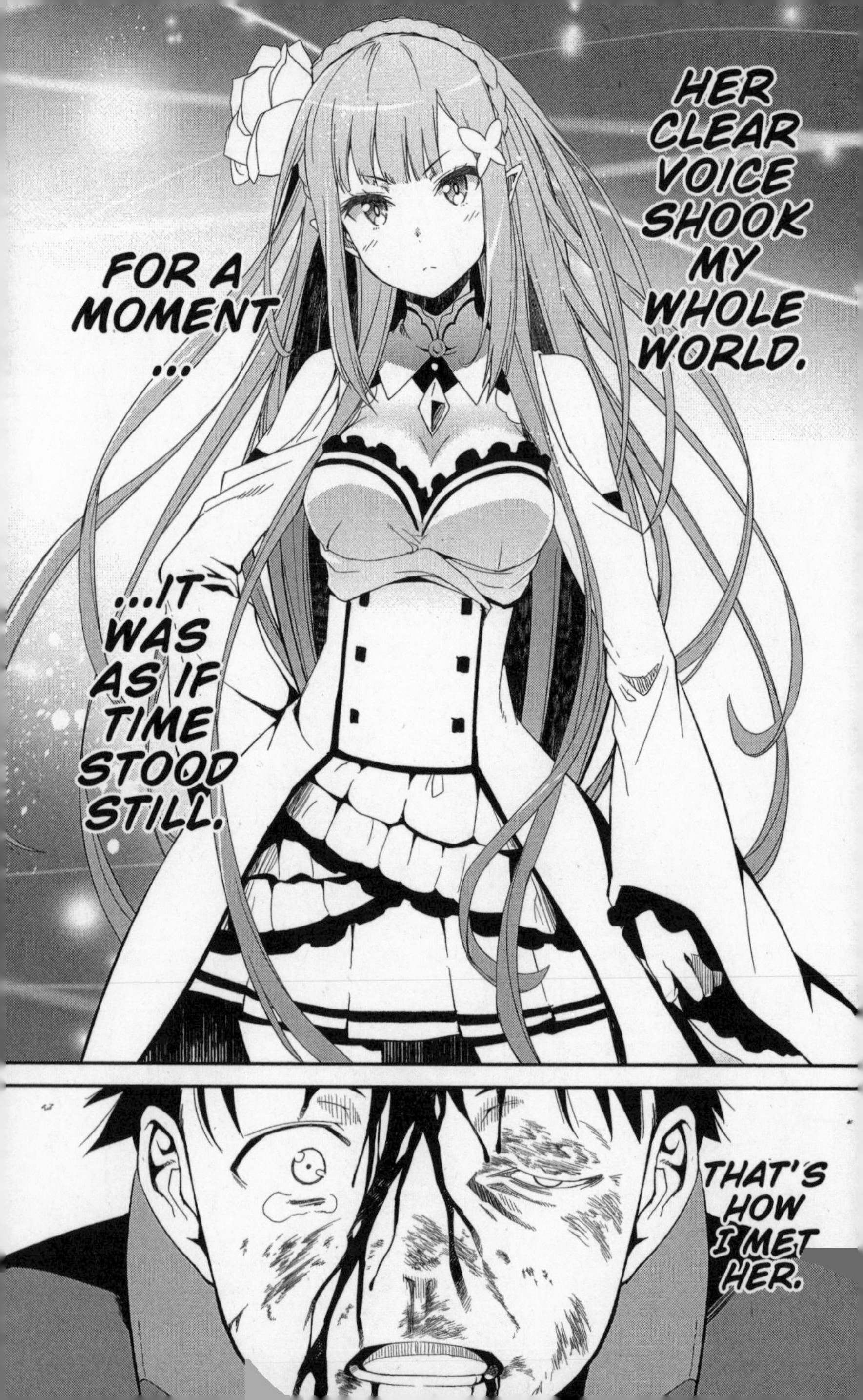
HER CLEAR VOICE SHOOK MY WHOLE WORLD.
FOR A MOMENT...
...IT WAS AS IF TIME STOOD STILL.
THAT'S HOW I MET HER.

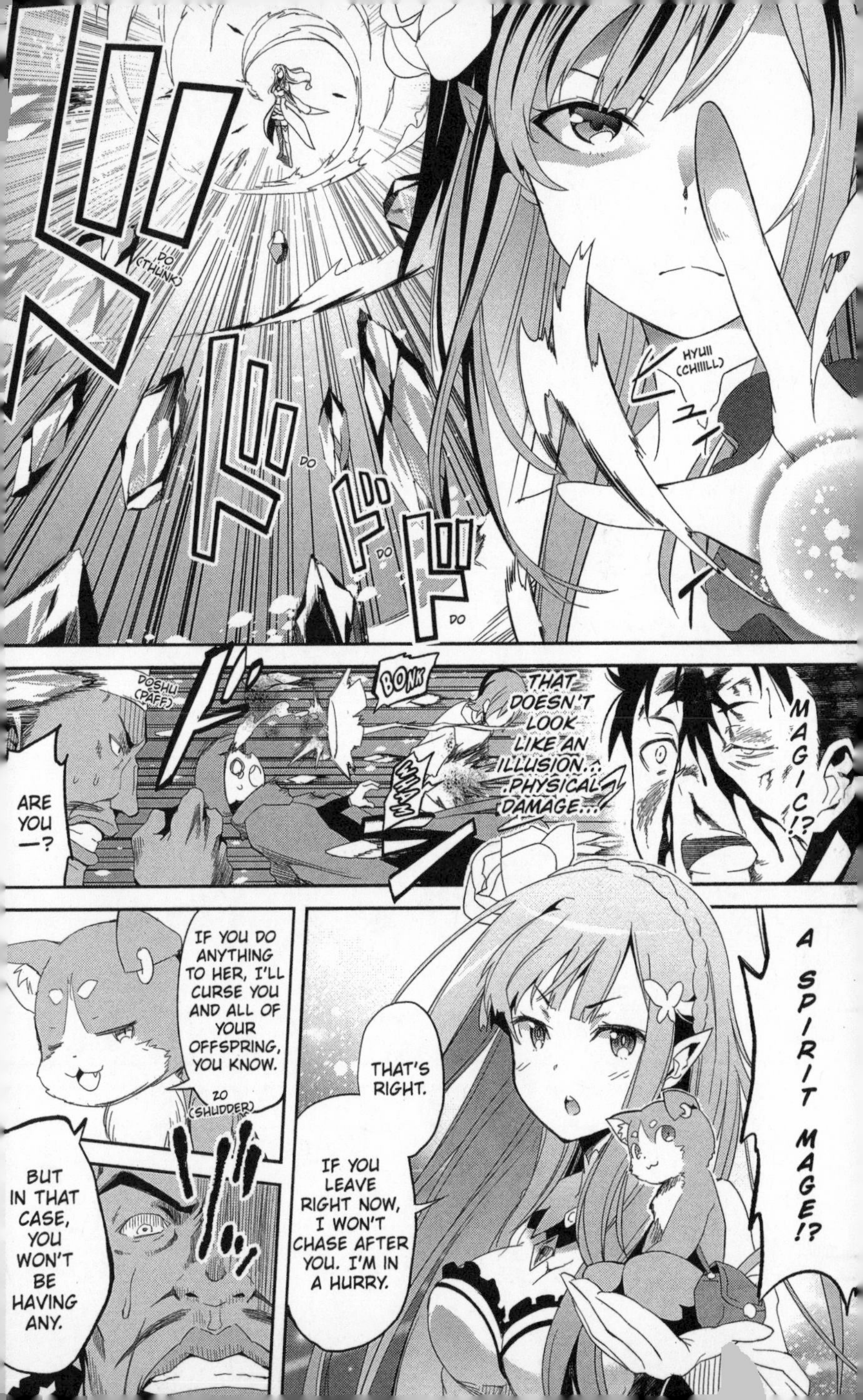
HYUII (CHIIILL)
DO (THUNK)
DO
DO
DO
MAGIC!?
THAT DOESN'T LOOK LIKE AN ILLUSION... PHYSICAL DAMAGE...!?
BONK
WHAM
DOSHU (PAFF)
ARE YOU—?
A SPIRIT MAGE!?
THAT'S RIGHT.
IF YOU LEAVE RIGHT NOW, I WON'T CHASE AFTER YOU. I'M IN A HURRY.
IF YOU DO ANYTHING TO HER, I'LL CURSE YOU AND ALL OF YOUR OFFSPRING, YOU KNOW.
ZO (SHUDDER)
BUT IN THAT CASE, YOU WON'T BE HAVING ANY.

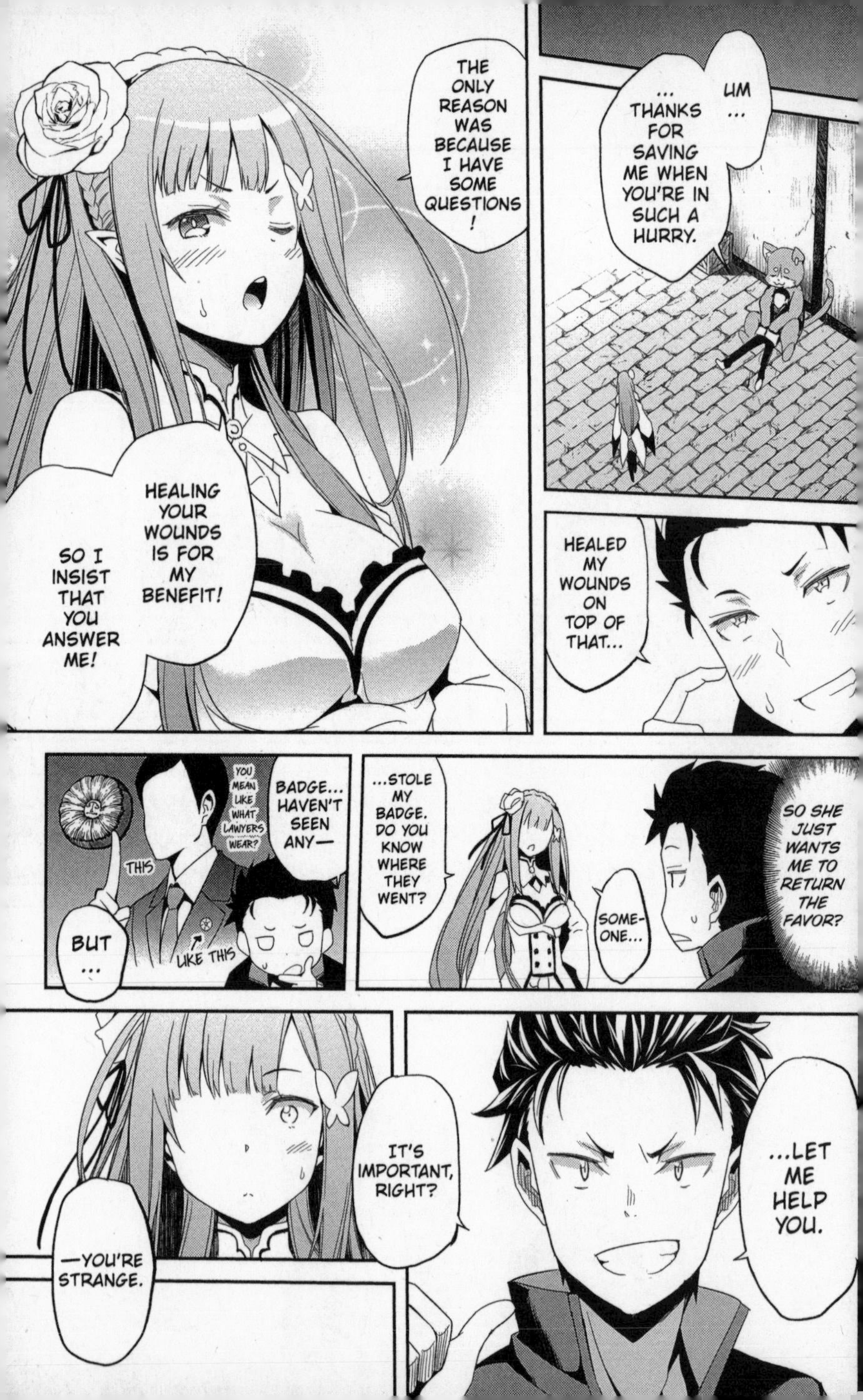
UM ...
... THANKS FOR SAVING ME WHEN YOU'RE IN SUCH A HURRY.
HEALED MY WOUNDS ON TOP OF THAT...
THE ONLY REASON WAS BECAUSE I HAVE SOME QUESTIONS!
HEALING YOUR WOUNDS IS FOR MY BENEFIT!
SO I INSIST THAT YOU ANSWER ME!
SO SHE JUST WANTS ME TO RETURN THE FAVOR?
SOME-ONE...
...STOLE MY BADGE. DO YOU KNOW WHERE THEY WENT?
BADGE... HAVEN'T SEEN ANY—
YOU MEAN LIKE WHAT LAWYERS WEAR?
THIS
LIKE THIS
BUT ...
...LET ME HELP YOU.
IT'S IMPORTANT, RIGHT?
—YOU'RE STRANGE.

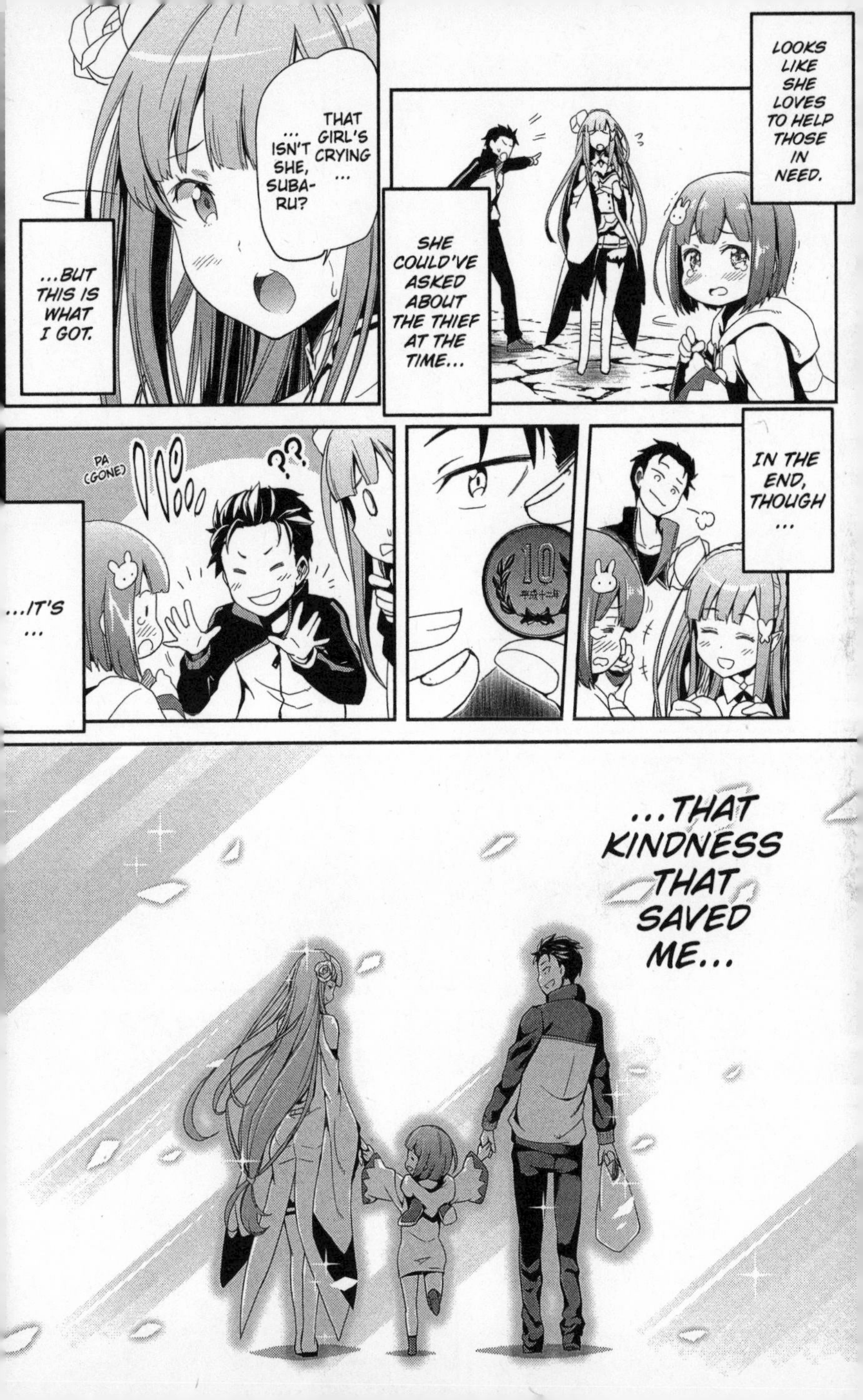
LOOKS LIKE SHE LOVES TO HELP THOSE IN NEED.
SHE COULD'VE ASKED ABOUT THE THIEF AT THE TIME...
THAT GIRL'S CRYING ... ISN'T SHE, SUBA-RU?
...BUT THIS IS WHAT I GOT.
IN THE END, THOUGH ...
10
PA (GONE)
...IT'S ...
...THAT KINDNESS THAT SAVED ME...

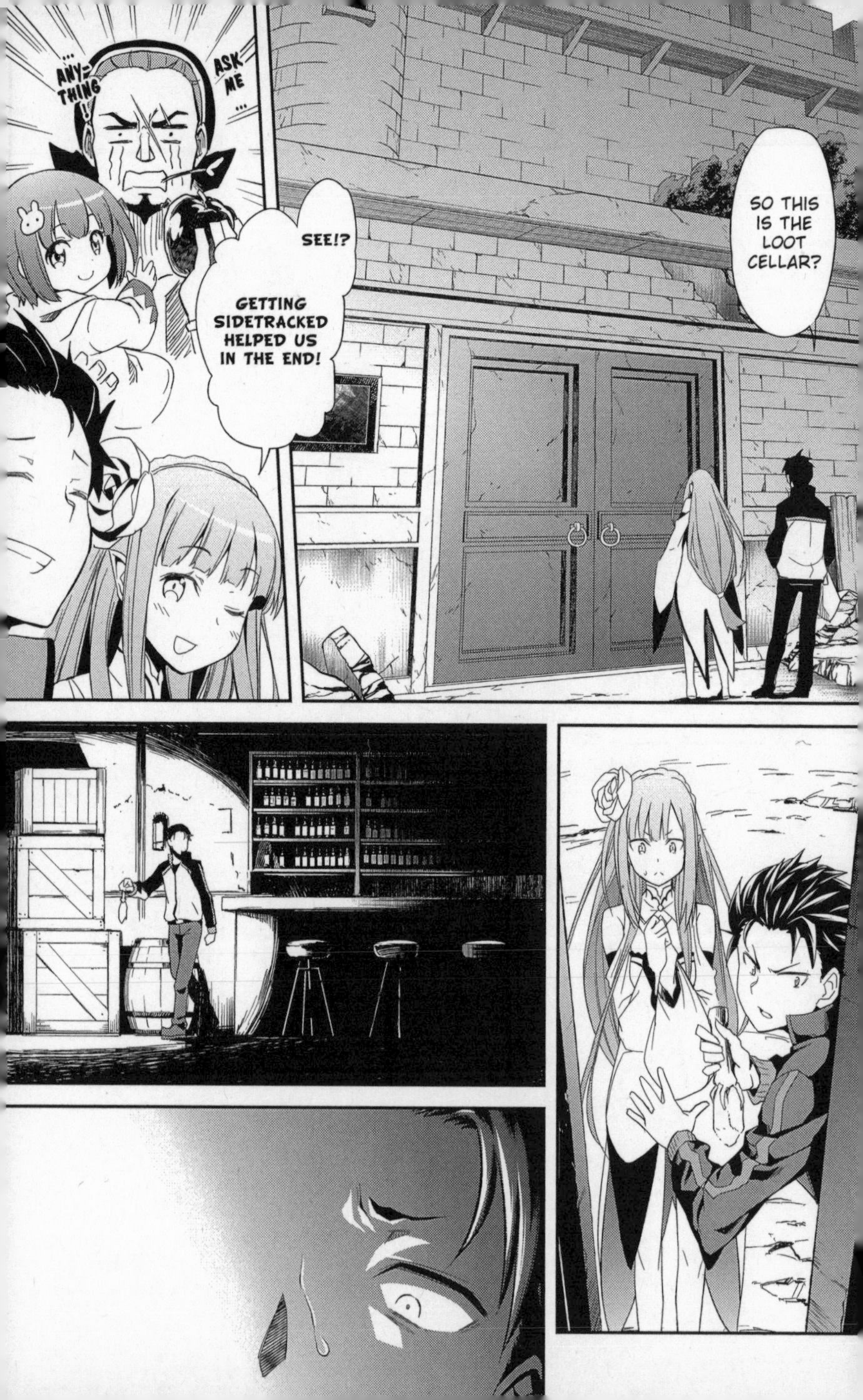
SO THIS IS THE LOOT CELLAR?
ASK ME ...
... ANY-THING!
SEE!?
GETTING SIDETRACKED HELPED US IN THE END!

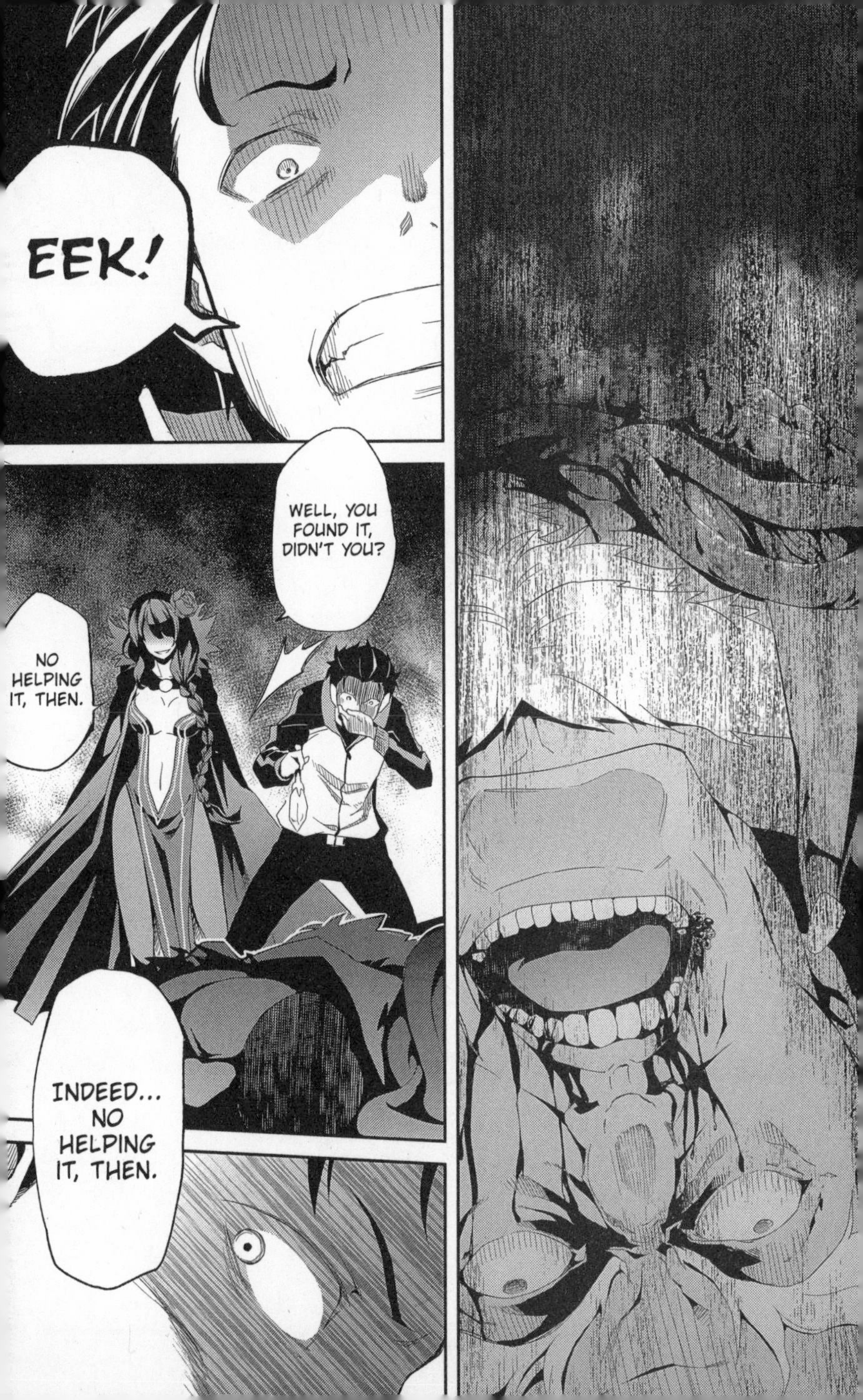
EEK!
WELL, YOU FOUND IT, DIDN'T YOU?
NO HELPING IT, THEN.
INDEED... NO HELPING IT, THEN.

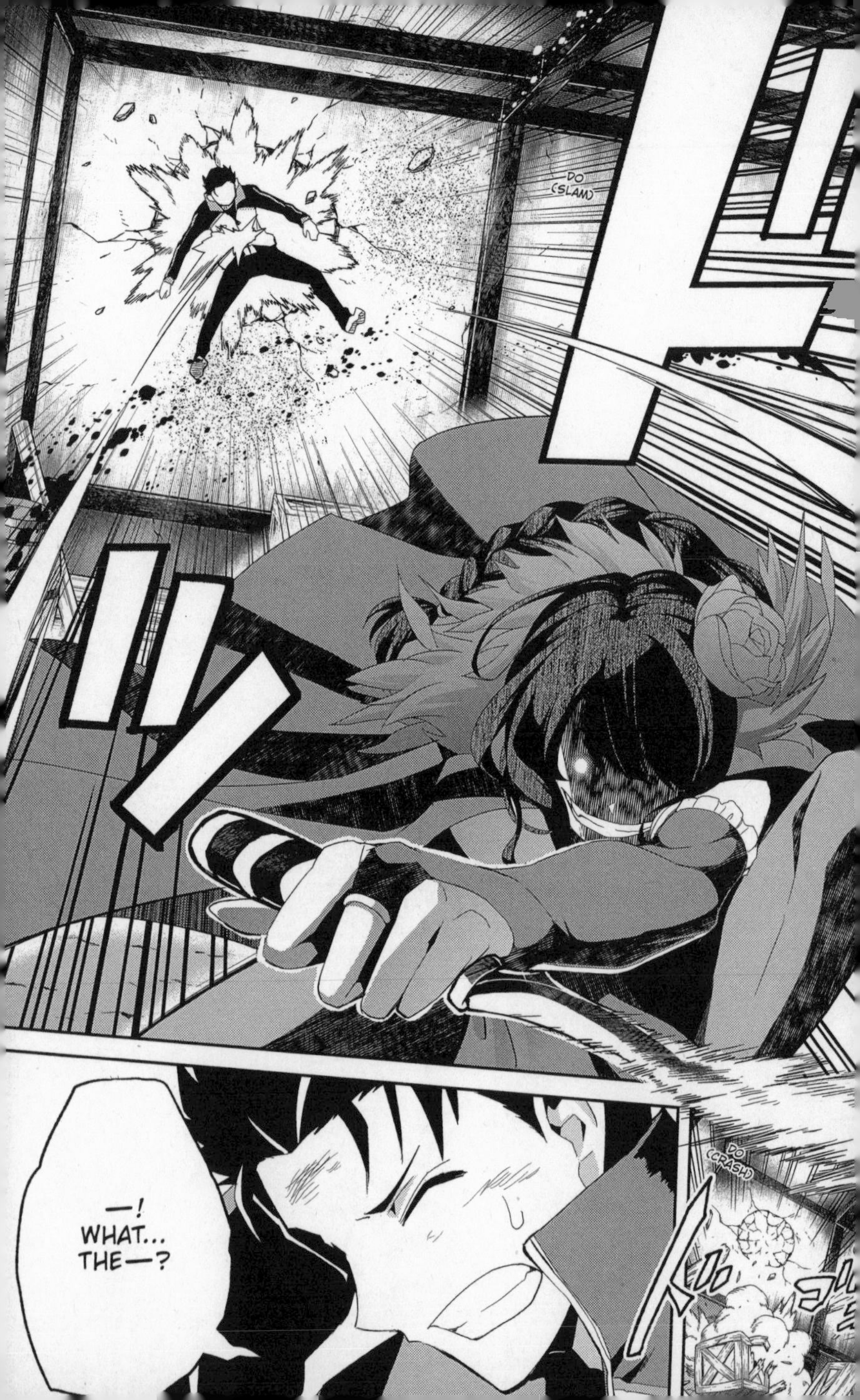
DO
(SLAM)
DO
(CRASH)
—!
WHAT...
THE—?

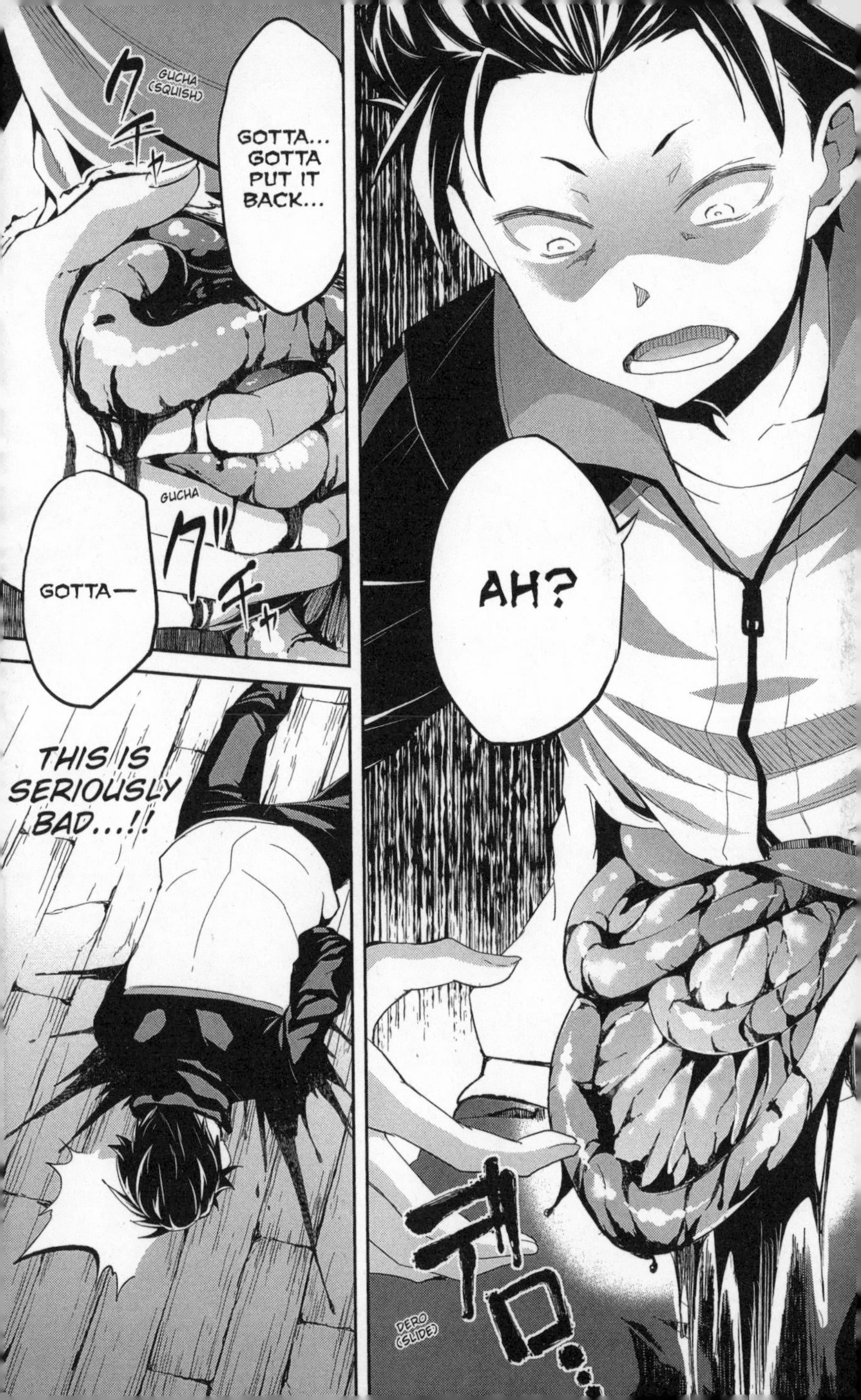
AH?
DERO (SLIDE)
GOTTA... GOTTA PUT IT BACK...
GUCHA (SQUISH)
GUCHA
GOTTA—
THIS IS SERIOUSLY BAD...!!

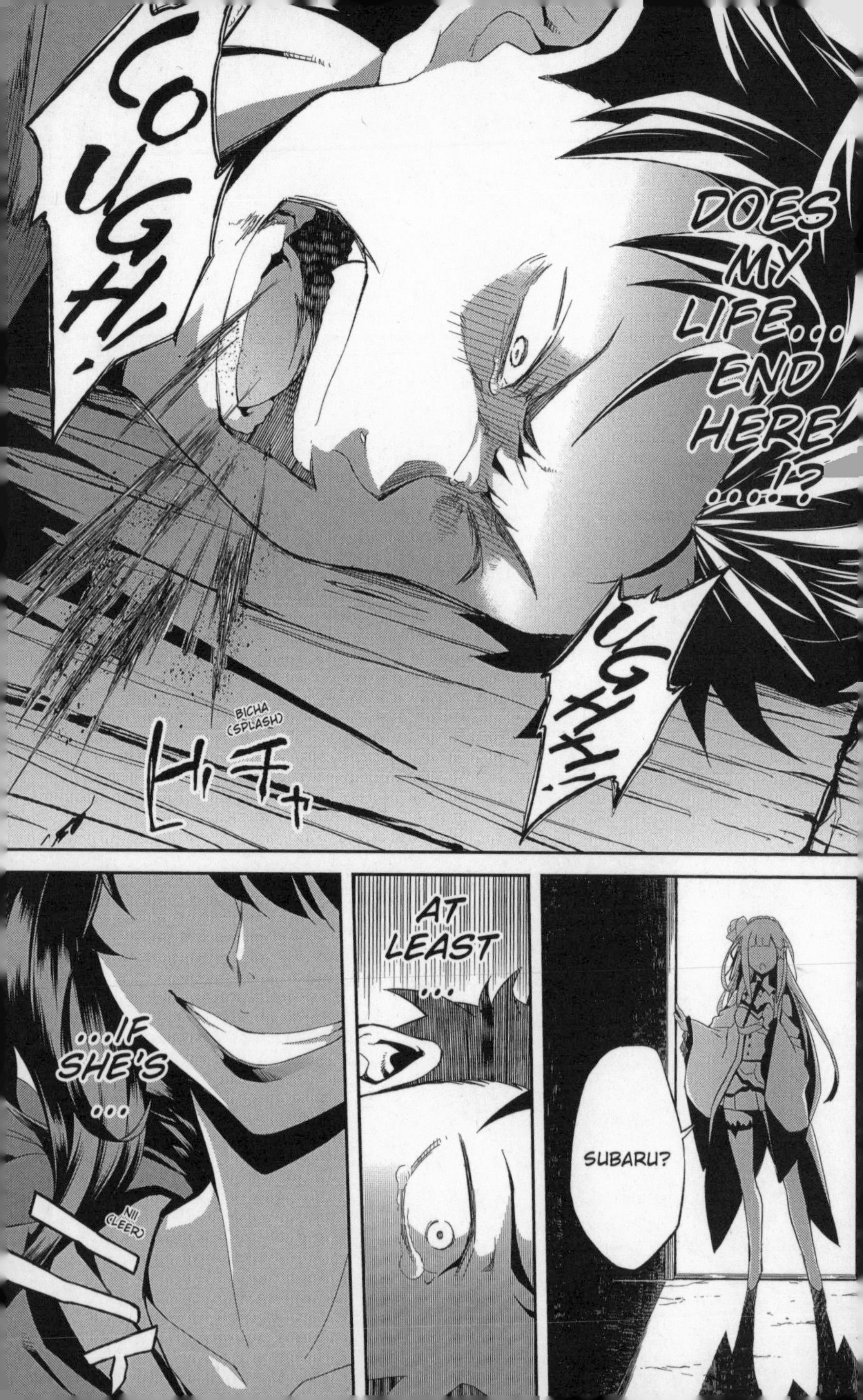
DOES MY LIFE... END HERE ...!?
COUGH! UGH!
UGHH!!
BICHA (SPLASH)
ビチャ
SUBARU?
AT LEAST...
...IF SHE'S...
NII (LEER)

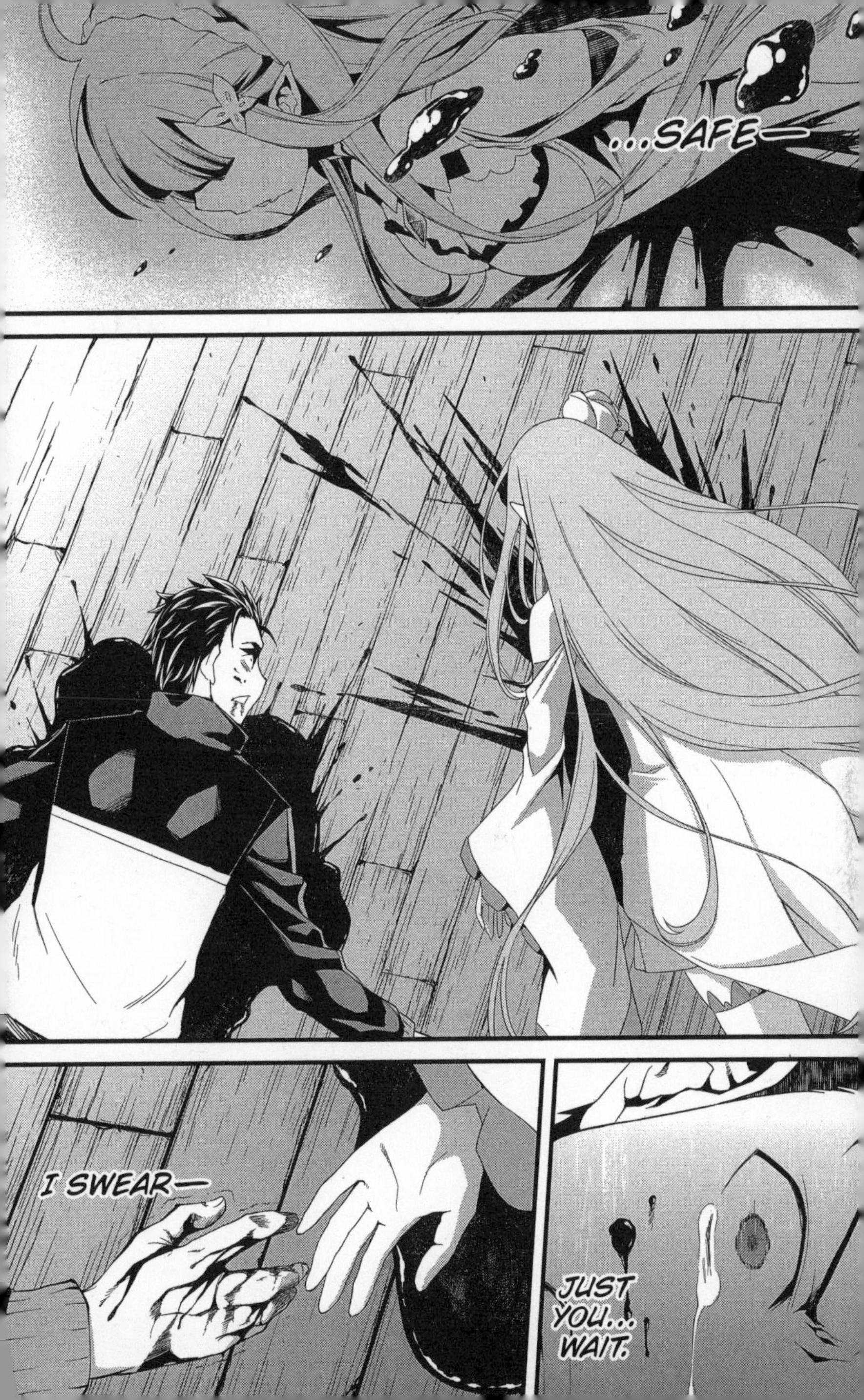
...SAFE—
JUST YOU... WAIT.
I SWEAR—

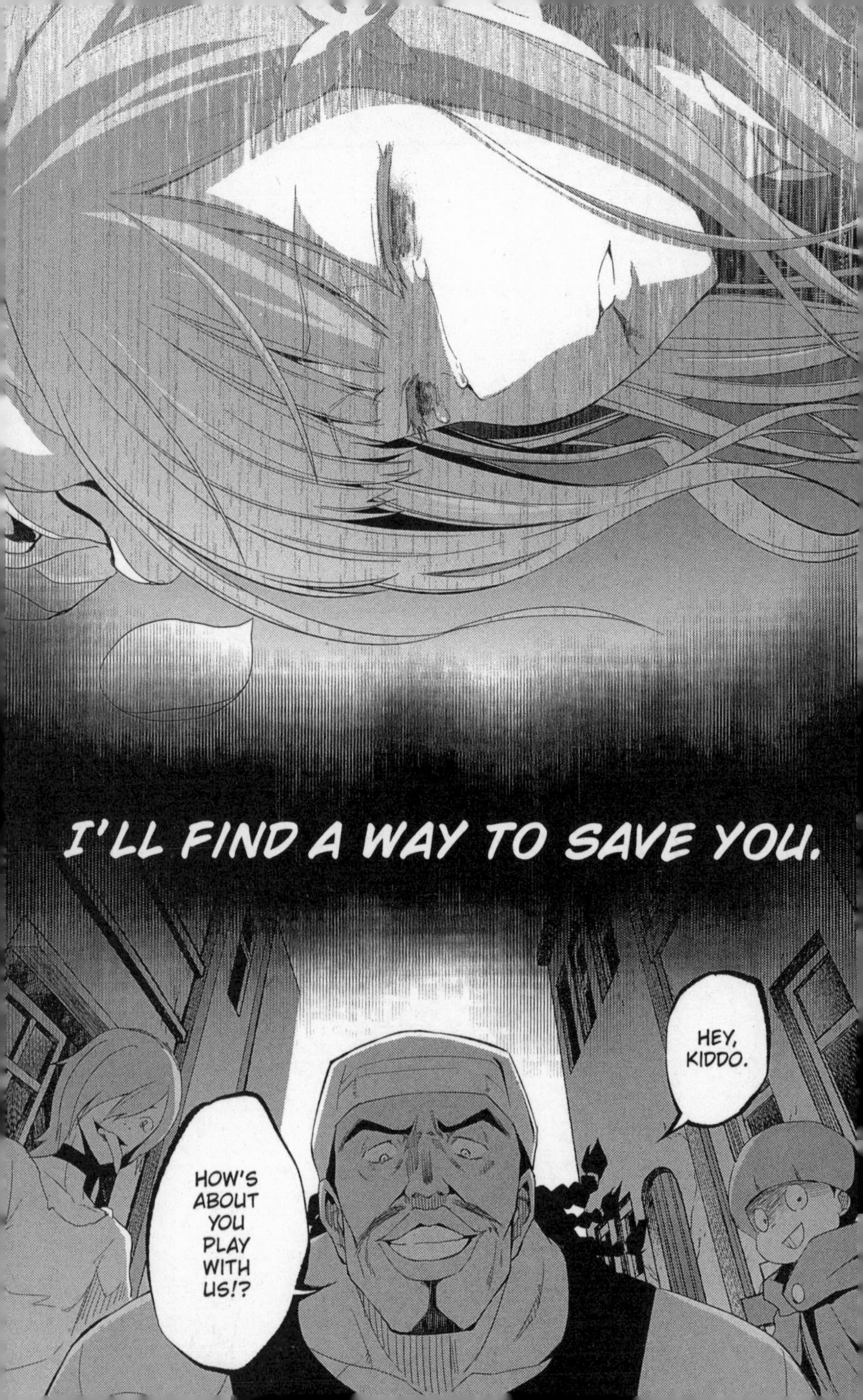
I'LL FIND A WAY TO SAVE YOU.
HEY, KIDDO.
HOW'S ABOUT YOU PLAY WITH US!?

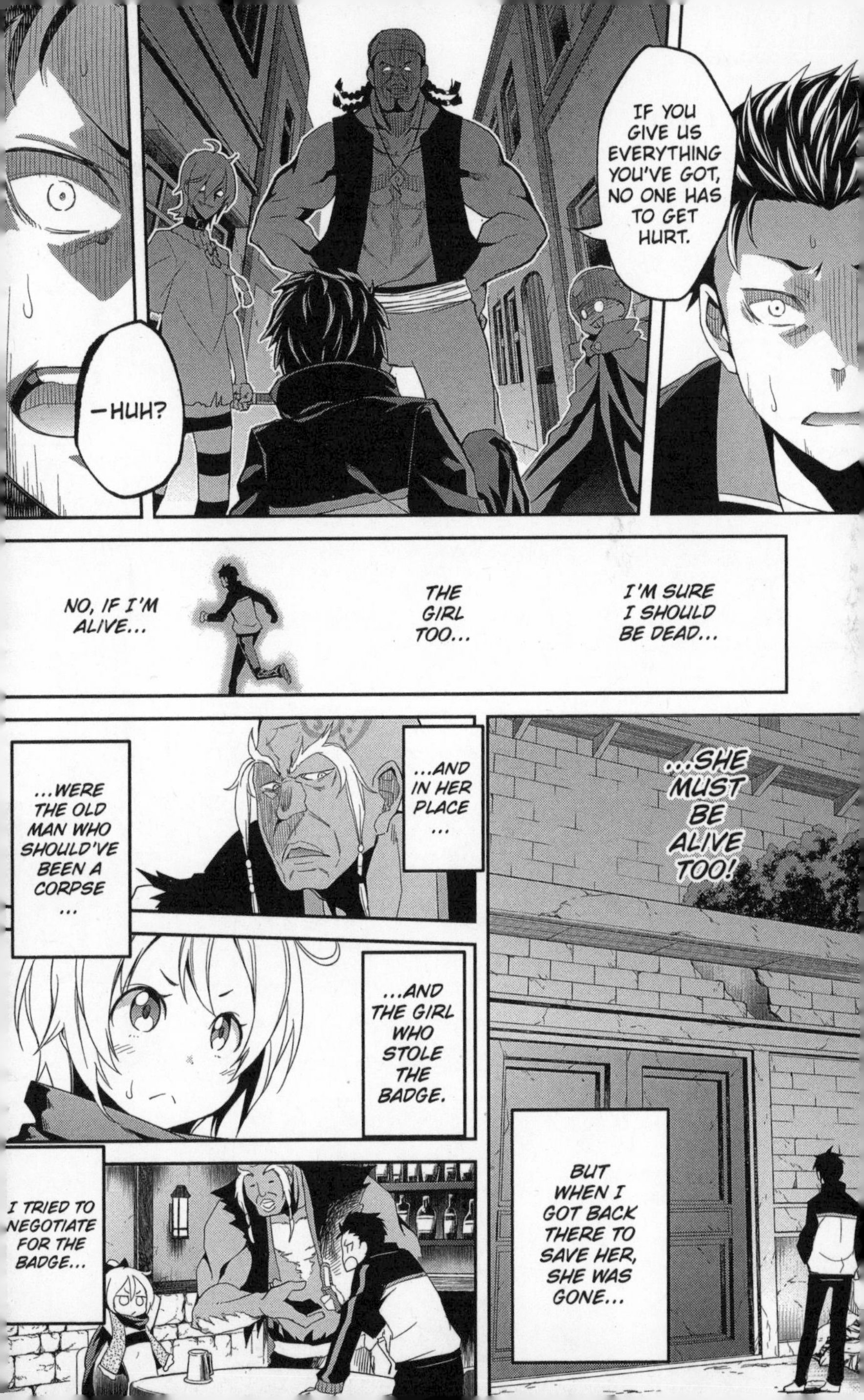
IF YOU GIVE US EVERYTHING YOU'VE GOT, NO ONE HAS TO GET HURT.
—HUH?
I'M SURE I SHOULD BE DEAD...
THE GIRL TOO...
NO, IF I'M ALIVE...
...SHE MUST BE ALIVE TOO!
BUT WHEN I GOT BACK THERE TO SAVE HER, SHE WAS GONE...
...AND IN HER PLACE...
...WERE THE OLD MAN WHO SHOULD'VE BEEN A CORPSE...
...AND THE GIRL WHO STOLE THE BADGE.
I TRIED TO NEGOTIATE FOR THE BADGE...

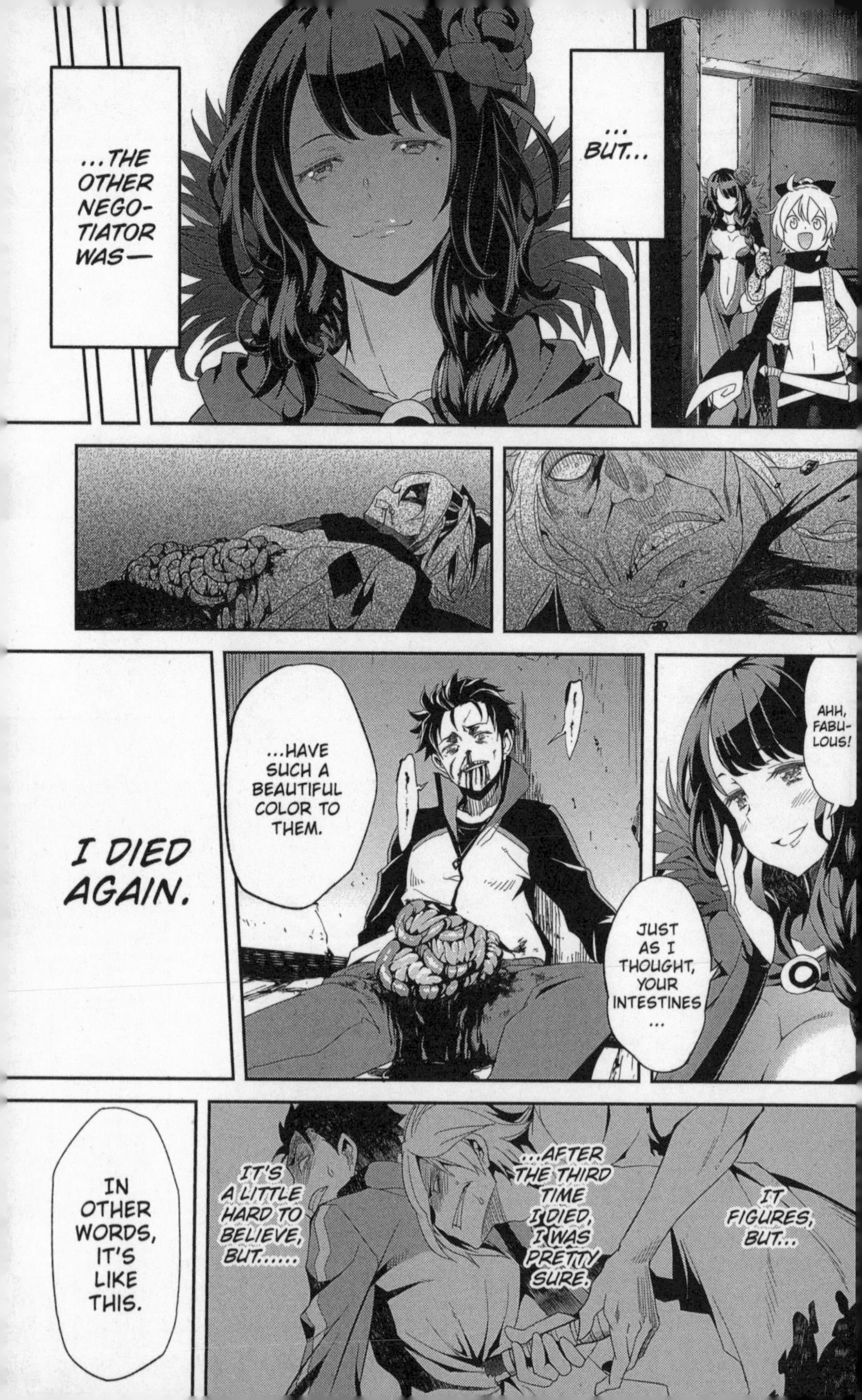
...BUT...
...THE OTHER NEGO-TIATOR WAS—
AHH, FABU-LOUS!
JUST AS I THOUGHT, YOUR INTESTINES...
...HAVE SUCH A BEAUTIFUL COLOR TO THEM.
I DIED AGAIN.
IT FIGURES, BUT...
...AFTER THE THIRD TIME I DIED, I WAS PRETTY SURE.
IT'S A LITTLE HARD TO BELIEVE, BUT......
IN OTHER WORDS, IT'S LIKE THIS.

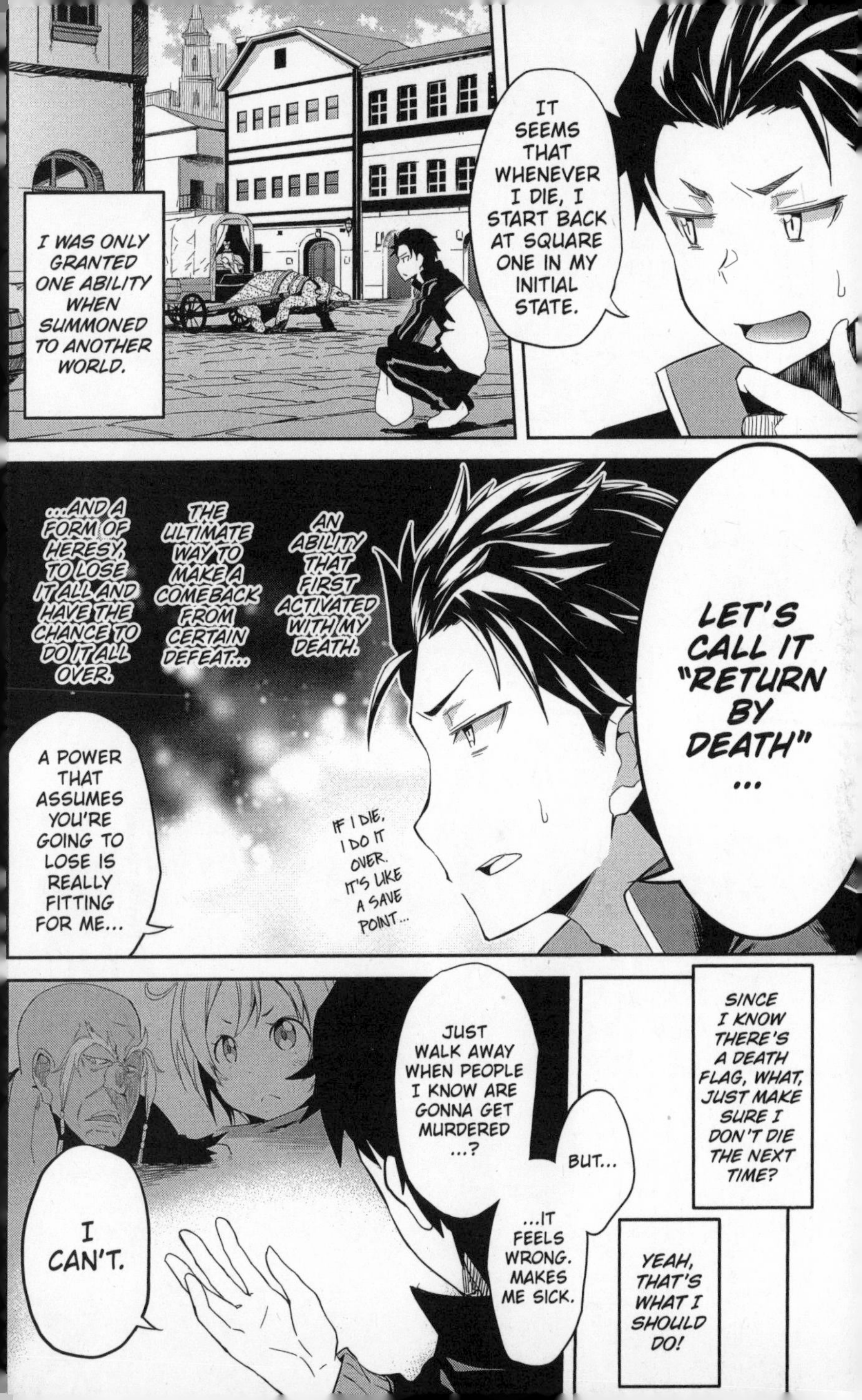
IT SEEMS THAT WHENEVER I DIE, I START BACK AT SQUARE ONE IN MY INITIAL STATE.
I WAS ONLY GRANTED ONE ABILITY WHEN SUMMONED TO ANOTHER WORLD.
LET'S CALL IT "RETURN BY DEATH"...
AN ABILITY THAT FIRST ACTIVATED WITH MY DEATH.
THE ULTIMATE WAY TO MAKE A COMEBACK FROM CERTAIN DEFEAT...
...AND A FORM OF HERESY, TO LOSE IT ALL AND HAVE THE CHANCE TO DO IT ALL OVER.
IF I DIE, I DO IT OVER. IT'S LIKE A SAVE POINT...
A POWER THAT ASSUMES YOU'RE GOING TO LOSE IS REALLY FITTING FOR ME...
SINCE I KNOW THERE'S A DEATH FLAG, WHAT, JUST MAKE SURE I DON'T DIE THE NEXT TIME?
YEAH, THAT'S WHAT I SHOULD DO!
JUST WALK AWAY WHEN PEOPLE I KNOW ARE GONNA GET MURDERED...?
BUT...
...IT FEELS WRONG. MAKES ME SICK.
I CAN'T.

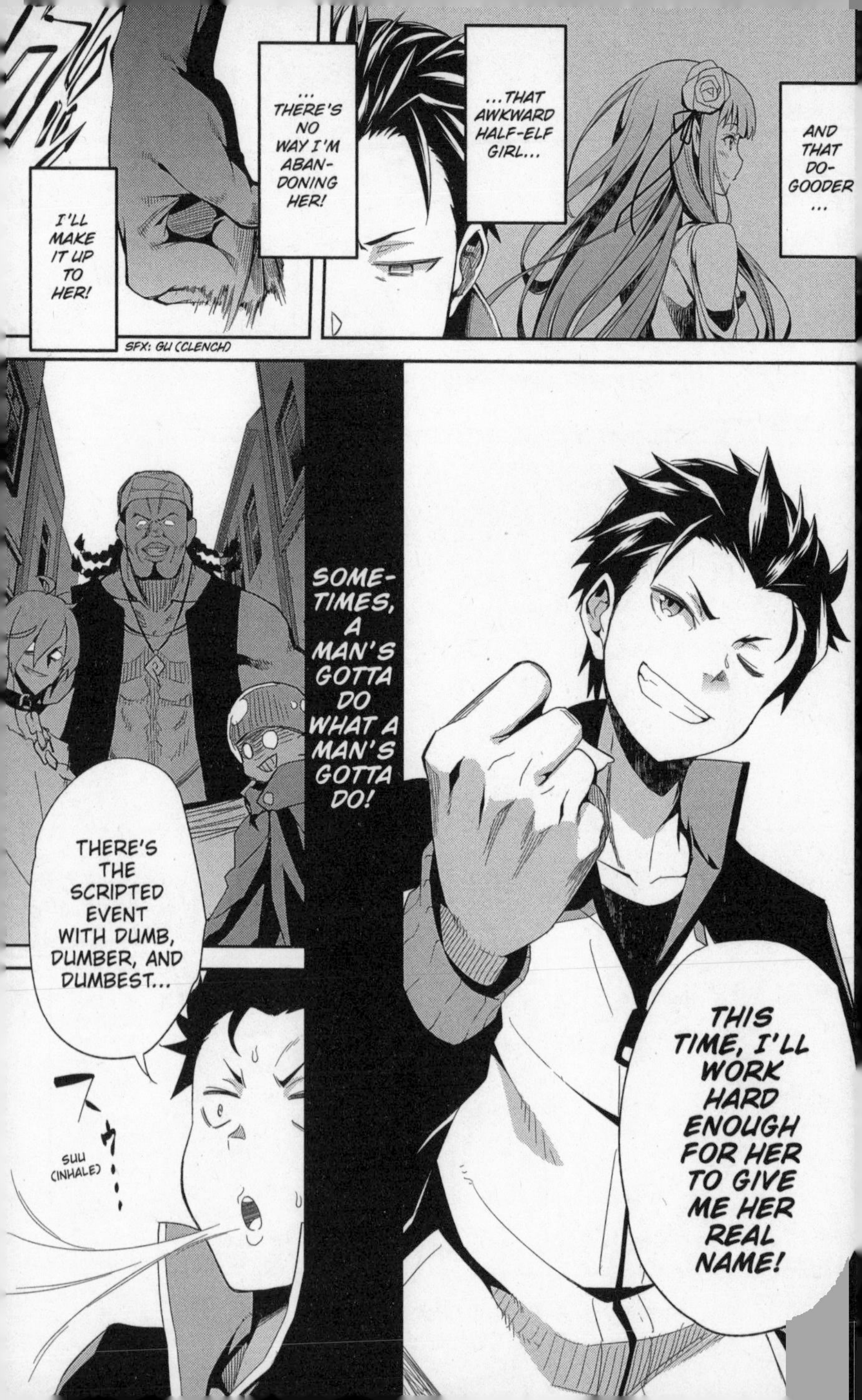

AND THAT DO-GOODER...
...THAT AWKWARD HALF-ELF GIRL...
...THERE'S NO WAY I'M ABAN-DONING HER!
I'LL MAKE IT UP TO HER!
SFX: GU (CLENCH)
SOME-TIMES, A MAN'S GOTTA DO WHAT A MAN'S GOTTA DO!
THIS TIME, I'LL WORK HARD ENOUGH FOR HER TO GIVE ME HER REAL NAME!
THERE'S THE SCRIPTED EVENT WITH DUMB, DUMBER, AND DUMBEST...
SUU (INHALE)

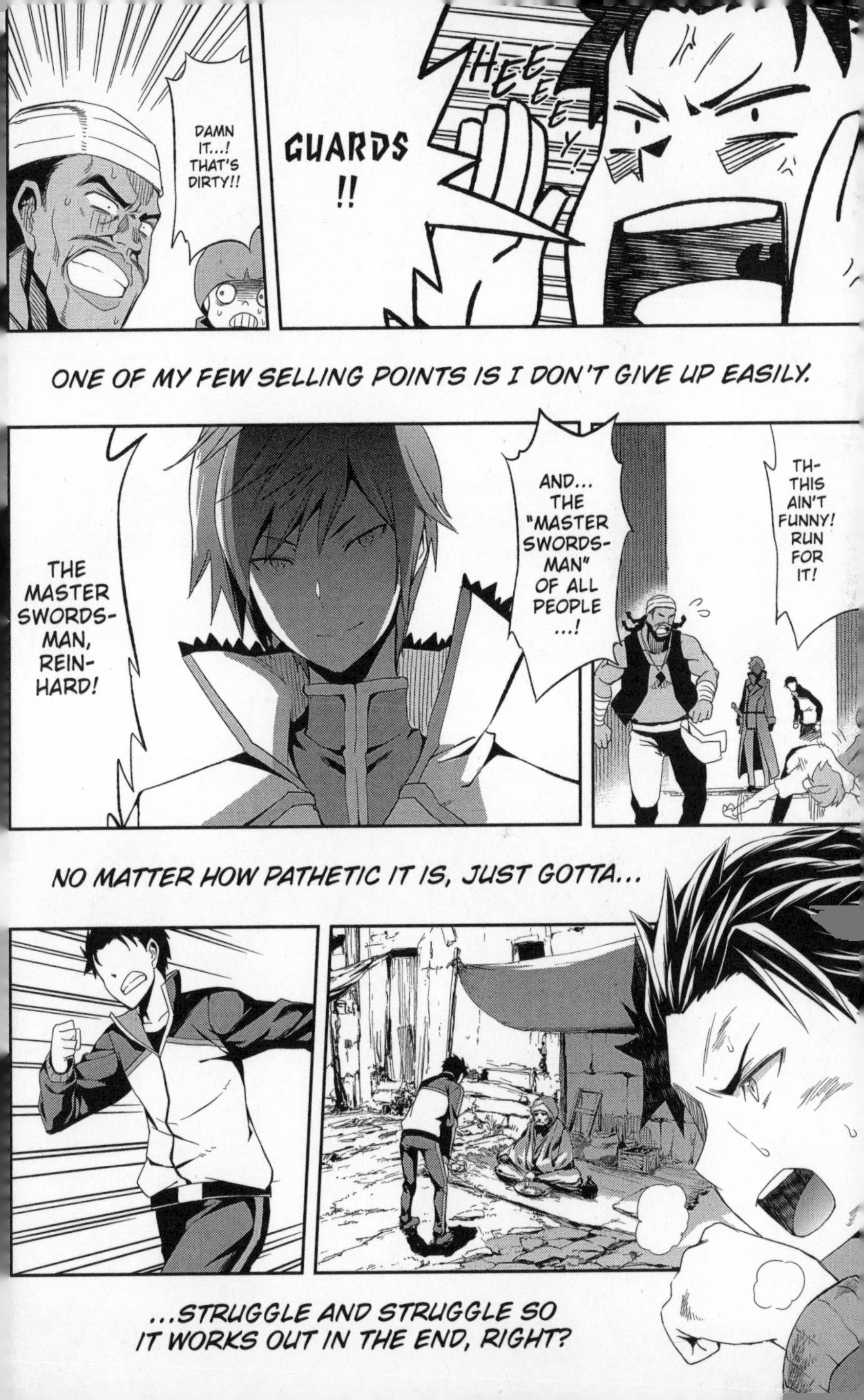
HEEEEEY!
GUARDS!!
DAMN IT...! THAT'S DIRTY!!
ONE OF MY FEW SELLING POINTS IS I DON'T GIVE UP EASILY.
TH-THIS AIN'T FUNNY! RUN FOR IT!
AND... THE "MASTER SWORDS-MAN" OF ALL PEOPLE...!
THE MASTER SWORDS-MAN, REIN-HARD!
NO MATTER HOW PATHETIC IT IS, JUST GOTTA...
...STRUGGLE AND STRUGGLE SO IT WORKS OUT IN THE END, RIGHT?

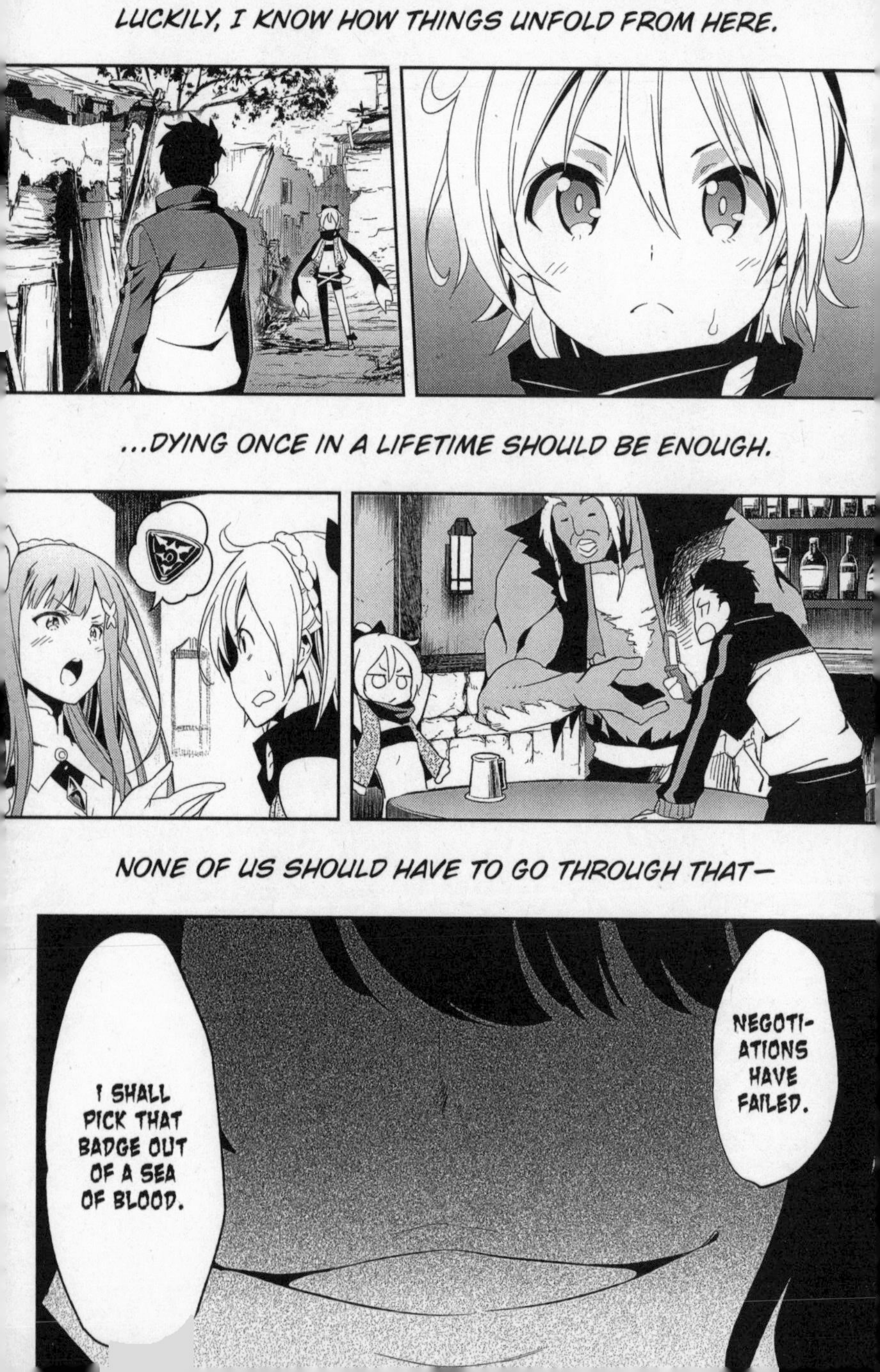
LUCKILY, I KNOW HOW THINGS UNFOLD FROM HERE.
...DYING ONCE IN A LIFETIME SHOULD BE ENOUGH.
NONE OF US SHOULD HAVE TO GO THROUGH THAT—
NEGOTI-ATIONS HAVE FAILED.
I SHALL PICK THAT BADGE OUT OF A SEA OF BLOOD.

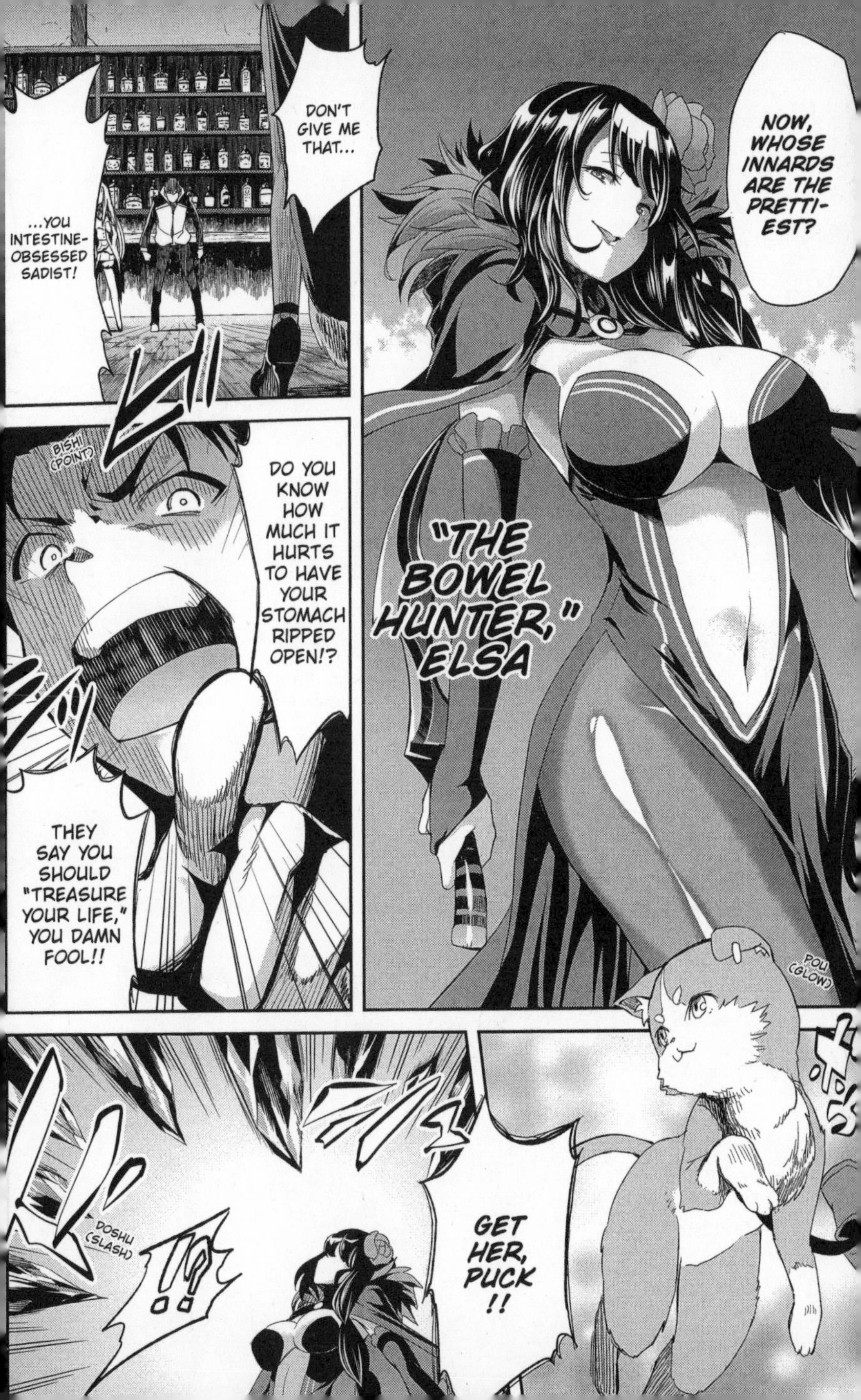
NOW, WHOSE INNARDS ARE THE PRETTI-EST?
"THE BOWEL HUNTER," ELSA
POU (GLOW)
DON'T GIVE ME THAT...
...YOU INTESTINE-OBSESSED SADIST!
BISHI (POINT)
DO YOU KNOW HOW MUCH IT HURTS TO HAVE YOUR STOMACH RIPPED OPEN!?
THEY SAY YOU SHOULD "TREASURE YOUR LIFE," YOU DAMN FOOL!!
GET HER, PUCK!!
DOSHU (SLASH)
!?

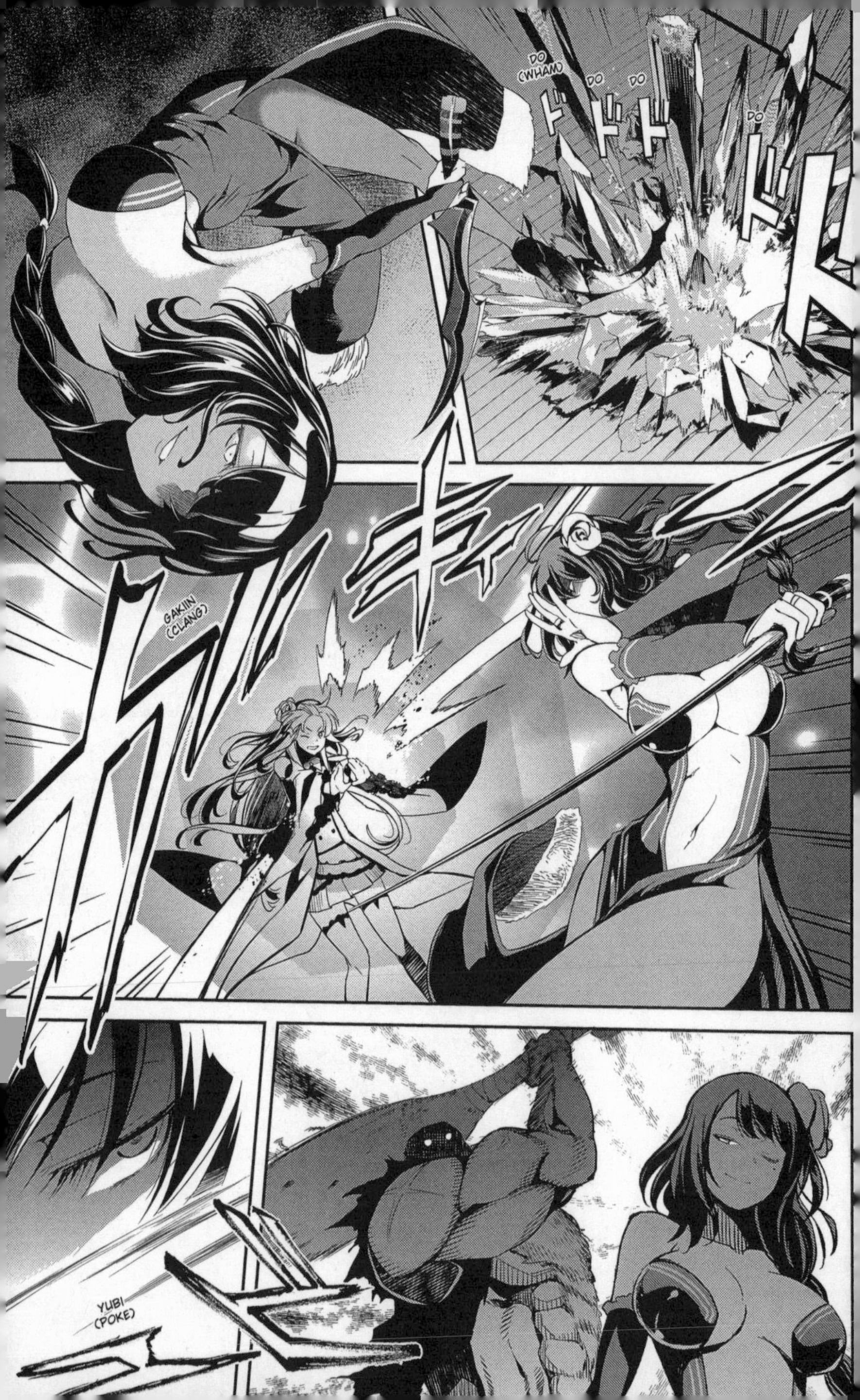
DO
(WHAM)
DO
DO
DO
GAKIIN
(CLANG)
YUBI
(POKE)

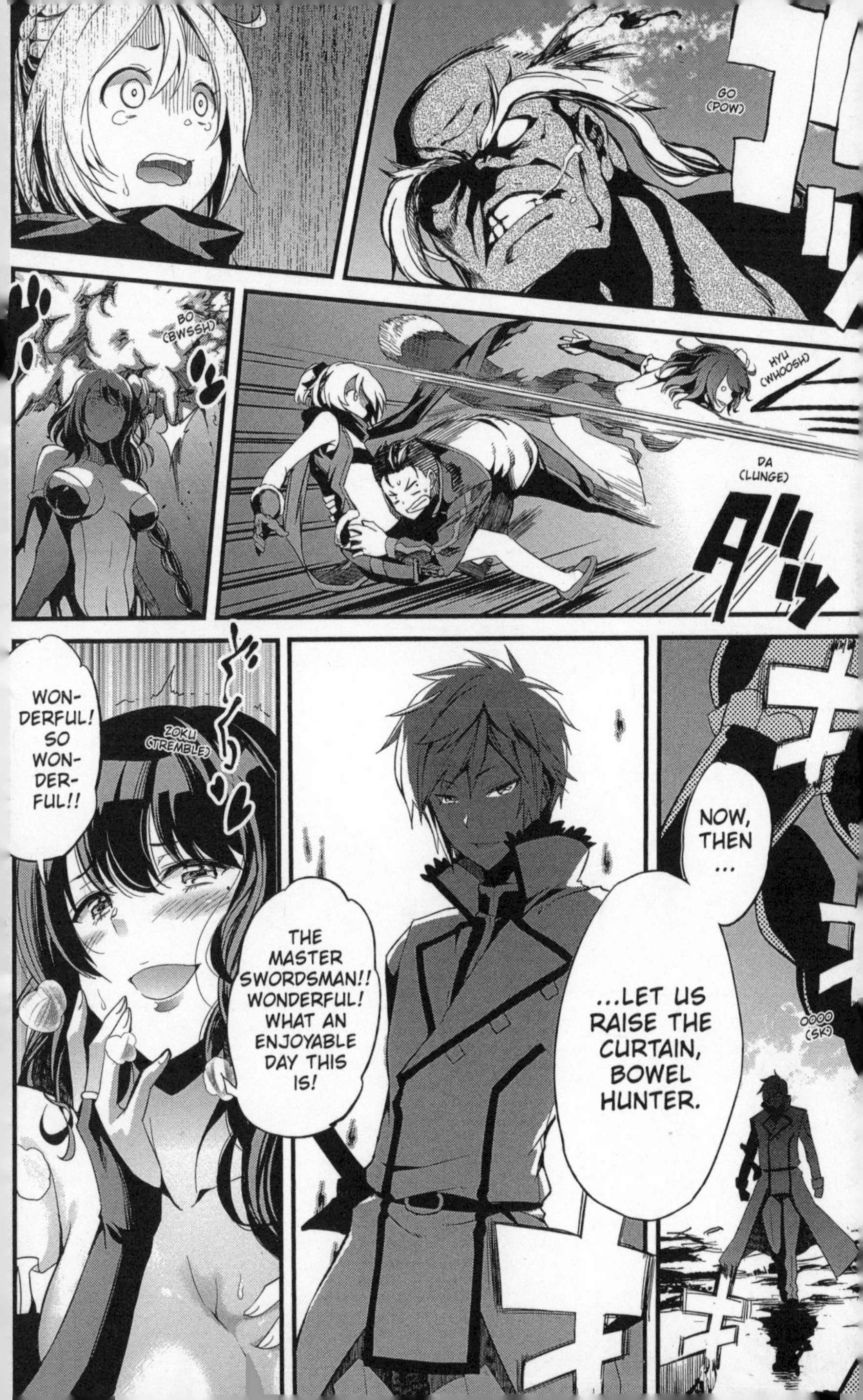
GO (POW)
HYU (WHOOSH)
DA (LUNGE)
BO (BWSSH)
OOOO (SK)
NOW, THEN...
...LET US RAISE THE CURTAIN, BOWEL HUNTER.
THE MASTER SWORDSMAN!! WONDERFUL! WHAT AN ENJOYABLE DAY THIS IS!
ZOKU (TREMBLE)
WON-DERFUL! SO WON-DER-FUL!!

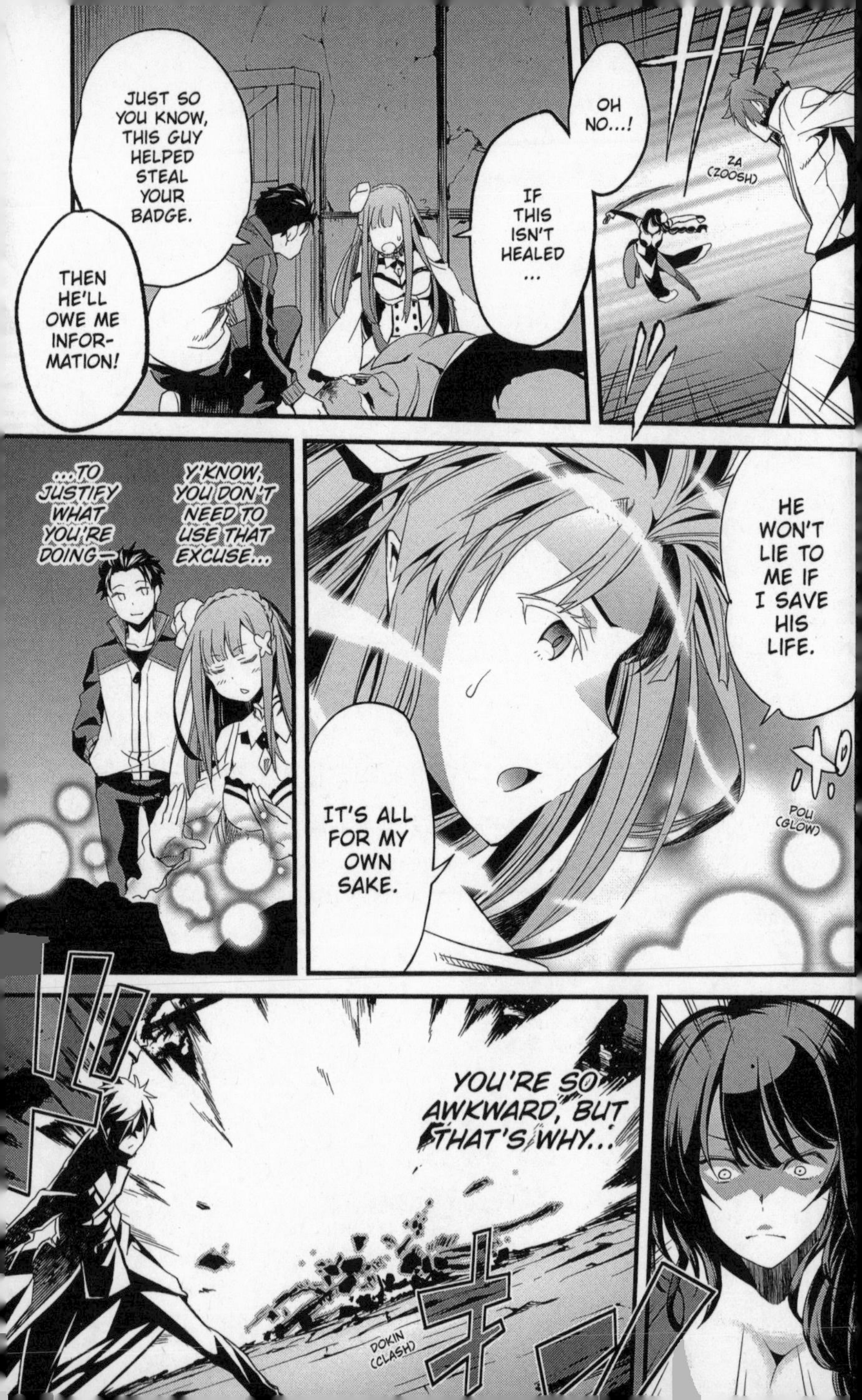
ZA (ZOOSH)
OH NO...!
IF THIS ISN'T HEALED...
JUST SO YOU KNOW, THIS GUY HELPED STEAL YOUR BADGE.
THEN HE'LL OWE ME INFORMATION!
HE WON'T LIE TO ME IF I SAVE HIS LIFE.
POU (GLOW)
IT'S ALL FOR MY OWN SAKE.
Y'KNOW, YOU DON'T NEED TO USE THAT EXCUSE...
...TO JUSTIFY WHAT YOU'RE DOING—
YOU'RE SO AWKWARD, BUT THAT'S WHY...
DOKIN (CLASH)

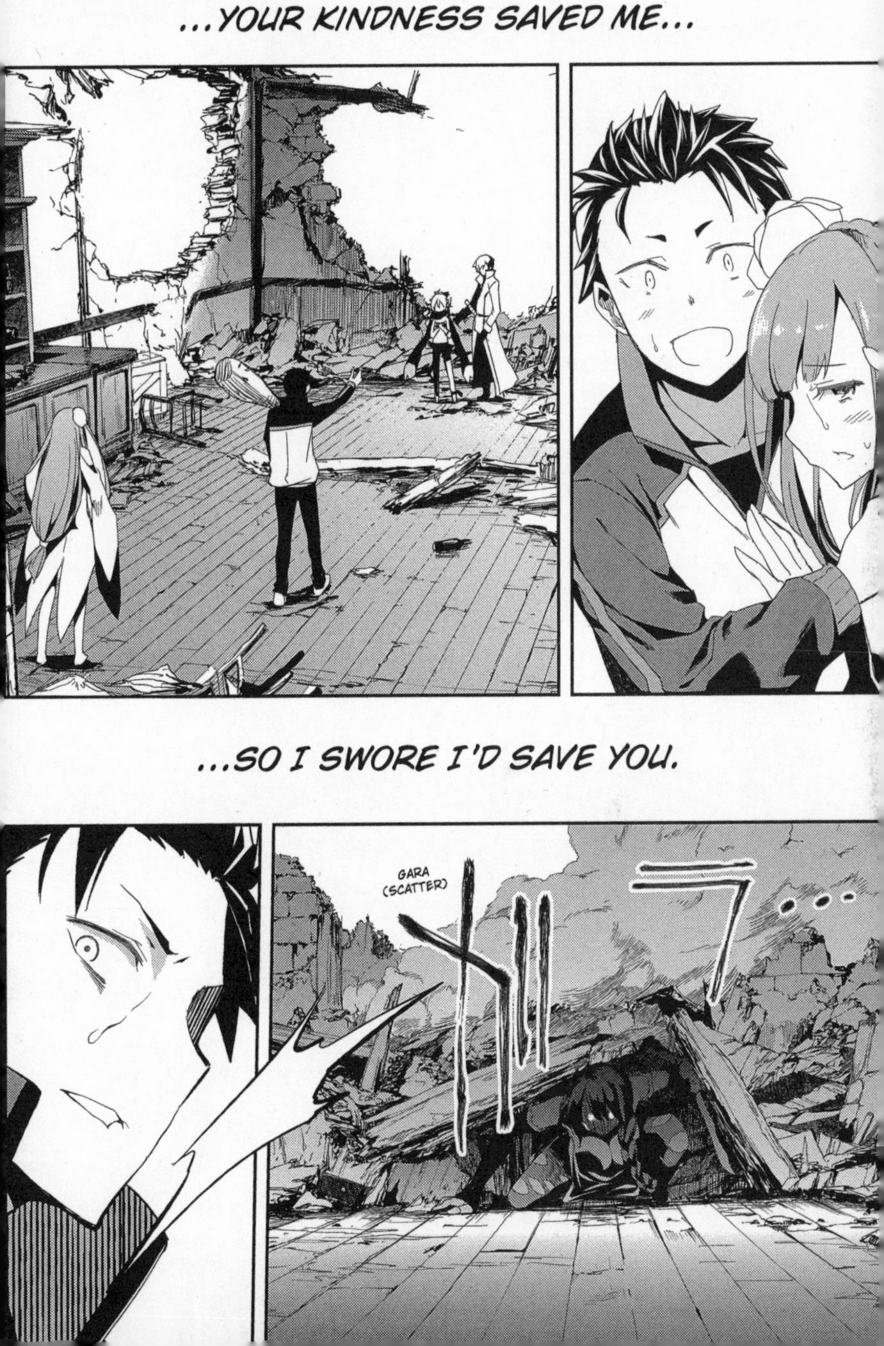
...YOUR KINDNESS SAVED ME...
...SO I SWORE I'D SAVE YOU.
GARA (SCATTER)

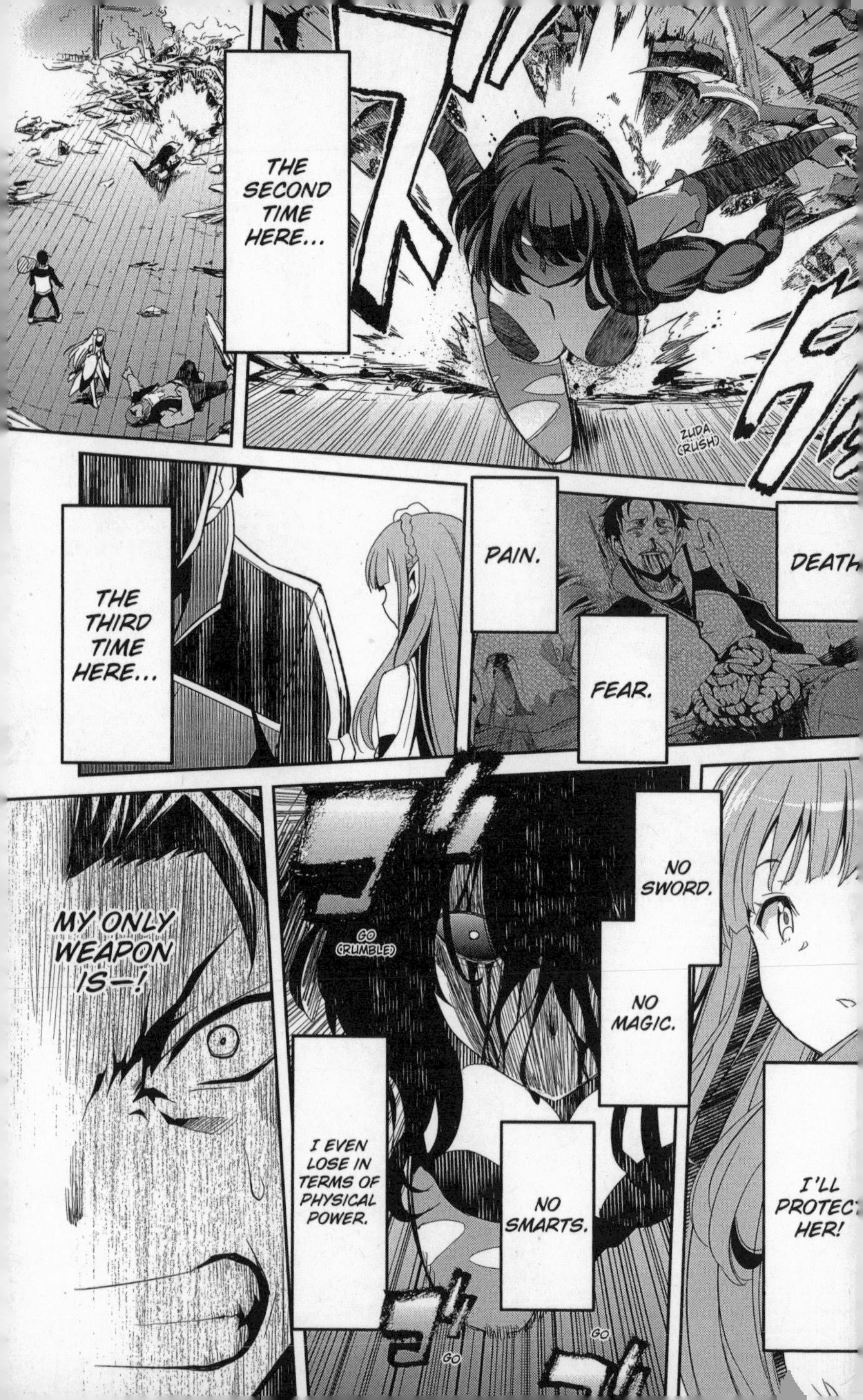
THE SECOND TIME HERE...
ZUDA (CRUSH)
DEATH
PAIN.
FEAR.
THE THIRD TIME HERE...
I'LL PROTEC HER!
NO SWORD.
NO MAGIC.
GO (RUMBLE)
NO SMARTS.
I EVEN LOSE IN TERMS OF PHYSICAL POWER.
GO
GO
MY ONLY WEAPON IS—!

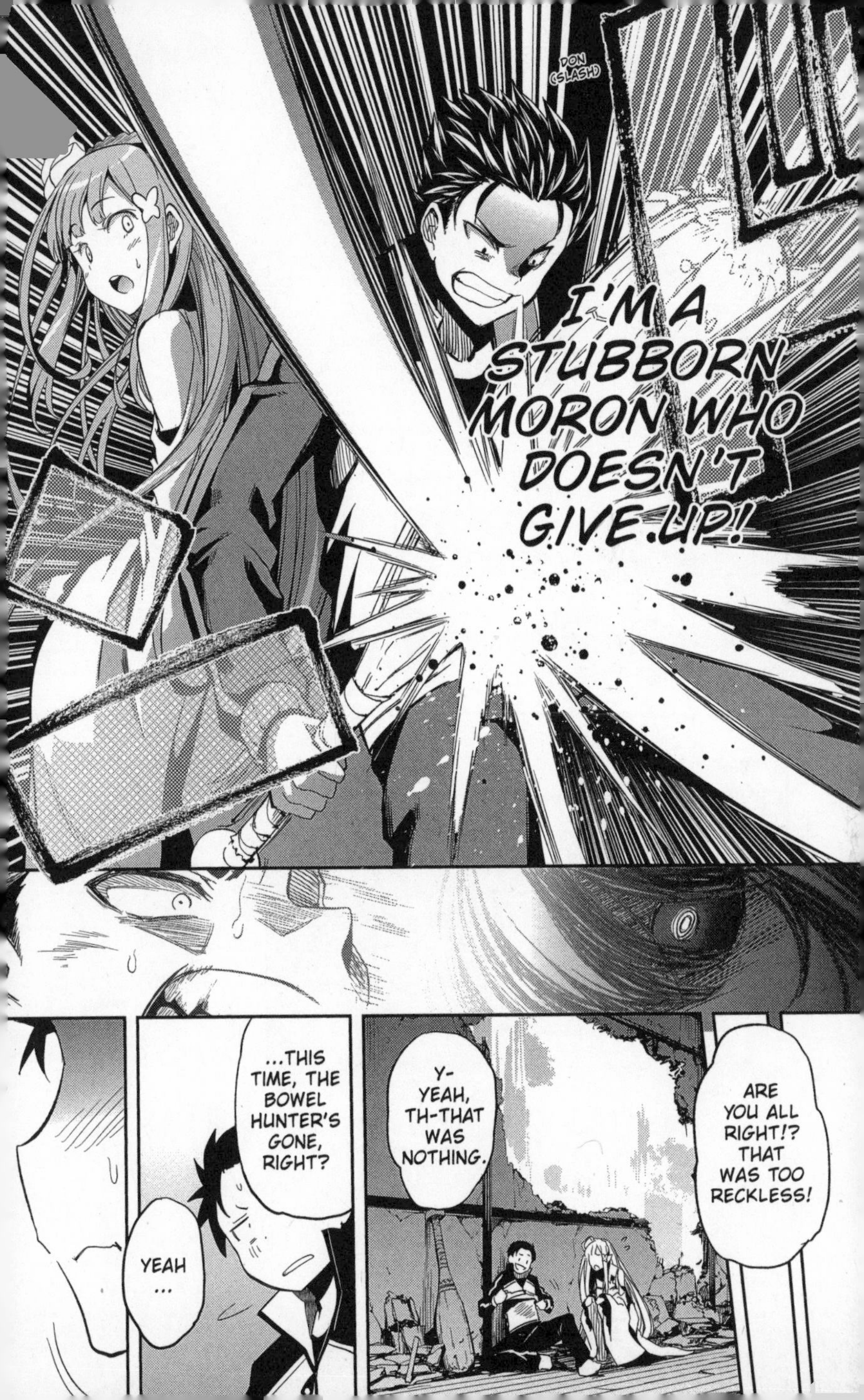
DON (SLASH)
I'M A STUBBORN MORON WHO DOESN'T GIVE UP!
ARE YOU ALL RIGHT!? THAT WAS TOO RECKLESS!
Y-YEAH, TH-THAT WAS NOTHING.
...THIS TIME, THE BOWEL HUNTER'S GONE, RIGHT?
YEAH...

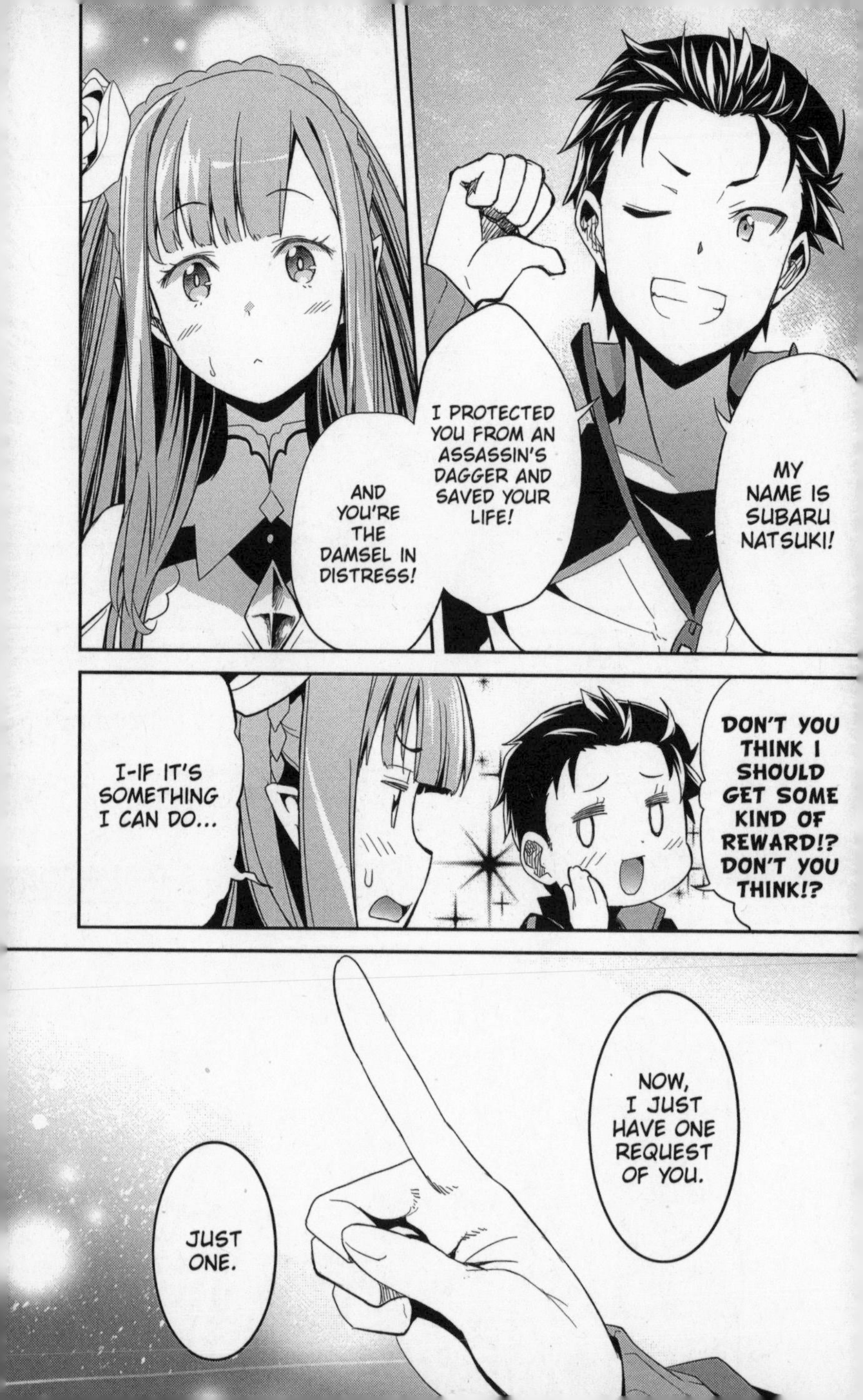
MY NAME IS SUBARU NATSUKI!
I PROTECTED YOU FROM AN ASSASSIN'S DAGGER AND SAVED YOUR LIFE!
AND YOU'RE THE DAMSEL IN DISTRESS!
DON'T YOU THINK I SHOULD GET SOME KIND OF REWARD!? DON'T YOU THINK!?
I-IF IT'S SOMETHING I CAN DO...
NOW, I JUST HAVE ONE REQUEST OF YOU.
JUST ONE.

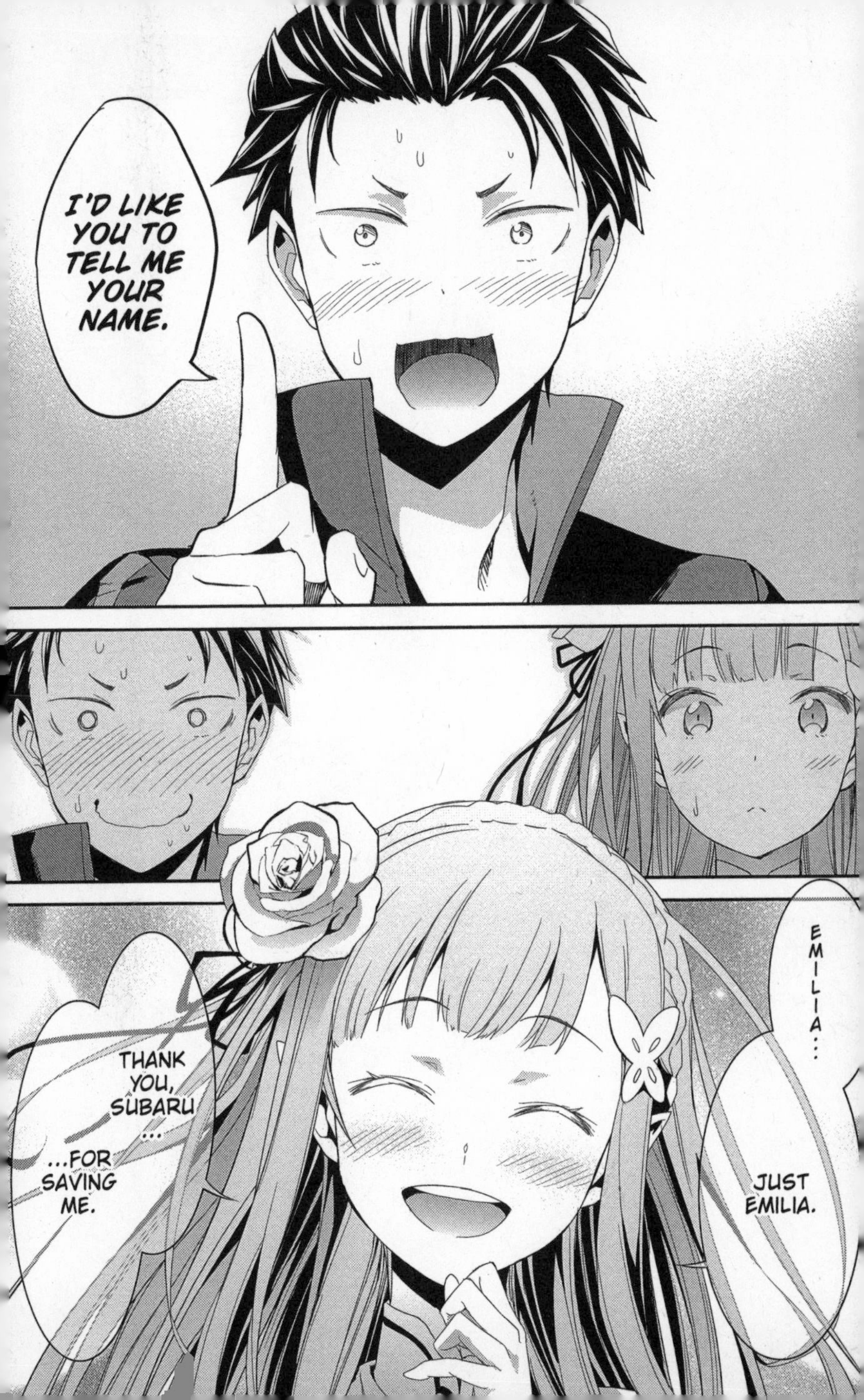
I'D LIKE YOU TO TELL ME YOUR NAME.
EMILIA...
JUST EMILIA.
THANK YOU, SUBARU...
...FOR SAVING ME.

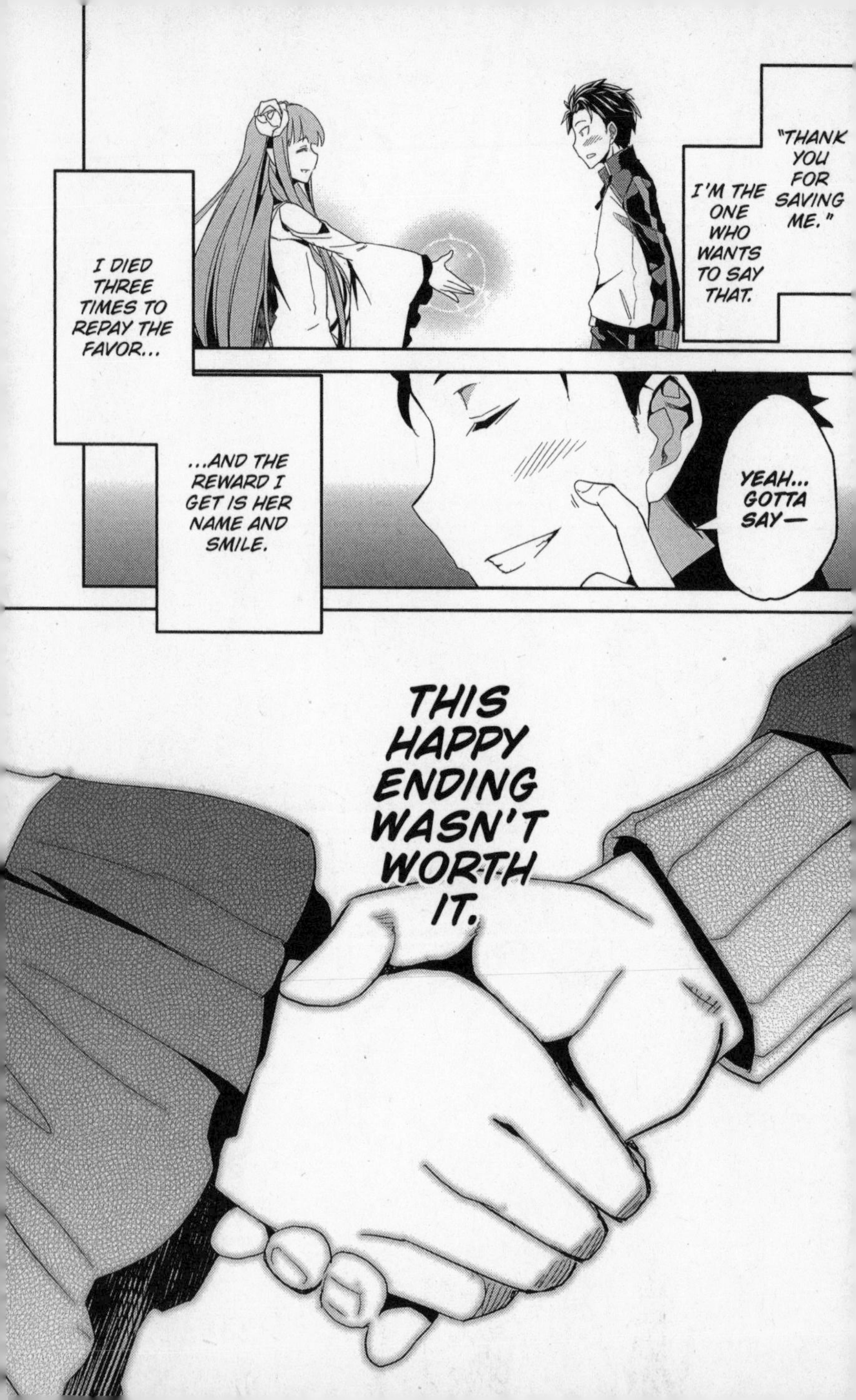
"THANK YOU FOR SAVING ME."
I'M THE ONE WHO WANTS TO SAY THAT.
I DIED THREE TIMES TO REPAY THE FAVOR...
YEAH... GOTTA SAY—
...AND THE REWARD I GET IS HER NAME AND SMILE.
THIS HAPPY ENDING WASN'T WORTH IT.

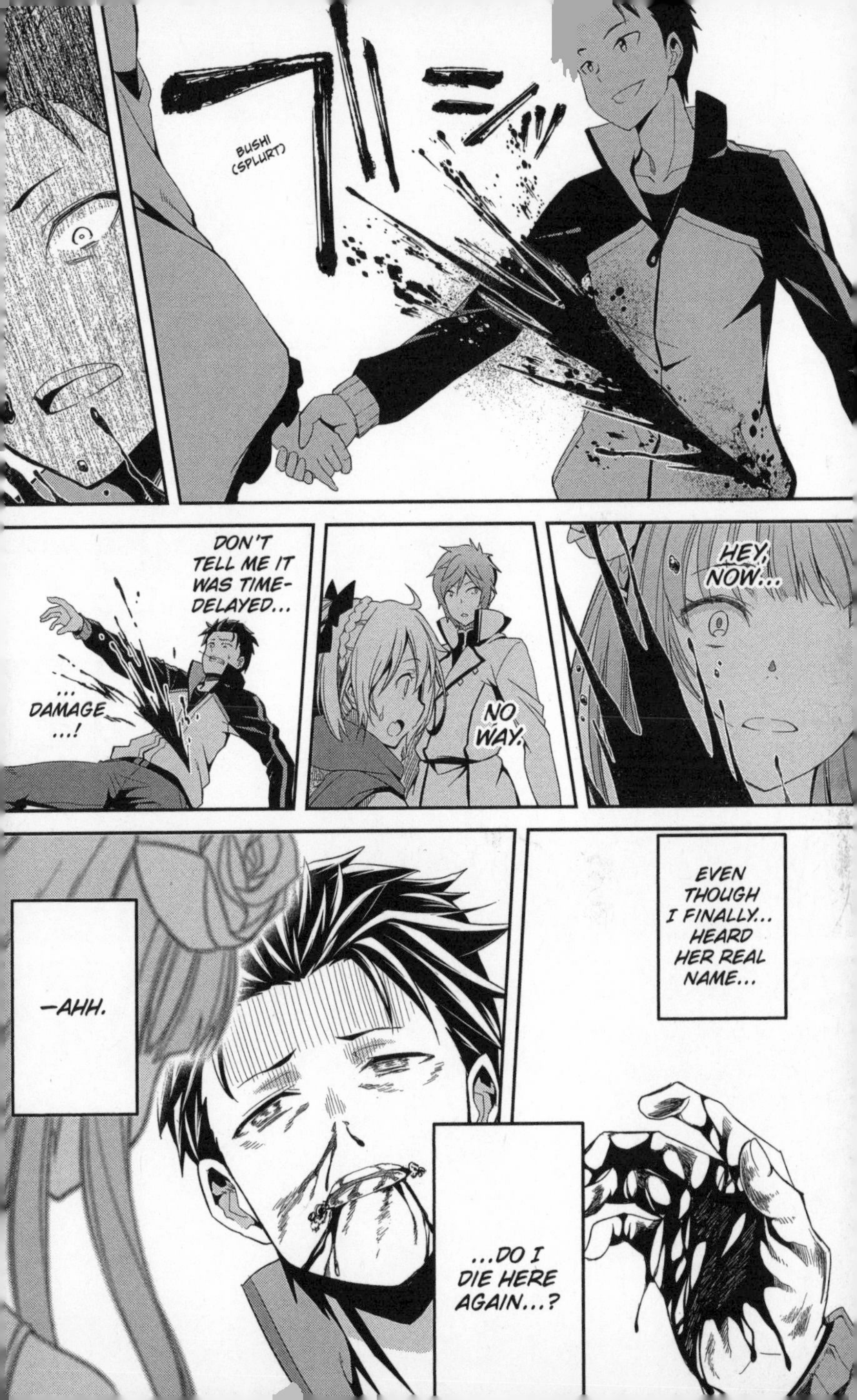
BUSHI (SPLURT)
HEY, NOW...
NO WAY.
DON'T TELL ME IT WAS TIME-DELAYED...
...DAMAGE...!
EVEN THOUGH I FINALLY... HEARD HER REAL NAME...
—AHH.
...DO I DIE HERE AGAIN...?

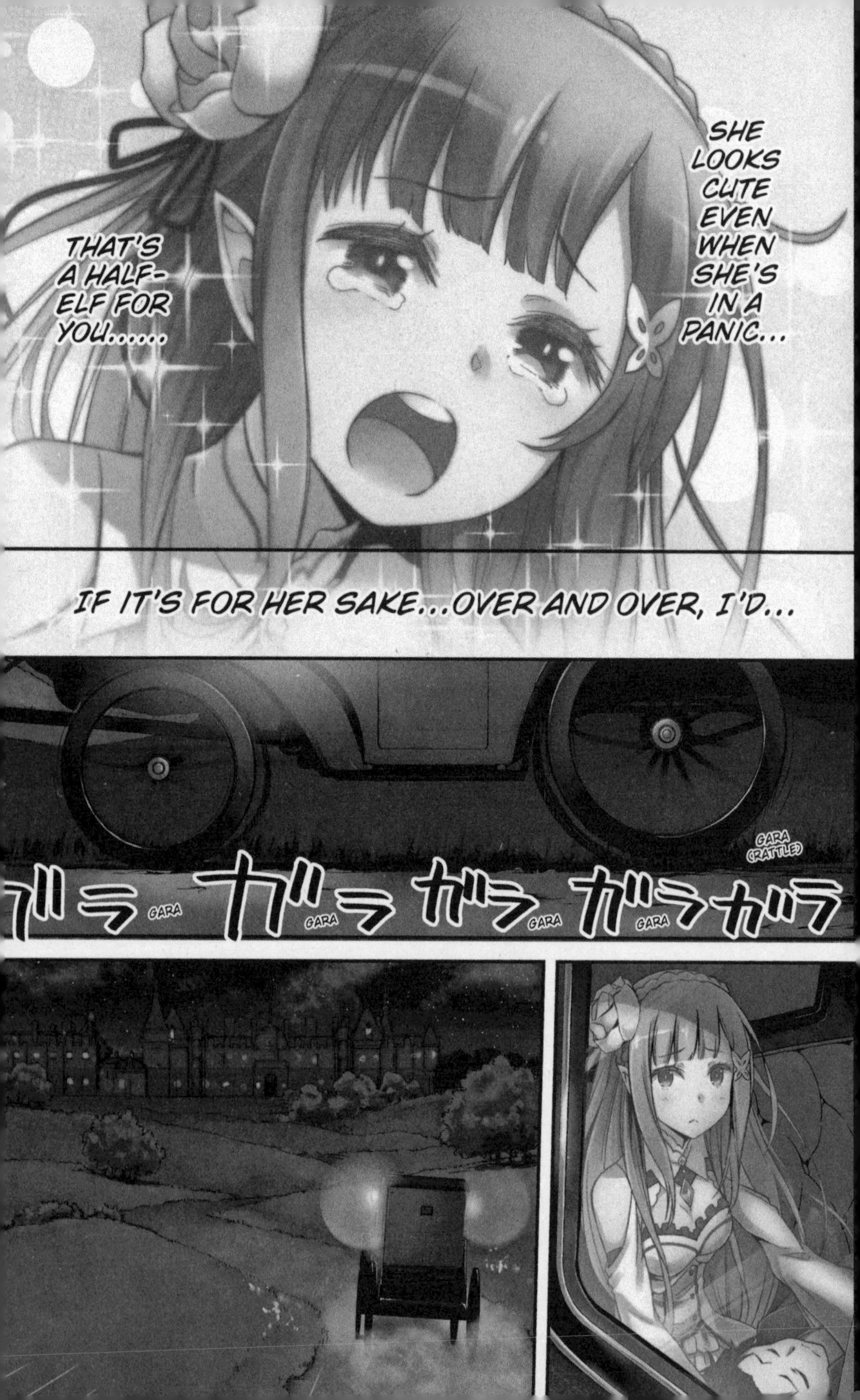
SHE LOOKS CUTE EVEN WHEN SHE'S IN A PANIC...
THAT'S A HALF-ELF FOR YOU......
IF IT'S FOR HER SAKE...OVER AND OVER, I'D...
GARA (RATTLE)
ガラガラ
GARA
ガラ
GARA
ガラ
GARA
ガラ
GARA
ガラ

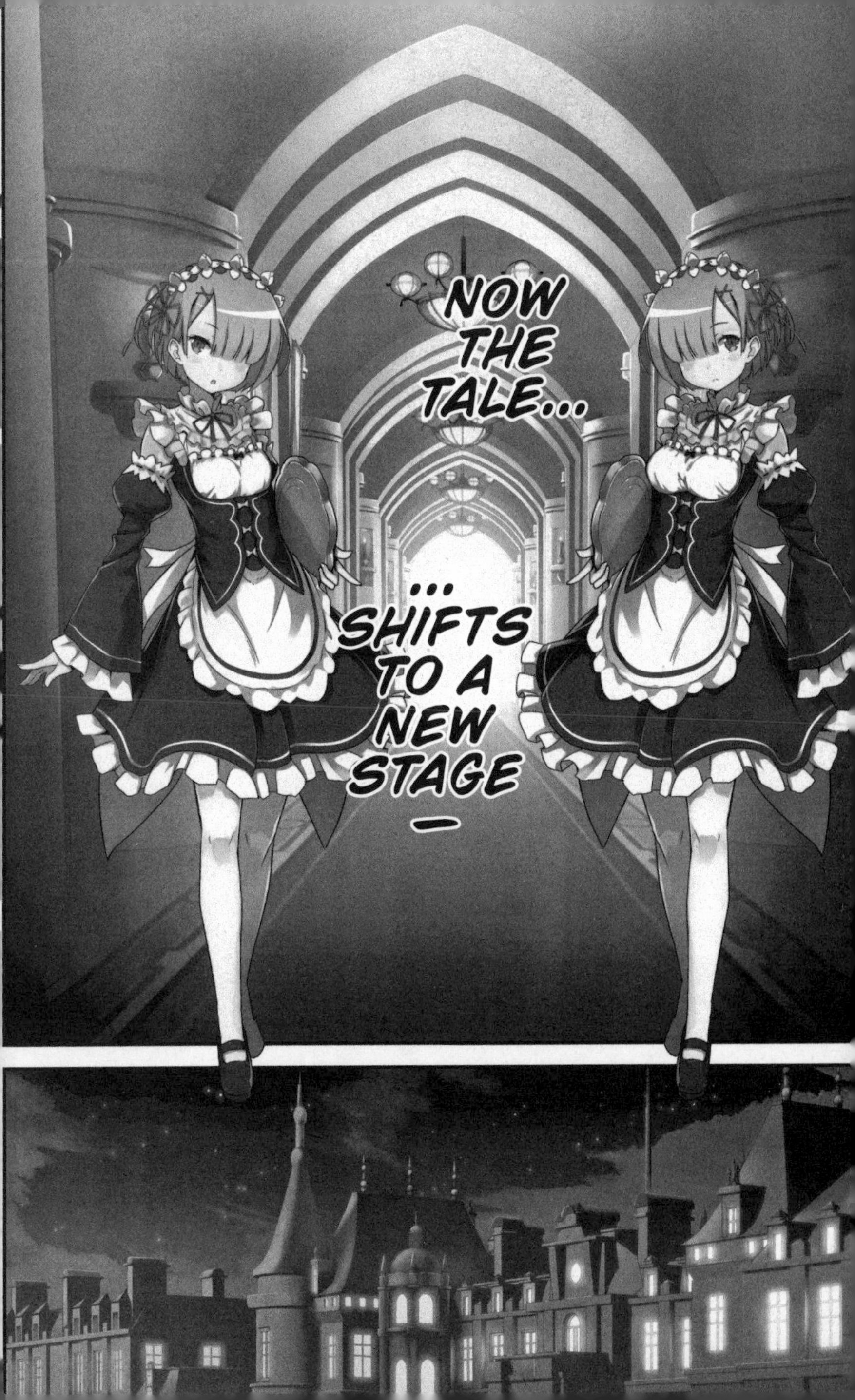
NOW THE TALE...
...SHIFTS TO A NEW STAGE —

It was quite an ordeal putting this digest of Chapter 1 of the novel together. Thanks to that, my version of Chapter 1 from the source material is a mess. I suppose the second and third are even more of a mess though.

Compared to this digest, Matsuse-sensei's comic adaptation of Chapter 1 conveys the charm of the original's first volume in ways I couldn't!

Re:ZeRo

-Starting Life in Another World-

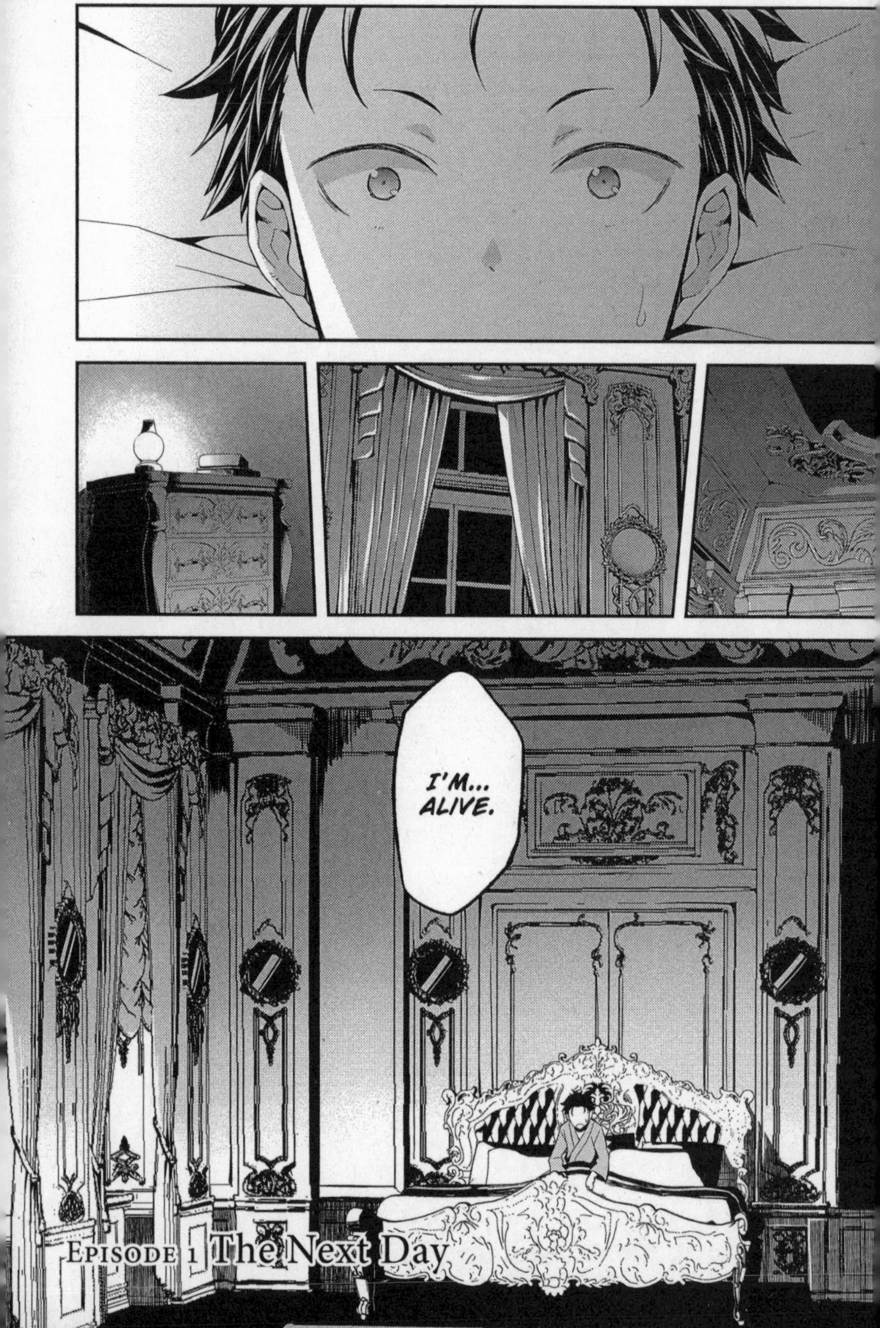
I'M... ALIVE.
EPISODE 1 The Next Day

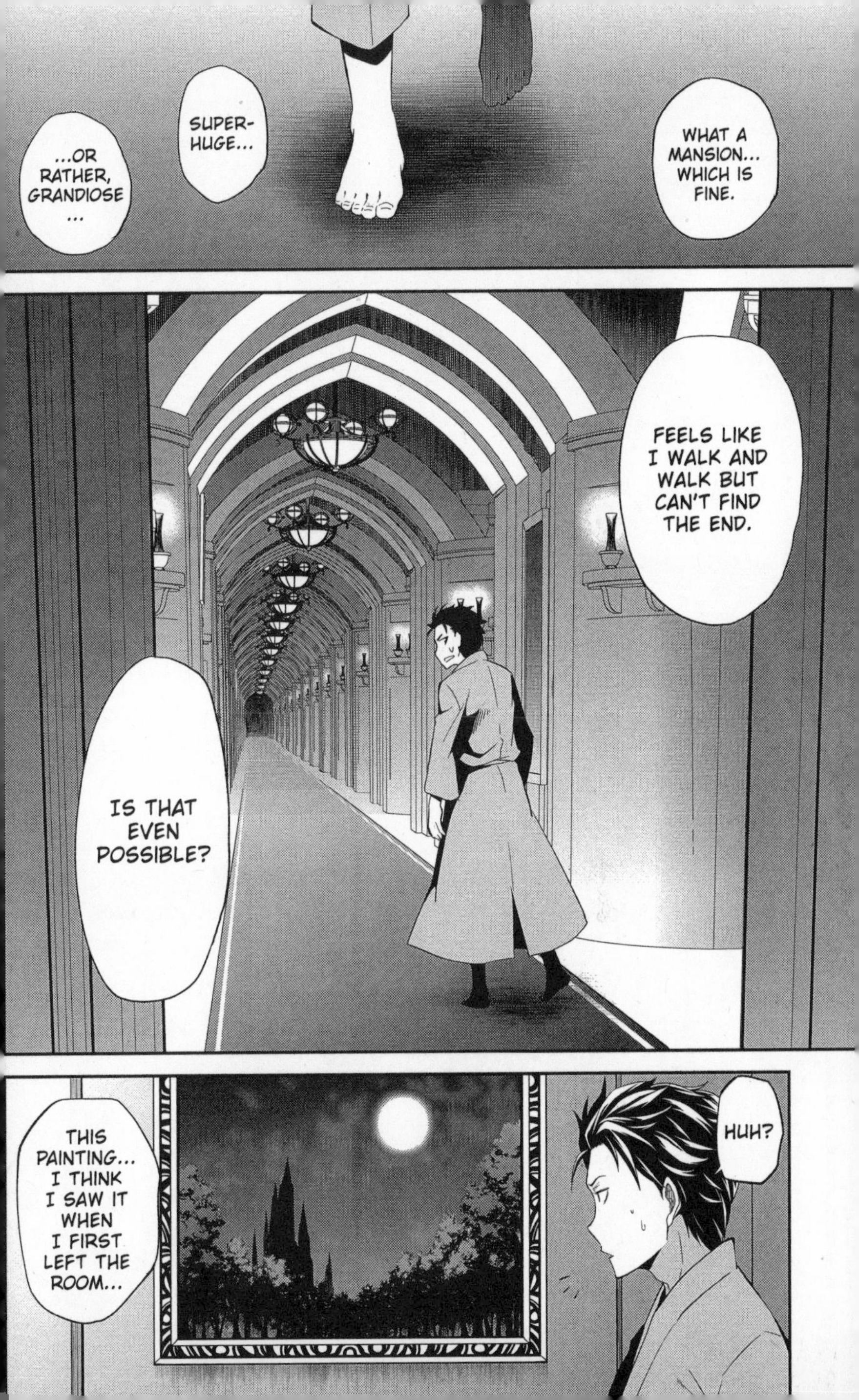
WHAT A MANSION... WHICH IS FINE.
SUPER-HUGE...
...OR RATHER, GRANDIOSE ...
FEELS LIKE I WALK AND WALK BUT CAN'T FIND THE END.
IS THAT EVEN POSSIBLE?
HUH?
THIS PAINTING... I THINK I SAW IT WHEN I FIRST LEFT THE ROOM...

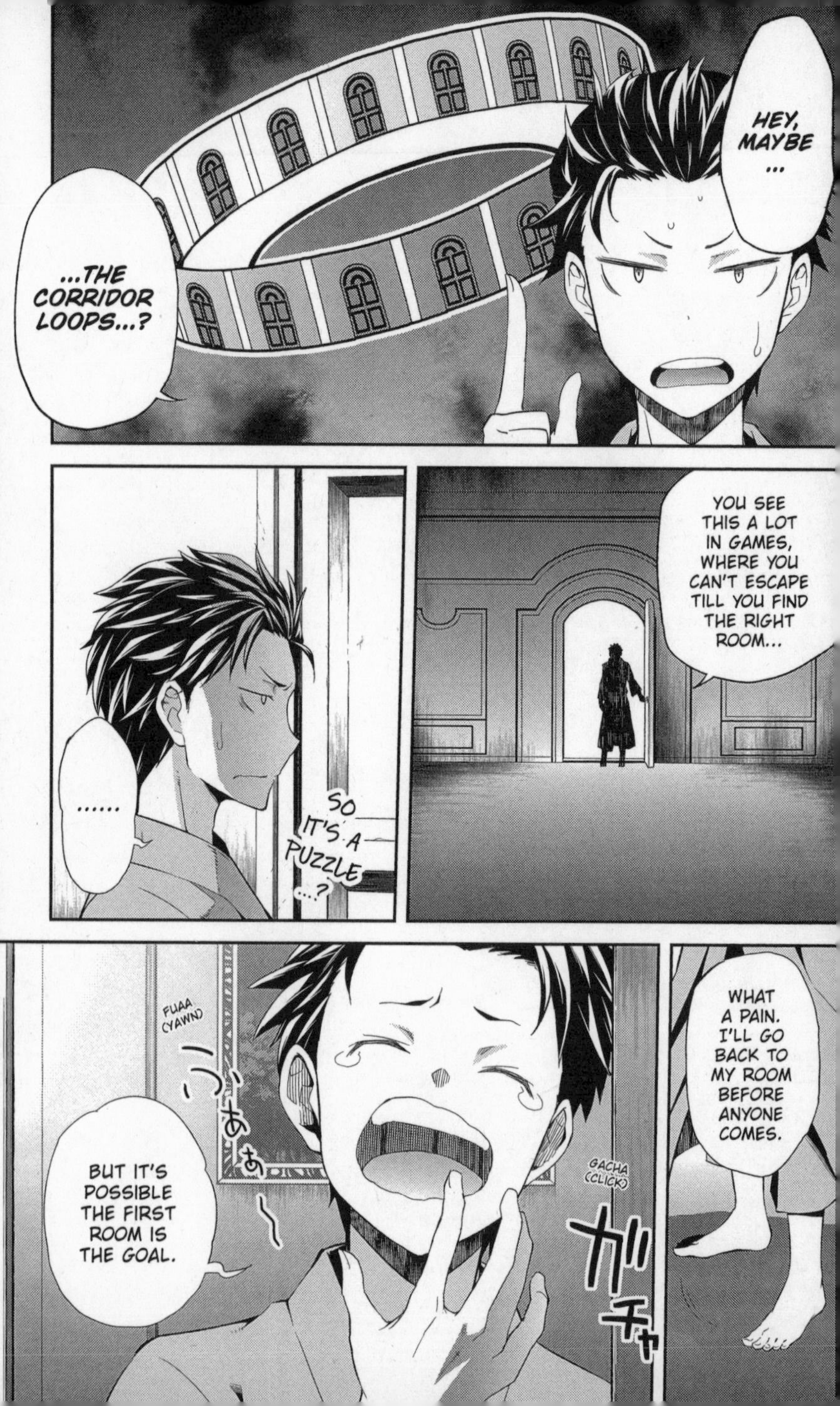
HEY, MAYBE ...
...THE CORRIDOR LOOPS...?
YOU SEE THIS A LOT IN GAMES, WHERE YOU CAN'T ESCAPE TILL YOU FIND THE RIGHT ROOM...
SO IT'S A PUZZLE ...?
......
WHAT A PAIN. I'LL GO BACK TO MY ROOM BEFORE ANYONE COMES.
ガチャ
GACHA (CLICK)
ふぁあ～
FUAA (YAWN)
BUT IT'S POSSIBLE THE FIRST ROOM IS THE GOAL.

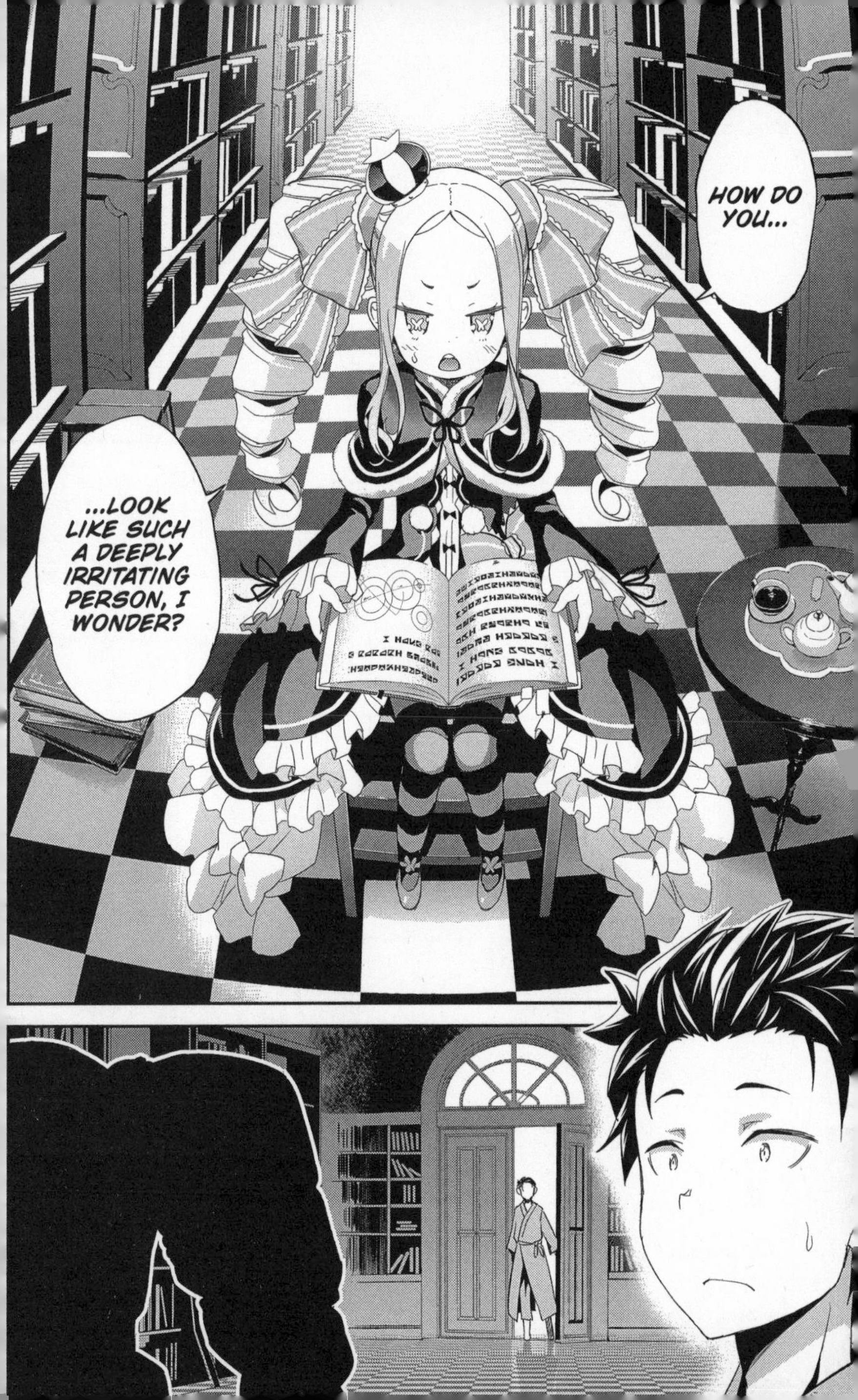
HOW DO YOU...
...LOOK LIKE SUCH A DEEPLY IRRITATING PERSON, I WONDER?

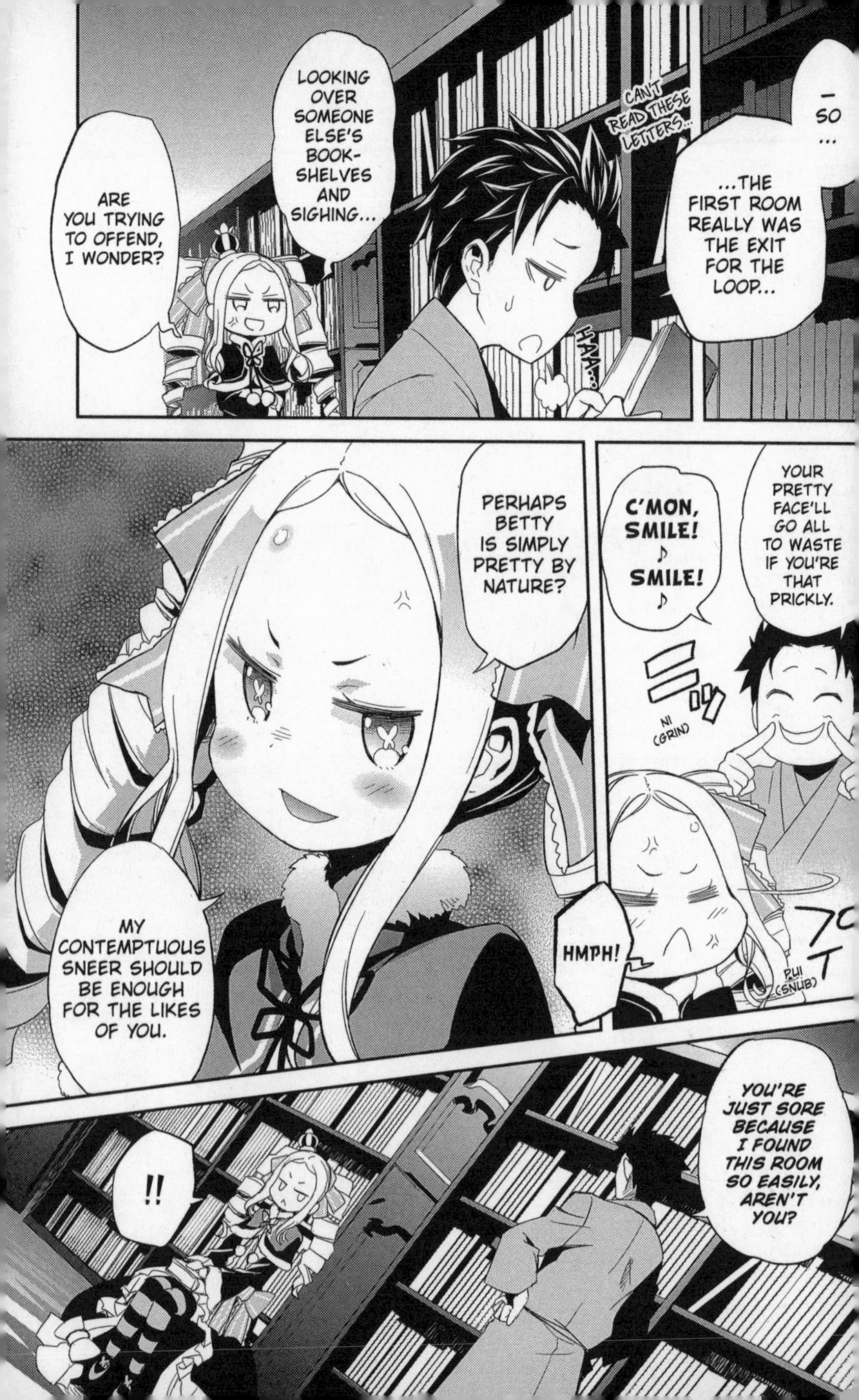
—SO...
...THE FIRST ROOM REALLY WAS THE EXIT FOR THE LOOP...
CAN'T READ THESE LETTERS...
HAA...
LOOKING OVER SOMEONE ELSE'S BOOK-SHELVES AND SIGHING...
ARE YOU TRYING TO OFFEND, I WONDER?
YOUR PRETTY FACE'LL GO ALL TO WASTE IF YOU'RE THAT PRICKLY.
C'MON, SMILE! ♪ SMILE! ♪
NI (GRIN)
HMPH!
PUI (SNUB)
PERHAPS BETTY IS SIMPLY PRETTY BY NATURE?
MY CONTEMPTUOUS SNEER SHOULD BE ENOUGH FOR THE LIKES OF YOU.
YOU'RE JUST SORE BECAUSE I FOUND THIS ROOM SO EASILY, AREN'T YOU?
!!

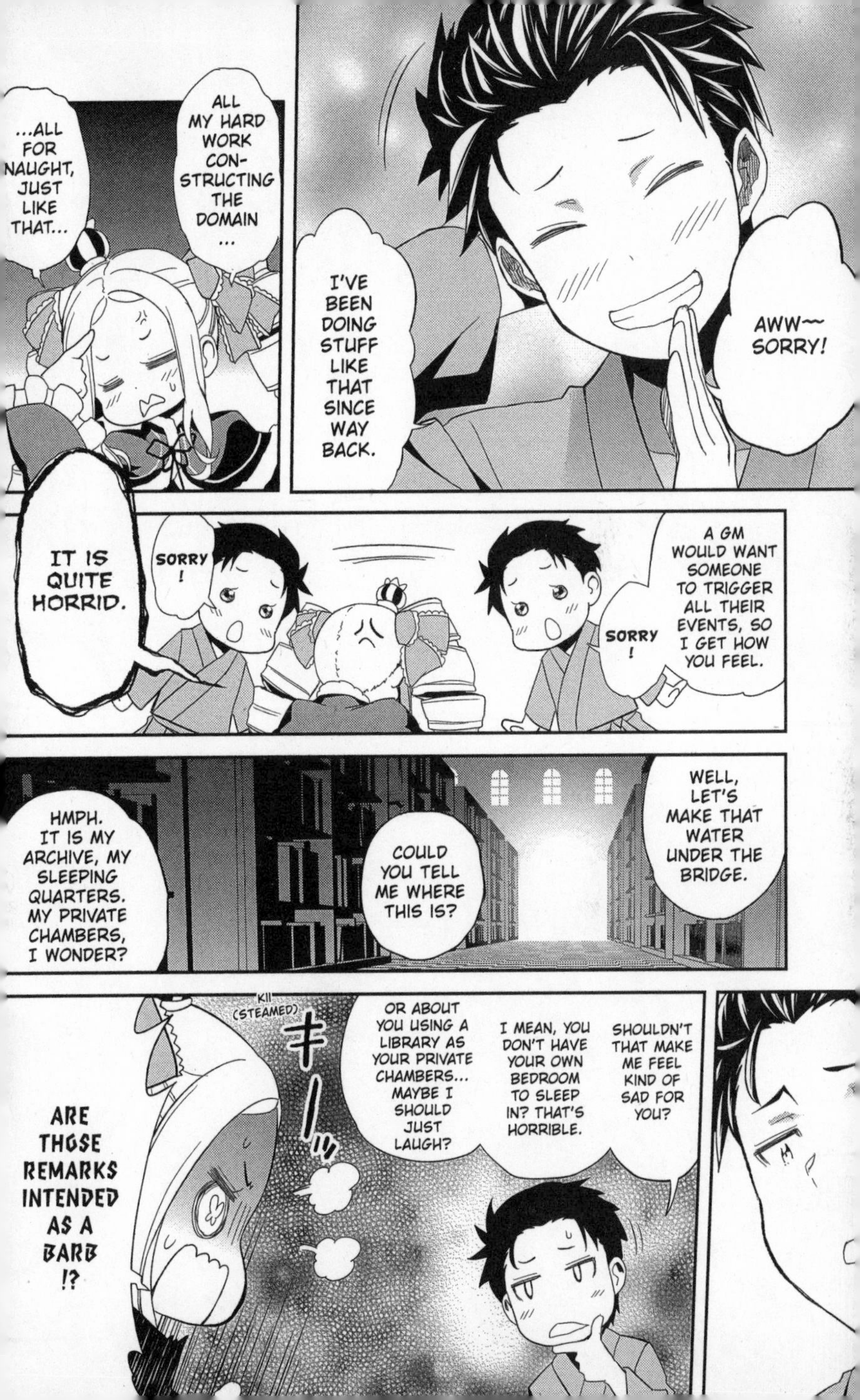
AWW~~ SORRY!
I'VE BEEN DOING STUFF LIKE THAT SINCE WAY BACK.
ALL MY HARD WORK CON-STRUCTING THE DOMAIN...
...ALL FOR NAUGHT, JUST LIKE THAT...
A GM WOULD WANT SOMEONE TO TRIGGER ALL THEIR EVENTS, SO I GET HOW YOU FEEL.
SORRY!
SORRY!
IT IS QUITE HORRID.
WELL, LET'S MAKE THAT WATER UNDER THE BRIDGE.
COULD YOU TELL ME WHERE THIS IS?
HMPH. IT IS MY ARCHIVE, MY SLEEPING QUARTERS. MY PRIVATE CHAMBERS, I WONDER?
SHOULDN'T THAT MAKE ME FEEL KIND OF SAD FOR YOU?
I MEAN, YOU DON'T HAVE YOUR OWN BEDROOM TO SLEEP IN? THAT'S HORRIBLE.
OR ABOUT YOU USING A LIBRARY AS YOUR PRIVATE CHAMBERS... MAYBE I SHOULD JUST LAUGH?
KII (STEAMED)
ARE THOSE REMARKS INTENDED AS A BARB!?

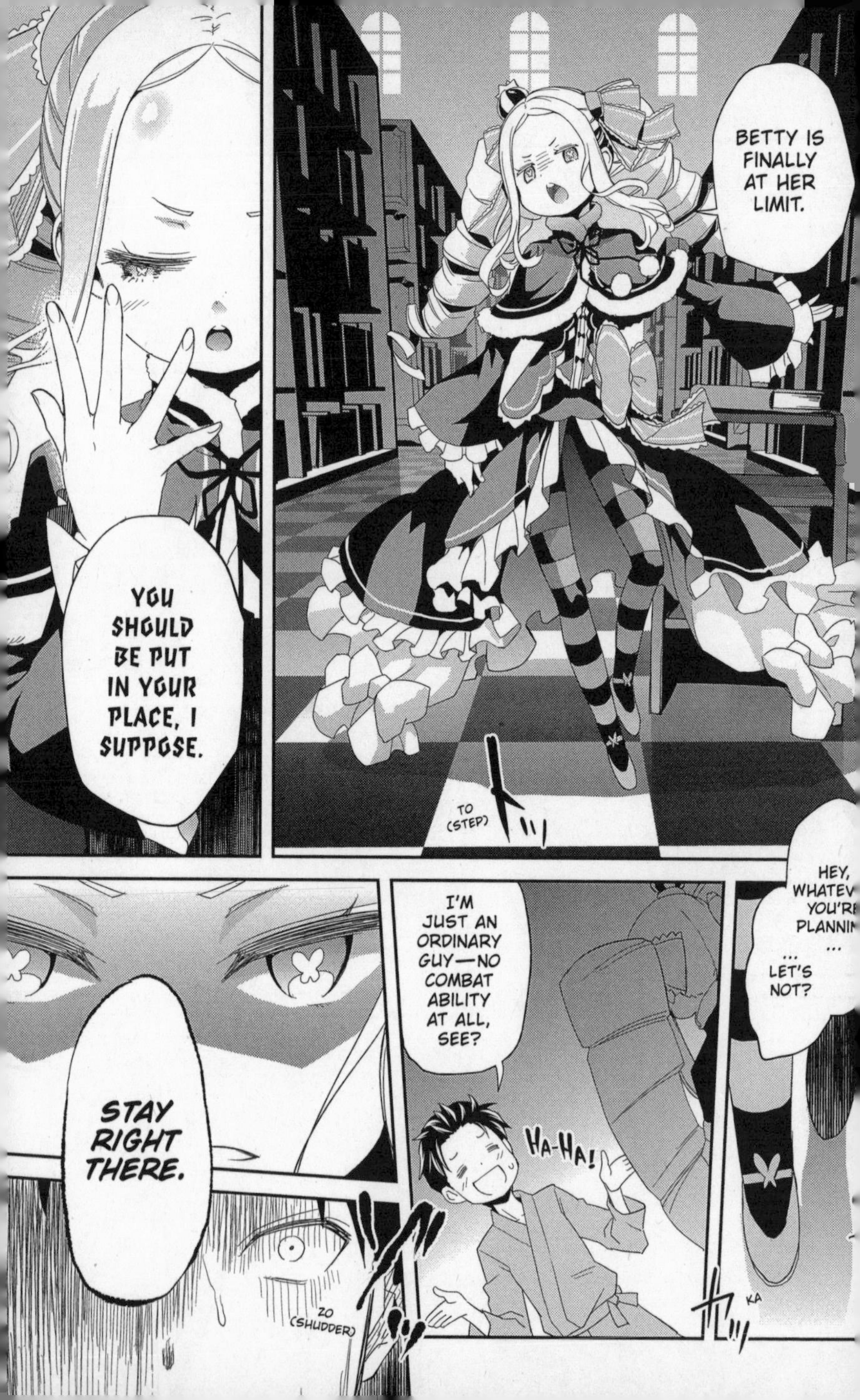
BETTY IS FINALLY AT HER LIMIT.
TO (STEP)
YOU SHOULD BE PUT IN YOUR PLACE, I SUPPOSE.
HEY, WHATEV YOU'R PLANNI ... LET'S NOT?
KA
I'M JUST AN ORDINARY GUY—NO COMBAT ABILITY AT ALL, SEE?
HA-HA!
STAY RIGHT THERE.
ZO (SHUDDER)

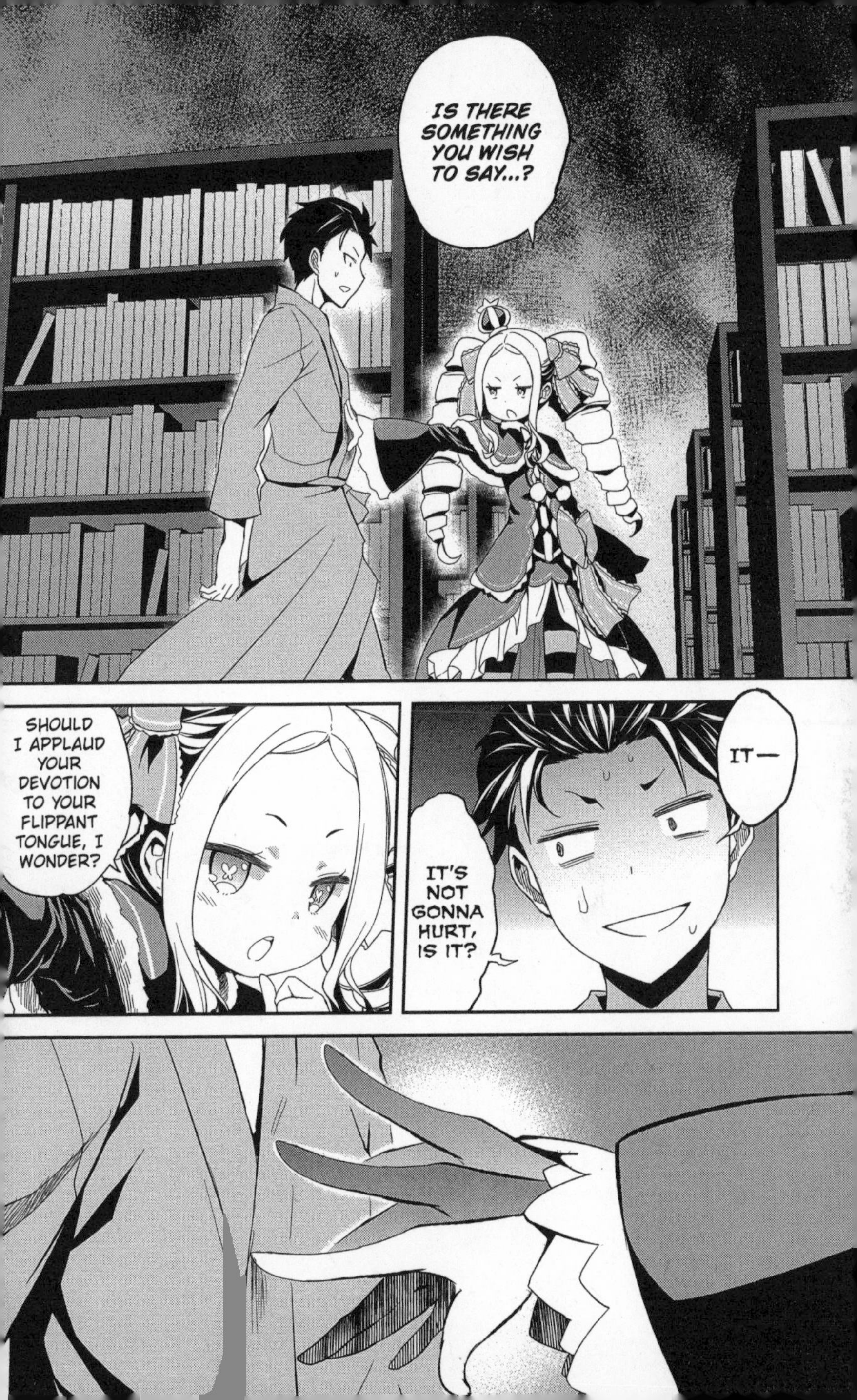
IS THERE SOMETHING YOU WISH TO SAY...?
IT—
IT'S NOT GONNA HURT, IS IT?
SHOULD I APPLAUD YOUR DEVOTION TO YOUR FLIPPANT TONGUE, I WONDER?

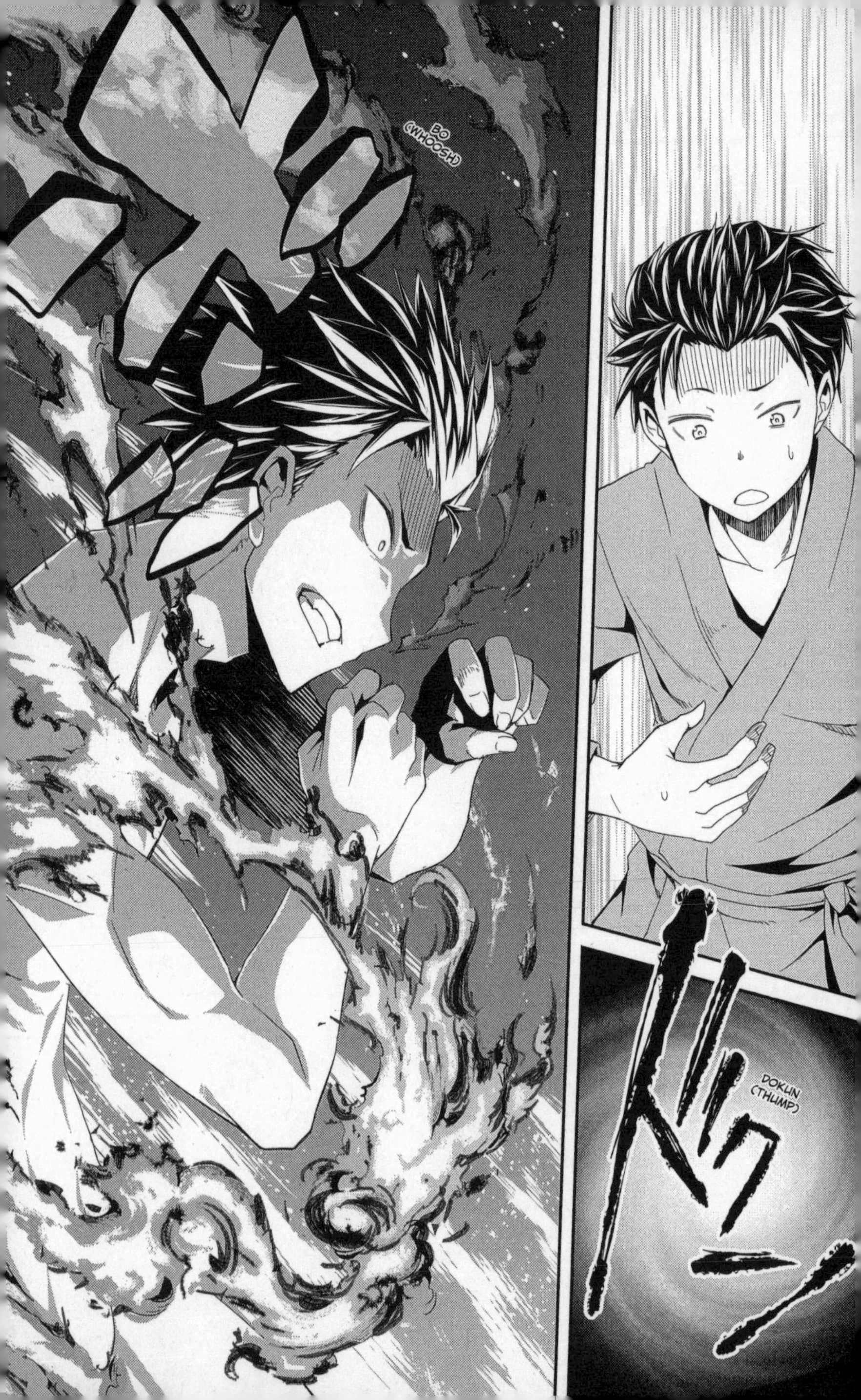
DOKUN (THUMP)
BO (WHOOSH)

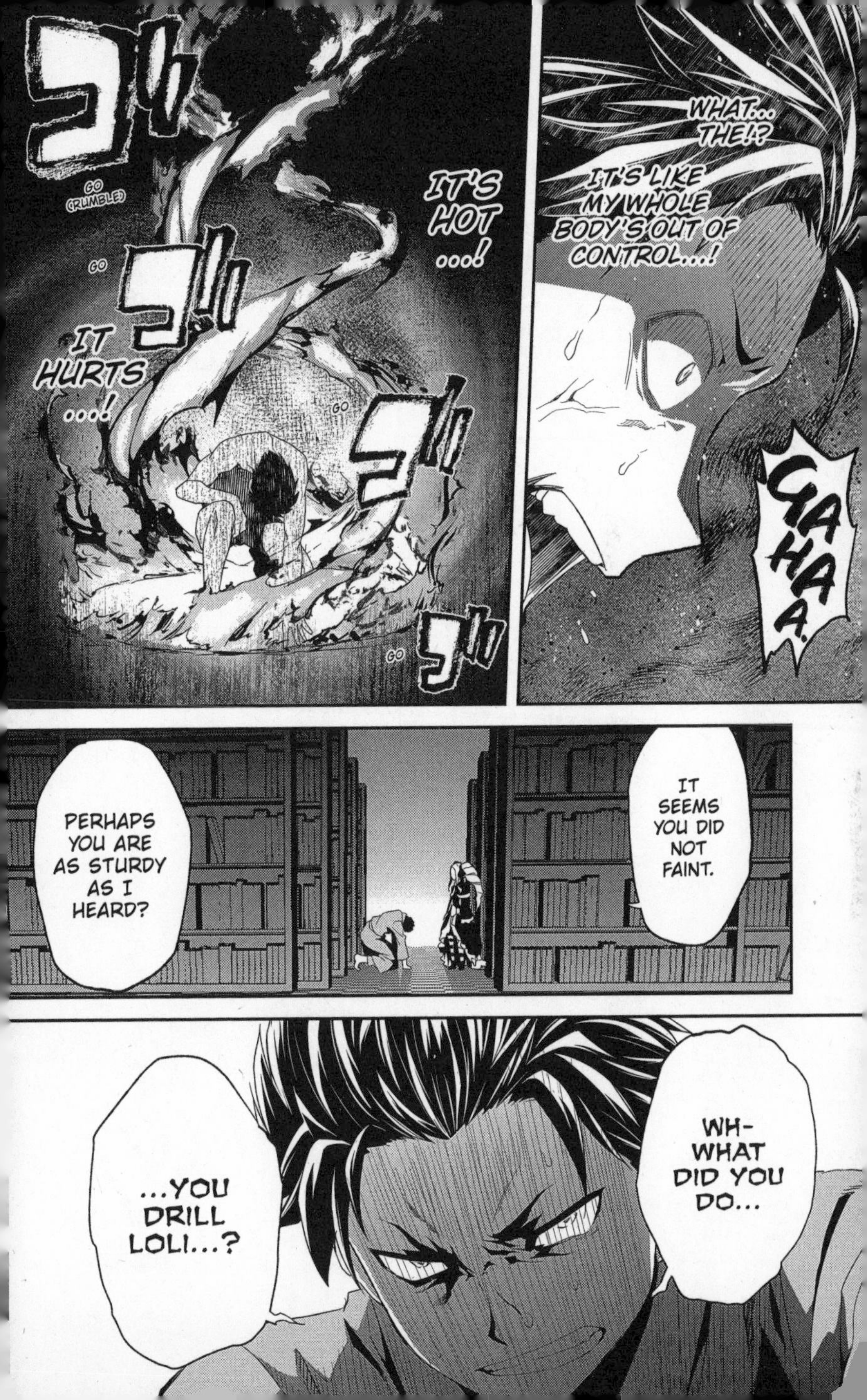
WHAT... THE!?
IT'S LIKE MY WHOLE BODY'S OUT OF CONTROL...!
GAHAAA.
GO (RUMBLE)
IT'S HOT...!
GO
IT HURTS...!
GO
GO
IT SEEMS YOU DID NOT FAINT.
PERHAPS YOU ARE AS STURDY AS I HEARD?
WH- WHAT DID YOU DO...
...YOU DRILL LOLI...?

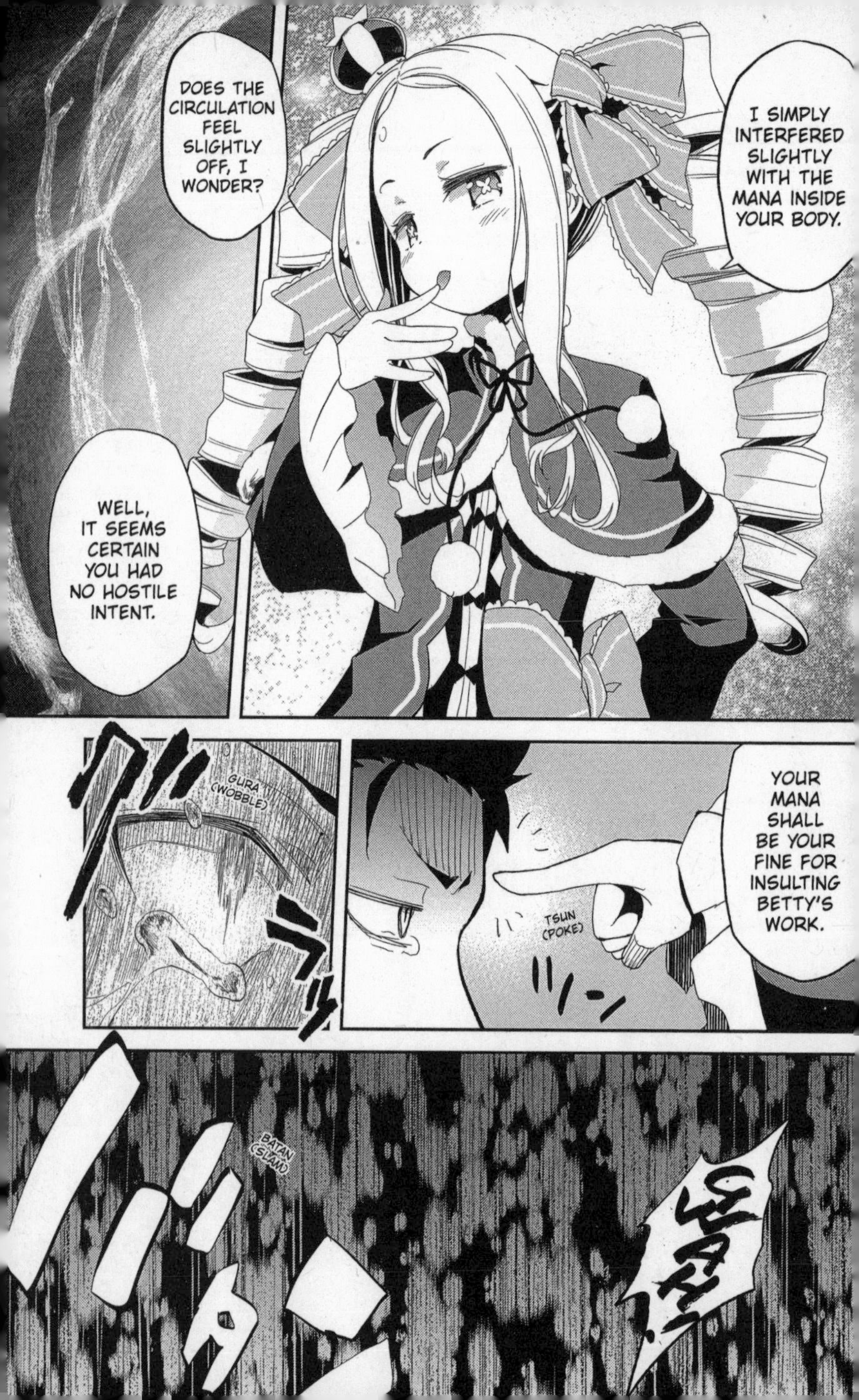
I SIMPLY INTERFERED SLIGHTLY WITH THE MANA INSIDE YOUR BODY.
DOES THE CIRCULATION FEEL SLIGHTLY OFF, I WONDER?
WELL, IT SEEMS CERTAIN YOU HAD NO HOSTILE INTENT.
YOUR MANA SHALL BE YOUR FINE FOR INSULTING BETTY'S WORK.
TSUN (POKE)
GURA (WOBBLE)
SMACK!
BATAN (SLAM)

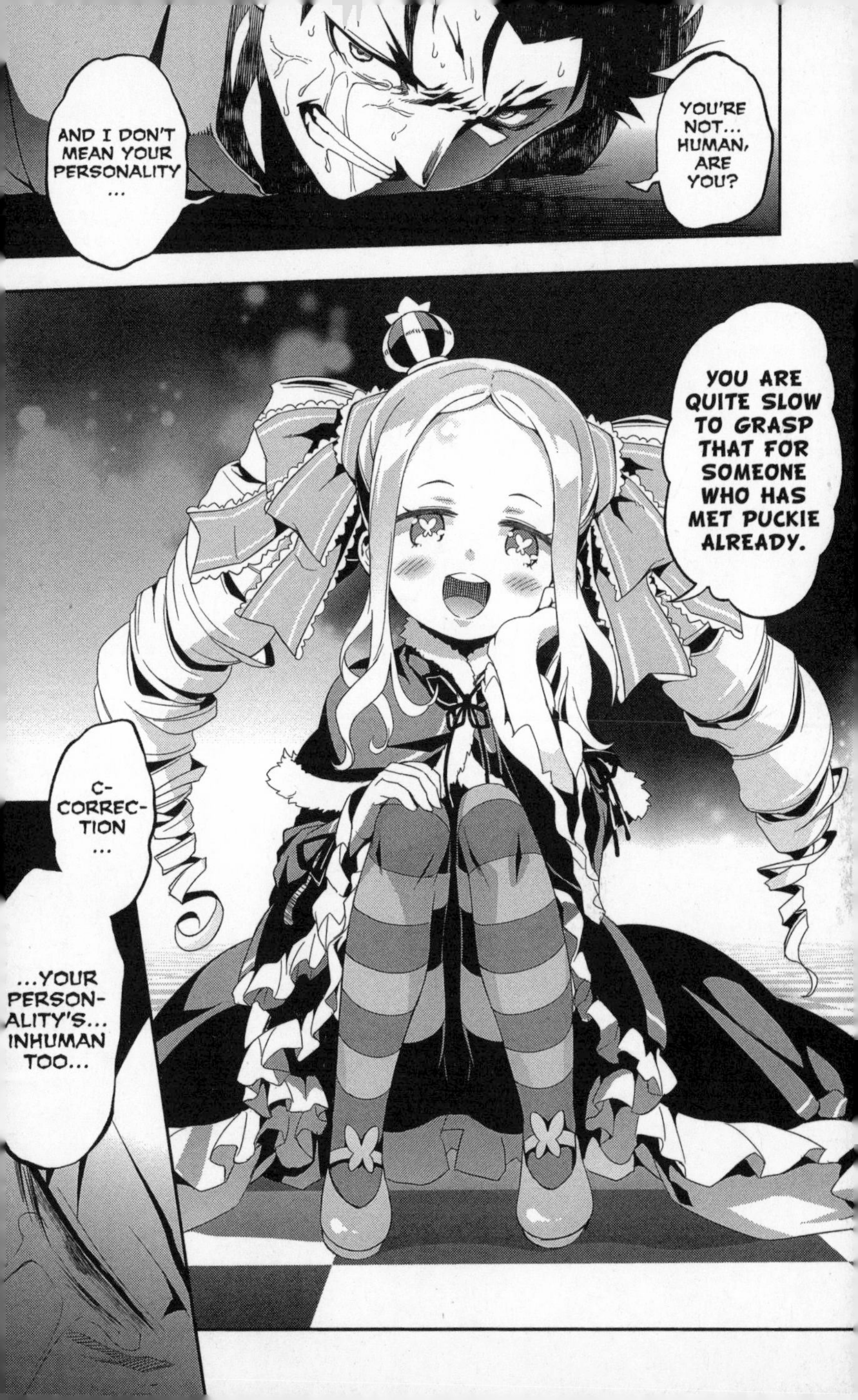
YOU'RE NOT... HUMAN, ARE YOU?
AND I DON'T MEAN YOUR PERSONALITY...
YOU ARE QUITE SLOW TO GRASP THAT FOR SOMEONE WHO HAS MET PUCKIE ALREADY.
C-CORREC-TION...
...YOUR PERSON-ALITY'S... INHUMAN TOO...

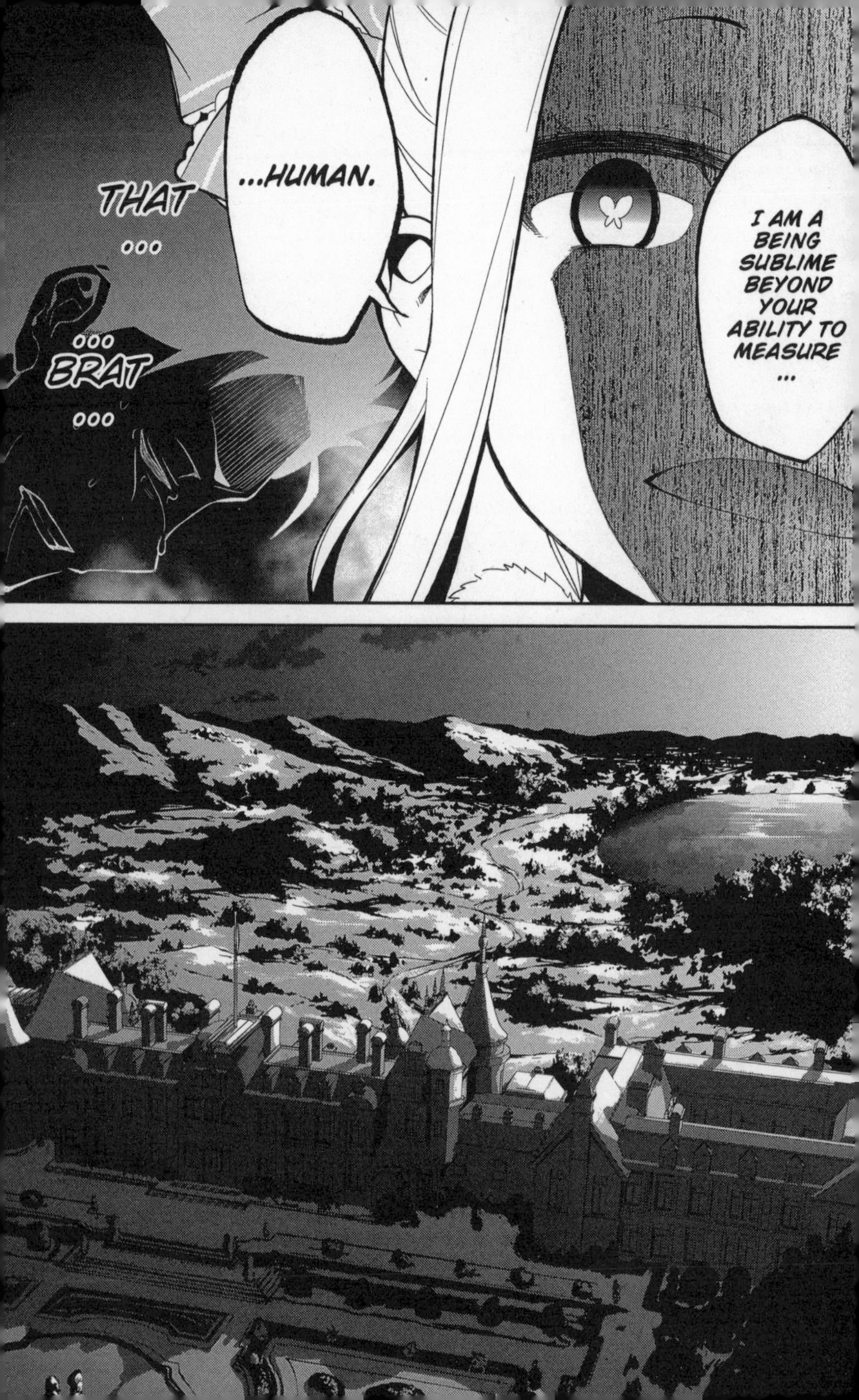
I AM A BEING SUBLIME BEYOND YOUR ABILITY TO MEASURE ...
...HUMAN.
THAT
BRAT

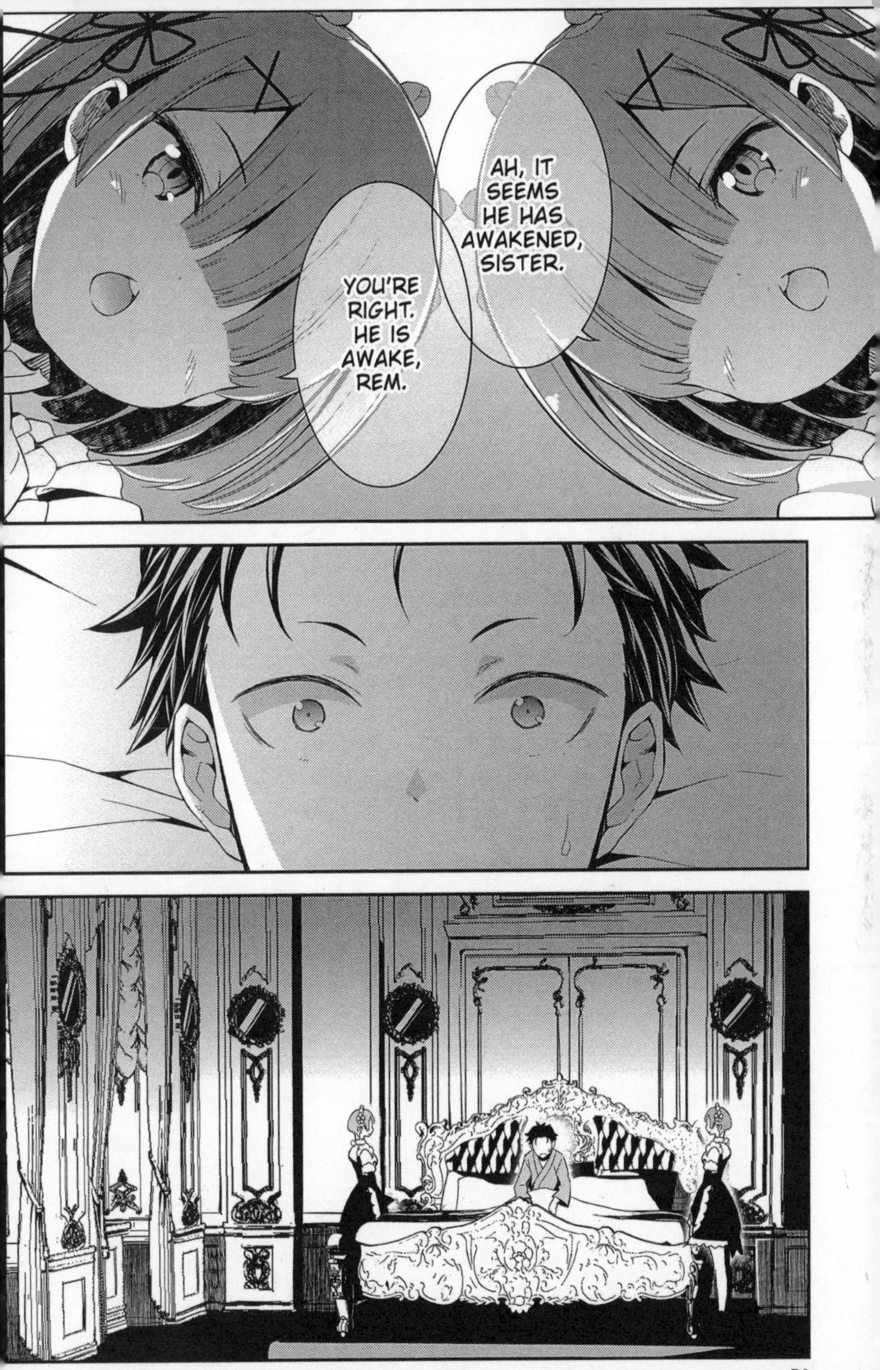
AH, IT SEEMS HE HAS AWAKENED, SISTER.
YOU'RE RIGHT. HE IS AWAKE, REM.

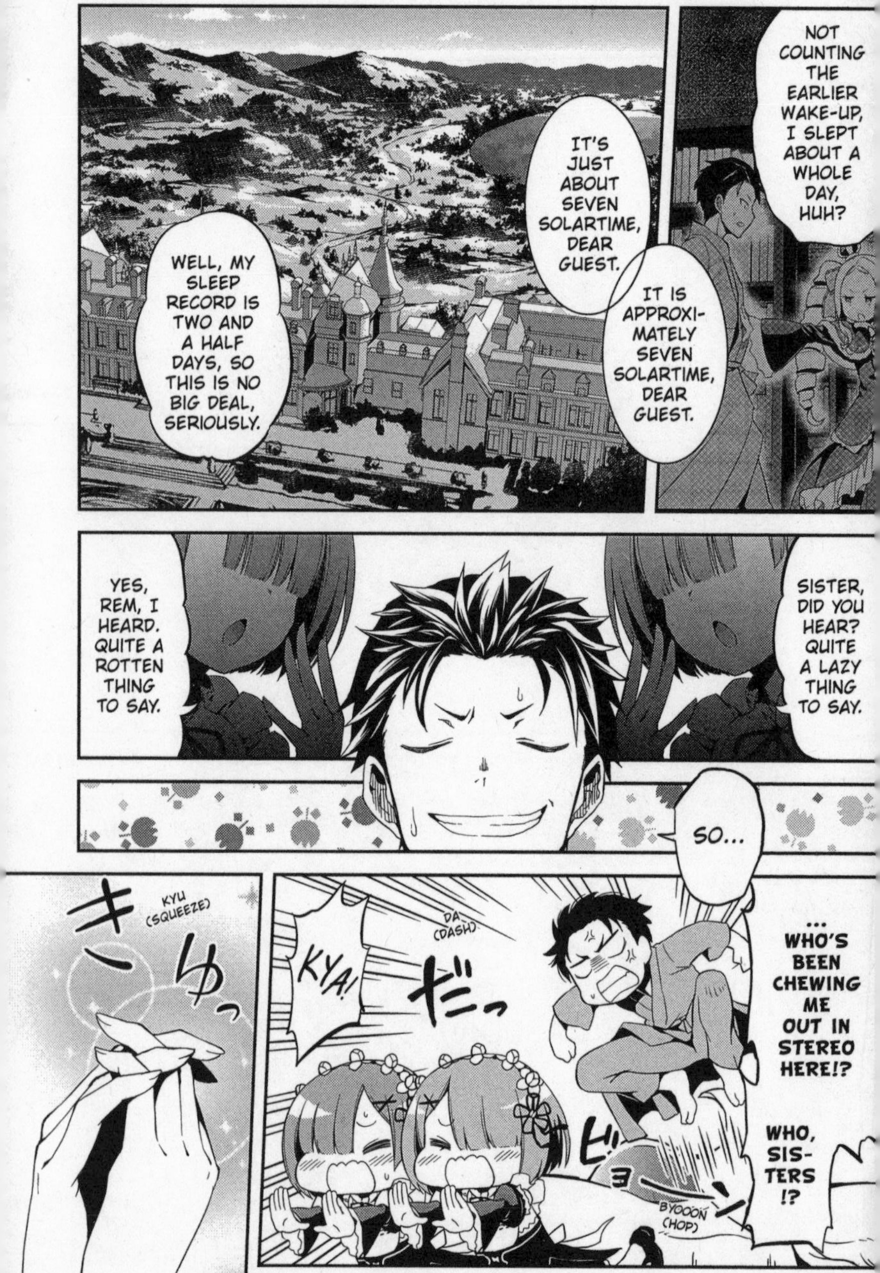
NOT COUNTING THE EARLIER WAKE-UP, I SLEPT ABOUT A WHOLE DAY, HUH?
IT'S JUST ABOUT SEVEN SOLARTIME, DEAR GUEST.
IT IS APPROXI-MATELY SEVEN SOLARTIME, DEAR GUEST.
WELL, MY SLEEP RECORD IS TWO AND A HALF DAYS, SO THIS IS NO BIG DEAL, SERIOUSLY.
SISTER, DID YOU HEAR? QUITE A LAZY THING TO SAY.
YES, REM, I HEARD. QUITE A ROTTEN THING TO SAY.
SO...
...WHO'S BEEN CHEWING ME OUT IN STEREO HERE!?
WHO, SIS-TERS!?
DA (DASH)
KYA!
BYOOON (HOP)
KYU (SQUEEZE)

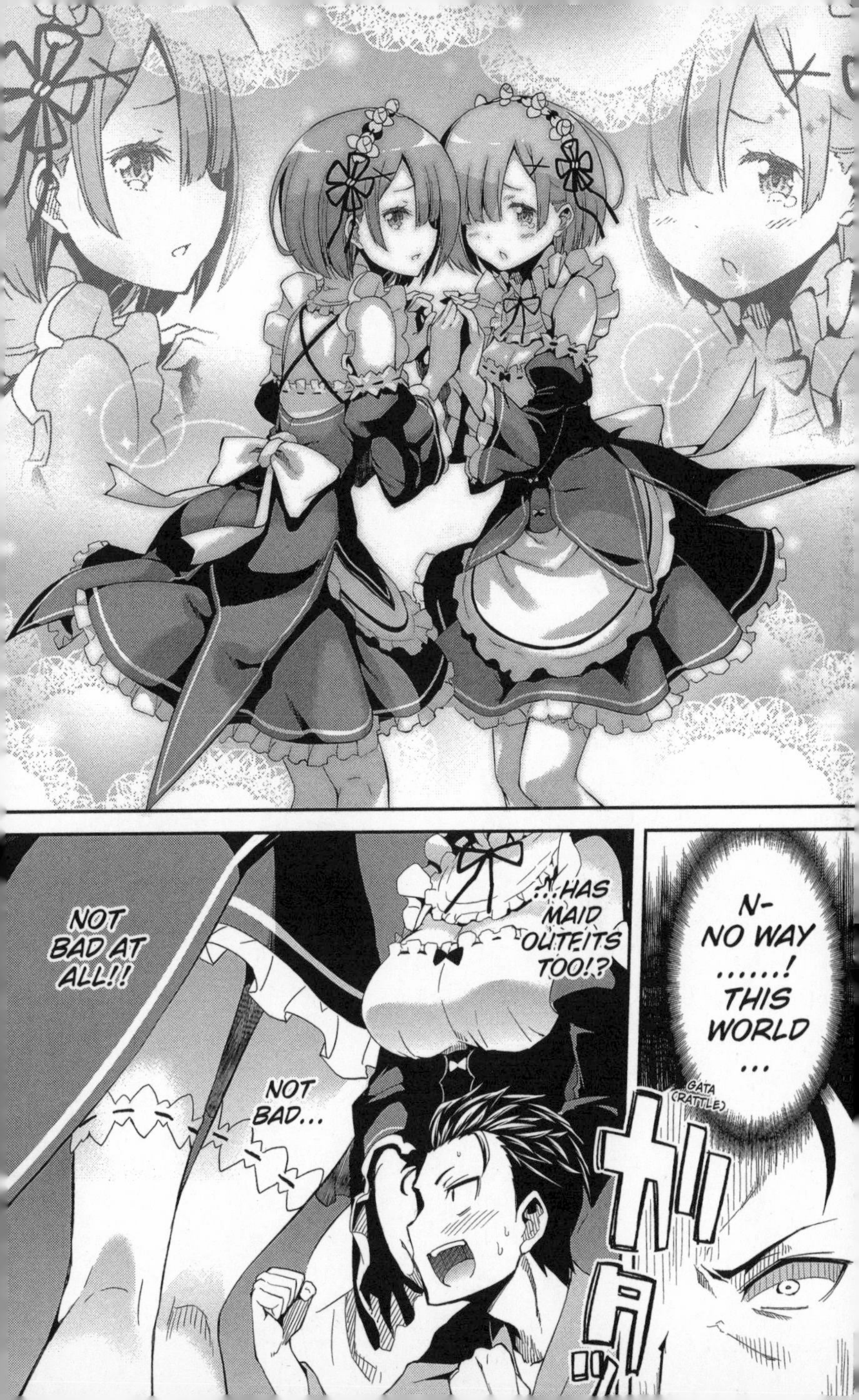
N-
NO WAY
......!
THIS
WORLD
...
GATA
(RATTLE)
...HAS
MAID
OUTFITS
TOO!?
NOT
BAD...
NOT
BAD AT
ALL!!

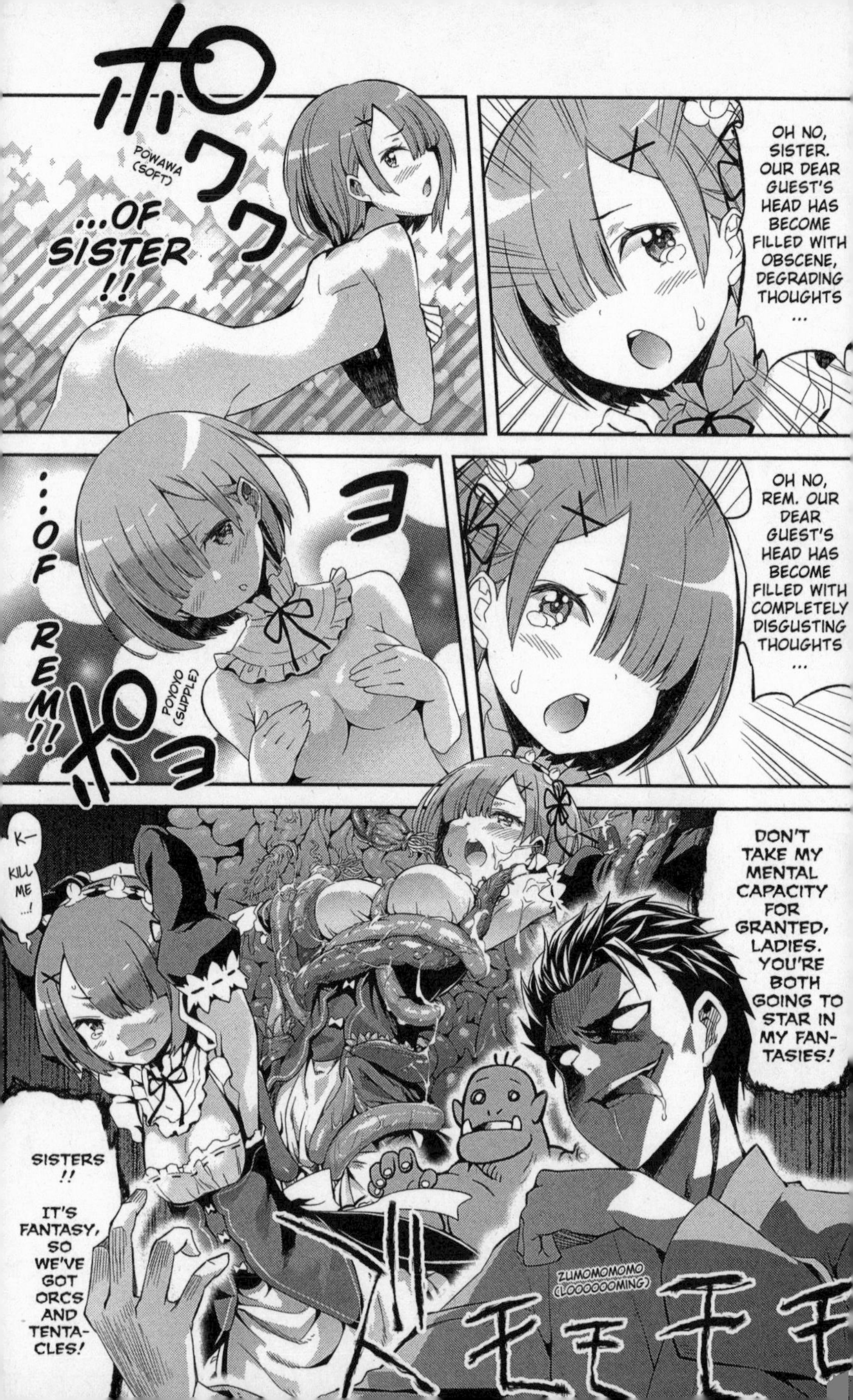
OH NO, SISTER. OUR DEAR GUEST'S HEAD HAS BECOME FILLED WITH OBSCENE, DEGRADING THOUGHTS...
POWAWA (SOFT)
...OF SISTER!!
OH NO, REM. OUR DEAR GUEST'S HEAD HAS BECOME FILLED WITH COMPLETELY DISGUSTING THOUGHTS...
...OF REM!!
POYOYO (SUPPLE)
DON'T TAKE MY MENTAL CAPACITY FOR GRANTED, LADIES. YOU'RE BOTH GOING TO STAR IN MY FAN-TASIES!
K—
KILL ME...!
ZUMOMOMOMO (LOOOOOOMING)
SISTERS!!
IT'S FANTASY, SO WE'VE GOT ORCS AND TENTA-CLES!

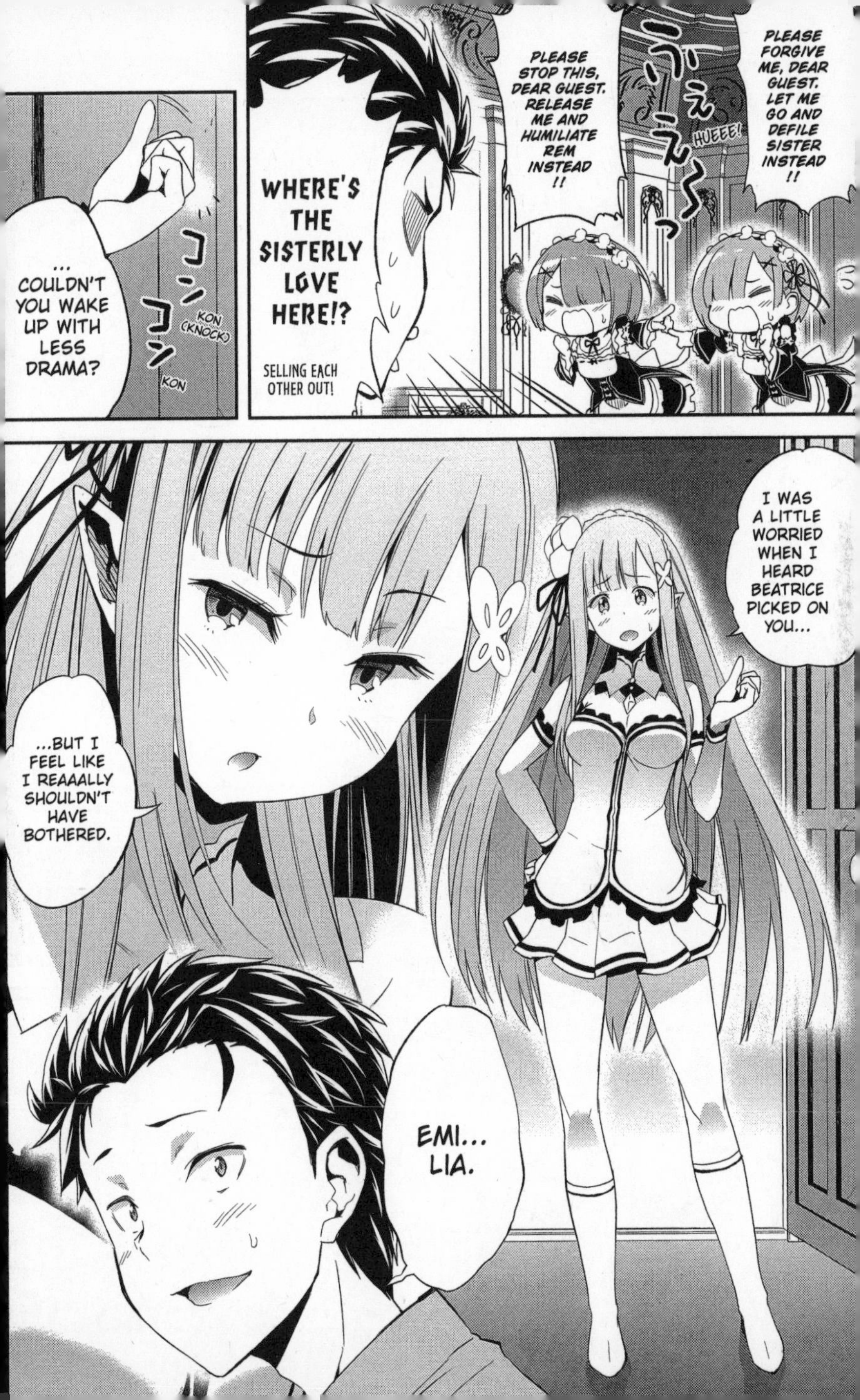
PLEASE FORGIVE ME, DEAR GUEST. LET ME GO AND DEFILE SISTER INSTEAD !!
HUEEE!
PLEASE STOP THIS, DEAR GUEST. RELEASE ME AND HUMILIATE REM INSTEAD !!
WHERE'S THE SISTERLY LOVE HERE!?
SELLING EACH OTHER OUT!
コンコン
KON (KNOCK)
KON
... COULDN'T YOU WAKE UP WITH LESS DRAMA?
I WAS A LITTLE WORRIED WHEN I HEARD BEATRICE PICKED ON YOU...
...BUT I FEEL LIKE I REAAALLY SHOULDN'T HAVE BOTHERED.
EMI... LIA.

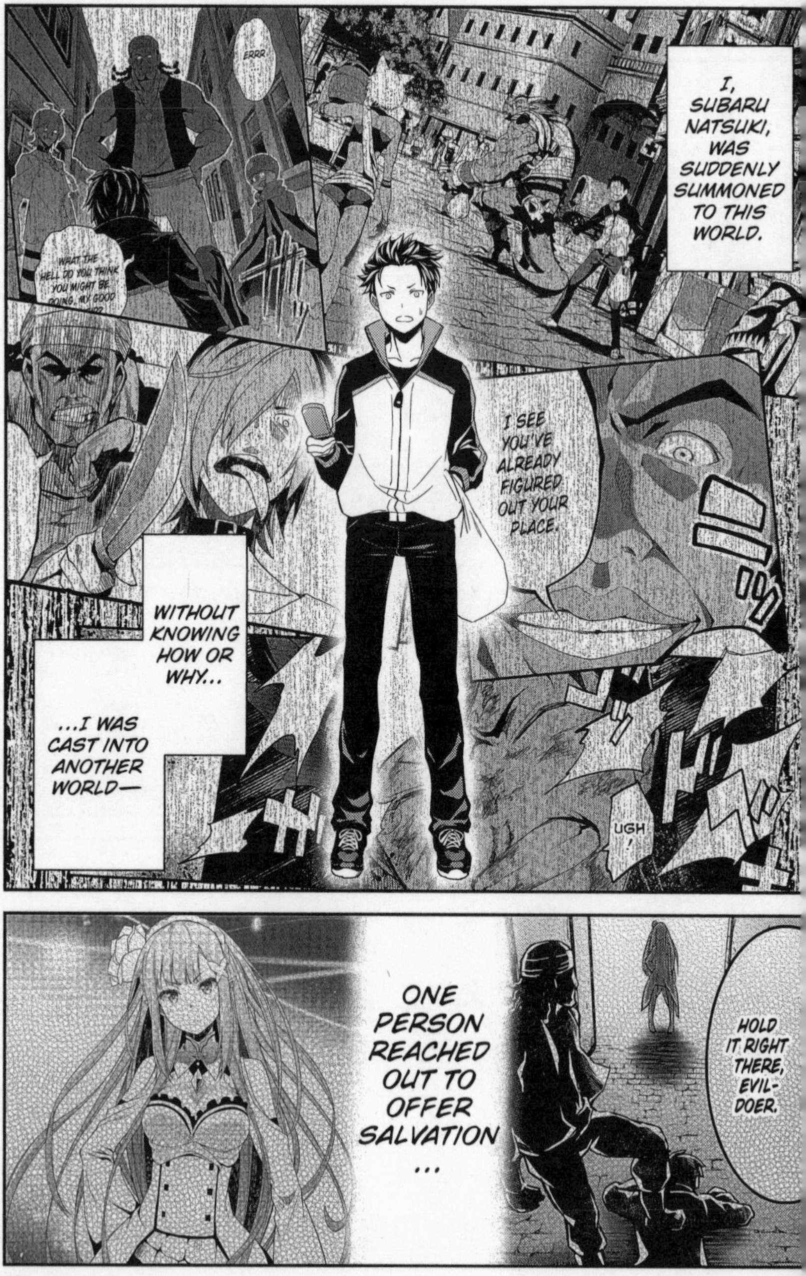
I, SUBARU NATSUKI, WAS SUDDENLY SUMMONED TO THIS WORLD.
ERRR...
WHAT THE HELL DO YOU THINK YOU MIGHT BE DOING, MY GOOD
I SEE YOU'VE ALREADY FIGURED OUT YOUR PLACE.
UGH!
WITHOUT KNOWING HOW OR WHY...
...I WAS CAST INTO ANOTHER WORLD—
HOLD IT RIGHT THERE, EVIL-DOER.
ONE PERSON REACHED OUT TO OFFER SALVATION ...

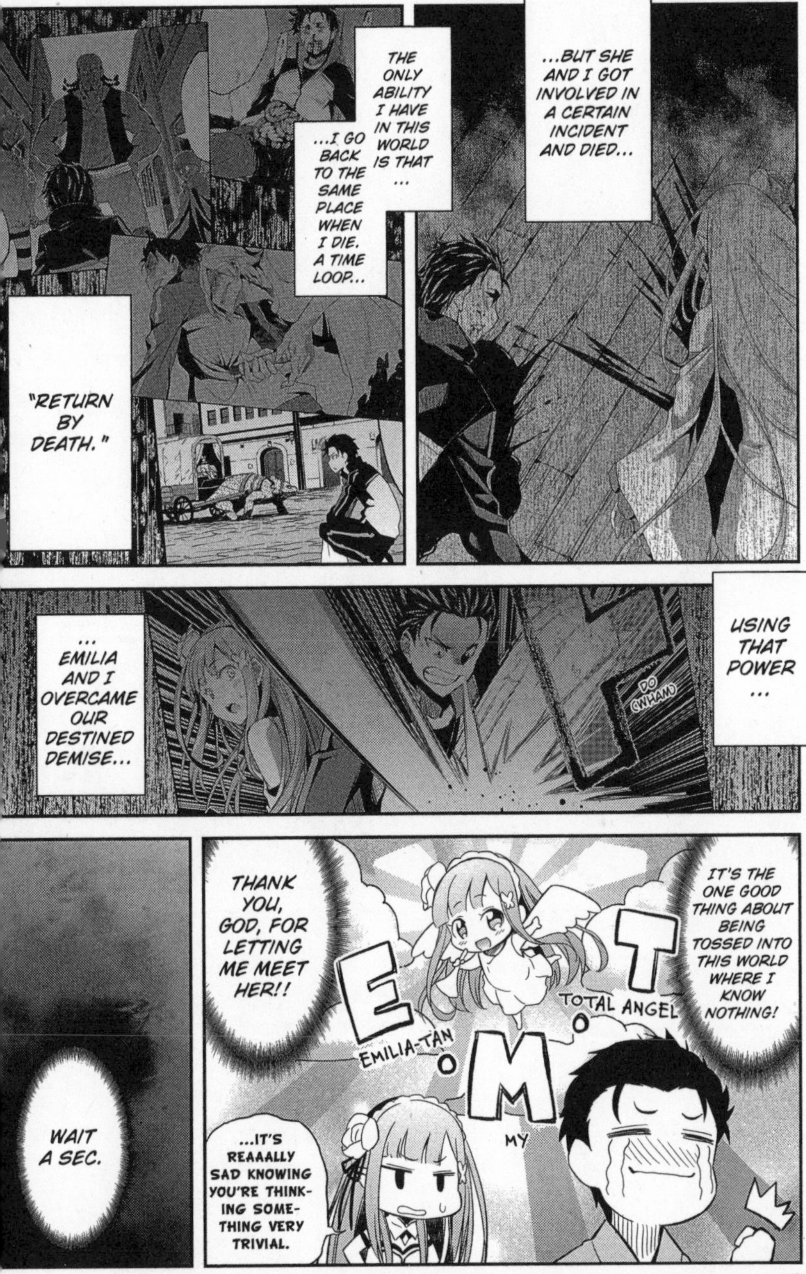
...BUT SHE AND I GOT INVOLVED IN A CERTAIN INCIDENT AND DIED...
THE ONLY ABILITY I HAVE IN THIS WORLD IS THAT ...
...I GO BACK TO THE SAME PLACE WHEN I DIE. A TIME LOOP...
"RETURN BY DEATH."
USING THAT POWER ...
DO (WHAM)
... EMILIA AND I OVERCAME OUR DESTINED DEMISE...
IT'S THE ONE GOOD THING ABOUT BEING TOSSED INTO THIS WORLD WHERE I KNOW NOTHING!
THANK YOU, GOD, FOR LETTING ME MEET HER!!
T
TOTAL ANGEL
O
E
EMILIA-TAN
O
M
MY
...IT'S REAAALLY SAD KNOWING YOU'RE THINKING SOMETHING VERY TRIVIAL.
WAIT A SEC.

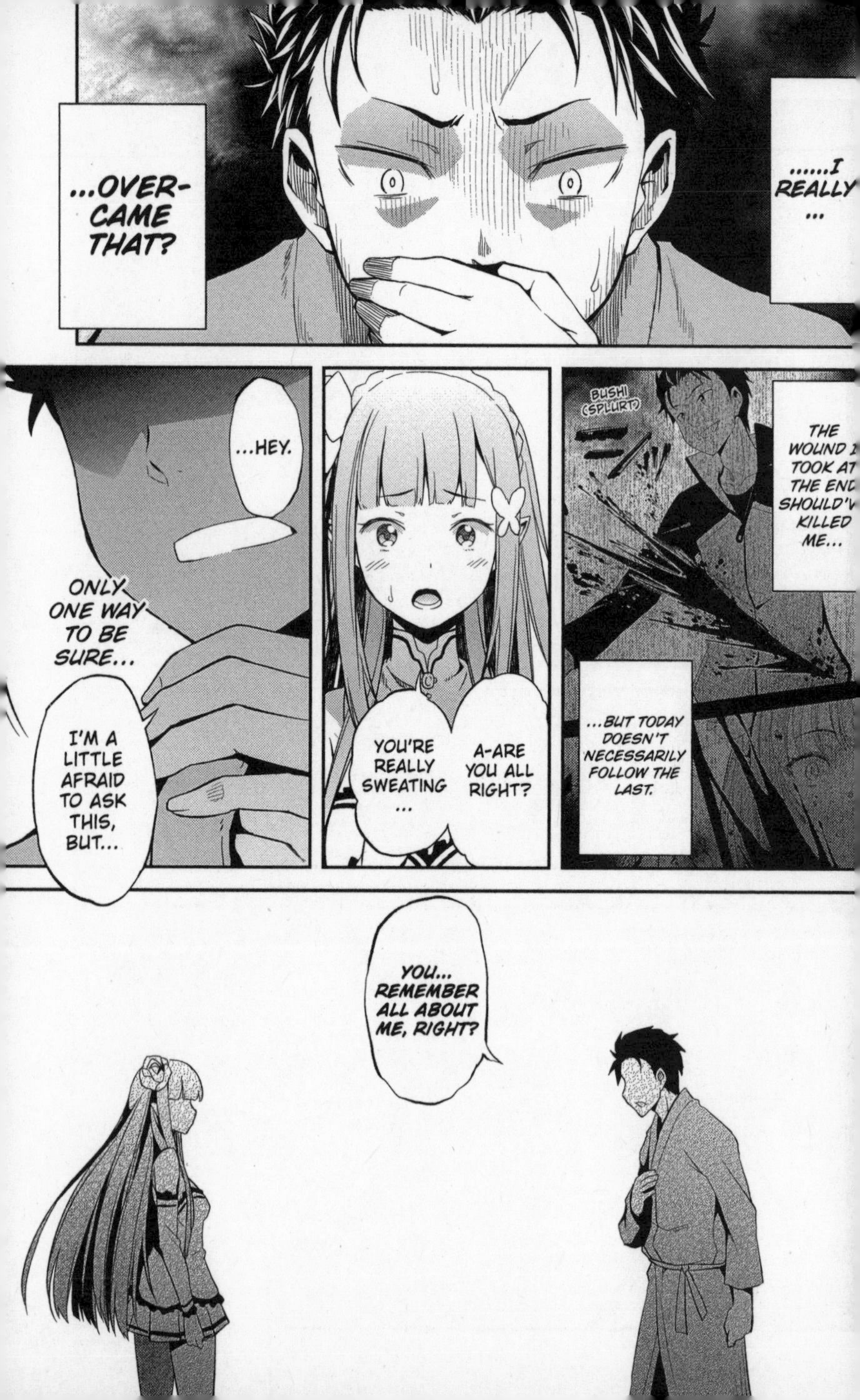
......I REALLY ...
...OVER-CAME THAT?
THE WOUND I TOOK AT THE END SHOULD'VE KILLED ME...
BUSHI (SPLURT)
...BUT TODAY DOESN'T NECESSARILY FOLLOW THE LAST.
A-ARE YOU ALL RIGHT?
YOU'RE REALLY SWEATING ...
...HEY.
ONLY ONE WAY TO BE SURE...
I'M A LITTLE AFRAID TO ASK THIS, BUT...
YOU... REMEMBER ALL ABOUT ME, RIGHT?

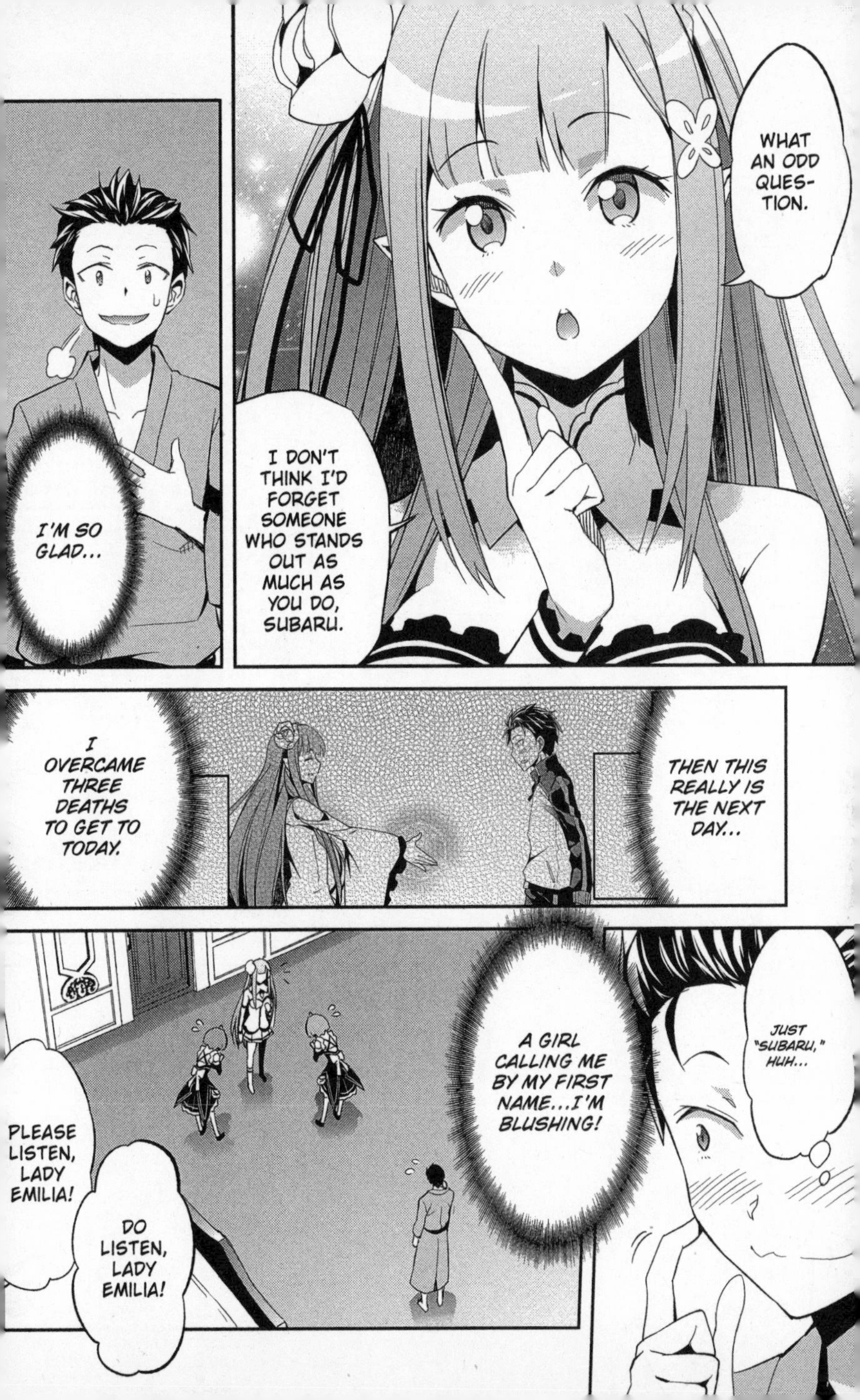
WHAT AN ODD QUES-TION.
I DON'T THINK I'D FORGET SOMEONE WHO STANDS OUT AS MUCH AS YOU DO, SUBARU.
I'M SO GLAD...
THEN THIS REALLY IS THE NEXT DAY...
I OVERCAME THREE DEATHS TO GET TO TODAY.
JUST "SUBARU," HUH...
A GIRL CALLING ME BY MY FIRST NAME...I'M BLUSHING!
PLEASE LISTEN, LADY EMILIA!
DO LISTEN, LADY EMILIA!

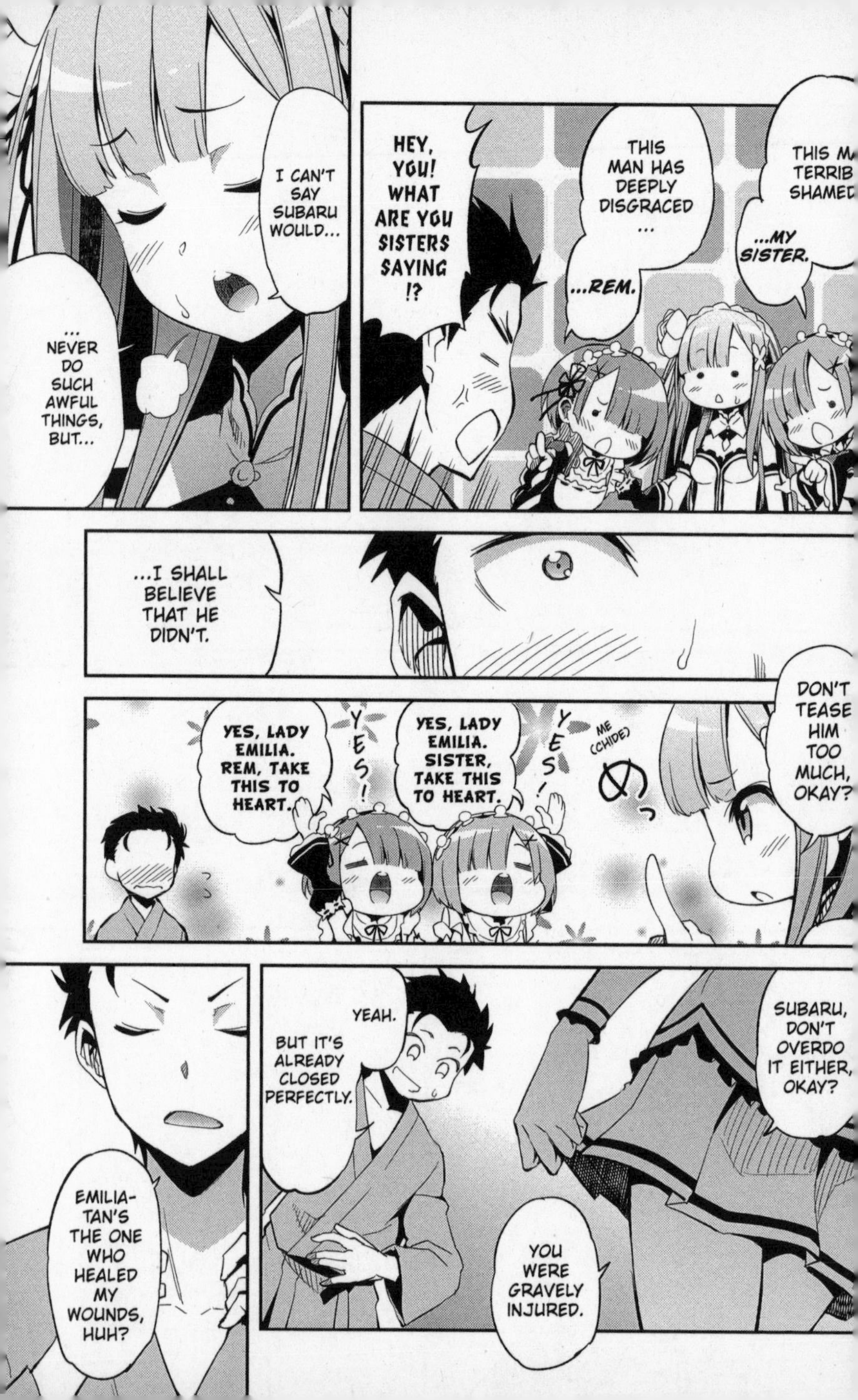
THIS MA TERRIB SHAMED
...MY SISTER.
THIS MAN HAS DEEPLY DISGRACED ...
...REM.
HEY, YOU! WHAT ARE YOU SISTERS SAYING !?
I CAN'T SAY SUBARU WOULD...
... NEVER DO SUCH AWFUL THINGS, BUT...
...I SHALL BELIEVE THAT HE DIDN'T.
DON'T TEASE HIM TOO MUCH, OKAY?
ME (CHIDE)
YES!
YES, LADY EMILIA. SISTER, TAKE THIS TO HEART.
YES!
YES, LADY EMILIA. REM, TAKE THIS TO HEART.
SUBARU, DON'T OVERDO IT EITHER, OKAY?
YEAH.
BUT IT'S ALREADY CLOSED PERFECTLY.
YOU WERE GRAVELY INJURED.
EMILIA-TAN'S THE ONE WHO HEALED MY WOUNDS, HUH?

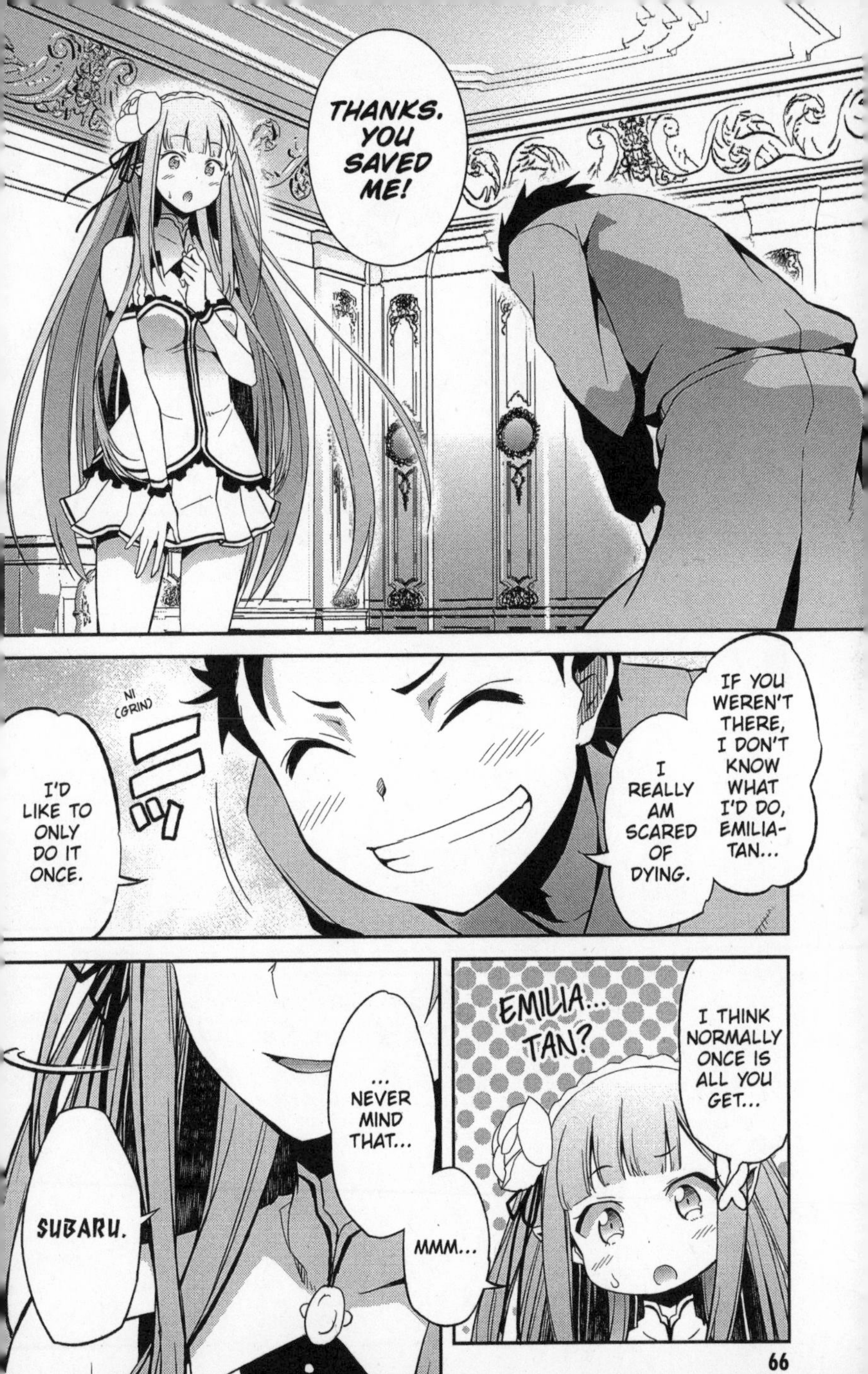
THANKS. YOU SAVED ME!
IF YOU WEREN'T THERE, I DON'T KNOW WHAT I'D DO, EMILIA-TAN...
I REALLY AM SCARED OF DYING.
NI (GRIN)
I'D LIKE TO ONLY DO IT ONCE.
I THINK NORMALLY ONCE IS ALL YOU GET...
EMILIA... TAN?
... NEVER MIND THAT...
MMM...
SUBARU.

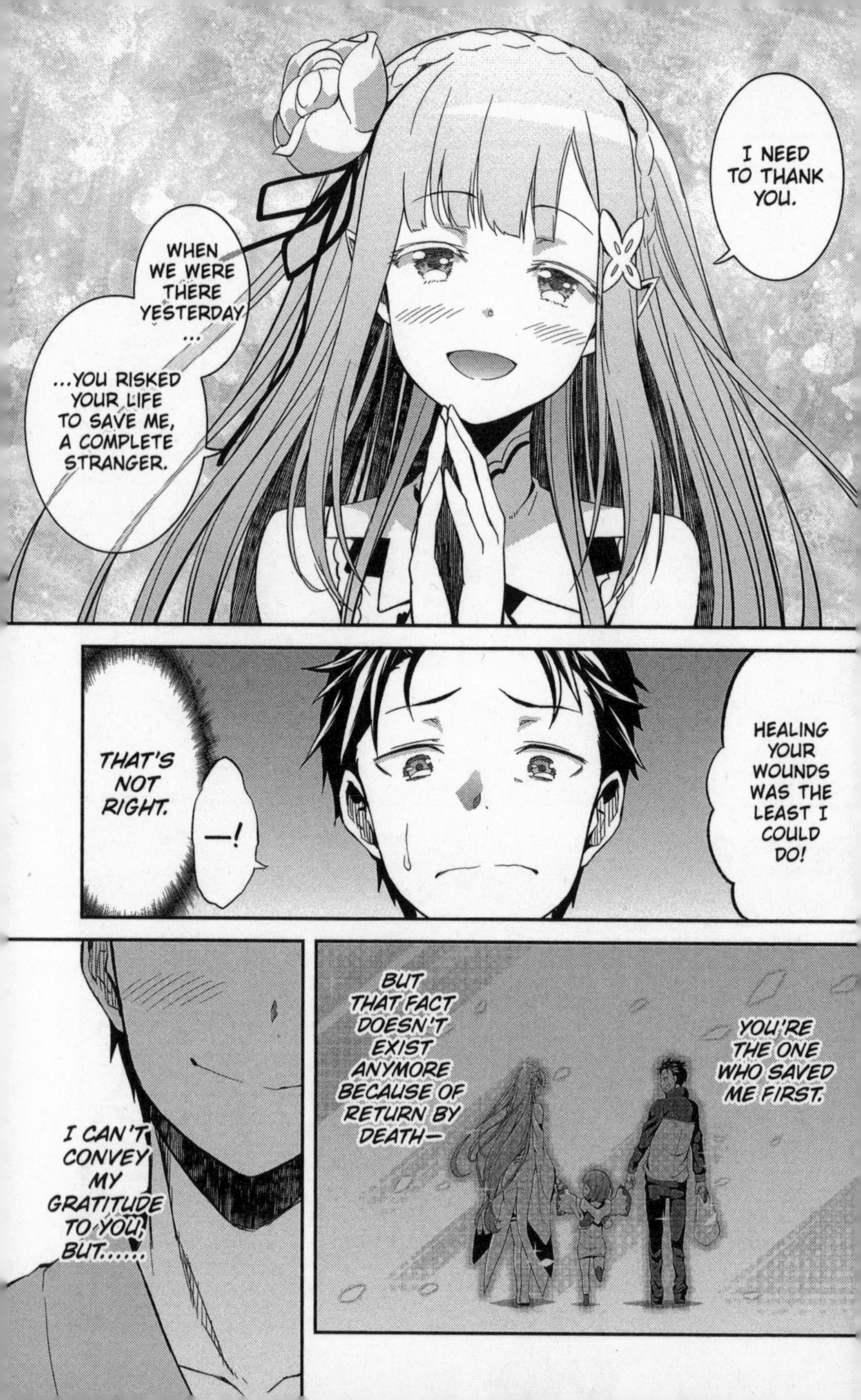
I NEED TO THANK YOU.
WHEN WE WERE THERE YESTERDAY...
...YOU RISKED YOUR LIFE TO SAVE ME, A COMPLETE STRANGER.
HEALING YOUR WOUNDS WAS THE LEAST I COULD DO!
—!
THAT'S NOT RIGHT.
YOU'RE THE ONE WHO SAVED ME FIRST.
BUT THAT FACT DOESN'T EXIST ANYMORE BECAUSE OF RETURN BY DEATH—
I CAN'T CONVEY MY GRATITUDE TO YOU, BUT......

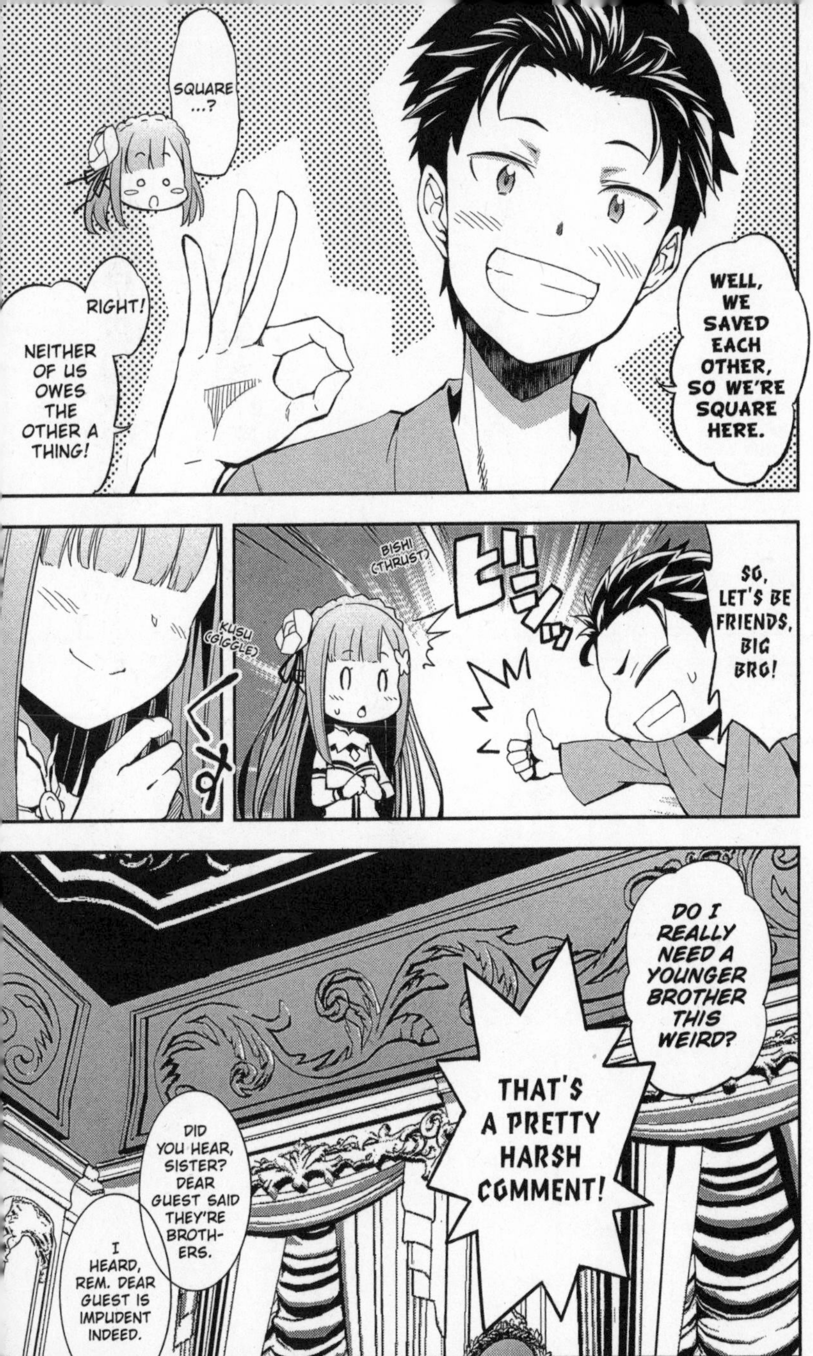
WELL, WE SAVED EACH OTHER, SO WE'RE SQUARE HERE.
SQUARE ...?
RIGHT!
NEITHER OF US OWES THE OTHER A THING!
SO, LET'S BE FRIENDS, BIG BRO!
BISHI (THRUST)
KUSU (GIGGLE)
DO I REALLY NEED A YOUNGER BROTHER THIS WEIRD?
THAT'S A PRETTY HARSH COMMENT!
DID YOU HEAR, SISTER? DEAR GUEST SAID THEY'RE BROTH-ERS.
I HEARD, REM. DEAR GUEST IS IMPUDENT INDEED.

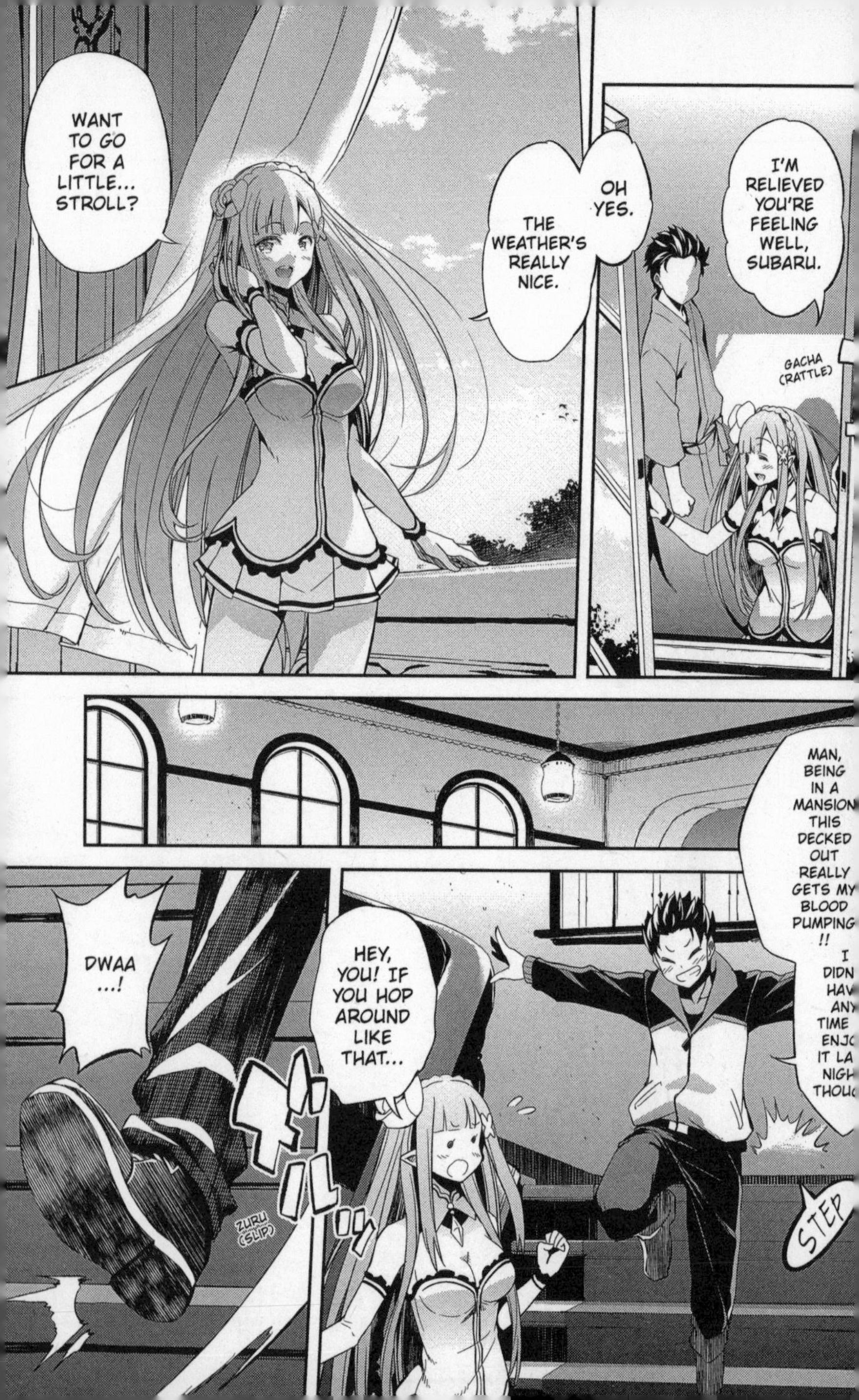
I'M RELIEVED YOU'RE FEELING WELL, SUBARU.
GACHA (RATTLE)
OH YES.
THE WEATHER'S REALLY NICE.
WANT TO GO FOR A LITTLE... STROLL?
MAN, BEING IN A MANSION THIS DECKED OUT REALLY GETS MY BLOOD PUMPING!!
I DIDN HAV ANY TIME ENJO IT LA NIGH THOU
STEP
HEY, YOU! IF YOU HOP AROUND LIKE THAT...
ZURU (SLIP)
DWAA...!

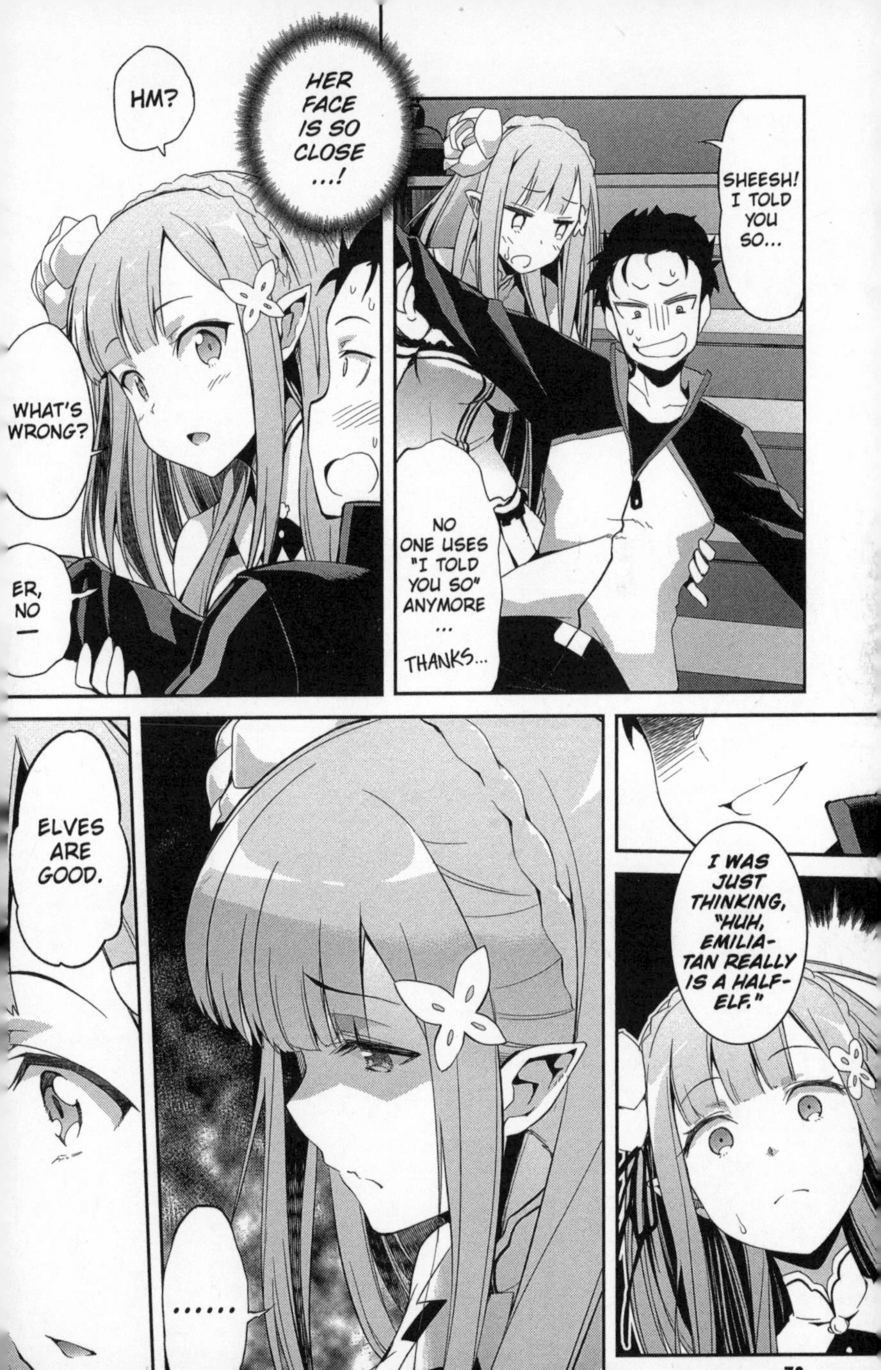
SHEESH! I TOLD YOU SO...
NO ONE USES "I TOLD YOU SO" ANYMORE... THANKS...
HER FACE IS SO CLOSE...!
HM?
WHAT'S WRONG?
ER, NO—
I WAS JUST THINKING, "HUH, EMILIA-TAN REALLY IS A HALF-ELF."
......
ELVES ARE GOOD.

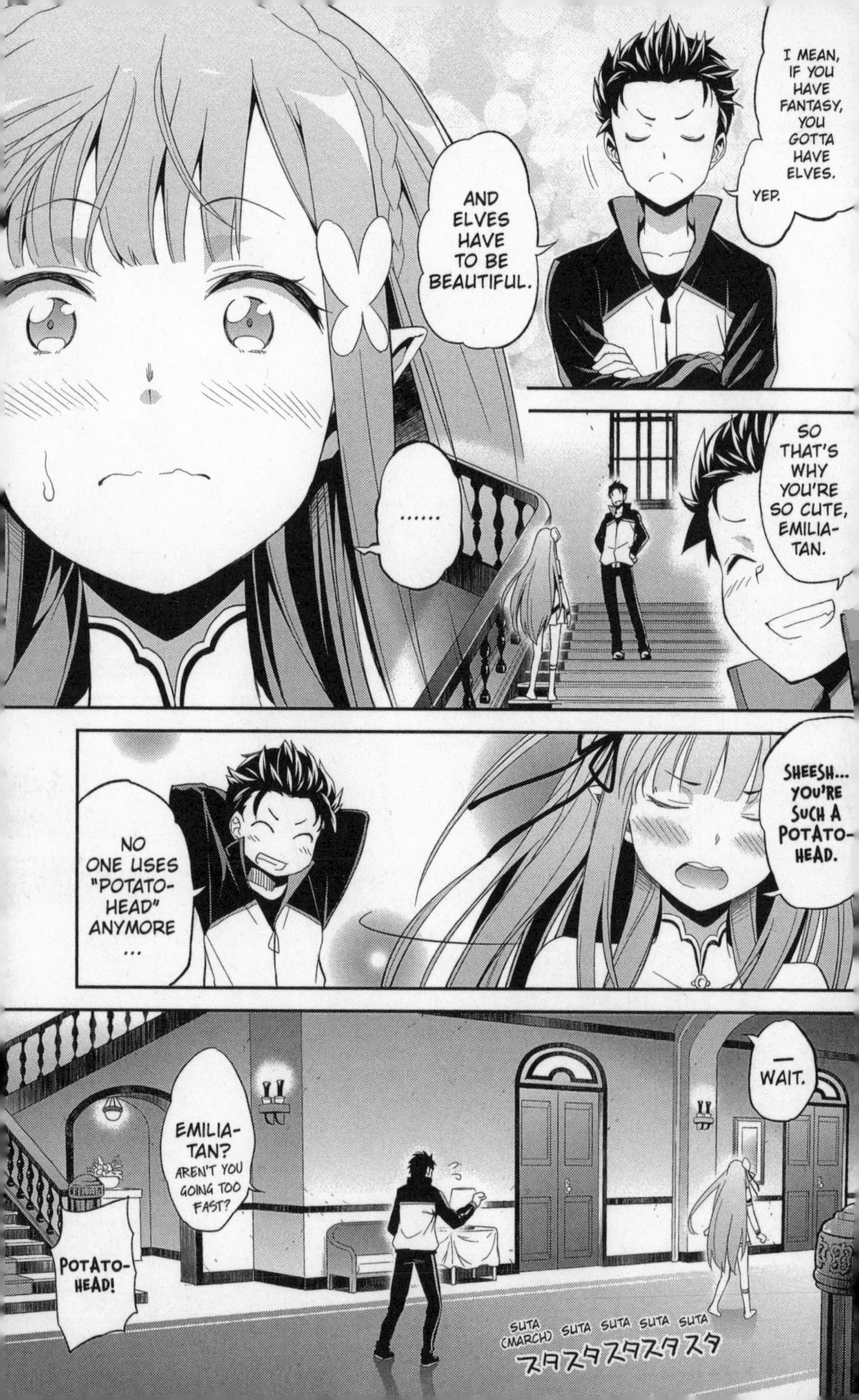
I MEAN, IF YOU HAVE FANTASY, YOU GOTTA HAVE ELVES.
YEP.
AND ELVES HAVE TO BE BEAUTIFUL.
SO THAT'S WHY YOU'RE SO CUTE, EMILIA-TAN.
......
SHEESH... YOU'RE SUCH A POTATO-HEAD.
NO ONE USES "POTATO-HEAD" ANYMORE ...
—WAIT.
EMILIA-TAN? AREN'T YOU GOING TOO FAST?
POTATO-HEAD!
SUTA (MARCH) SUTA SUTA SUTA SUTA
スタスタスタスタスタ

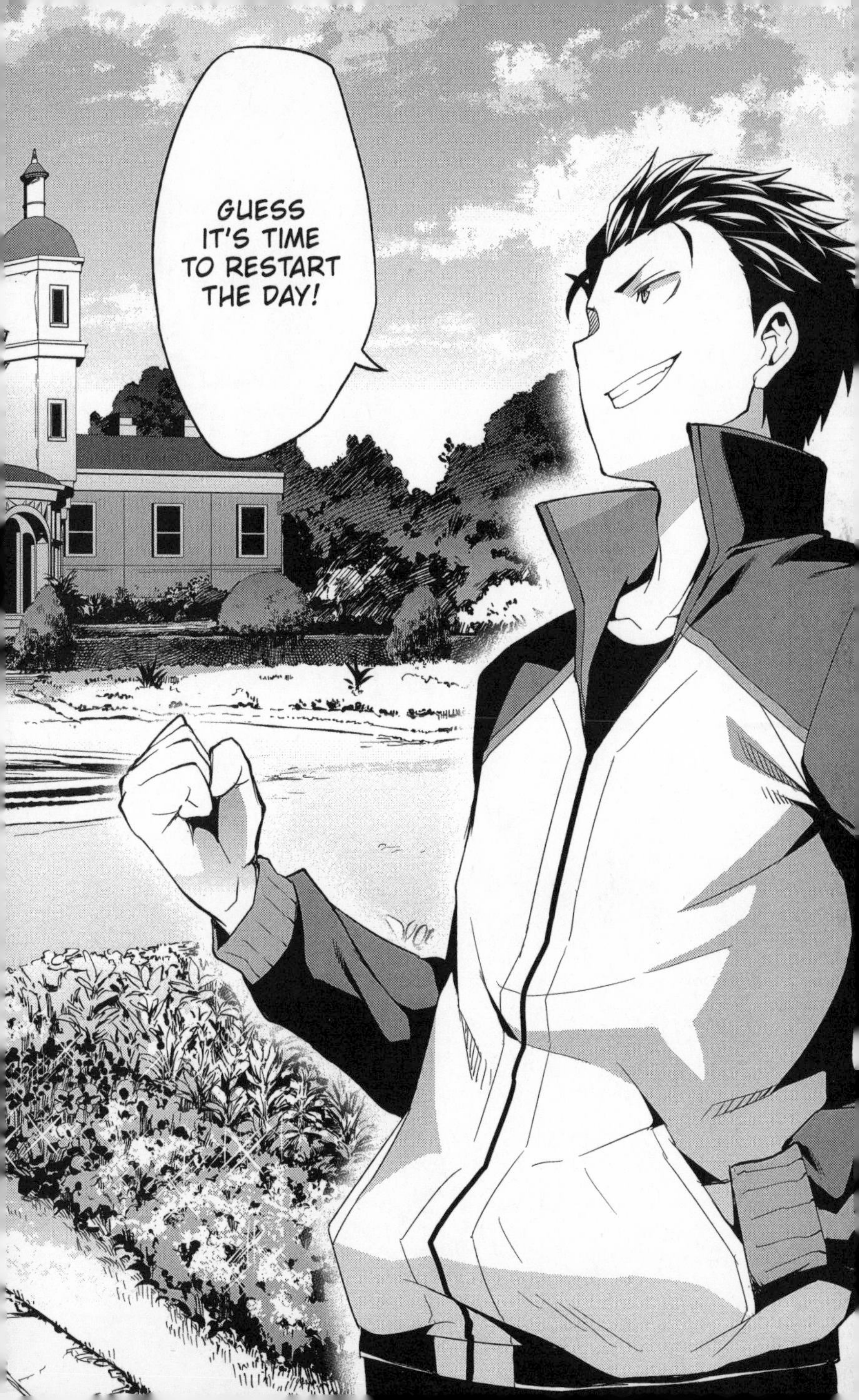
GUESS IT'S TIME TO RESTART THE DAY!

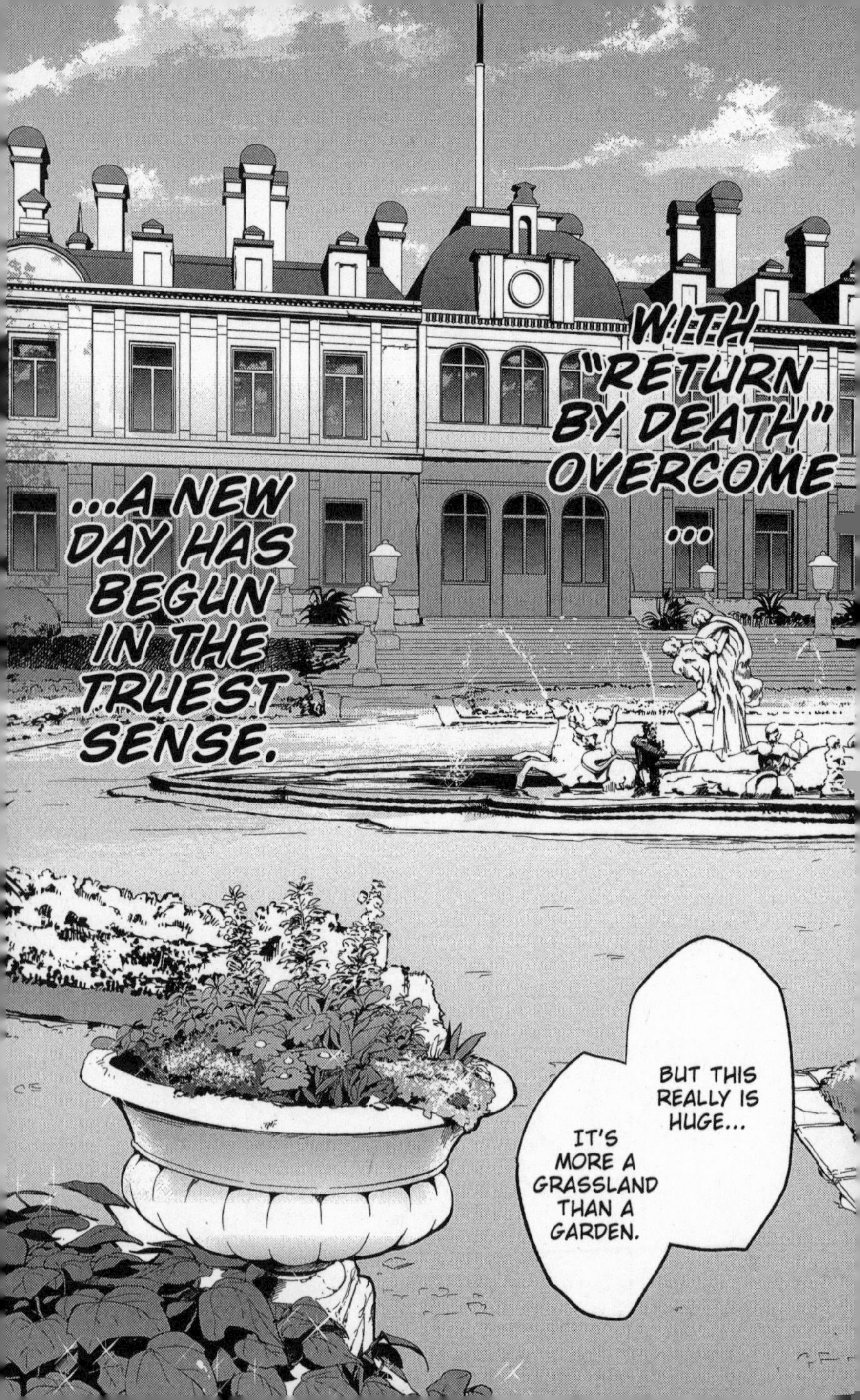
WITH "RETURN BY DEATH" OVERCOME...
...A NEW DAY HAS BEGUN IN THE TRUEST SENSE.
BUT THIS REALLY IS HUGE... IT'S MORE A GRASSLAND THAN A GARDEN.

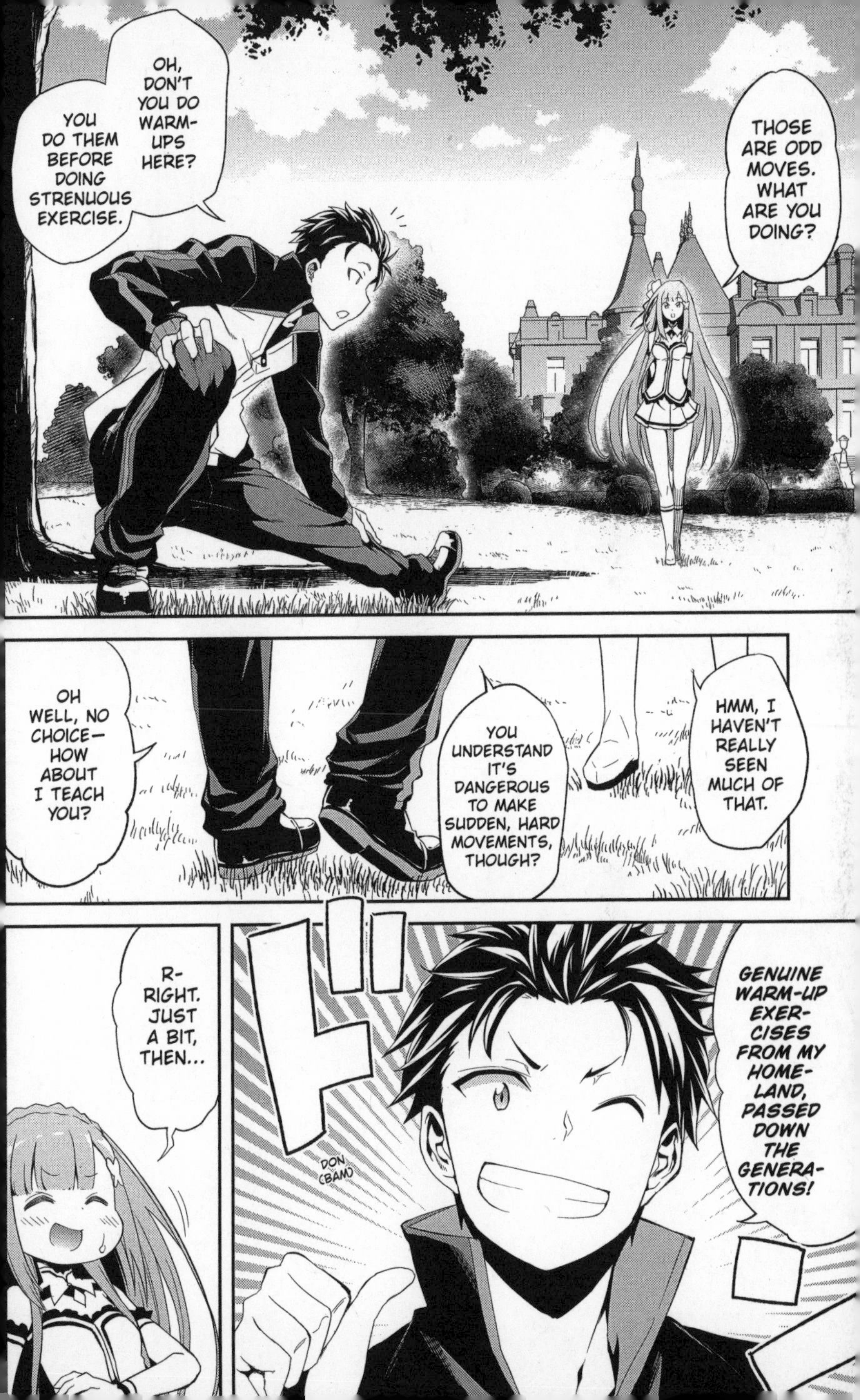
THOSE ARE ODD MOVES. WHAT ARE YOU DOING?
OH, DON'T YOU DO WARM-UPS HERE?
YOU DO THEM BEFORE DOING STRENUOUS EXERCISE.
HMM, I HAVEN'T REALLY SEEN MUCH OF THAT.
YOU UNDERSTAND IT'S DANGEROUS TO MAKE SUDDEN, HARD MOVEMENTS, THOUGH?
OH WELL, NO CHOICE—HOW ABOUT I TEACH YOU?
GENUINE WARM-UP EXER-CISES FROM MY HOME-LAND, PASSED DOWN THE GENERA-TIONS!
DON (BAM)
R-RIGHT. JUST A BIT, THEN...

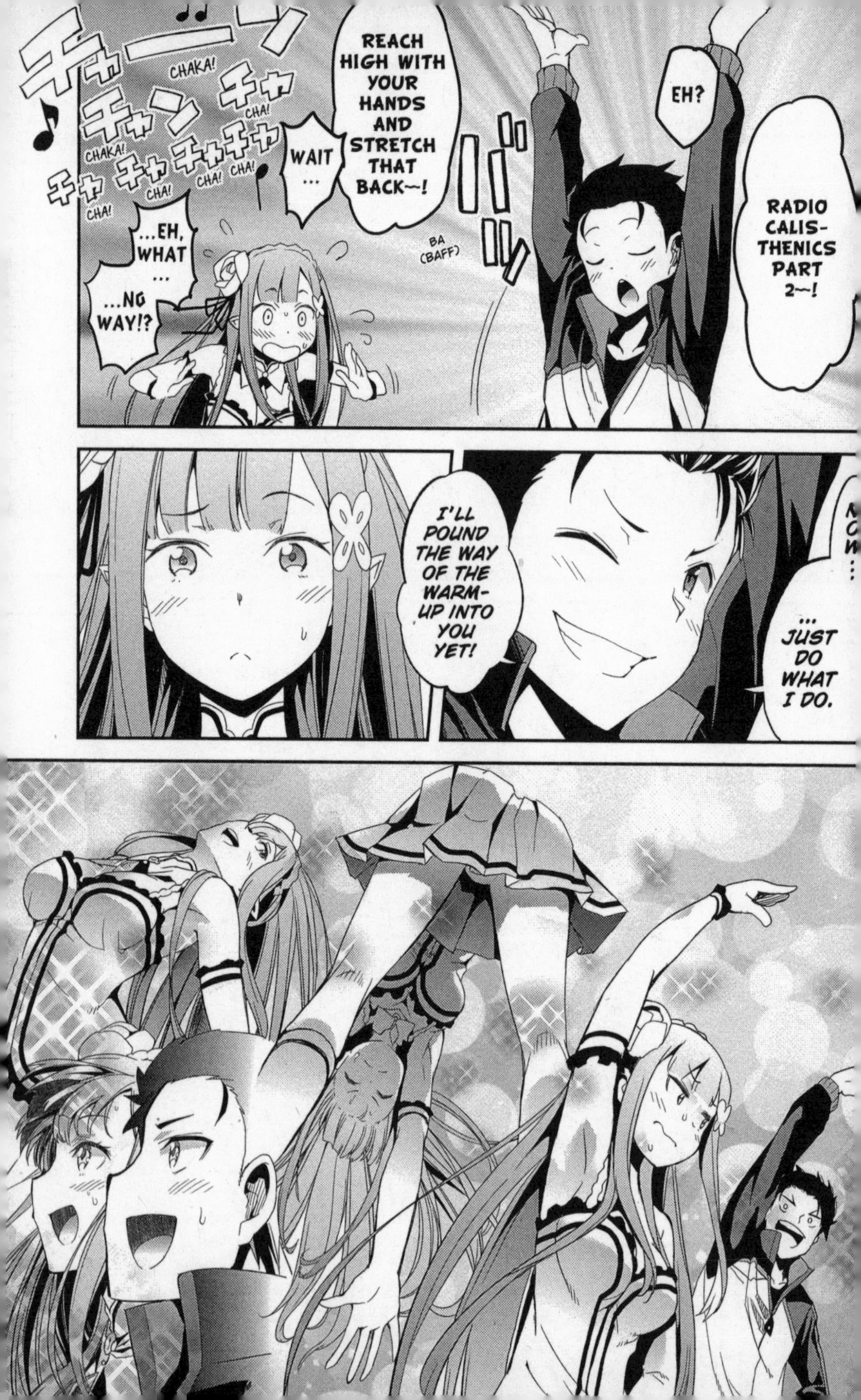
RADIO CALIS-THENICS PART 2~!
EH?
BA (BAFF)
REACH HIGH WITH YOUR HANDS AND STRETCH THAT BACK~!
WAIT ...
...EH, WHAT ... ...NO WAY!?
CHAKA!
CHA!
CHAKA!
CHA! CHA!
CHA!
CHA!
NOW...
... JUST DO WHAT I DO.
I'LL POUND THE WAY OF THE WARM-UP INTO YOU YET!

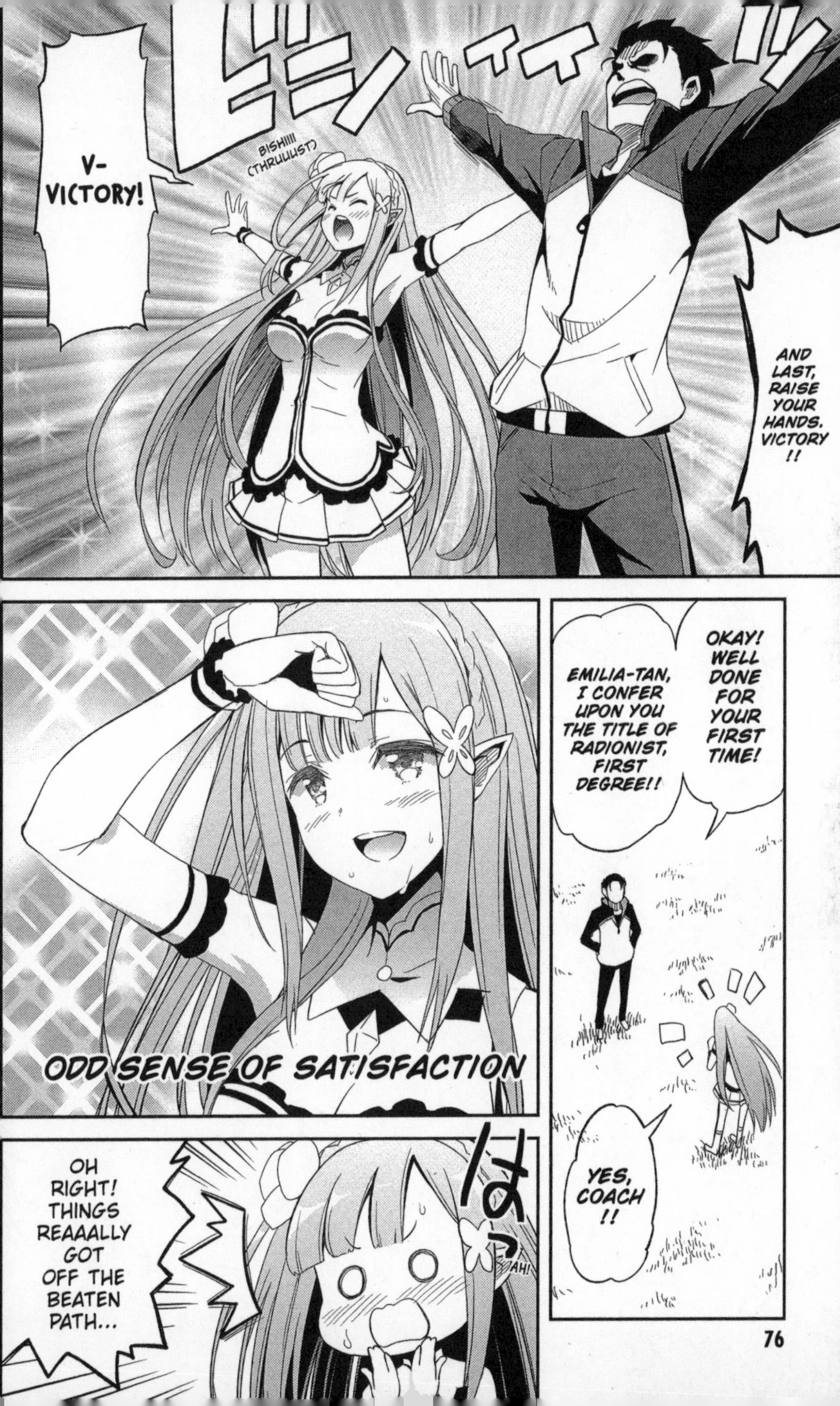
AND LAST, RAISE YOUR HANDS. VICTORY!!
ビシィィッ
BISHIIII (THRUUUST)
V-VICTORY!
OKAY! WELL DONE FOR YOUR FIRST TIME!
EMILIA-TAN, I CONFER UPON YOU THE TITLE OF RADIONIST, FIRST DEGREE!!
YES, COACH!!
ODD SENSE OF SATISFACTION
はっ
OH RIGHT! THINGS REAAALLY GOT OFF THE BEATEN PATH...

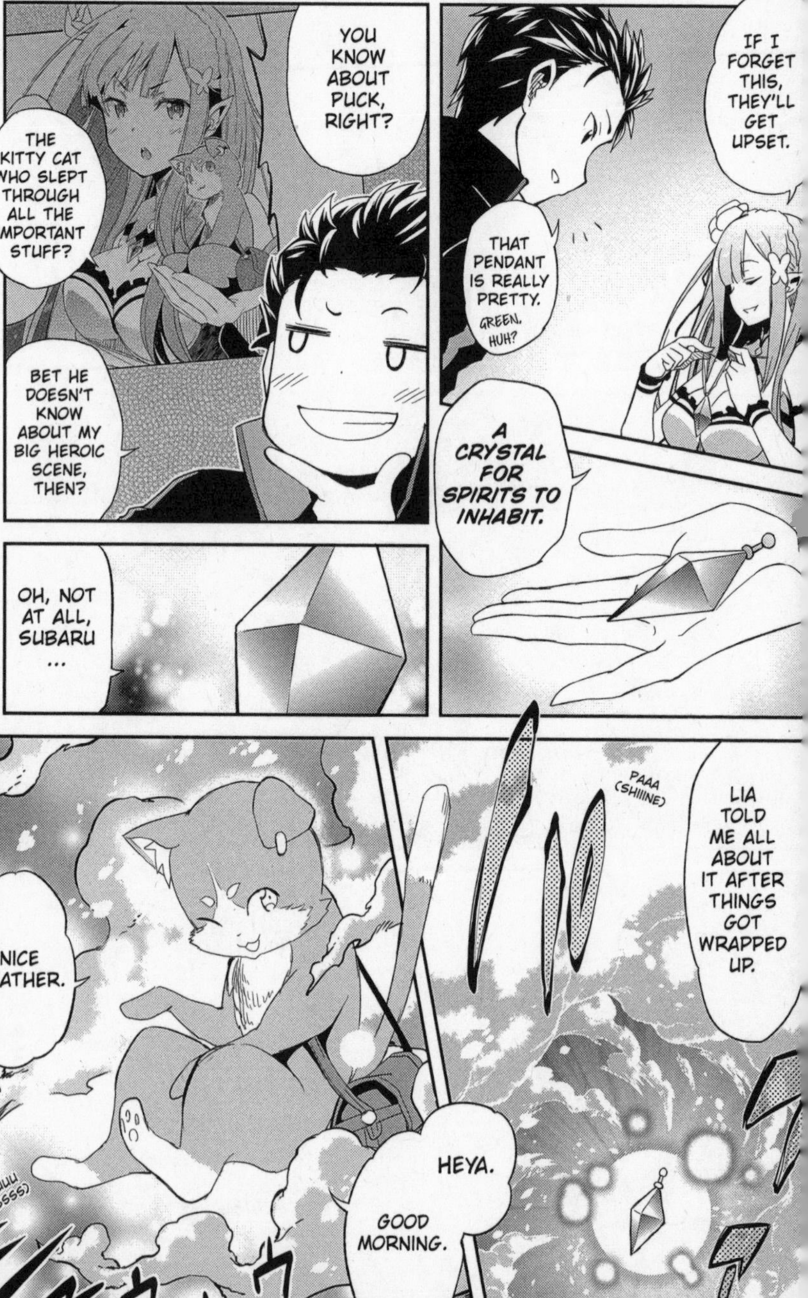
IF I FORGET THIS, THEY'LL GET UPSET.
THAT PENDANT IS REALLY PRETTY.
GREEN, HUH?
A CRYSTAL FOR SPIRITS TO INHABIT.
YOU KNOW ABOUT PUCK, RIGHT?
THE KITTY CAT WHO SLEPT THROUGH ALL THE IMPORTANT STUFF?
BET HE DOESN'T KNOW ABOUT MY BIG HEROIC SCENE, THEN?
OH, NOT AT ALL, SUBARU...
PAAA (SHIIINE)
LIA TOLD ME ALL ABOUT IT AFTER THINGS GOT WRAPPED UP.
HEYA.
GOOD MORNING.
NICE WEATHER.
SHUUUU (SSSSSS)

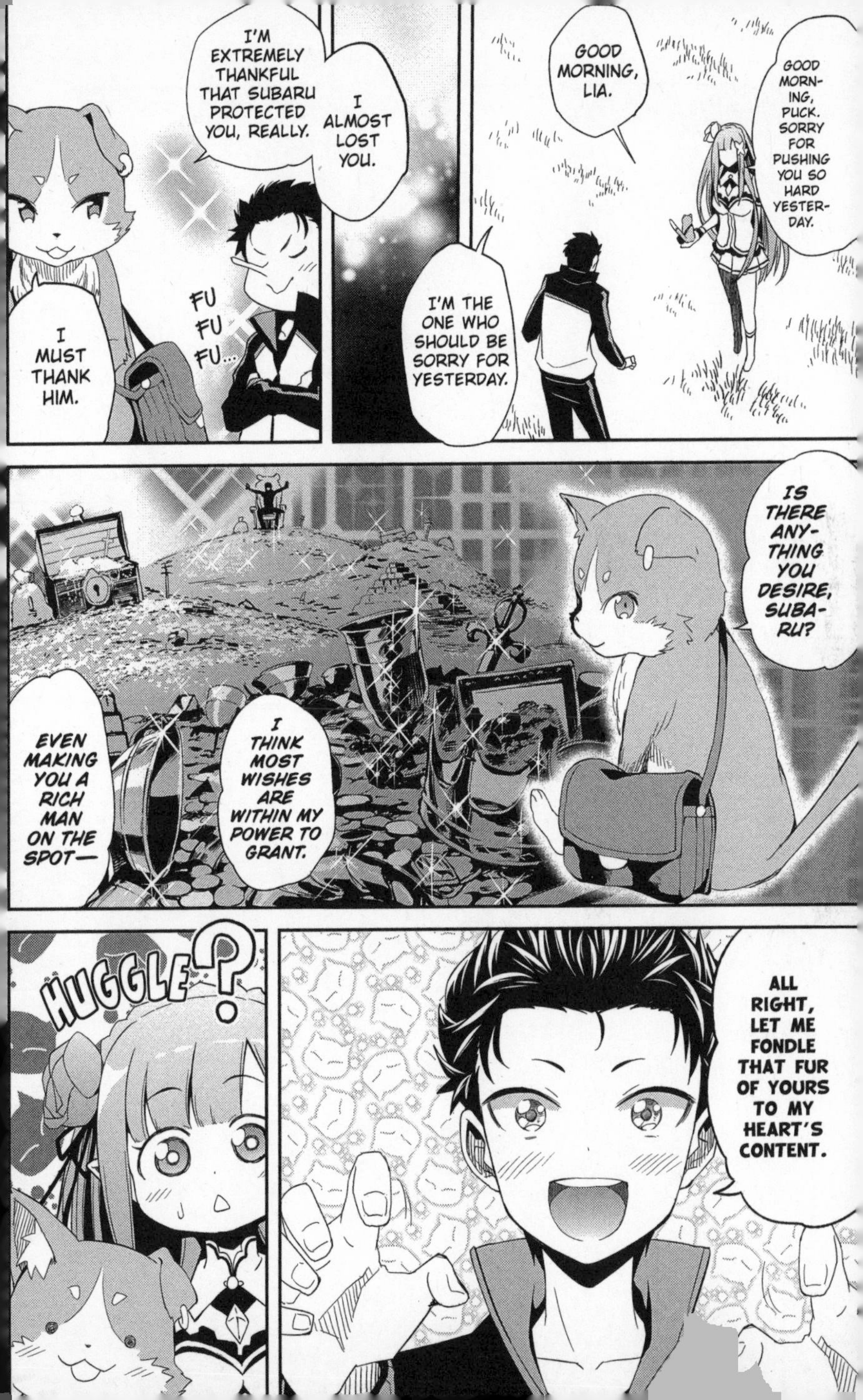
GOOD MORNING, PUCK. SORRY FOR PUSHING YOU SO HARD YESTERDAY.
GOOD MORNING, LIA.
I'M THE ONE WHO SHOULD BE SORRY FOR YESTERDAY.
I ALMOST LOST YOU.
I'M EXTREMELY THANKFUL THAT SUBARU PROTECTED YOU, REALLY.
FU FU FU...
I MUST THANK HIM.
IS THERE ANYTHING YOU DESIRE, SUBARU?
I THINK MOST WISHES ARE WITHIN MY POWER TO GRANT.
EVEN MAKING YOU A RICH MAN ON THE SPOT—
ALL RIGHT, LET ME FONDLE THAT FUR OF YOURS TO MY HEART'S CONTENT.
HUGGLE?

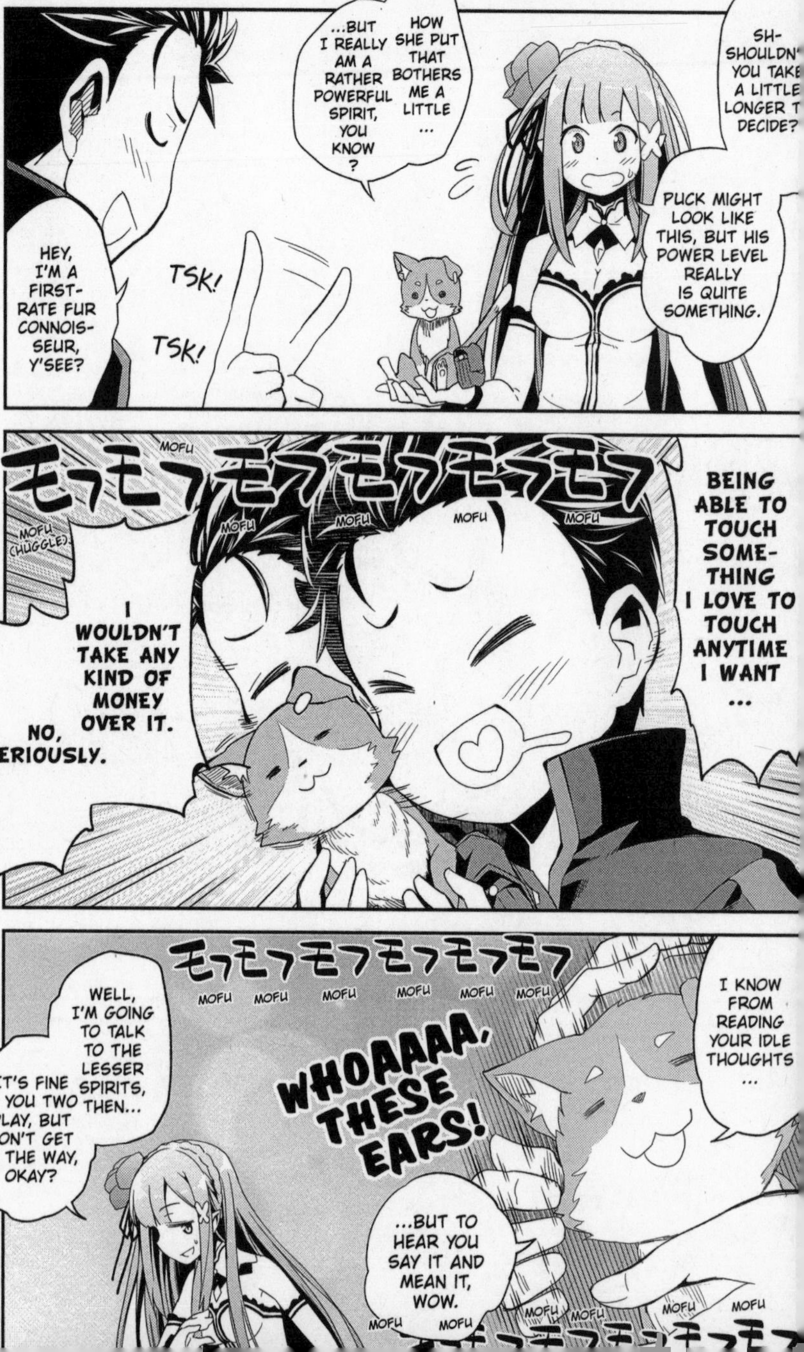
SH- SHOULDN' YOU TAKE A LITTLE LONGER T DECIDE?
PUCK MIGHT LOOK LIKE THIS, BUT HIS POWER LEVEL REALLY IS QUITE SOMETHING.
HOW SHE PUT THAT BOTHERS ME A LITTLE ...
...BUT I REALLY AM A RATHER POWERFUL SPIRIT, YOU KNOW ?
TSK!
TSK!
HEY, I'M A FIRST-RATE FUR CONNOIS-SEUR, Y'SEE?
モフモフモフモフモフモフ
MOFU MOFU MOFU MOFU MOFU
MOFU (HUGGLE)
BEING ABLE TO TOUCH SOME-THING I LOVE TO TOUCH ANYTIME I WANT ...
I WOULDN'T TAKE ANY KIND OF MONEY OVER IT.
NO, SERIOUSLY.
モフモフモフモフモフモフ
MOFU MOFU MOFU MOFU MOFU MOFU
I KNOW FROM READING YOUR IDLE THOUGHTS ...
WHOAAAA, THESE EARS!
...BUT TO HEAR YOU SAY IT AND MEAN IT, WOW.
MOFU MOFU MOFU MOFU MOFU MOFU
WELL, I'M GOING TO TALK TO THE LESSER SPIRITS, THEN...
IT'S FINE IF YOU TWO PLAY, BUT DON'T GET IN THE WAY, OKAY?

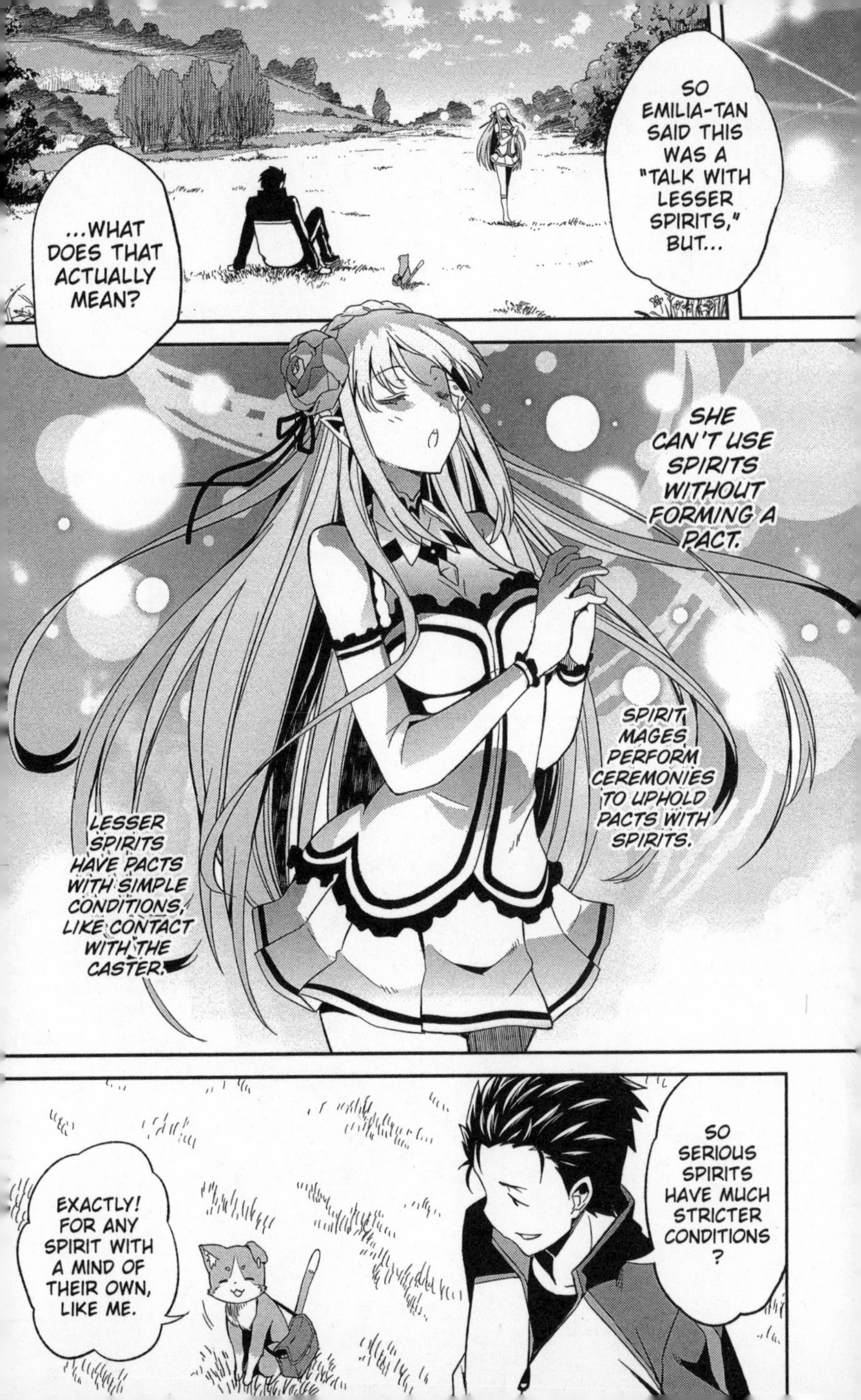
SO EMILIA-TAN SAID THIS WAS A "TALK WITH LESSER SPIRITS," BUT...
...WHAT DOES THAT ACTUALLY MEAN?
SHE CAN'T USE SPIRITS WITHOUT FORMING A PACT.
SPIRIT MAGES PERFORM CEREMONIES TO UPHOLD PACTS WITH SPIRITS.
LESSER SPIRITS HAVE PACTS WITH SIMPLE CONDITIONS, LIKE CONTACT WITH THE CASTER.
SO SERIOUS SPIRITS HAVE MUCH STRICTER CONDITIONS?
EXACTLY! FOR ANY SPIRIT WITH A MIND OF THEIR OWN, LIKE ME.

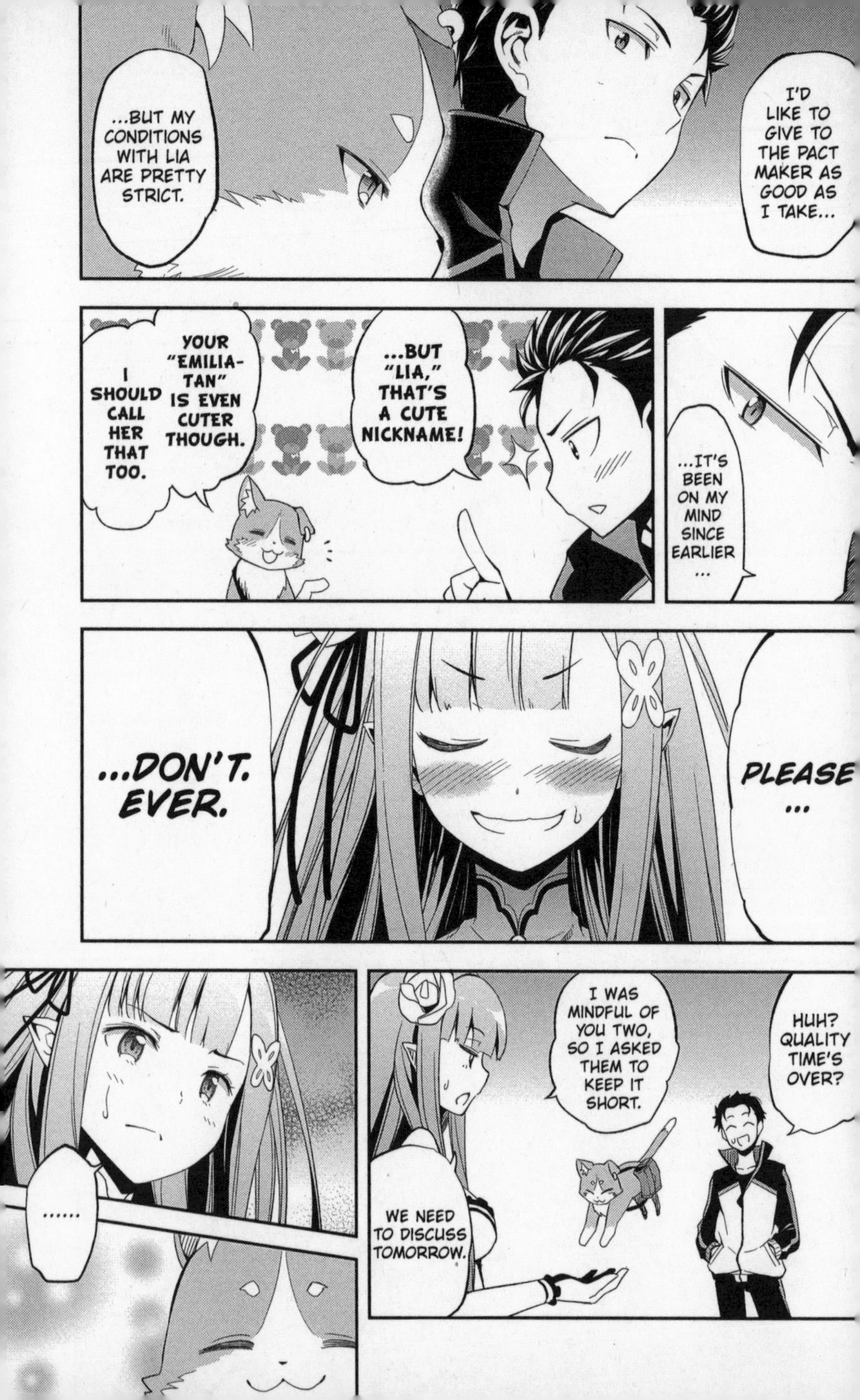
I'D LIKE TO GIVE TO THE PACT MAKER AS GOOD AS I TAKE...
...BUT MY CONDITIONS WITH LIA ARE PRETTY STRICT.
...IT'S BEEN ON MY MIND SINCE EARLIER ...
...BUT "LIA," THAT'S A CUTE NICKNAME!
YOUR "EMILIA-TAN" IS EVEN CUTER THOUGH.
I SHOULD CALL HER THAT TOO.
PLEASE ...
...DON'T. EVER.
HUH? QUALITY TIME'S OVER?
I WAS MINDFUL OF YOU TWO, SO I ASKED THEM TO KEEP IT SHORT.
WE NEED TO DISCUSS TOMORROW.
......

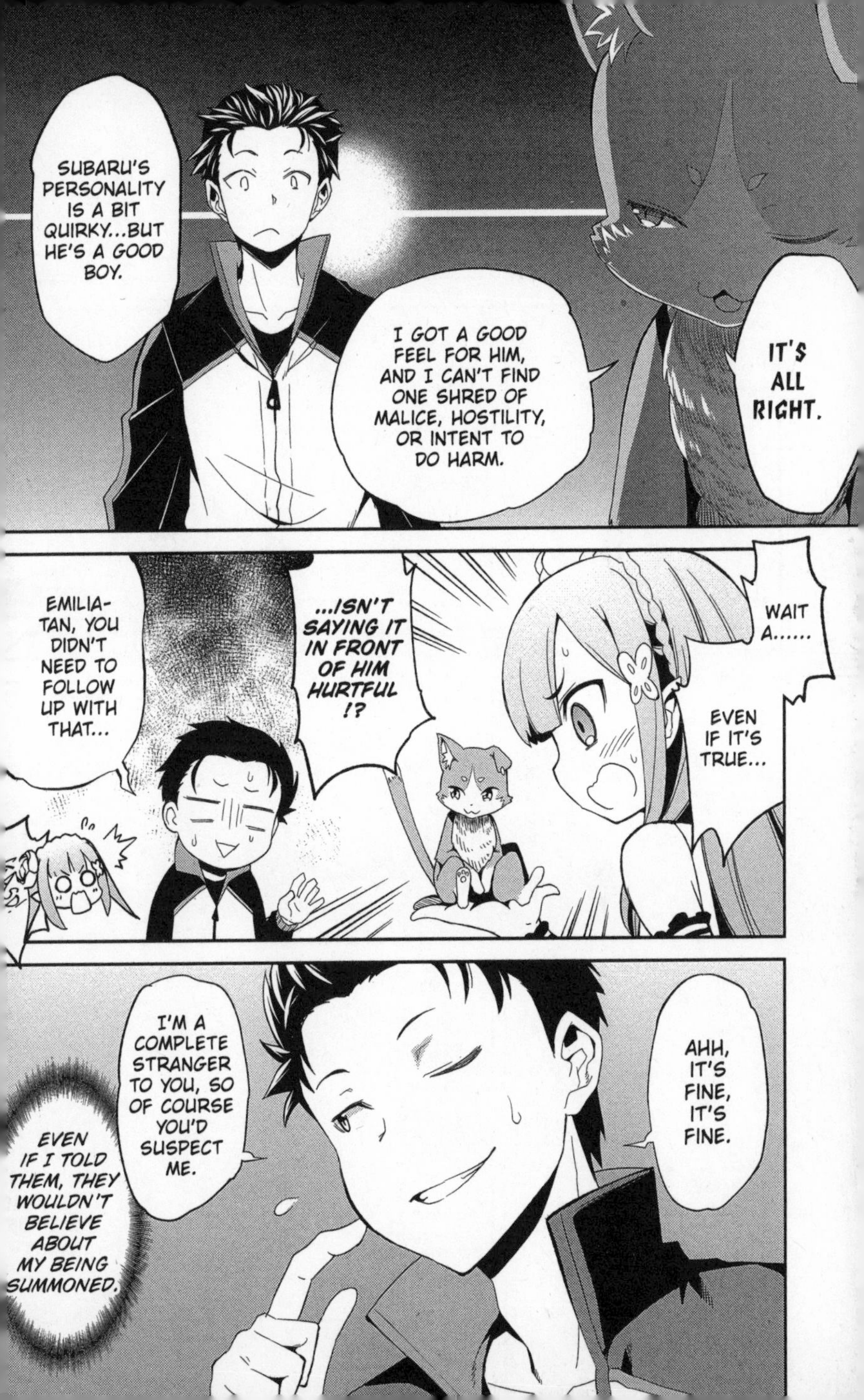
IT'S ALL RIGHT.
I GOT A GOOD FEEL FOR HIM, AND I CAN'T FIND ONE SHRED OF MALICE, HOSTILITY, OR INTENT TO DO HARM.
SUBARU'S PERSONALITY IS A BIT QUIRKY...BUT HE'S A GOOD BOY.
WAIT A......
EVEN IF IT'S TRUE...
...ISN'T SAYING IT IN FRONT OF HIM HURTFUL!?
EMILIA-TAN, YOU DIDN'T NEED TO FOLLOW UP WITH THAT...
AHH, IT'S FINE, IT'S FINE.
I'M A COMPLETE STRANGER TO YOU, SO OF COURSE YOU'D SUSPECT ME.
EVEN IF I TOLD THEM, THEY WOULDN'T BELIEVE ABOUT MY BEING SUMMONED.

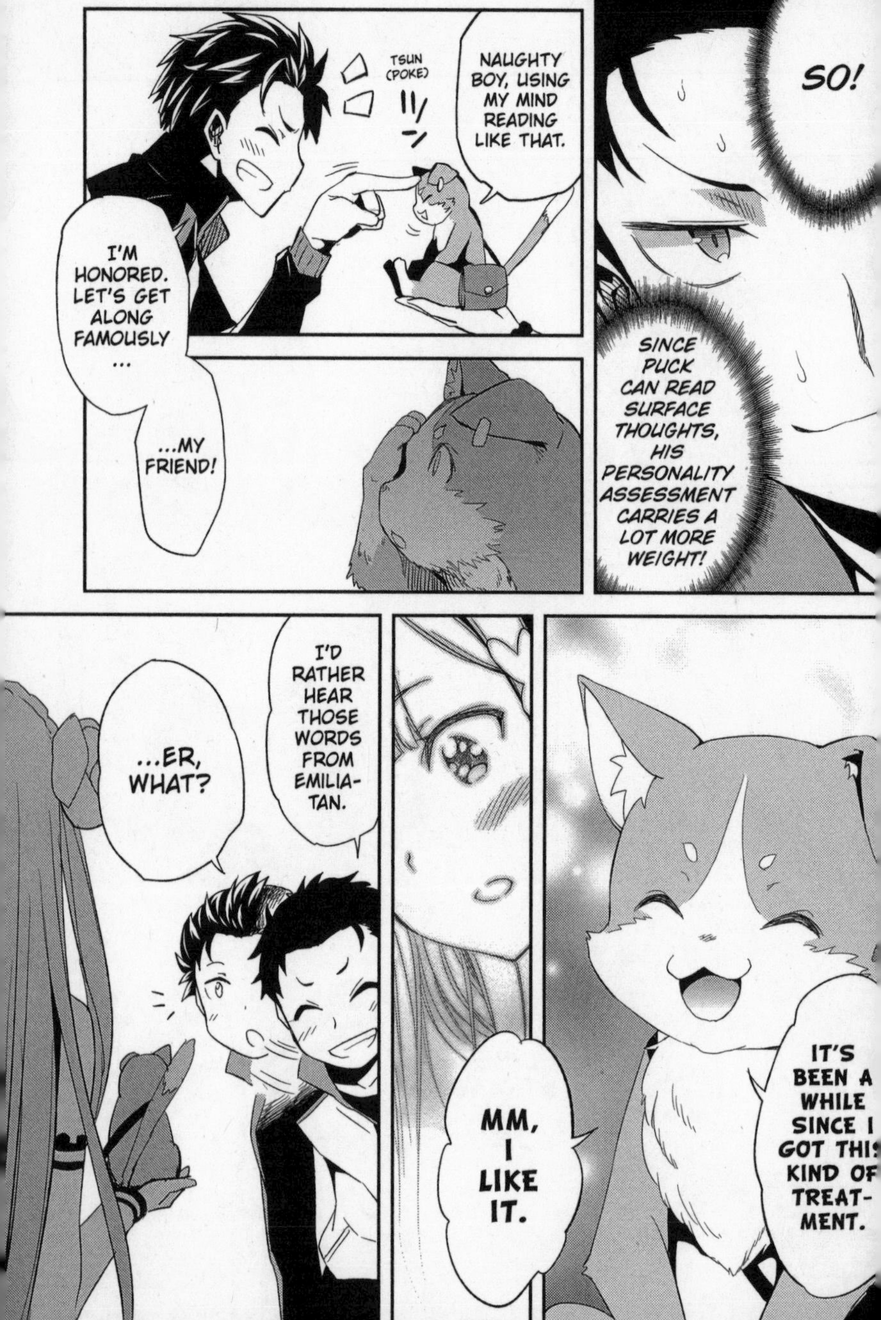
SO!
SINCE PUCK CAN READ SURFACE THOUGHTS, HIS PERSONALITY ASSESSMENT CARRIES A LOT MORE WEIGHT!
NAUGHTY BOY, USING MY MIND READING LIKE THAT.
TSUN (POKE)
I'M HONORED. LET'S GET ALONG FAMOUSLY...
...MY FRIEND!
IT'S BEEN A WHILE SINCE I GOT THIS KIND OF TREAT-MENT.
MM, I LIKE IT.
I'D RATHER HEAR THOSE WORDS FROM EMILIA-TAN.
...ER, WHAT?

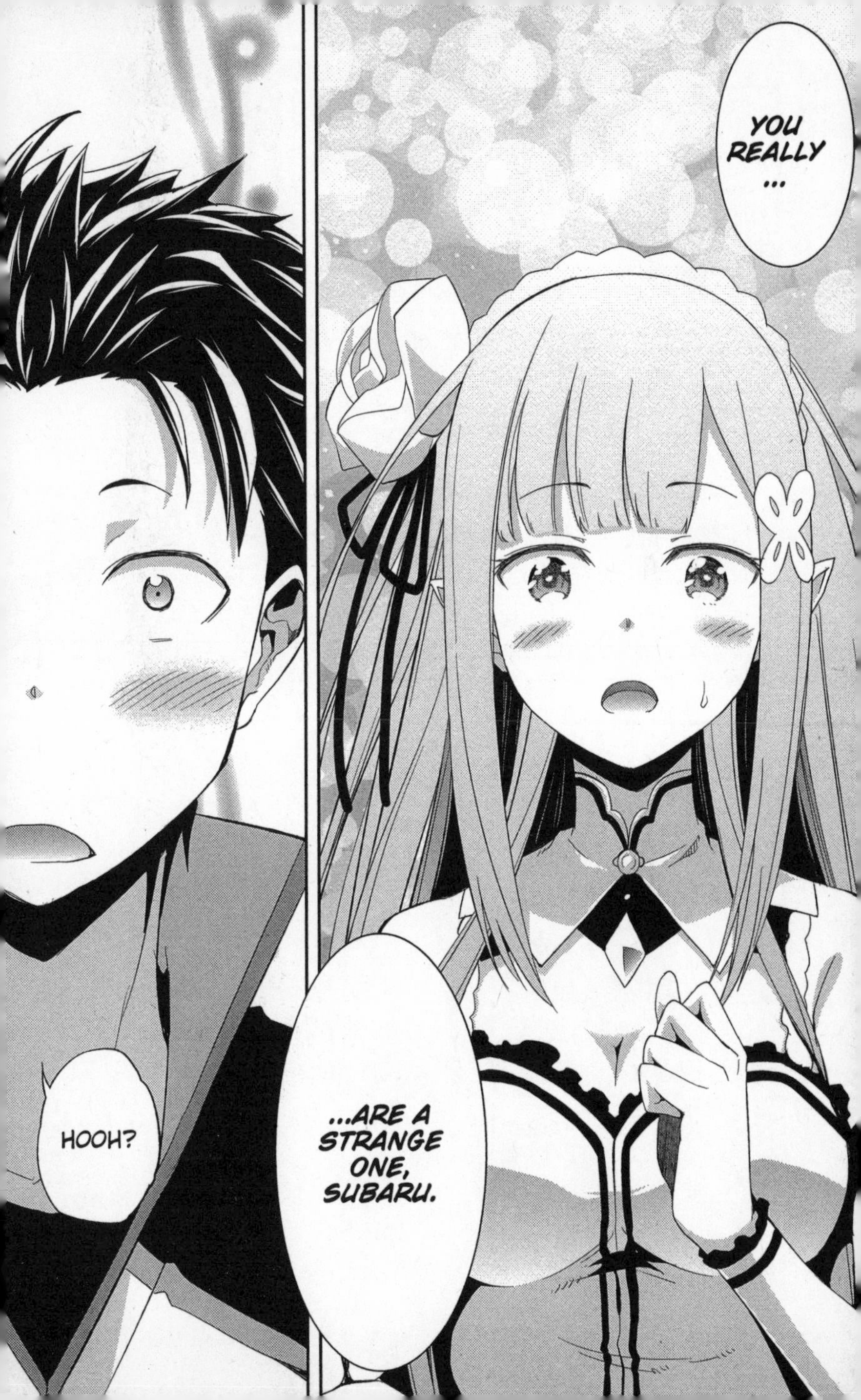
YOU REALLY ...
...ARE A STRANGE ONE, SUBARU.
HOOH?

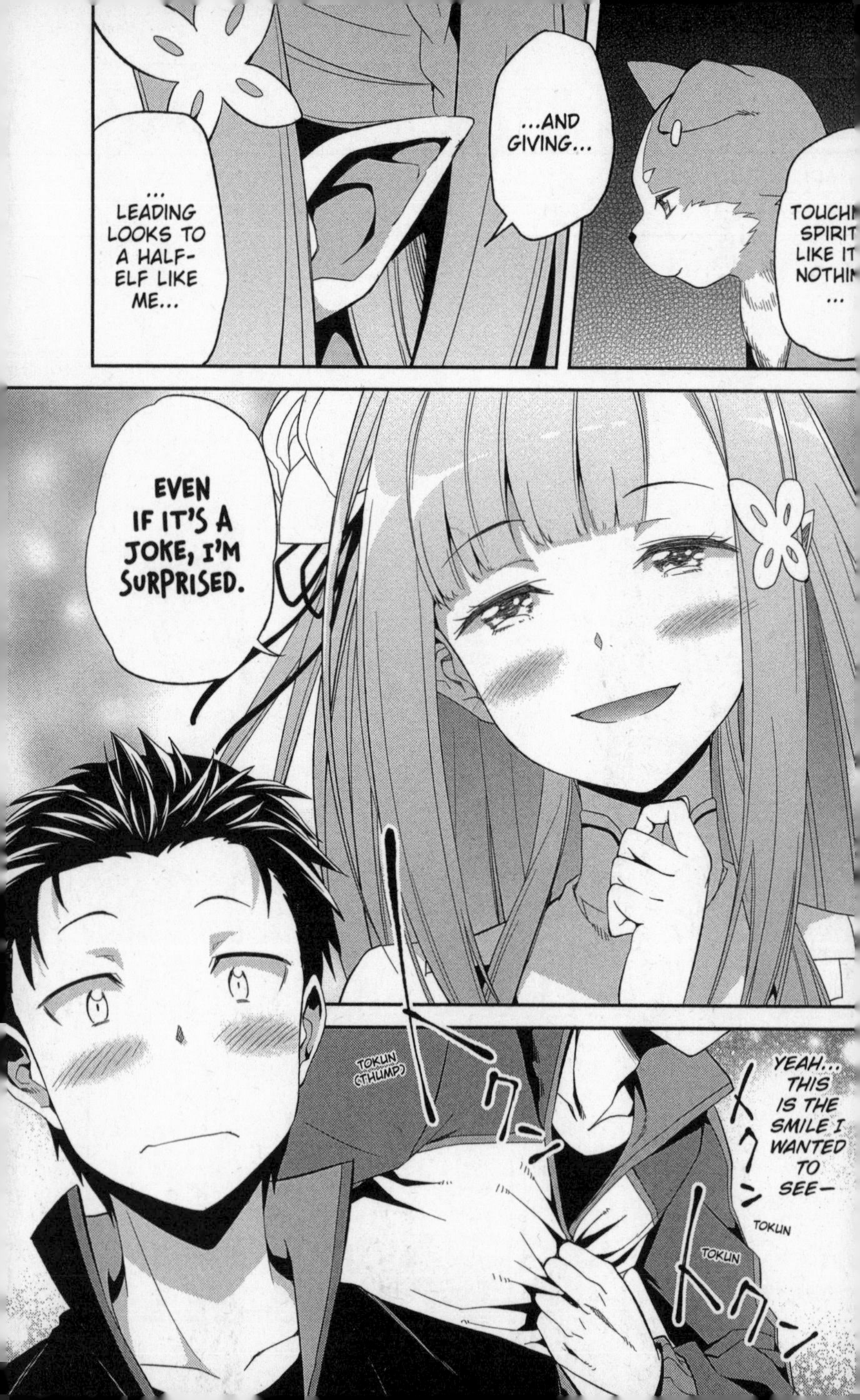
TOUCHI
SPIRIT
LIKE IT
NOTHI
...
...AND GIVING...
... LEADING LOOKS TO A HALF-ELF LIKE ME...
EVEN IF IT'S A JOKE, I'M SURPRISED.
YEAH... THIS IS THE SMILE I WANTED TO SEE—
TOKUN
TOKUN
TOKUN (THUMP)

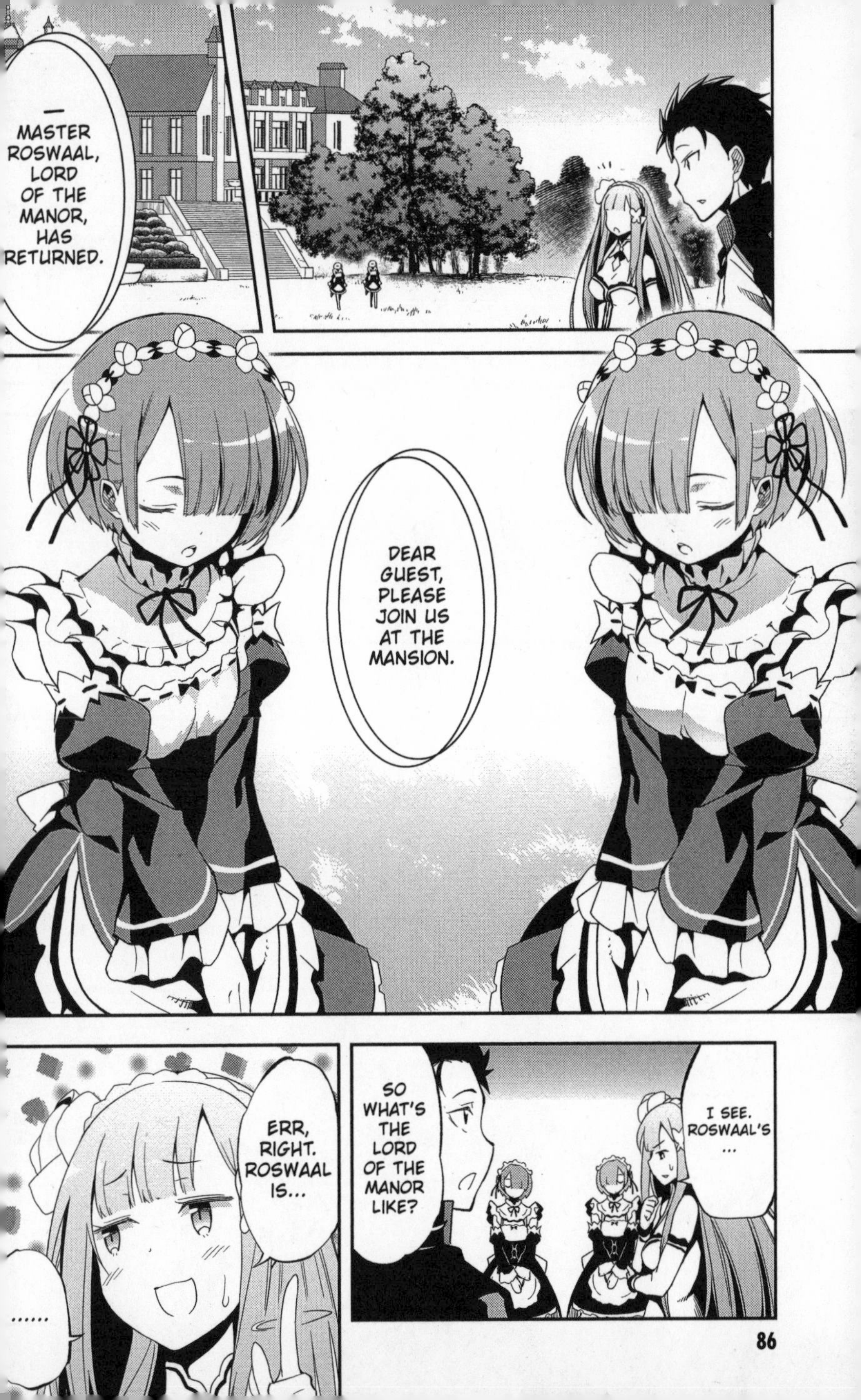
—MASTER ROSWAAL, LORD OF THE MANOR, HAS RETURNED.
DEAR GUEST, PLEASE JOIN US AT THE MANSION.
I SEE. ROSWAAL'S ...
SO WHAT'S THE LORD OF THE MANOR LIKE?
ERR, RIGHT. ROSWAAL IS...
......

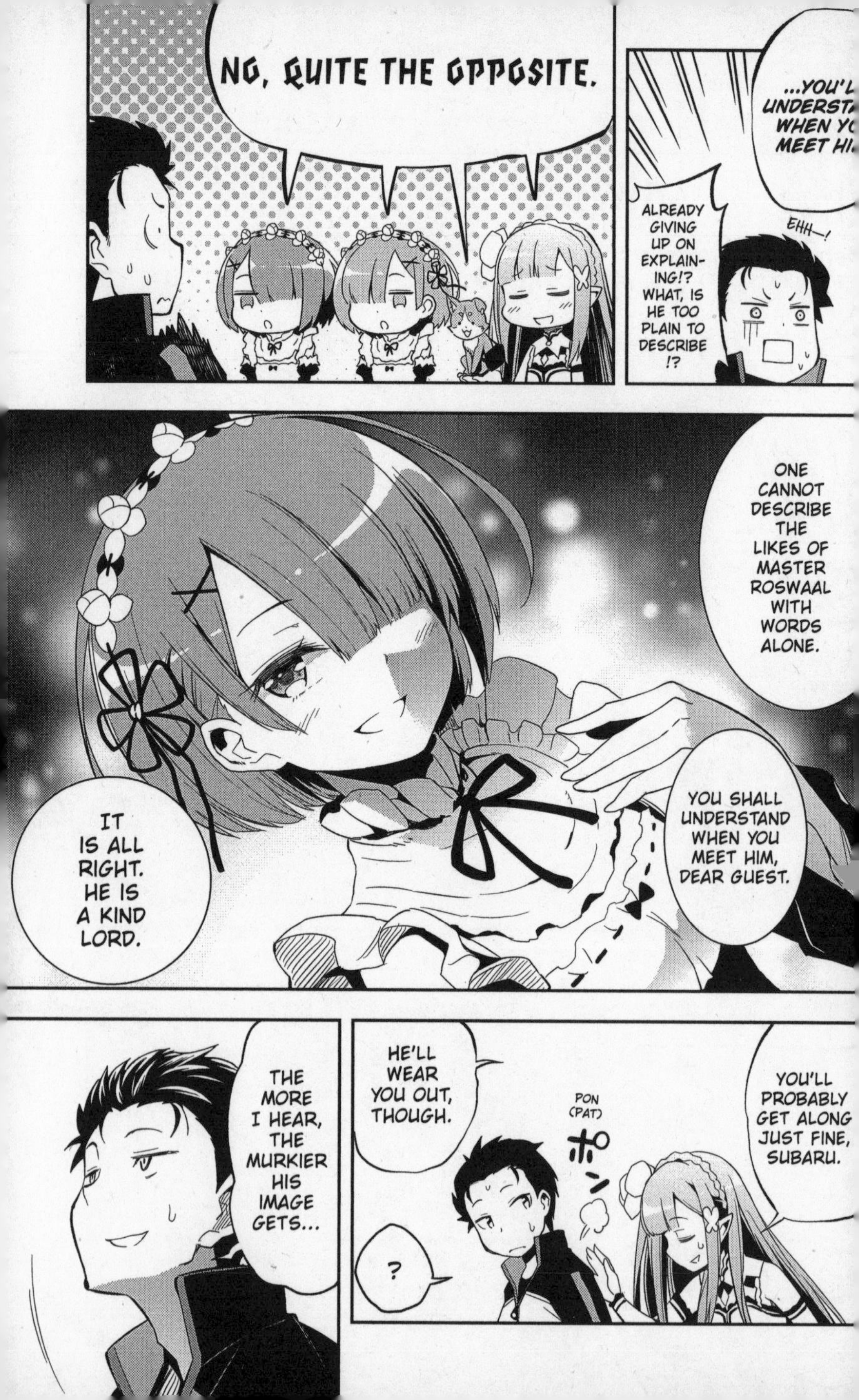
...YOU'L UNDERST WHEN YO MEET HI
EHH—!
ALREADY GIVING UP ON EXPLAIN-ING!? WHAT, IS HE TOO PLAIN TO DESCRIBE !?
NO, QUITE THE OPPOSITE.
ONE CANNOT DESCRIBE THE LIKES OF MASTER ROSWAAL WITH WORDS ALONE.
YOU SHALL UNDERSTAND WHEN YOU MEET HIM, DEAR GUEST.
IT IS ALL RIGHT. HE IS A KIND LORD.
YOU'LL PROBABLY GET ALONG JUST FINE, SUBARU.
PON (PAT)
HE'LL WEAR YOU OUT, THOUGH.
?
THE MORE I HEAR, THE MURKIER HIS IMAGE GETS...

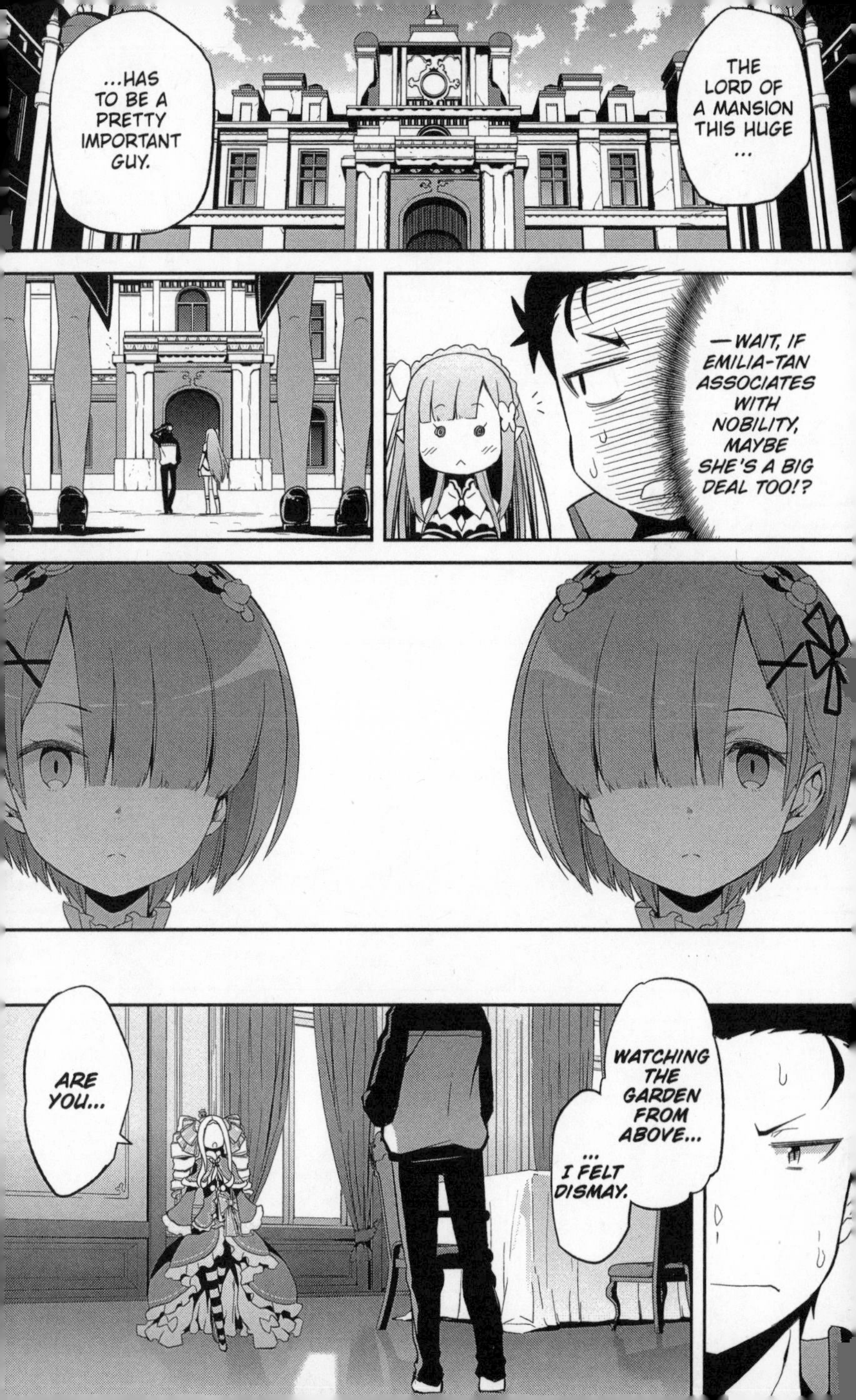
THE LORD OF A MANSION THIS HUGE ...
...HAS TO BE A PRETTY IMPORTANT GUY.
—WAIT, IF EMILIA-TAN ASSOCIATES WITH NOBILITY, MAYBE SHE'S A BIG DEAL TOO!?
WATCHING THE GARDEN FROM ABOVE...
... I FELT DISMAY.
ARE YOU...

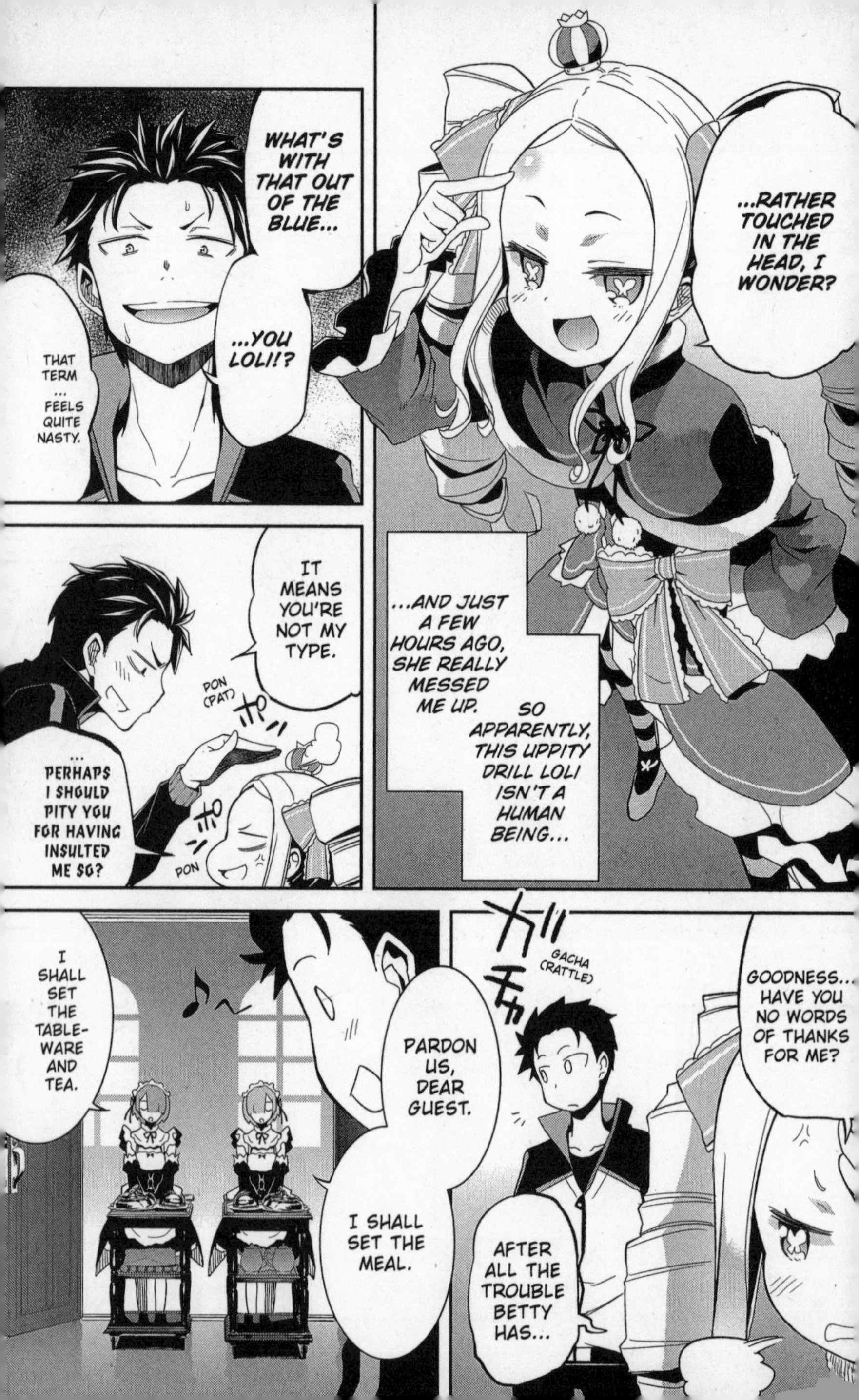
...RATHER TOUCHED IN THE HEAD, I WONDER?
...AND JUST A FEW HOURS AGO, SHE REALLY MESSED ME UP.
SO APPARENTLY, THIS UPPITY DRILL LOLI ISN'T A HUMAN BEING...
WHAT'S WITH THAT OUT OF THE BLUE...
...YOU LOLI!?
THAT TERM ... FEELS QUITE NASTY.
IT MEANS YOU'RE NOT MY TYPE.
PON (PAT)
... PERHAPS I SHOULD PITY YOU FOR HAVING INSULTED ME SO?
PON
GACHA (RATTLE)
GOODNESS... HAVE YOU NO WORDS OF THANKS FOR ME?
AFTER ALL THE TROUBLE BETTY HAS...
PARDON US, DEAR GUEST.
I SHALL SET THE MEAL.
I SHALL SET THE TABLE-WARE AND TEA.

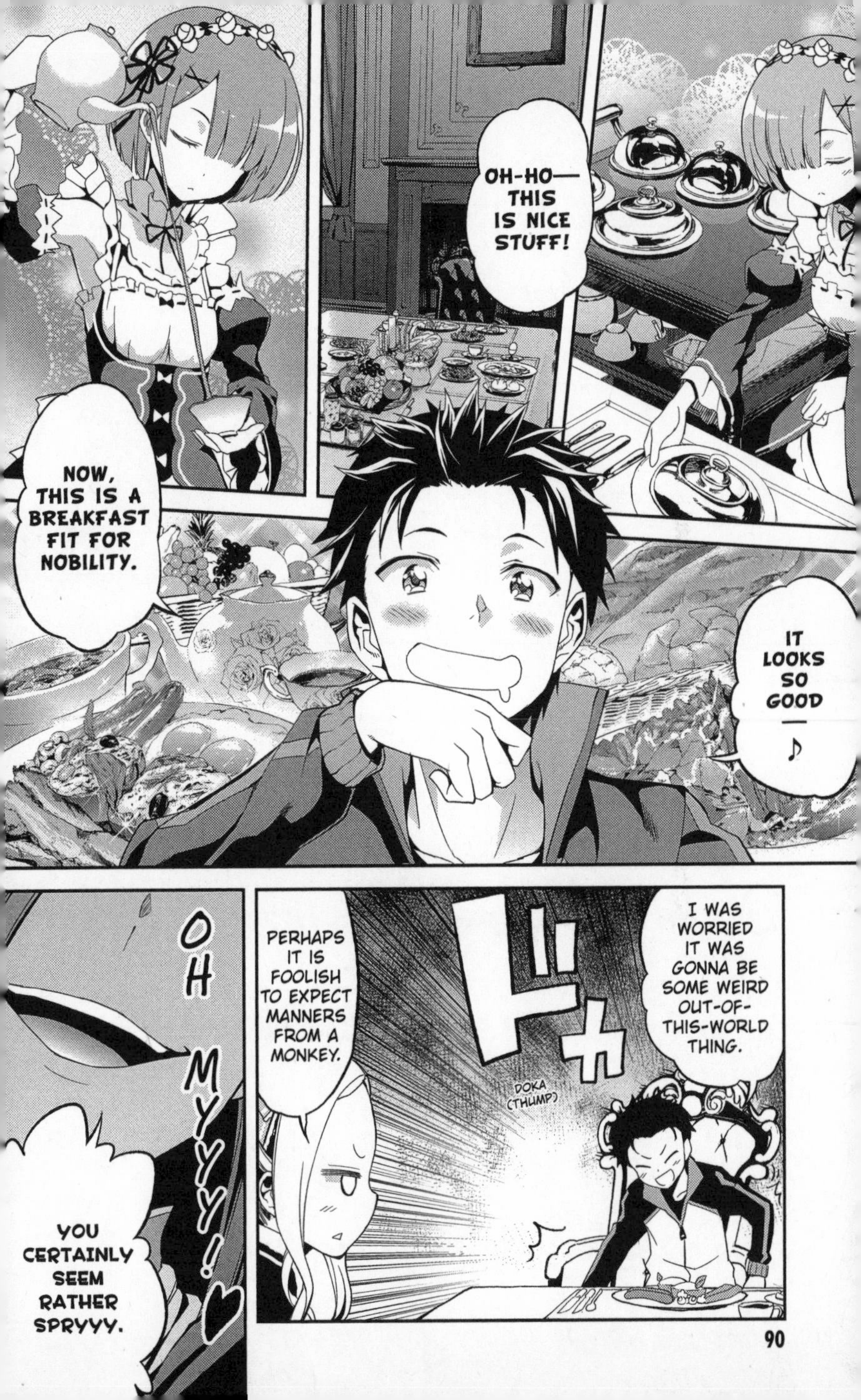
OH-HO— THIS IS NICE STUFF!
NOW, THIS IS A BREAKFAST FIT FOR NOBILITY.
IT LOOKS SO GOOD —♪
I WAS WORRIED IT WAS GONNA BE SOME WEIRD OUT-OF-THIS-WORLD THING.
DOKA (THUMP)
PERHAPS IT IS FOOLISH TO EXPECT MANNERS FROM A MONKEY.
OH MYYY!♥
YOU CERTAINLY SEEM RATHER SPRYYY.

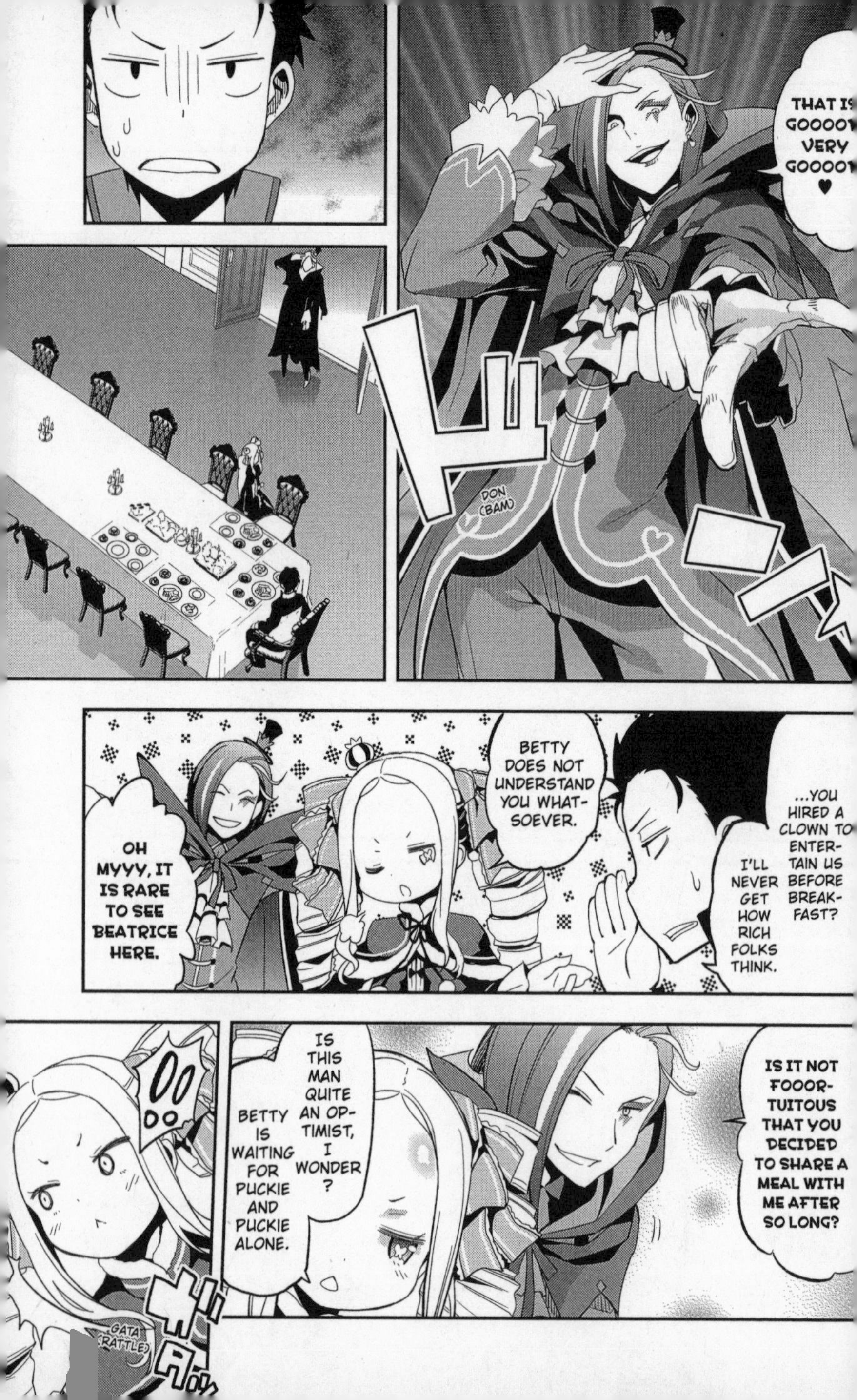
THAT IS GOOOO VERY GOOOO ♥
DON (BAM)
...YOU HIRED A CLOWN TO ENTERTAIN US BEFORE BREAKFAST?
I'LL NEVER GET HOW RICH FOLKS THINK.
BETTY DOES NOT UNDERSTAND YOU WHATSOEVER.
OH MYYY, IT IS RARE TO SEE BEATRICE HERE.
IS IT NOT FOOORTUITOUS THAT YOU DECIDED TO SHARE A MEAL WITH ME AFTER SO LONG?
IS THIS MAN QUITE AN OPTIMIST, I WONDER?
BETTY IS WAITING FOR PUCKIE AND PUCKIE ALONE.
GATA (RATTLE)

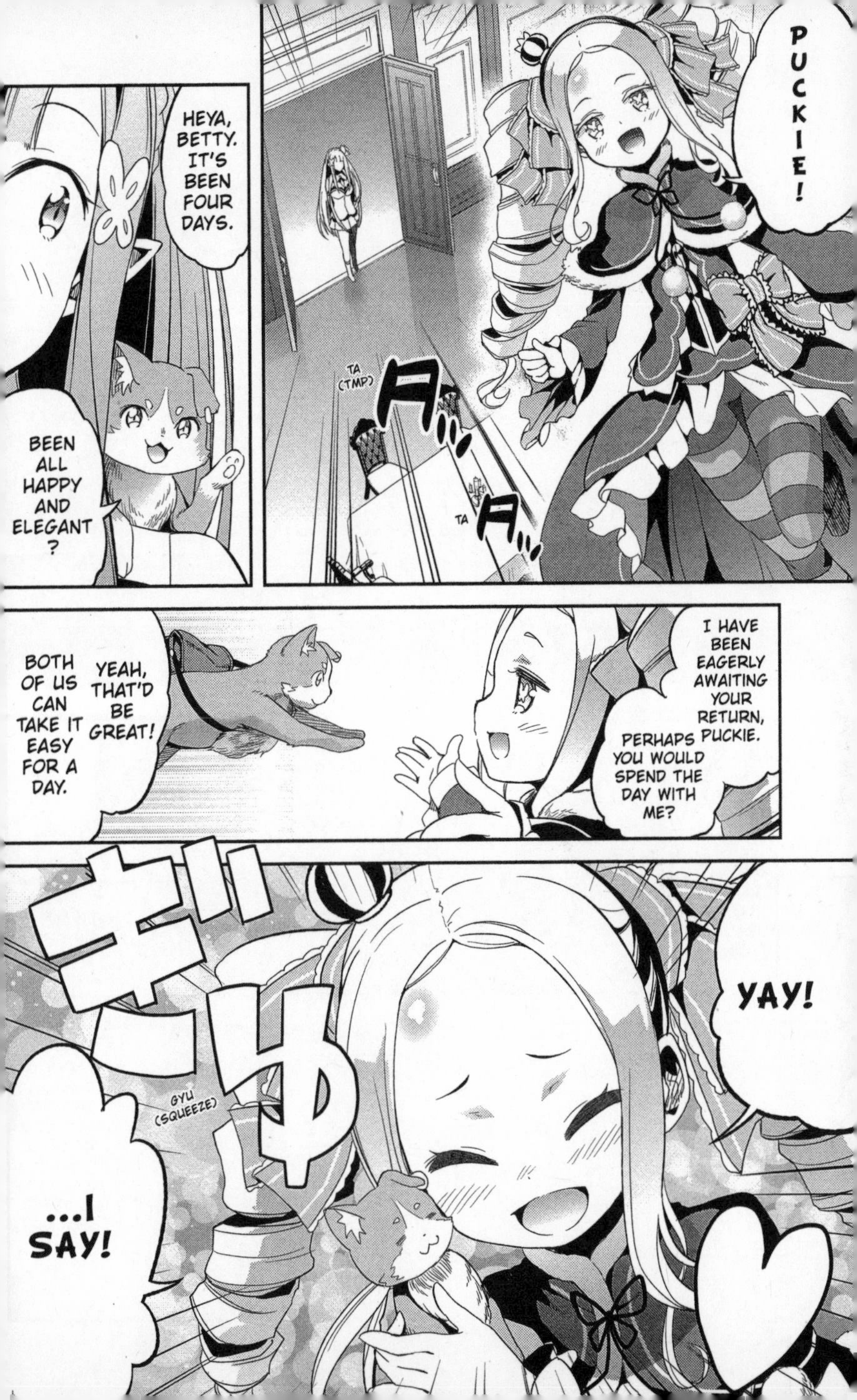
PUCKIE!
TA (TMP)
TA
HEYA, BETTY. IT'S BEEN FOUR DAYS.
BEEN ALL HAPPY AND ELEGANT?
I HAVE BEEN EAGERLY AWAITING YOUR RETURN, PUCKIE.
PERHAPS YOU WOULD SPEND THE DAY WITH ME?
YEAH, THAT'D BE GREAT!
BOTH OF US CAN TAKE IT EASY FOR A DAY.
YAY!
GYU (SQUEEZE)
...I SAY!

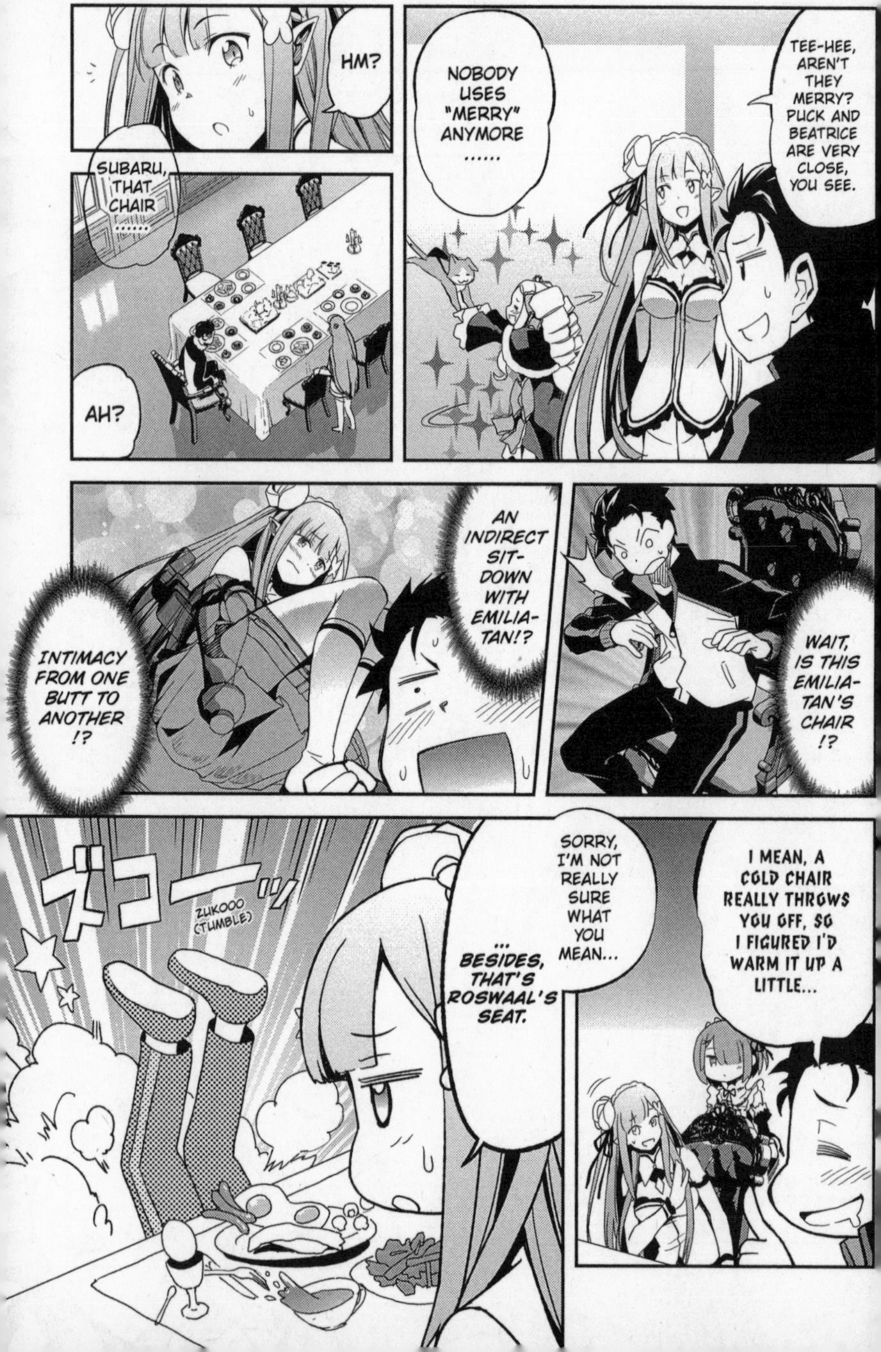
TEE-HEE, AREN'T THEY MERRY? PUCK AND BEATRICE ARE VERY CLOSE, YOU SEE.
NOBODY USES "MERRY" ANYMORE ......
HM?
SUBARU, THAT CHAIR ......
AH?
WAIT, IS THIS EMILIA-TAN'S CHAIR !?
AN INDIRECT SIT-DOWN WITH EMILIA-TAN!?
INTIMACY FROM ONE BUTT TO ANOTHER !?
I MEAN, A COLD CHAIR REALLY THROWS YOU OFF, SO I FIGURED I'D WARM IT UP A LITTLE...
SORRY, I'M NOT REALLY SURE WHAT YOU MEAN...
... BESIDES, THAT'S ROSWAAL'S SEAT.
ズコーッ
ZUKOOO (TUMBLE)

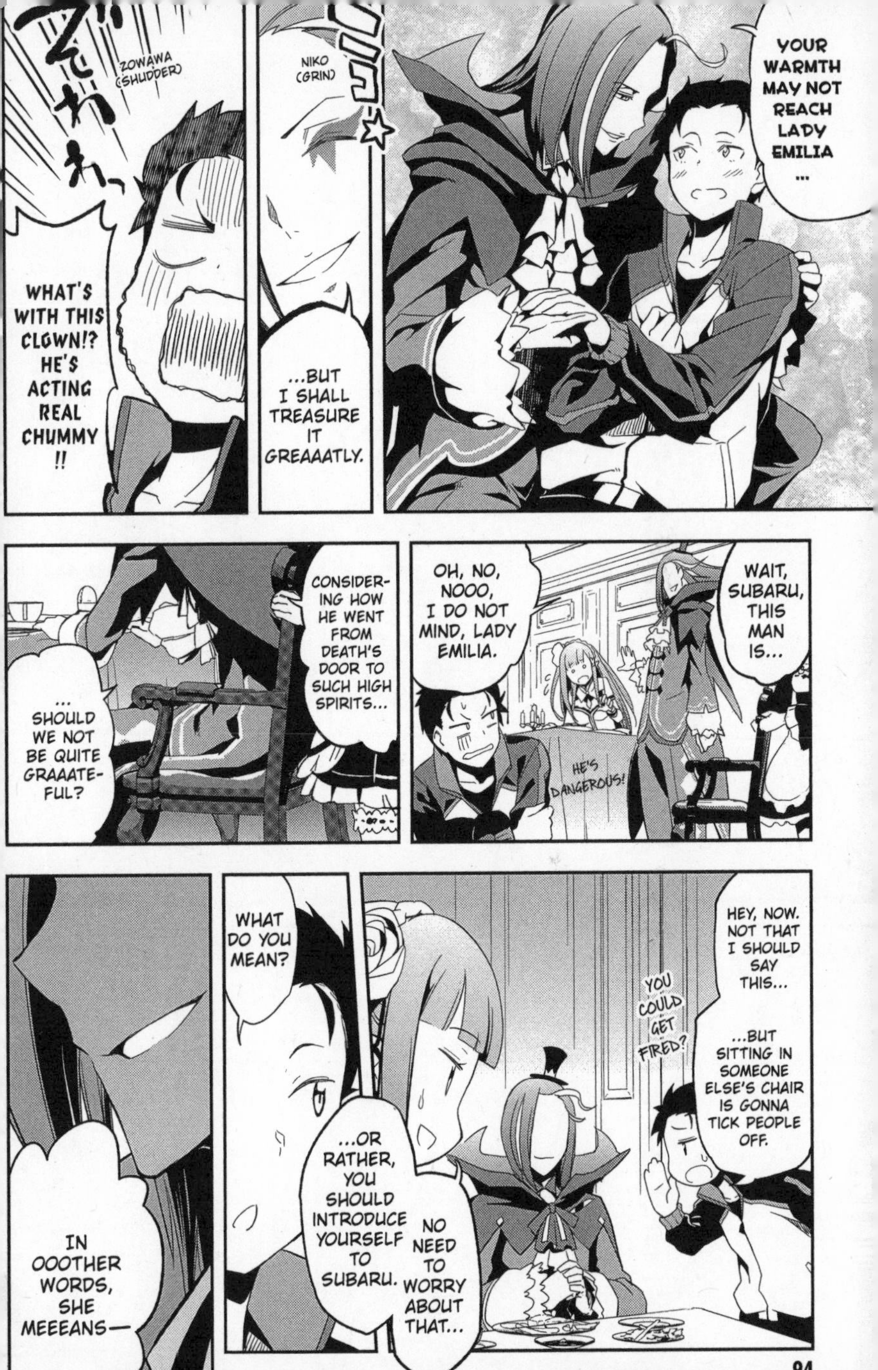
YOUR WARMTH MAY NOT REACH LADY EMILIA ...
NIKO (GRIN)
...BUT I SHALL TREASURE IT GREAAATLY.
ZOWAWA (SHUDDER)
WHAT'S WITH THIS CLOWN!? HE'S ACTING REAL CHUMMY !!
WAIT, SUBARU, THIS MAN IS...
HE'S DANGEROUS!
OH, NO, NOOO, I DO NOT MIND, LADY EMILIA.
CONSIDER-ING HOW HE WENT FROM DEATH'S DOOR TO SUCH HIGH SPIRITS...
... SHOULD WE NOT BE QUITE GRAAATE-FUL?
HEY, NOW. NOT THAT I SHOULD SAY THIS...
...BUT SITTING IN SOMEONE ELSE'S CHAIR IS GONNA TICK PEOPLE OFF.
YOU COULD GET FIRED?
NO NEED TO WORRY ABOUT THAT...
WHAT DO YOU MEAN?
...OR RATHER, YOU SHOULD INTRODUCE YOURSELF TO SUBARU.
IN OOOTHER WORDS, SHE MEEEANS—

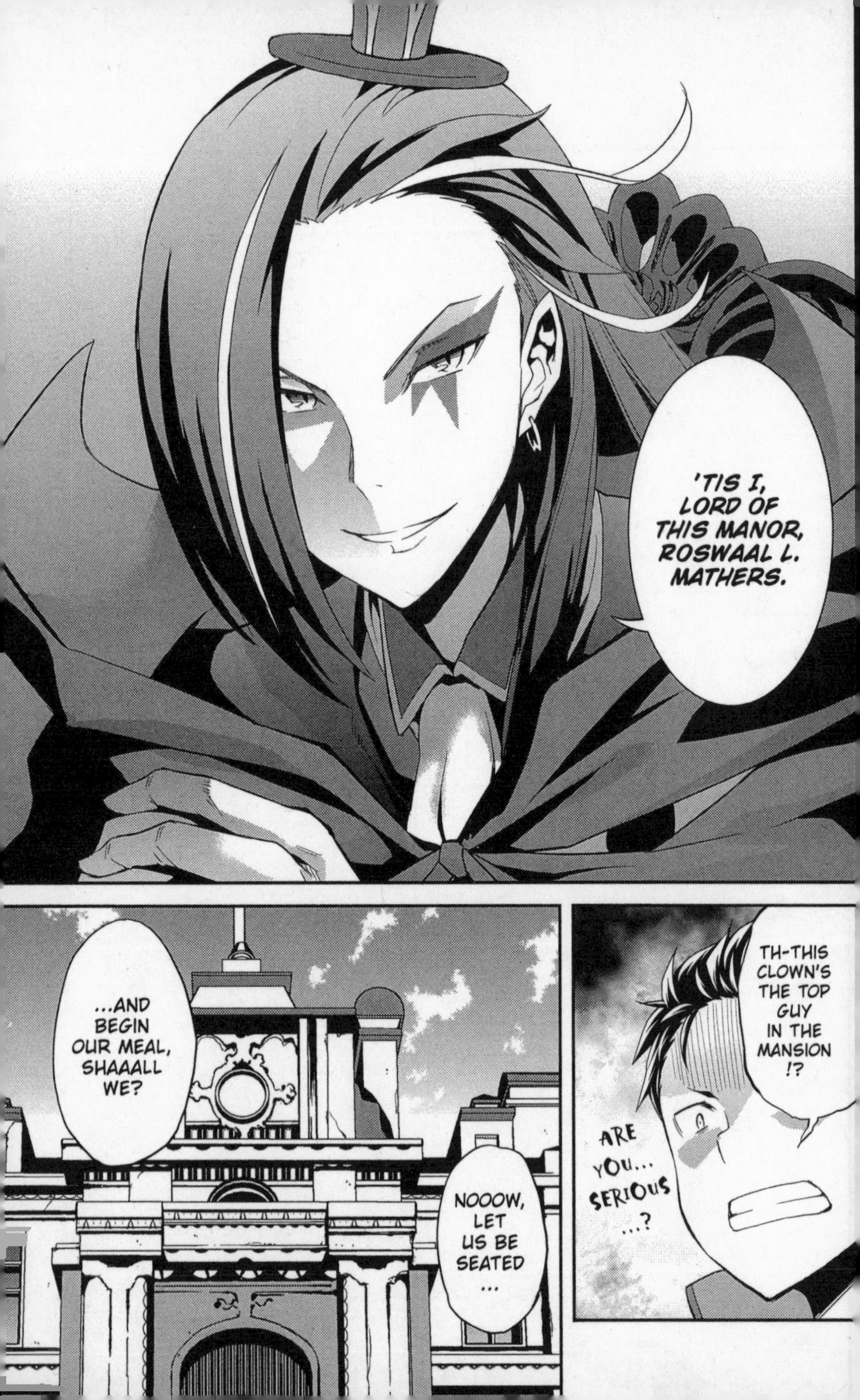
'TIS I, LORD OF THIS MANOR, ROSWAAL L. MATHERS.
TH-THIS CLOWN'S THE TOP GUY IN THE MANSION!?
ARE YOU... SERIOUS...?
NOOOW, LET US BE SEATED...
...AND BEGIN OUR MEAL, SHAAALL WE?

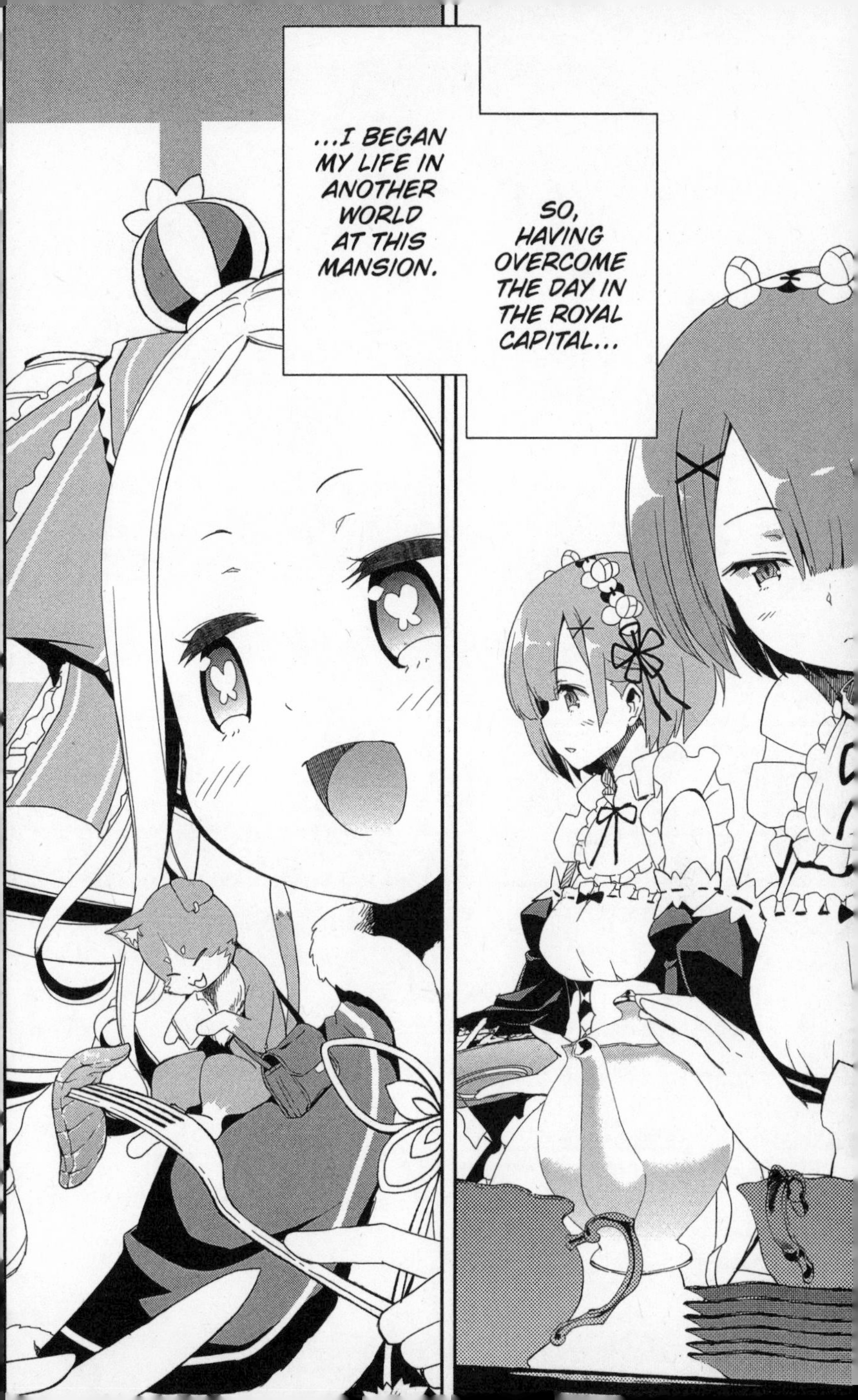
SO, HAVING OVERCOME THE DAY IN THE ROYAL CAPITAL...
...I BEGAN MY LIFE IN ANOTHER WORLD AT THIS MANSION.

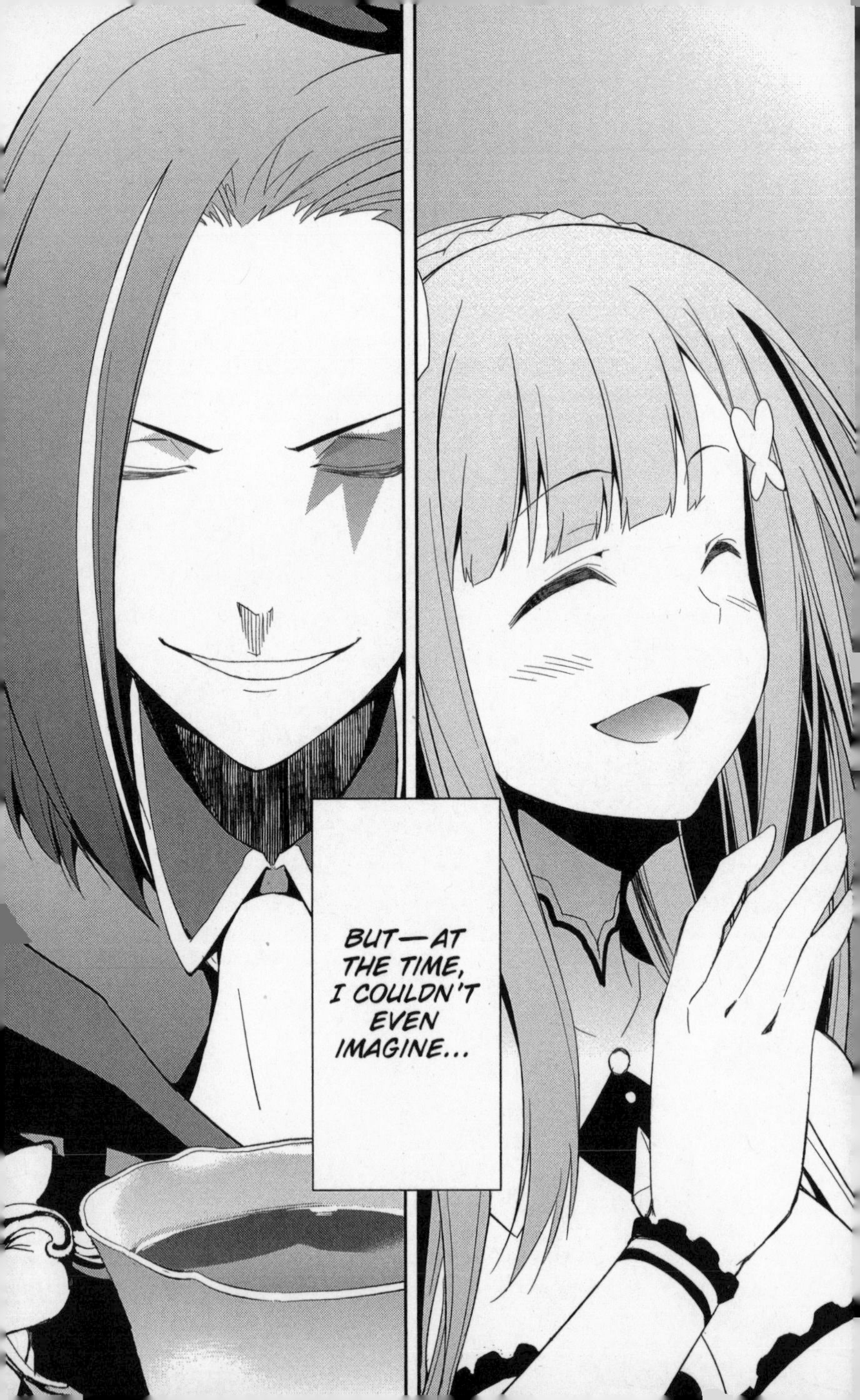
BUT—AT THE TIME, I COULDN'T EVEN IMAGINE...

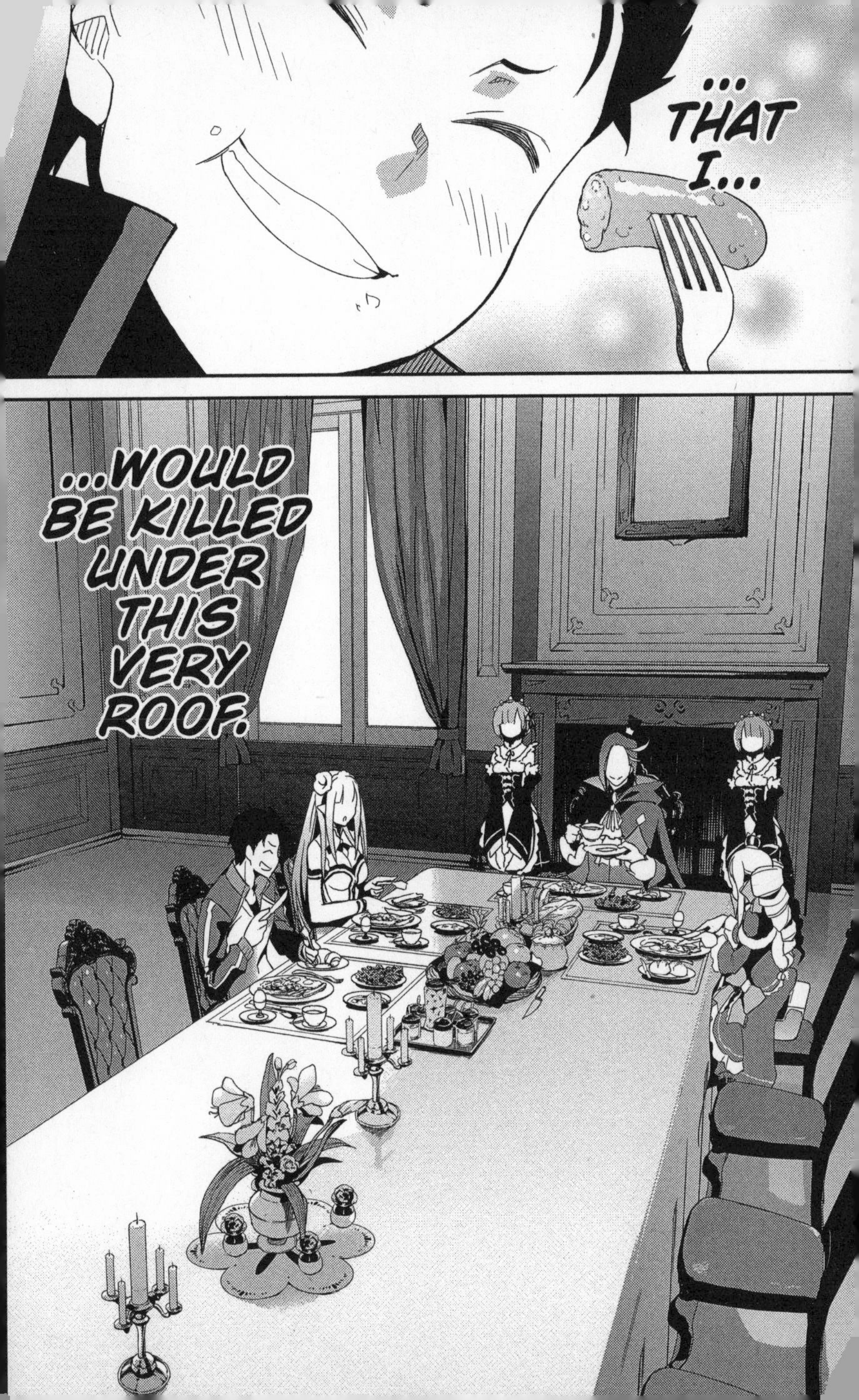
...THAT I...
...WOULD BE KILLED UNDER THIS VERY ROOF.

And now begins the second story arc!
Please enjoy the beginning of "A Week at the Mansion."

The only ability Subaru Natsuki gets when he's summoned to another world is time travel via his own death. But to save her, he'll die as many times as it takes.

Re:ZERO -Starting Life in Another World-

A Week at the Mansion

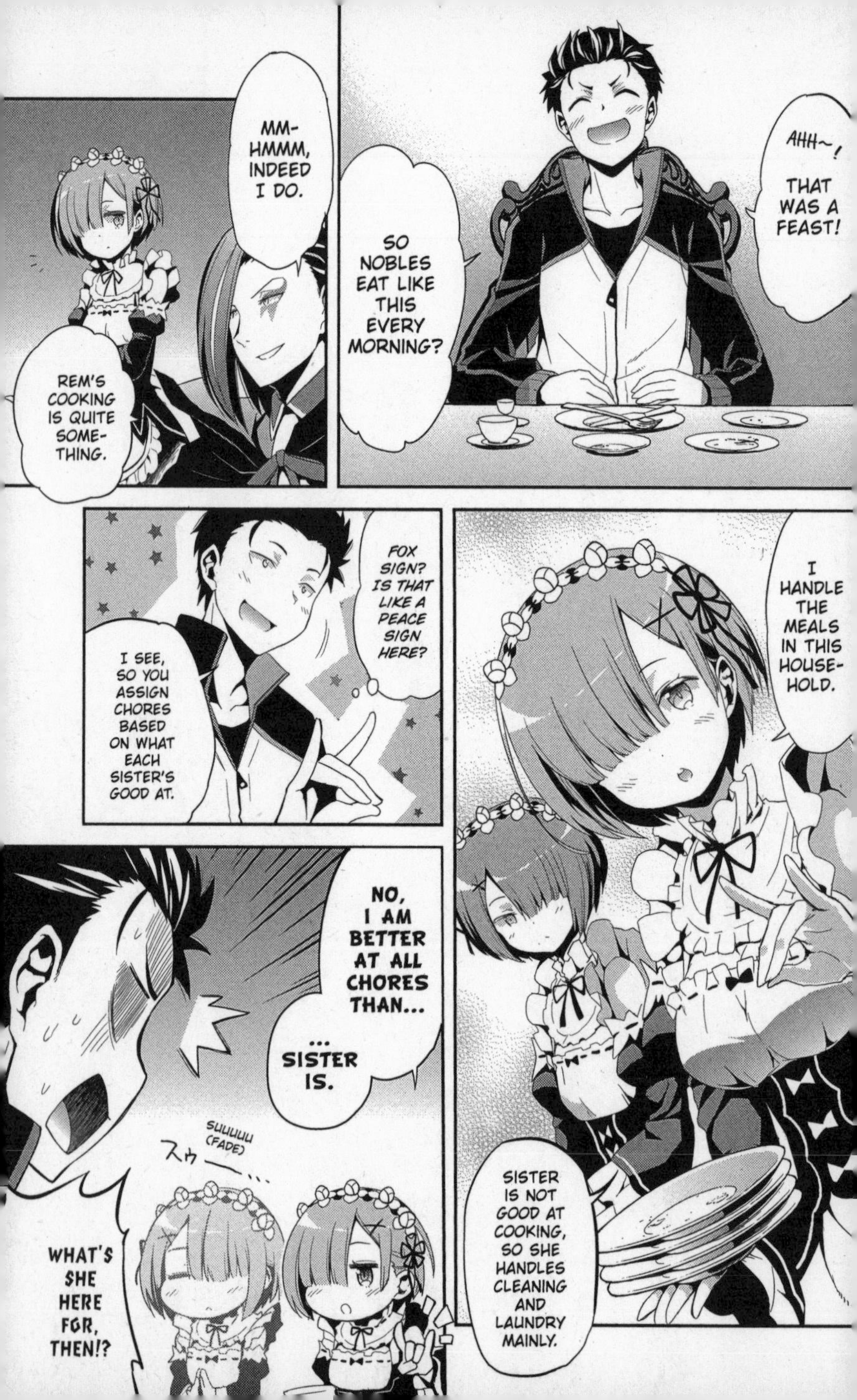
AHH~! THAT WAS A FEAST!
SO NOBLES EAT LIKE THIS EVERY MORNING?
MM-HMMM, INDEED I DO.
REM'S COOKING IS QUITE SOME-THING.
I HANDLE THE MEALS IN THIS HOUSE-HOLD.
SISTER IS NOT GOOD AT COOKING, SO SHE HANDLES CLEANING AND LAUNDRY MAINLY.
FOX SIGN? IS THAT LIKE A PEACE SIGN HERE?
I SEE, SO YOU ASSIGN CHORES BASED ON WHAT EACH SISTER'S GOOD AT.
NO, I AM BETTER AT ALL CHORES THAN...
... SISTER IS.
SUUUUU (FADE)
スゥー…
WHAT'S SHE HERE FOR, THEN!?

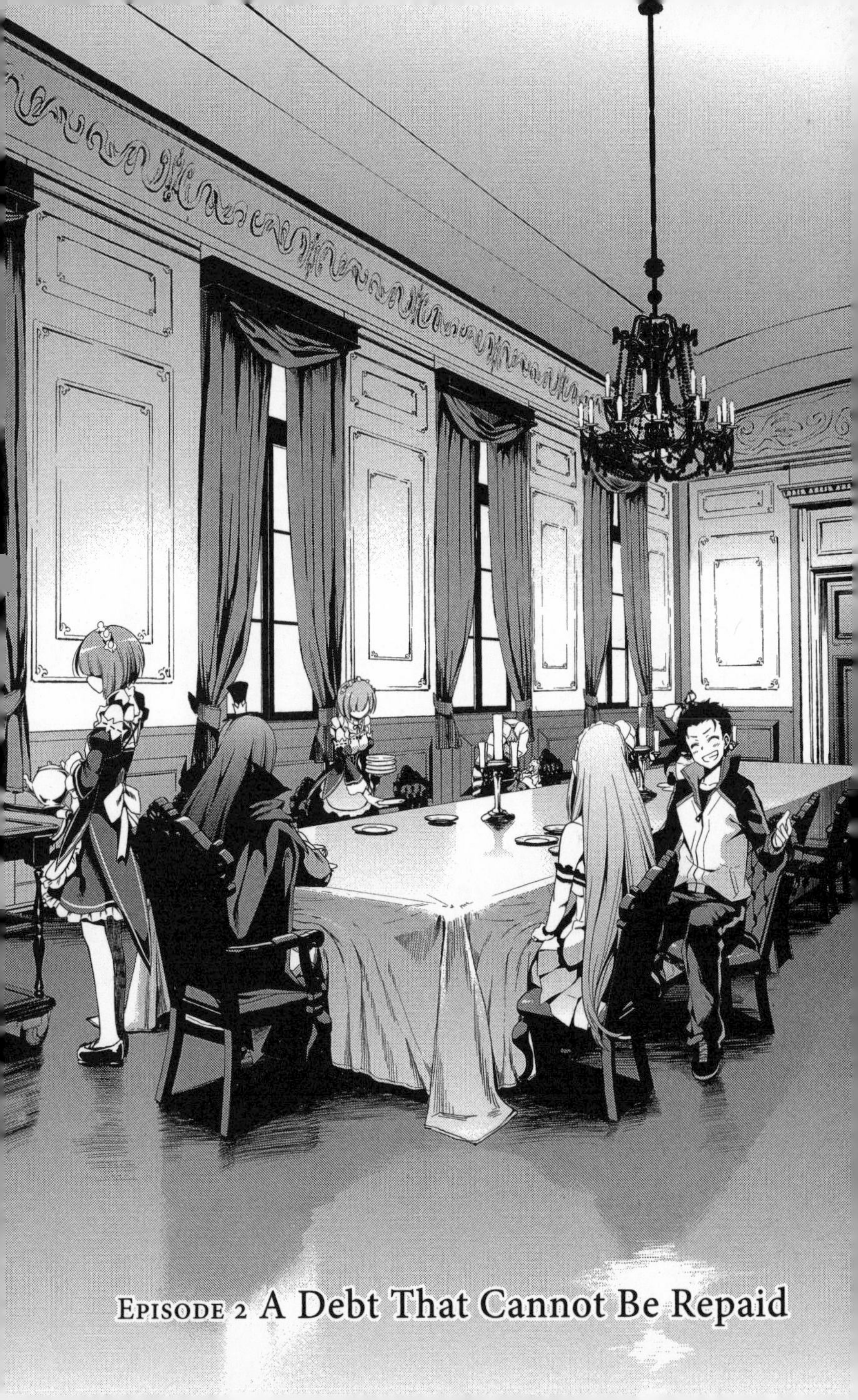

Episode 2 A Debt That Cannot Be Repaid

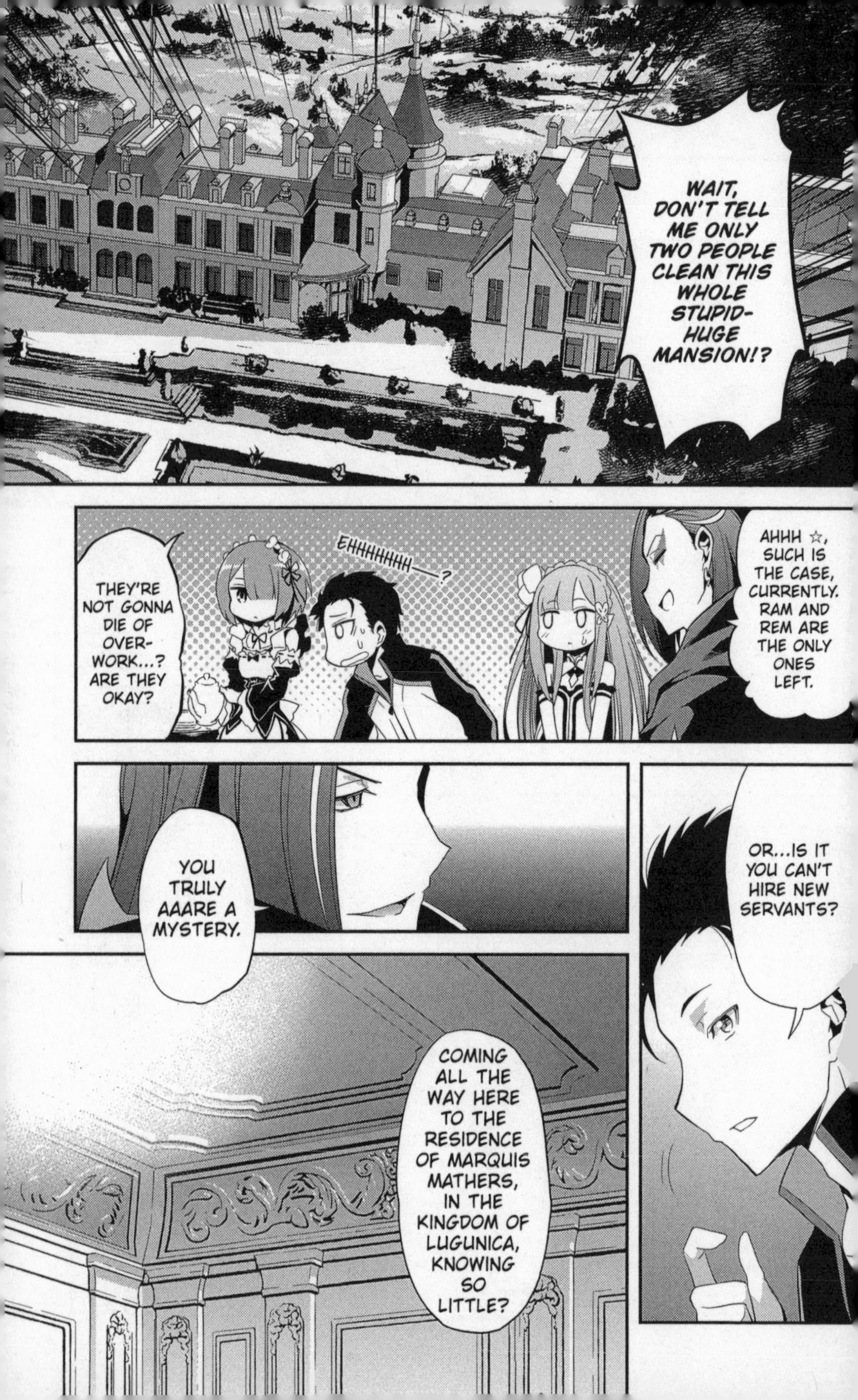
WAIT, DON'T TELL ME ONLY TWO PEOPLE CLEAN THIS WHOLE STUPID-HUGE MANSION!?
AHHH ☆, SUCH IS THE CASE, CURRENTLY. RAM AND REM ARE THE ONLY ONES LEFT.
EHHHHHHHH—?
THEY'RE NOT GONNA DIE OF OVER-WORK...? ARE THEY OKAY?
OR...IS IT YOU CAN'T HIRE NEW SERVANTS?
YOU TRULY AAARE A MYSTERY.
COMING ALL THE WAY HERE TO THE RESIDENCE OF MARQUIS MATHERS, IN THE KINGDOM OF LUGUNICA, KNOWING SO LITTLE?

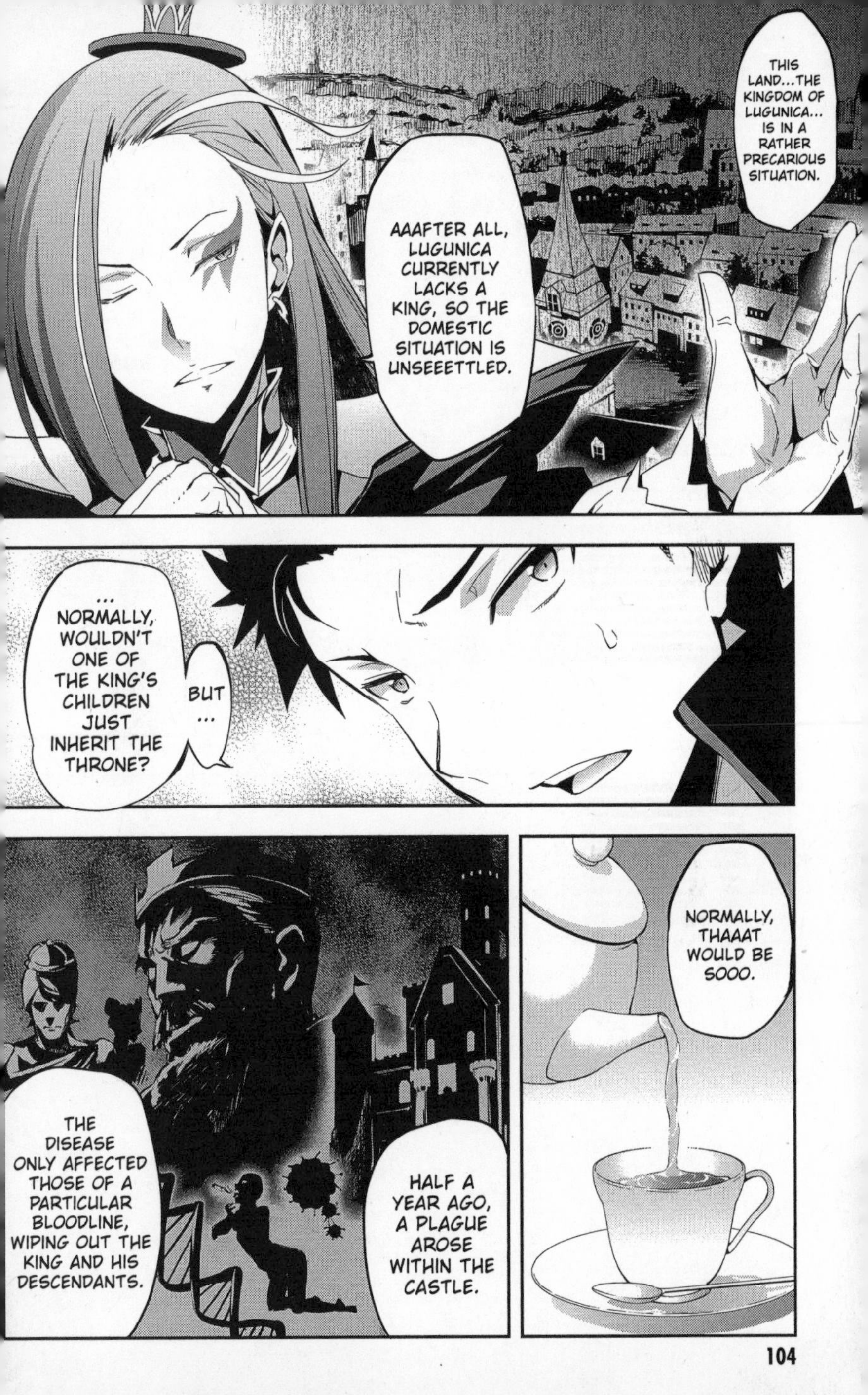
THIS LAND...THE KINGDOM OF LUGUNICA... IS IN A RATHER PRECARIOUS SITUATION.
AAAFTER ALL, LUGUNICA CURRENTLY LACKS A KING, SO THE DOMESTIC SITUATION IS UNSEEETTLED.
BUT ...
... NORMALLY, WOULDN'T ONE OF THE KING'S CHILDREN JUST INHERIT THE THRONE?
NORMALLY, THAAAT WOULD BE SOOO.
HALF A YEAR AGO, A PLAGUE AROSE WITHIN THE CASTLE.
THE DISEASE ONLY AFFECTED THOSE OF A PARTICULAR BLOODLINE, WIPING OUT THE KING AND HIS DESCENDANTS.

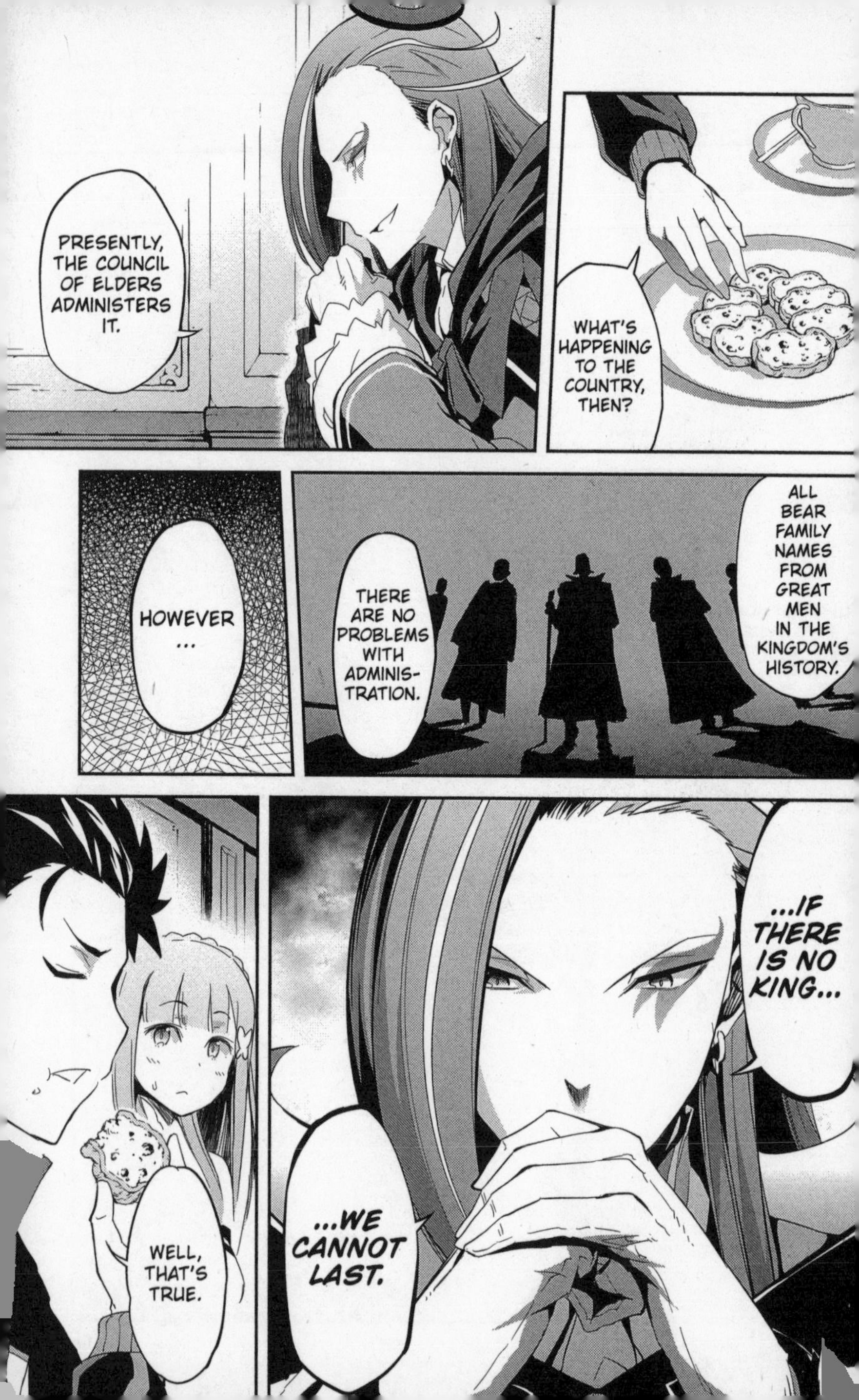
WHAT'S HAPPENING TO THE COUNTRY, THEN?
PRESENTLY, THE COUNCIL OF ELDERS ADMINISTERS IT.
ALL BEAR FAMILY NAMES FROM GREAT MEN IN THE KINGDOM'S HISTORY.
THERE ARE NO PROBLEMS WITH ADMINIS-TRATION.
HOWEVER ...
...IF THERE IS NO KING...
...WE CANNOT LAST.
WELL, THAT'S TRUE.

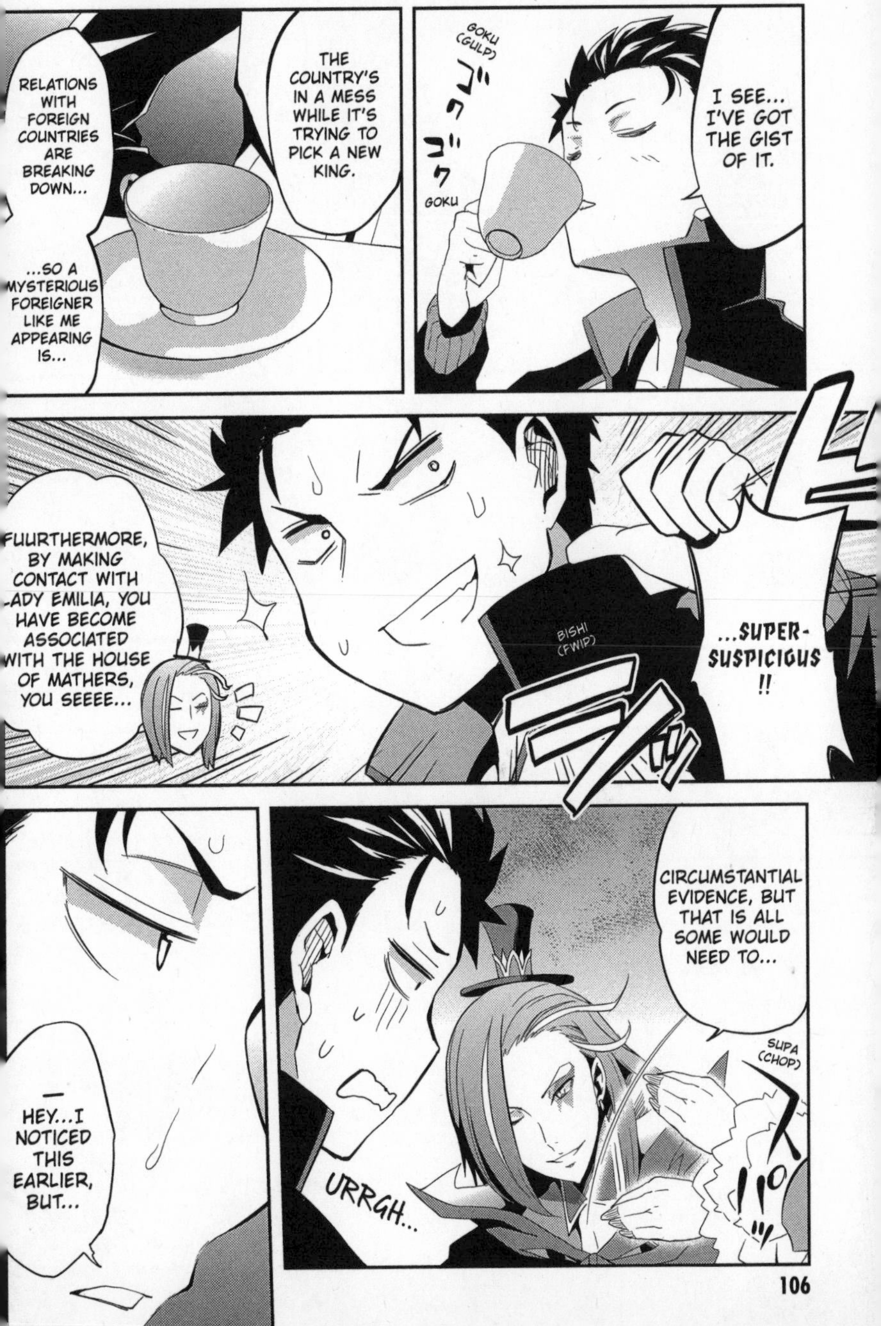
I SEE... I'VE GOT THE GIST OF IT.
GOKU (GULP)
GOKU
THE COUNTRY'S IN A MESS WHILE IT'S TRYING TO PICK A NEW KING.
RELATIONS WITH FOREIGN COUNTRIES ARE BREAKING DOWN...
...SO A MYSTERIOUS FOREIGNER LIKE ME APPEARING IS...
...SUPER-SUSPICIOUS !!
BISHI (FWIP)
FUURTHERMORE, BY MAKING CONTACT WITH LADY EMILIA, YOU HAVE BECOME ASSOCIATED WITH THE HOUSE OF MATHERS, YOU SEEEE...
CIRCUMSTANTIAL EVIDENCE, BUT THAT IS ALL SOME WOULD NEED TO...
SUPA (CHOP)
URRGH...
—HEY...I NOTICED THIS EARLIER, BUT...

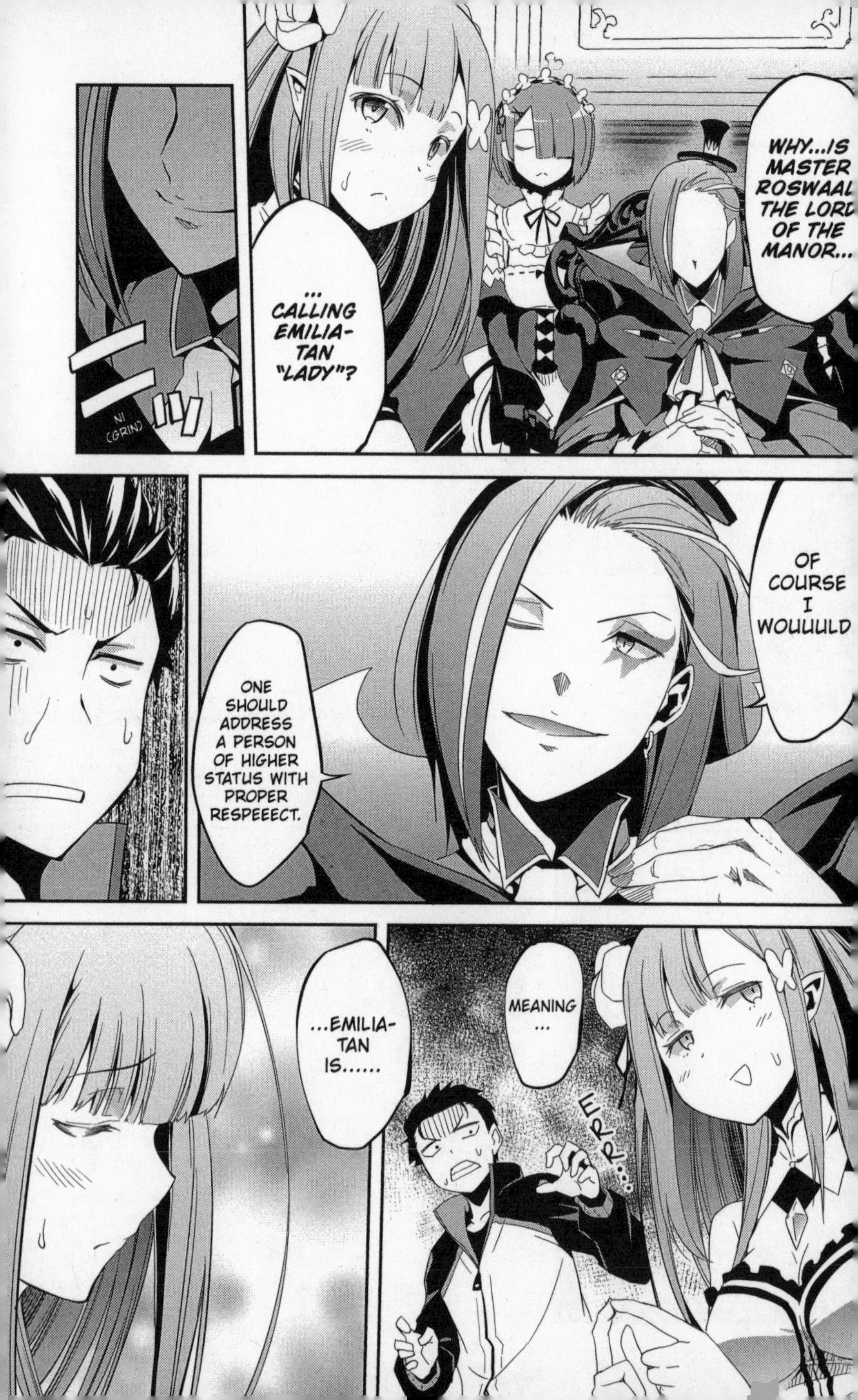
WHY...IS MASTER ROSWAAL THE LORD OF THE MANOR...
...CALLING EMILIA-TAN "LADY"?
NI (GRIND)
OF COURSE I WOUUULD
ONE SHOULD ADDRESS A PERSON OF HIGHER STATUS WITH PROPER RESPEEECT.
MEANING...
...EMILIA-TAN IS......
ERRR...

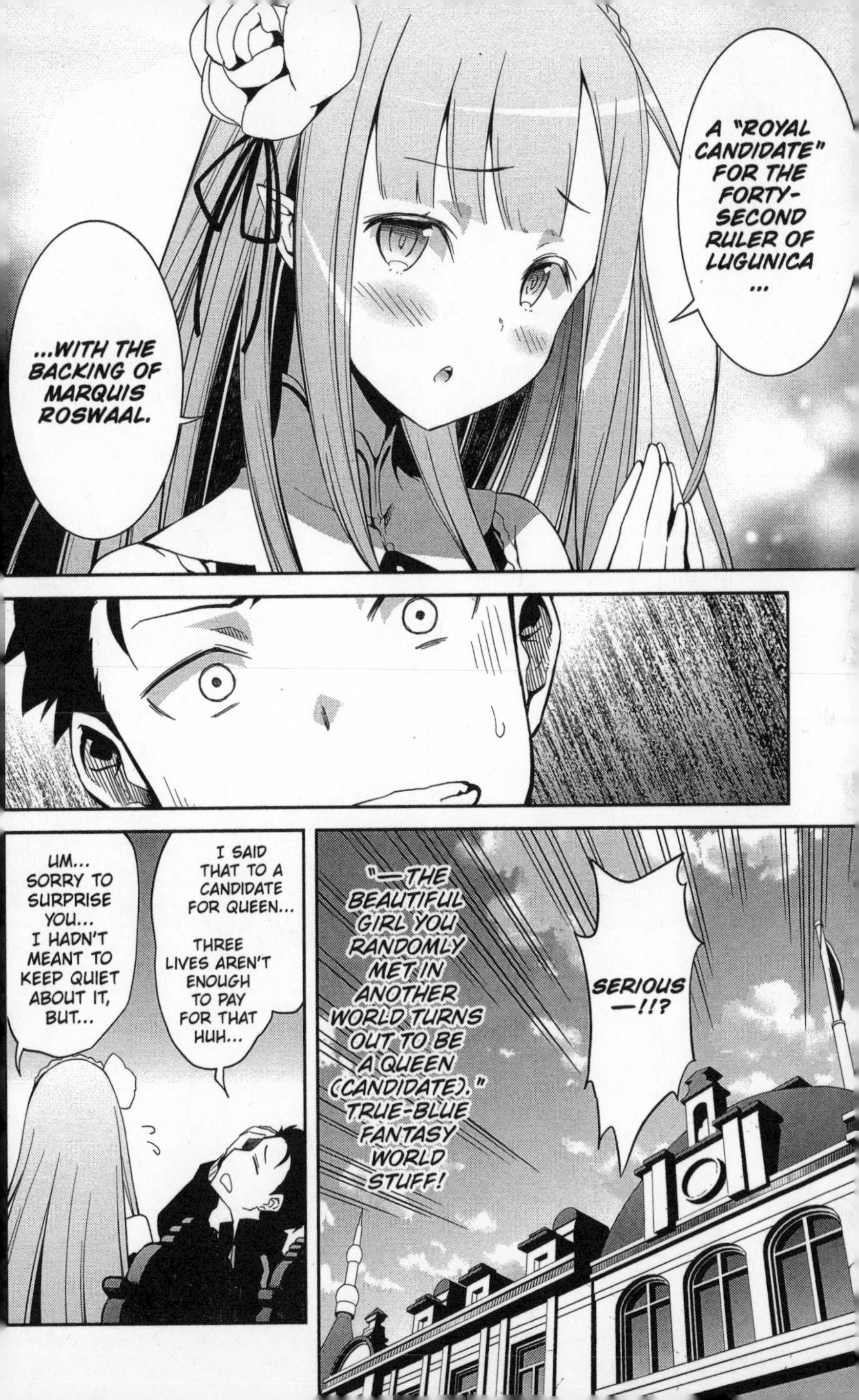
A "ROYAL CANDIDATE" FOR THE FORTY-SECOND RULER OF LUGUNICA ...
...WITH THE BACKING OF MARQUIS ROSWAAL.
SERIOUS—!!?
"—THE BEAUTIFUL GIRL YOU RANDOMLY MET IN ANOTHER WORLD TURNS OUT TO BE A QUEEN (CANDIDATE)." TRUE-BLUE FANTASY WORLD STUFF!
I SAID THAT TO A CANDIDATE FOR QUEEN...
THREE LIVES AREN'T ENOUGH TO PAY FOR THAT HUH...
UM... SORRY TO SURPRISE YOU... I HADN'T MEANT TO KEEP QUIET ABOUT IT, BUT...

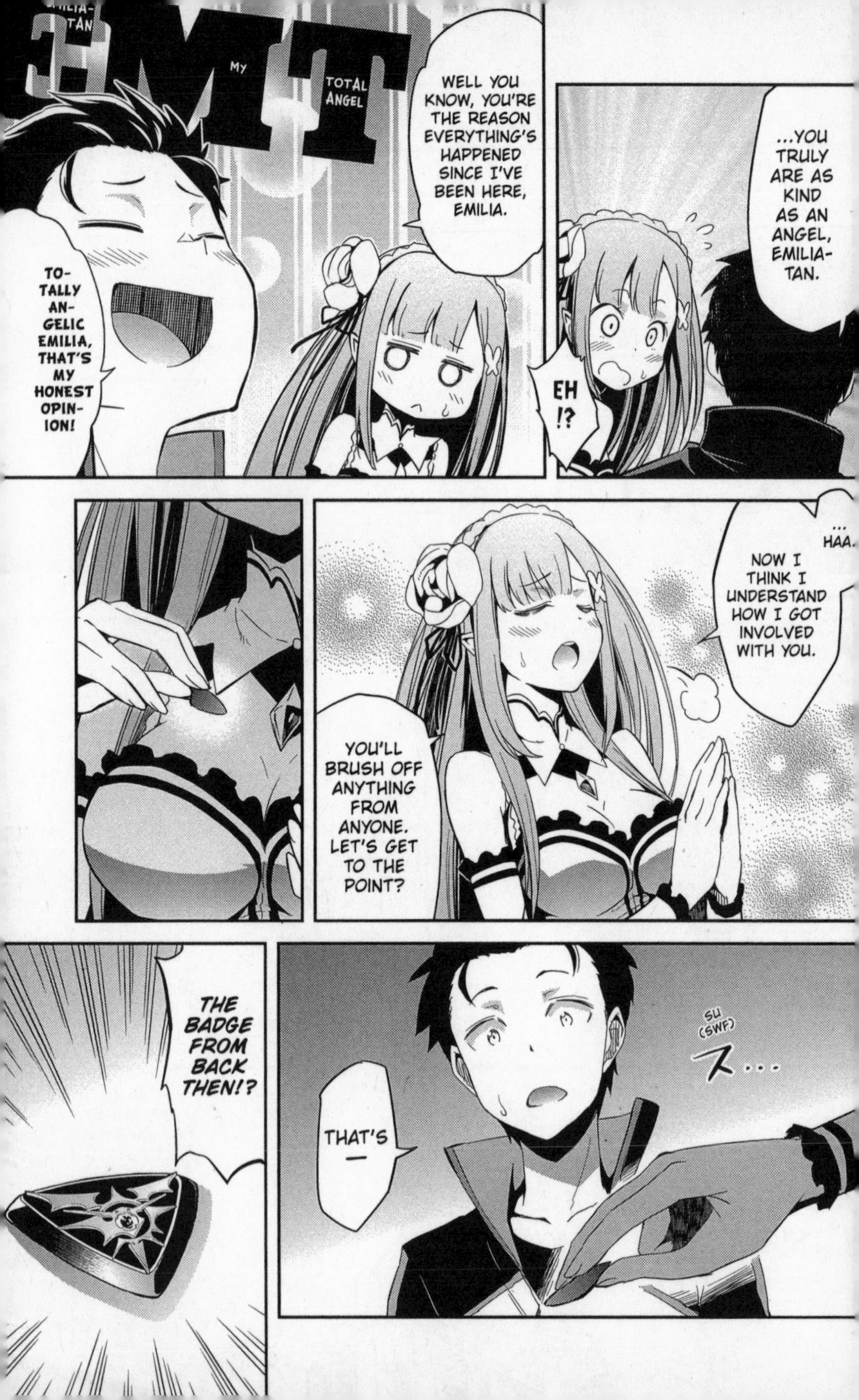

...YOU TRULY ARE AS KIND AS AN ANGEL, EMILIA-TAN.
EH!?
WELL YOU KNOW, YOU'RE THE REASON EVERYTHING'S HAPPENED SINCE I'VE BEEN HERE, EMILIA.
EMILIA-TAN
MY
TOTAL ANGEL
EMT
TO-TALLY AN-GELIC EMILIA, THAT'S MY HONEST OPIN-ION!
... HAA.
NOW I THINK I UNDERSTAND HOW I GOT INVOLVED WITH YOU.
YOU'LL BRUSH OFF ANYTHING FROM ANYONE. LET'S GET TO THE POINT?
SU (SWF)
ス...
THAT'S—
THE BADGE FROM BACK THEN!?

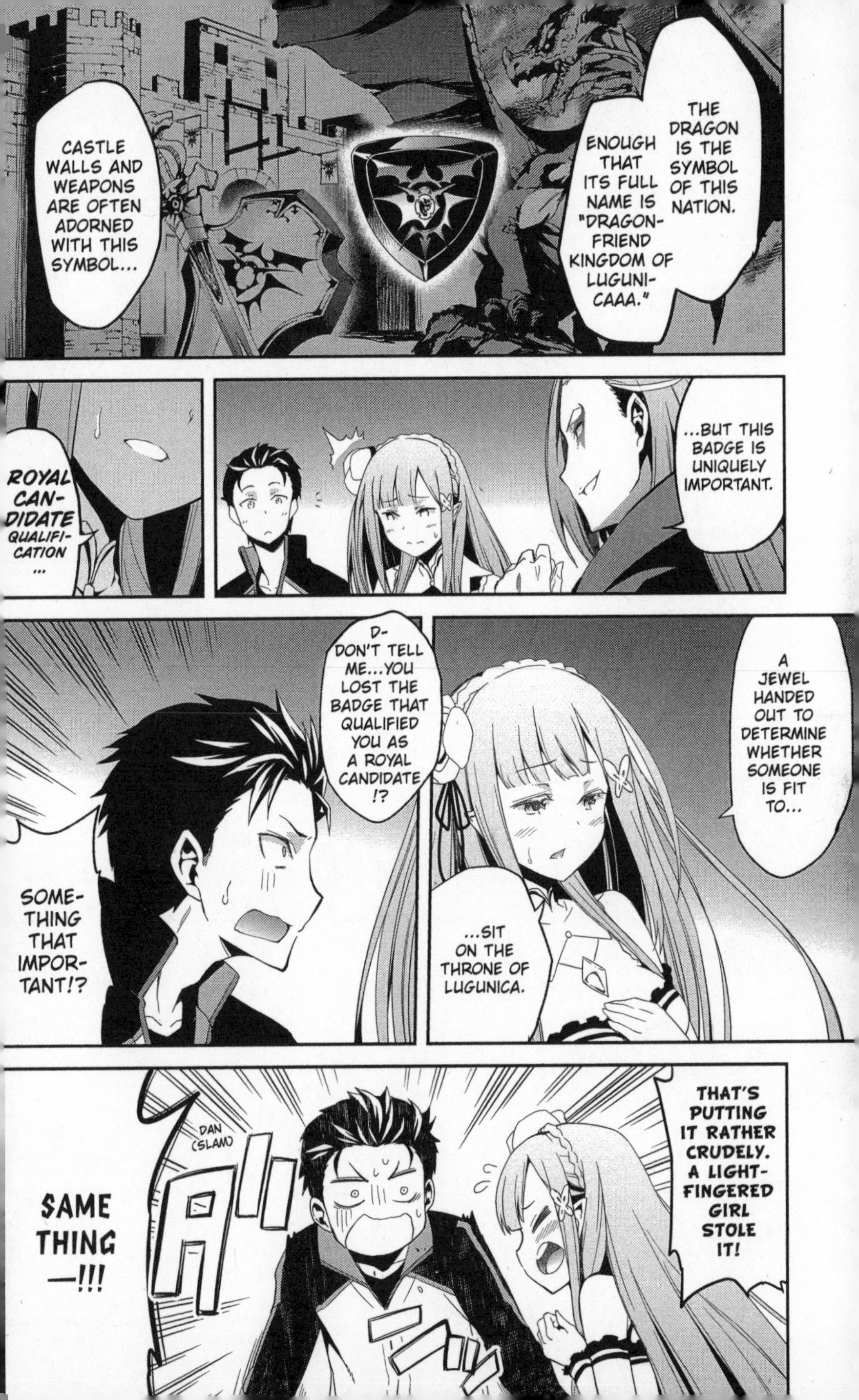
THE DRAGON IS THE SYMBOL OF THIS NATION.
ENOUGH THAT ITS FULL NAME IS "DRAGON-FRIEND KINGDOM OF LUGUNICAAA."
CASTLE WALLS AND WEAPONS ARE OFTEN ADORNED WITH THIS SYMBOL...
...BUT THIS BADGE IS UNIQUELY IMPORTANT.
ROYAL CANDIDATE QUALIFICATION...
A JEWEL HANDED OUT TO DETERMINE WHETHER SOMEONE IS FIT TO...
...SIT ON THE THRONE OF LUGUNICA.
D-DON'T TELL ME...YOU LOST THE BADGE THAT QUALIFIED YOU AS A ROYAL CANDIDATE!?
SOMETHING THAT IMPORTANT!?
THAT'S PUTTING IT RATHER CRUDELY. A LIGHT-FINGERED GIRL STOLE IT!
DAN (SLAM)
SAME THING—!!!

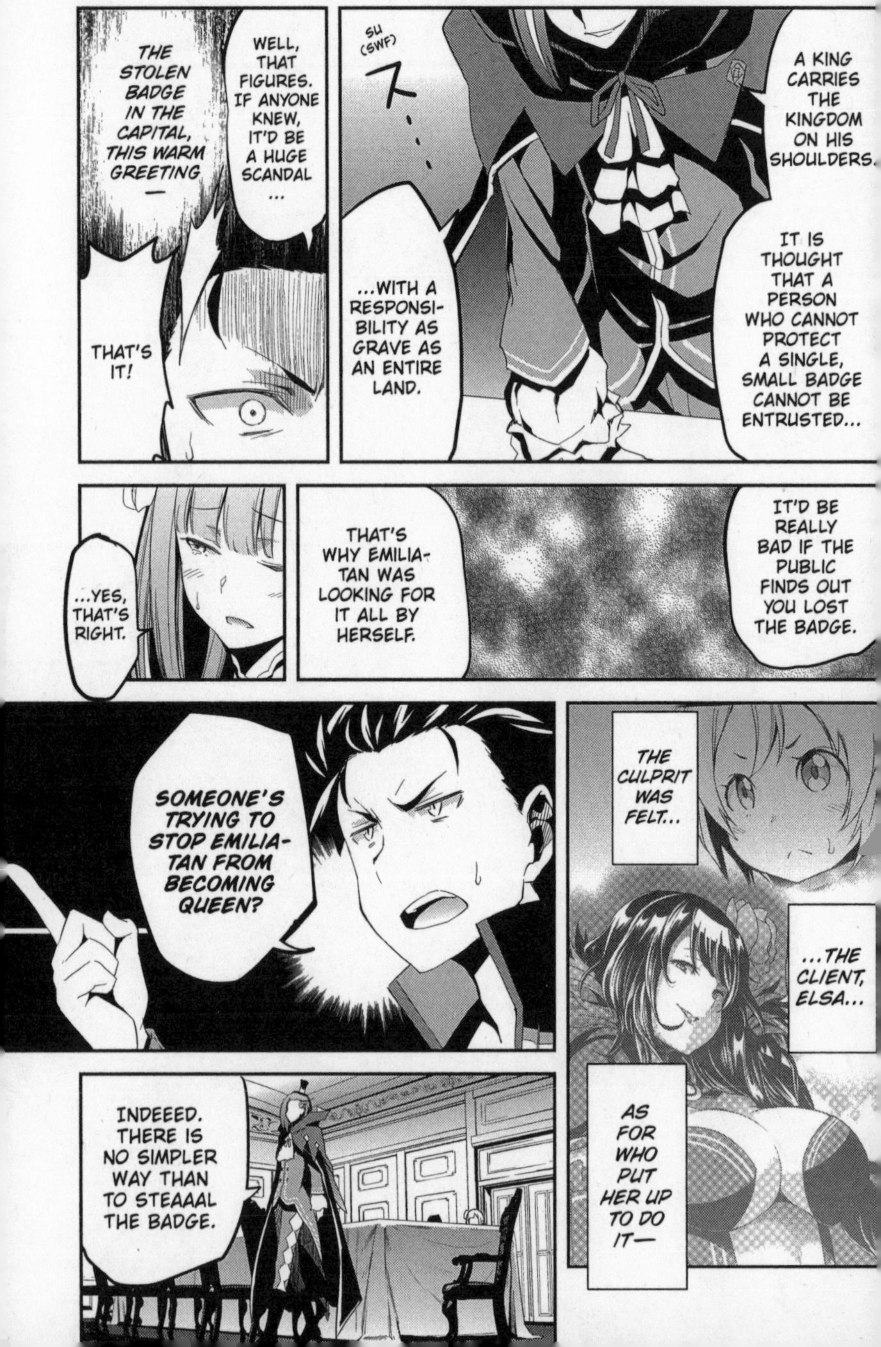
SU (SWF)
A KING CARRIES THE KINGDOM ON HIS SHOULDERS.
...WITH A RESPONSIBILITY AS GRAVE AS AN ENTIRE LAND.
IT IS THOUGHT THAT A PERSON WHO CANNOT PROTECT A SINGLE, SMALL BADGE CANNOT BE ENTRUSTED...
WELL, THAT FIGURES. IF ANYONE KNEW, IT'D BE A HUGE SCANDAL...
THE STOLEN BADGE IN THE CAPITAL, THIS WARM GREETING—
THAT'S IT!
IT'D BE REALLY BAD IF THE PUBLIC FINDS OUT YOU LOST THE BADGE.
THAT'S WHY EMILIA-TAN WAS LOOKING FOR IT ALL BY HERSELF.
...YES, THAT'S RIGHT.
THE CULPRIT WAS FELT...
...THE CLIENT, ELSA...
AS FOR WHO PUT HER UP TO DO IT—
SOMEONE'S TRYING TO STOP EMILIA-TAN FROM BECOMING QUEEN?
INDEEED. THERE IS NO SIMPLER WAY THAN TO STEAAAL THE BADGE.

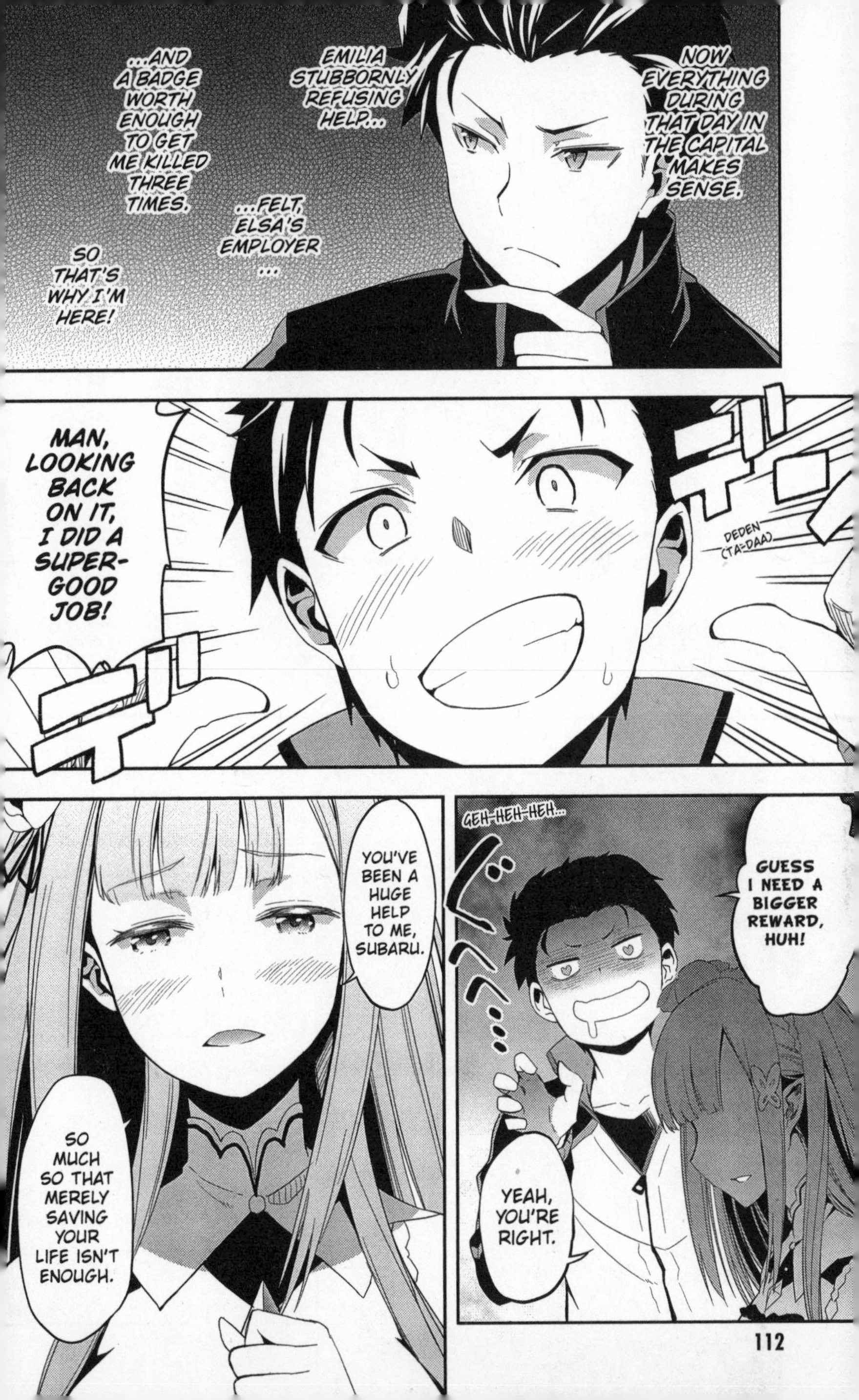
NOW EVERYTHING DURING THAT DAY IN THE CAPITAL MAKES SENSE.
EMILIA STUBBORNLY REFUSING HELP...
...FELT, ELSA'S EMPLOYER...
...AND A BADGE WORTH ENOUGH TO GET ME KILLED THREE TIMES.
SO THAT'S WHY I'M HERE!
DEDEN (TA-DAA)
MAN, LOOKING BACK ON IT, I DID A SUPER-GOOD JOB!
GUESS I NEED A BIGGER REWARD, HUH!
GEH-HEH-HEH...
YEAH, YOU'RE RIGHT.
YOU'VE BEEN A HUGE HELP TO ME, SUBARU.
SO MUCH SO THAT MERELY SAVING YOUR LIFE ISN'T ENOUGH.

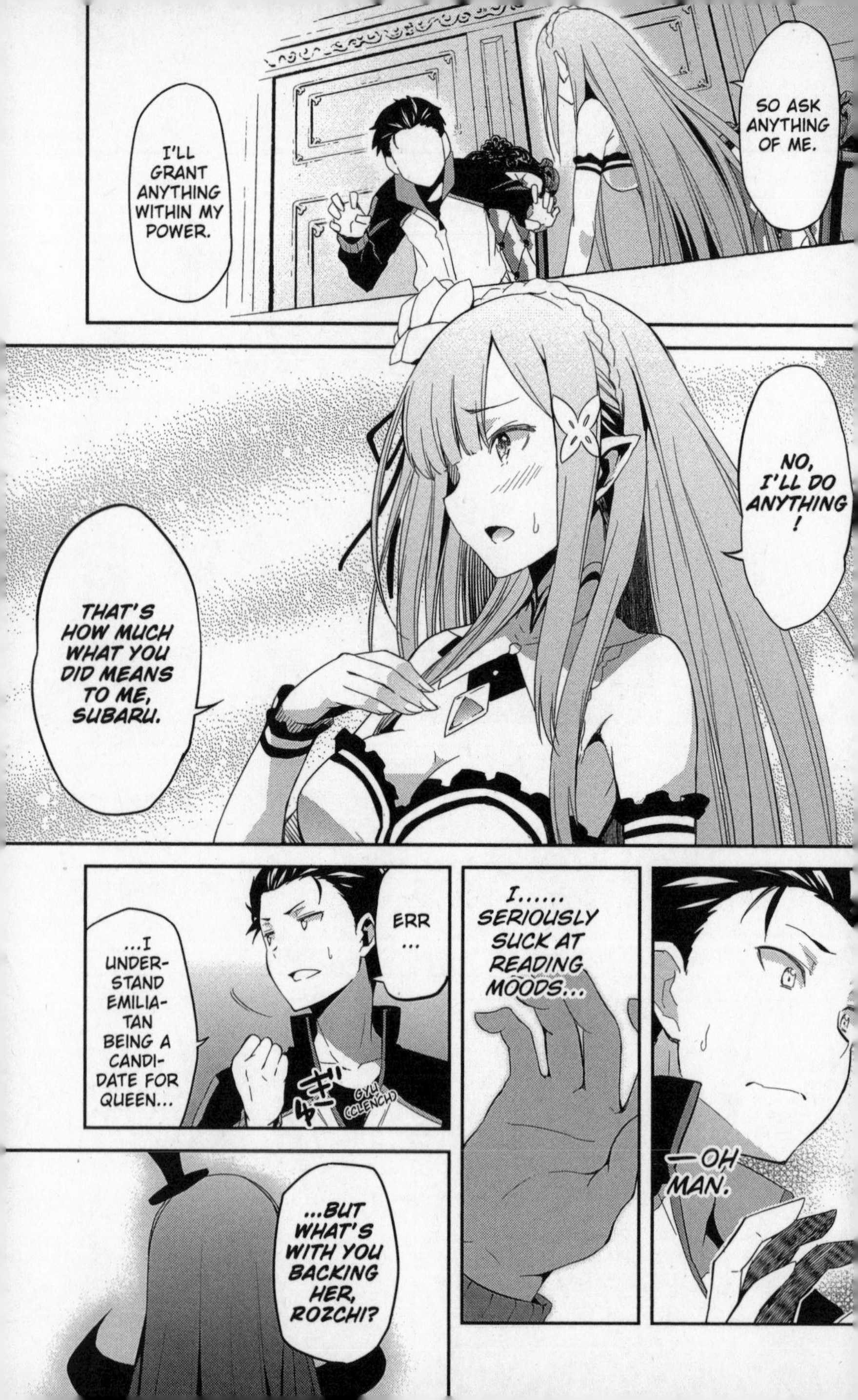
SO ASK ANYTHING OF ME.
I'LL GRANT ANYTHING WITHIN MY POWER.
NO, I'LL DO ANYTHING!
THAT'S HOW MUCH WHAT YOU DID MEANS TO ME, SUBARU.
—OH MAN.
I...... SERIOUSLY SUCK AT READING MOODS...
ERR...
...I UNDERSTAND EMILIA-TAN BEING A CANDIDATE FOR QUEEN...
GYU (CLENCH)
...BUT WHAT'S WITH YOU BACKING HER, ROZCHI?

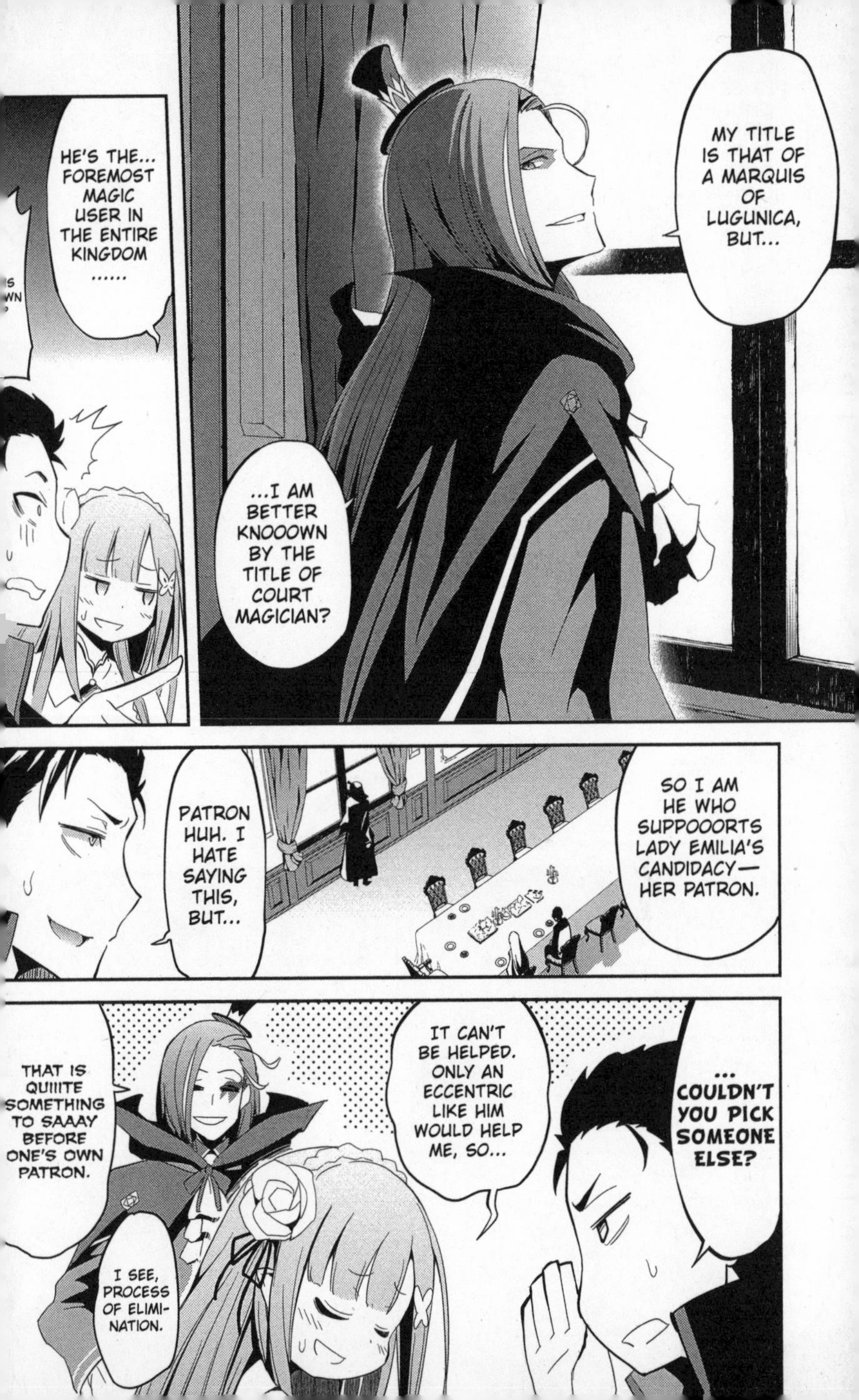
MY TITLE IS THAT OF A MARQUIS OF LUGUNICA, BUT...
...I AM BETTER KNOOOWN BY THE TITLE OF COURT MAGICIAN?
HE'S THE... FOREMOST MAGIC USER IN THE ENTIRE KINGDOM ......
SO I AM HE WHO SUPPOOORTS LADY EMILIA'S CANDIDACY— HER PATRON.
PATRON HUH. I HATE SAYING THIS, BUT...
...COULDN'T YOU PICK SOMEONE ELSE?
IT CAN'T BE HELPED. ONLY AN ECCENTRIC LIKE HIM WOULD HELP ME, SO...
THAT IS QUIIITE SOMETHING TO SAAAY BEFORE ONE'S OWN PATRON.
I SEE, PROCESS OF ELIMINATION.

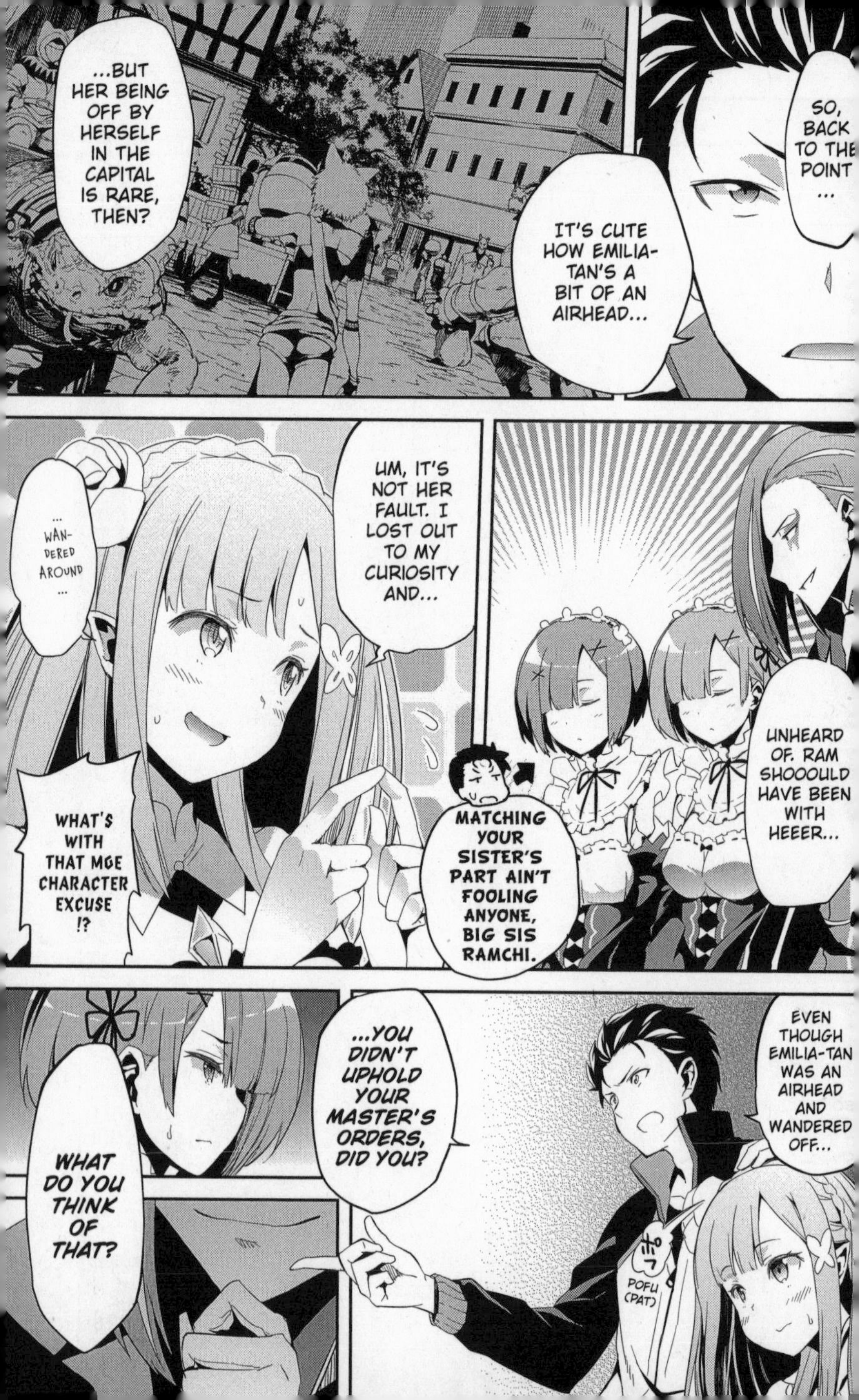
SO, BACK TO THE POINT...
IT'S CUTE HOW EMILIA-TAN'S A BIT OF AN AIRHEAD...
...BUT HER BEING OFF BY HERSELF IN THE CAPITAL IS RARE, THEN?
UNHEARD OF. RAM SHOOOULD HAVE BEEN WITH HEEER...
MATCHING YOUR SISTER'S PART AIN'T FOOLING ANYONE, BIG SIS RAMCHI.
UM, IT'S NOT HER FAULT. I LOST OUT TO MY CURIOSITY AND...
...WAN-DERED AROUND...
WHAT'S WITH THAT MOE CHARACTER EXCUSE!?
EVEN THOUGH EMILIA-TAN WAS AN AIRHEAD AND WANDERED OFF...
ポフ
POFU (PAT)
...YOU DIDN'T UPHOLD YOUR MASTER'S ORDERS, DID YOU?
WHAT DO YOU THINK OF THAT?

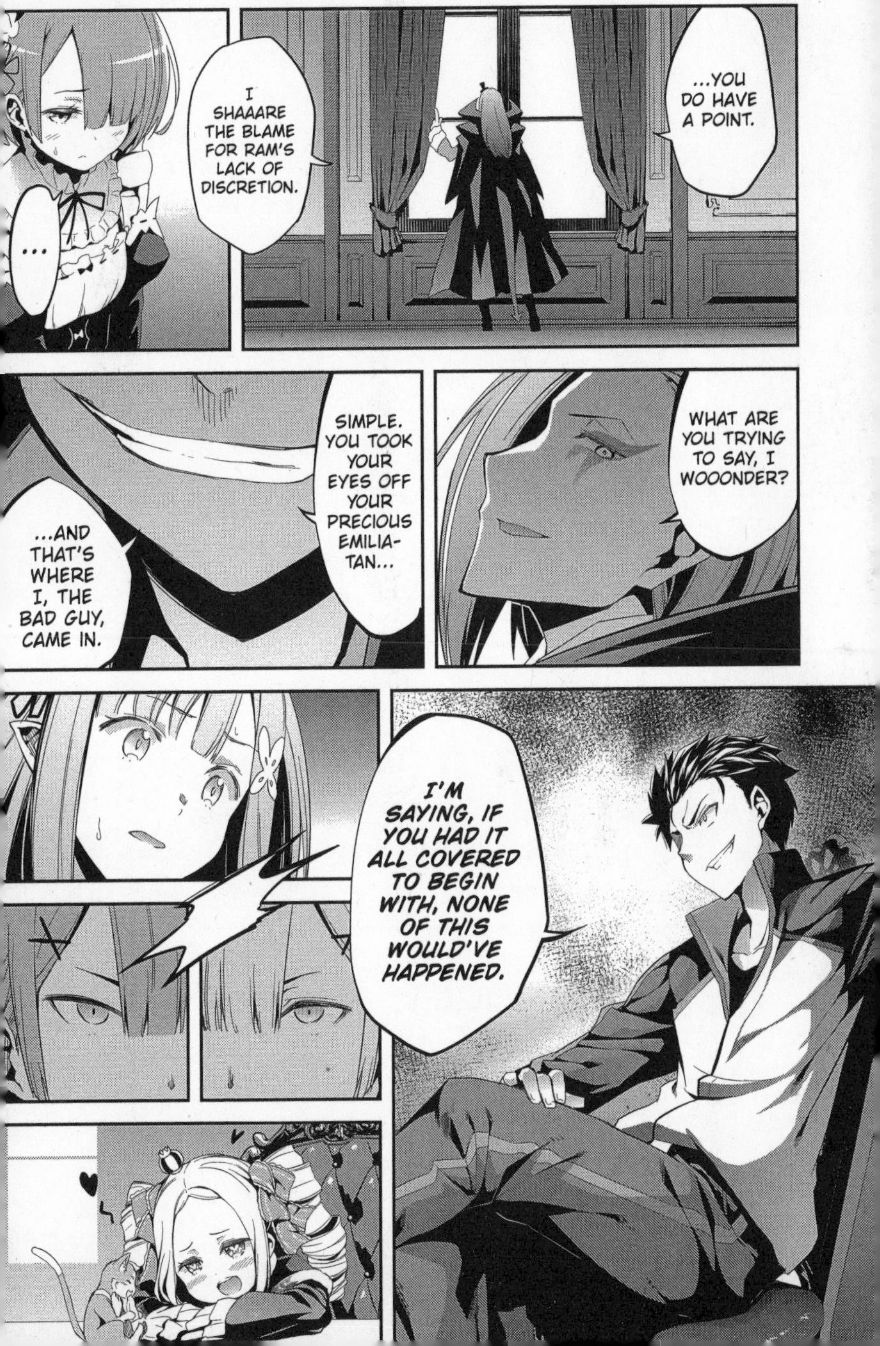
...YOU DO HAVE A POINT.
I SHAAARE THE BLAME FOR RAM'S LACK OF DISCRETION.
...
WHAT ARE YOU TRYING TO SAY, I WOOONDER?
SIMPLE. YOU TOOK YOUR EYES OFF YOUR PRECIOUS EMILIA-TAN...
...AND THAT'S WHERE I, THE BAD GUY, CAME IN.
I'M SAYING, IF YOU HAD IT ALL COVERED TO BEGIN WITH, NONE OF THIS WOULD'VE HAPPENED.

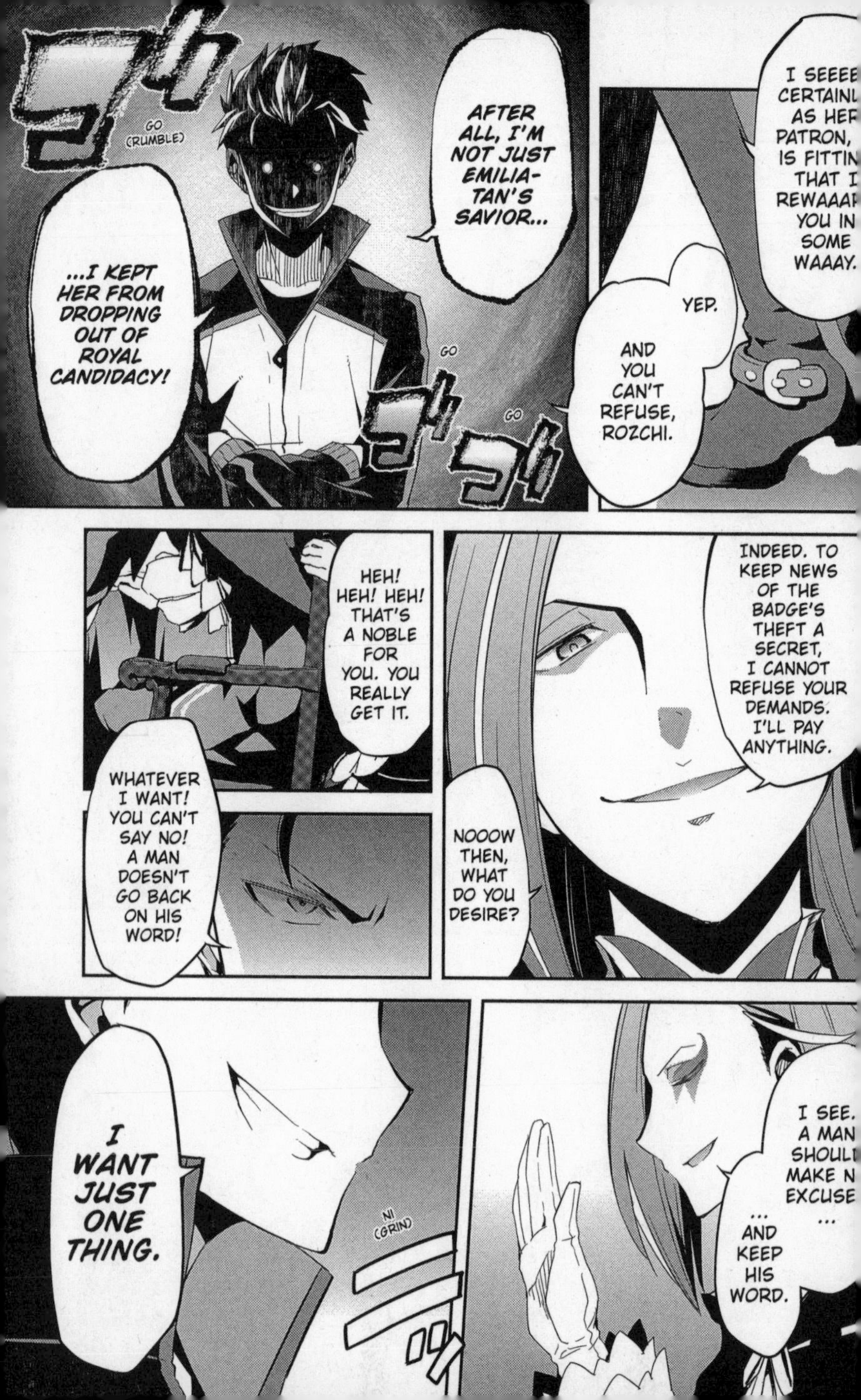
I SEEEE CERTAINL AS HER PATRON, IS FITTIN THAT I REWAAAR YOU IN SOME WAAAY.
YEP.
AND YOU CAN'T REFUSE, ROZCHI.
AFTER ALL, I'M NOT JUST EMILIA-TAN'S SAVIOR...
GO (RUMBLE)
...I KEPT HER FROM DROPPING OUT OF ROYAL CANDIDACY!
GO
GO
INDEED. TO KEEP NEWS OF THE BADGE'S THEFT A SECRET, I CANNOT REFUSE YOUR DEMANDS. I'LL PAY ANYTHING.
NOOOW THEN, WHAT DO YOU DESIRE?
HEH! HEH! HEH! THAT'S A NOBLE FOR YOU. YOU REALLY GET IT.
WHATEVER I WANT! YOU CAN'T SAY NO! A MAN DOESN'T GO BACK ON HIS WORD!
I SEE. A MAN SHOUL MAKE N EXCUSE ...
... AND KEEP HIS WORD.
NI (GRIN)
I WANT JUST ONE THING.

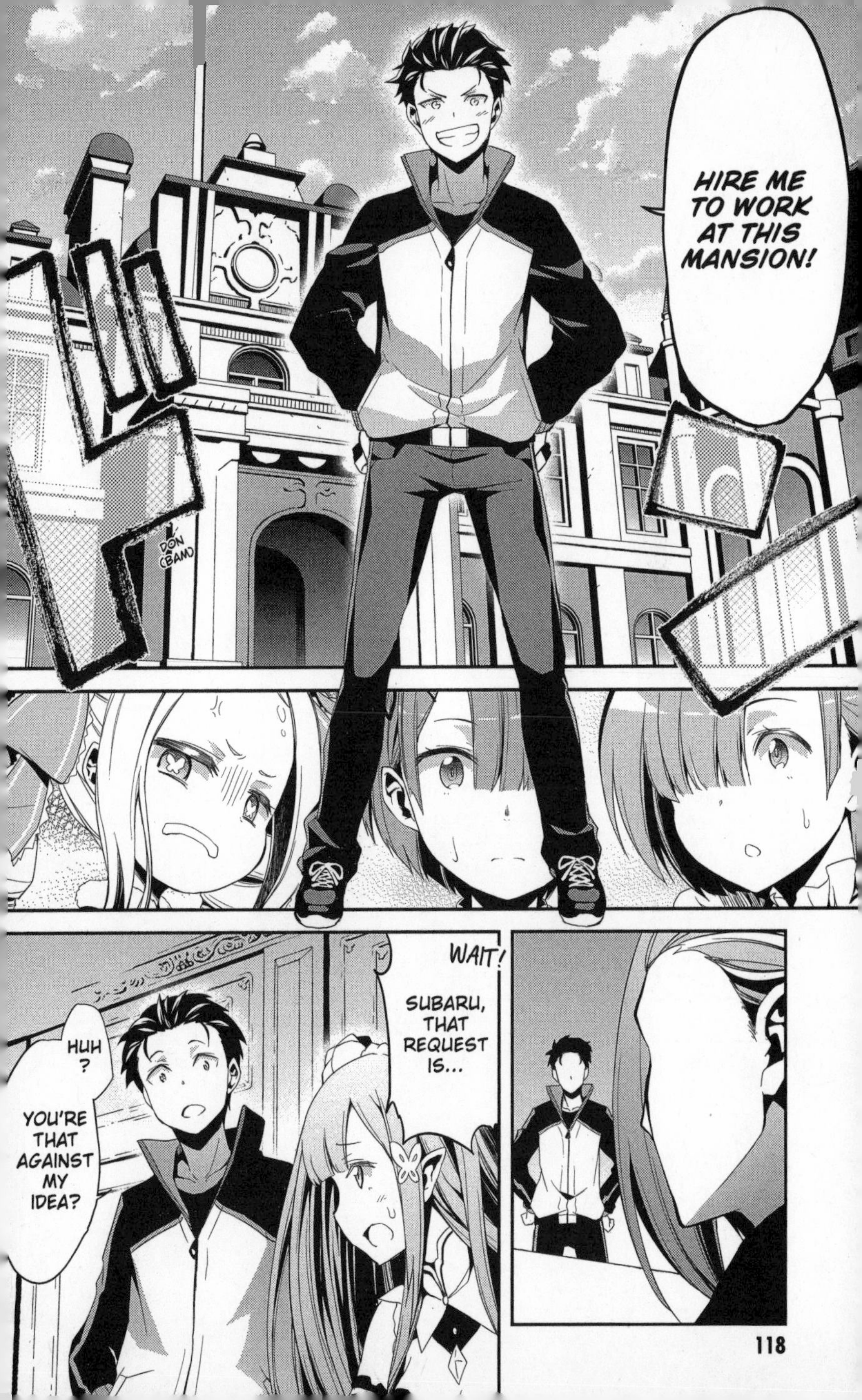
HIRE ME TO WORK AT THIS MANSION!
DON (BAM)
WAIT!
SUBARU, THAT REQUEST IS...
HUH?
YOU'RE THAT AGAINST MY IDEA?

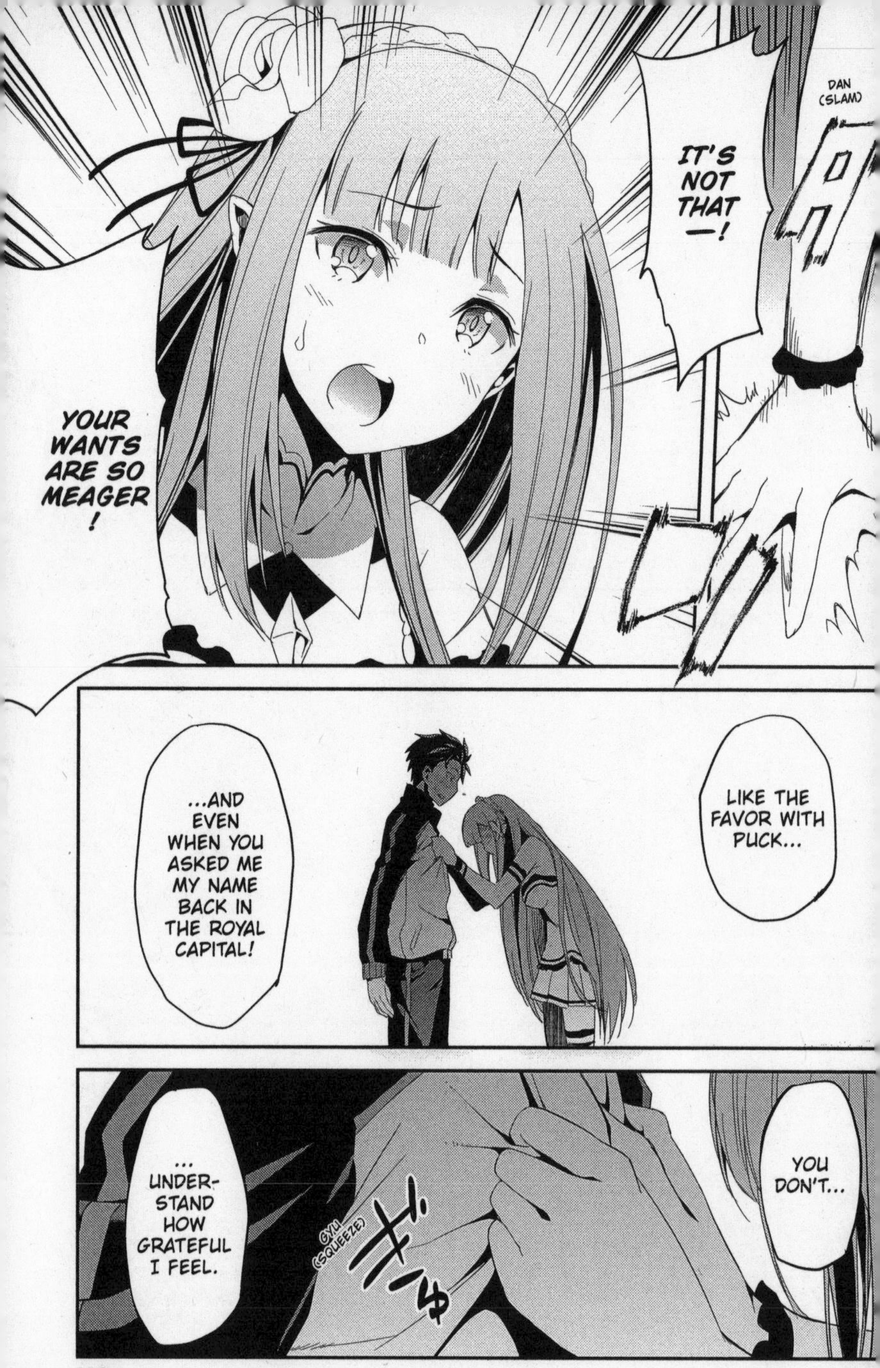
DAN (SLAM)
IT'S NOT THAT—!
YOUR WANTS ARE SO MEAGER!
LIKE THE FAVOR WITH PUCK...
...AND EVEN WHEN YOU ASKED ME MY NAME BACK IN THE ROYAL CAPITAL!
YOU DON'T...
GYU (SQUEEZE)
...UNDERSTAND HOW GRATEFUL I FEEL.

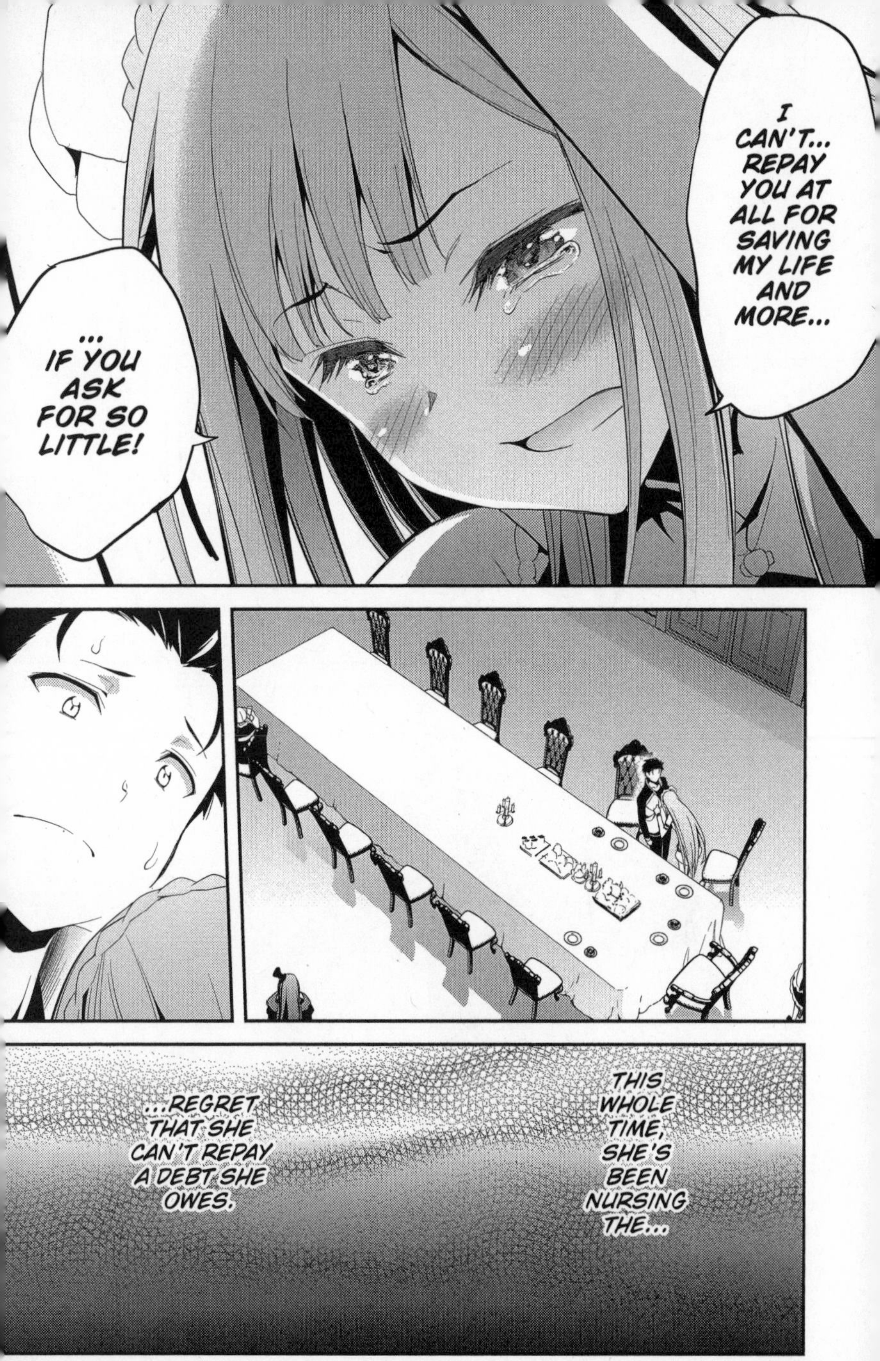
I CAN'T... REPAY YOU AT ALL FOR SAVING MY LIFE AND MORE...
... IF YOU ASK FOR SO LITTLE!
THIS WHOLE TIME, SHE'S BEEN NURSING THE...
...REGRET THAT SHE CAN'T REPAY A DEBT SHE OWES.

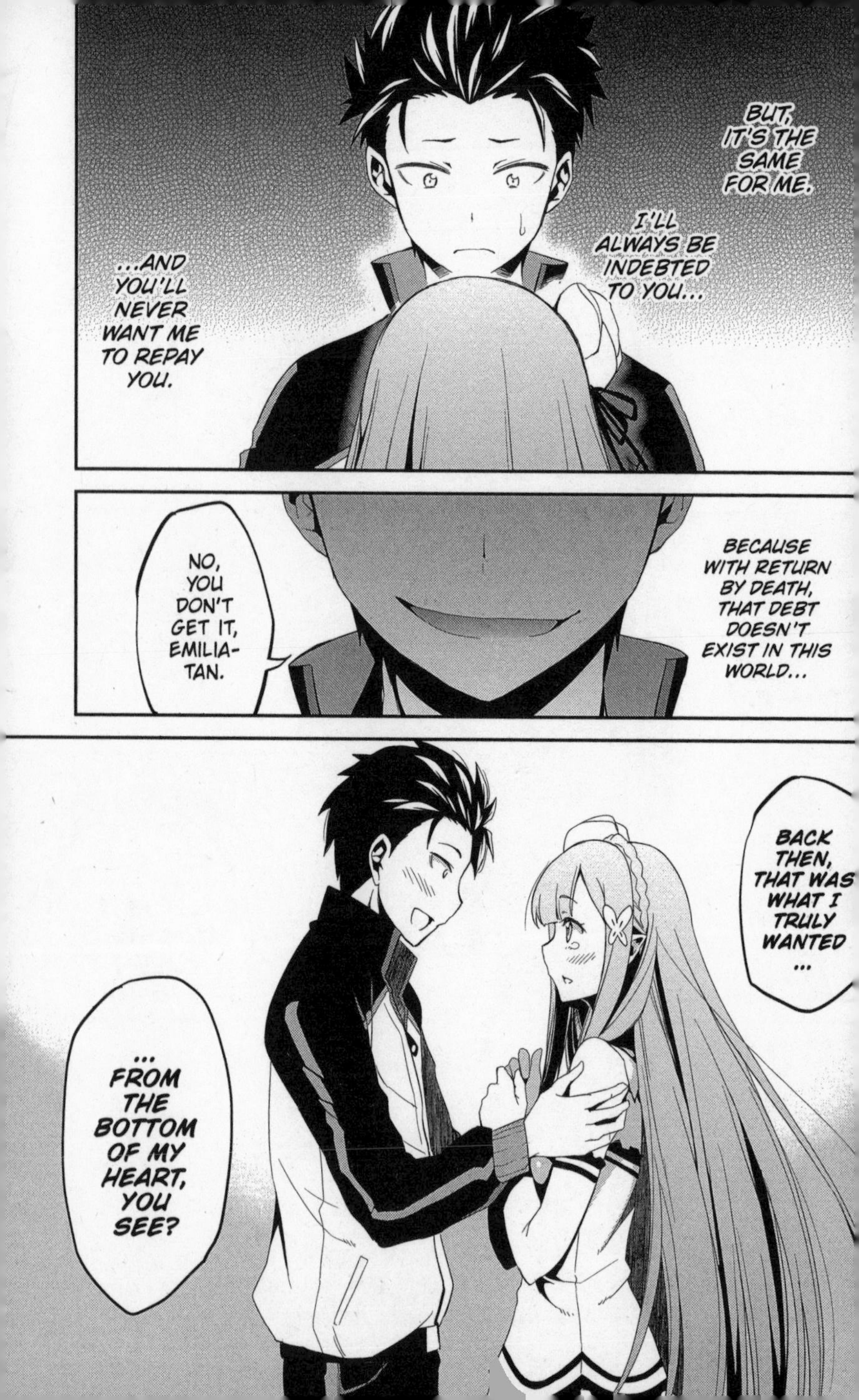
BUT, IT'S THE SAME FOR ME.
I'LL ALWAYS BE INDEBTED TO YOU...
...AND YOU'LL NEVER WANT ME TO REPAY YOU.
BECAUSE WITH RETURN BY DEATH, THAT DEBT DOESN'T EXIST IN THIS WORLD...
NO, YOU DON'T GET IT, EMILIA-TAN.
BACK THEN, THAT WAS WHAT I TRULY WANTED...
...FROM THE BOTTOM OF MY HEART, YOU SEE?

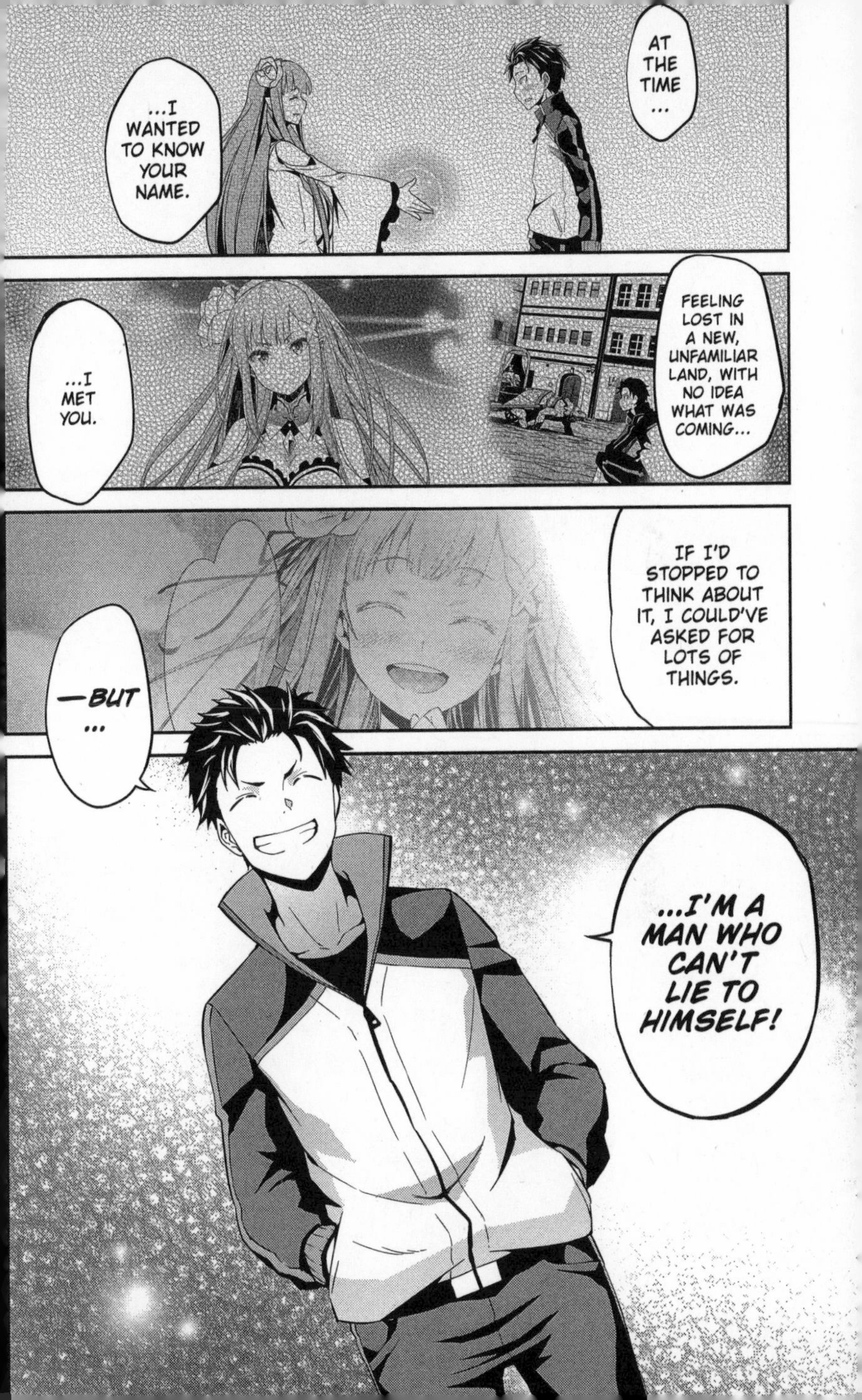
AT THE TIME...
...I WANTED TO KNOW YOUR NAME.
FEELING LOST IN A NEW, UNFAMILIAR LAND, WITH NO IDEA WHAT WAS COMING...
...I MET YOU.
IF I'D STOPPED TO THINK ABOUT IT, I COULD'VE ASKED FOR LOTS OF THINGS.
—BUT...
...I'M A MAN WHO CAN'T LIE TO HIMSELF!

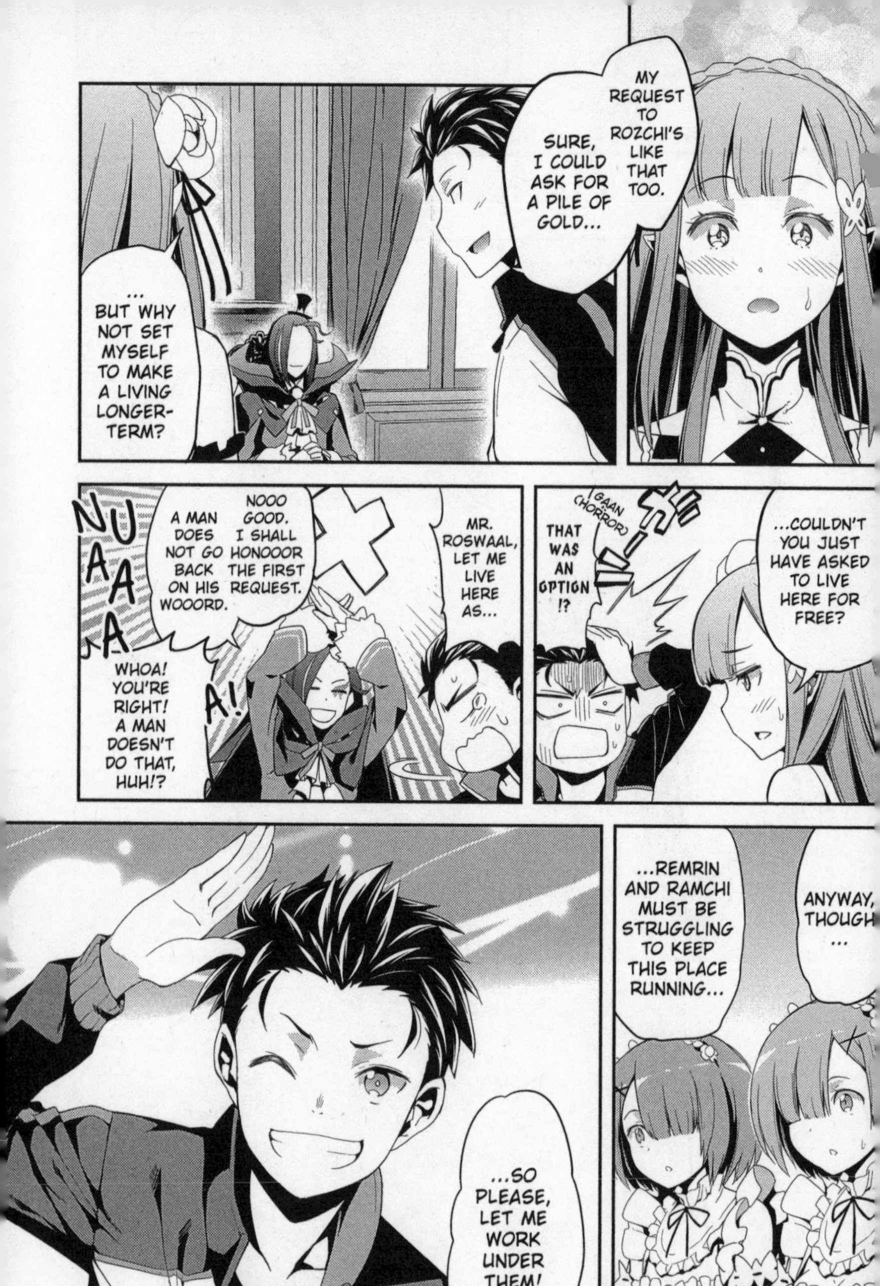
MY REQUEST TO ROZCHI'S LIKE THAT TOO.
SURE, I COULD ASK FOR A PILE OF GOLD...
...BUT WHY NOT SET MYSELF TO MAKE A LIVING LONGER-TERM?
...COULDN'T YOU JUST HAVE ASKED TO LIVE HERE FOR FREE?
GAAN (HORROR)
THAT WAS AN OPTION!?
MR. ROSWAAL, LET ME LIVE HERE AS...
NOOO GOOD. I SHALL HONOOOR THE FIRST REQUEST.
A MAN DOES NOT GO BACK ON HIS WOOORD.
NUAAAA!
WHOA! YOU'RE RIGHT! A MAN DOESN'T DO THAT, HUH!?
ANYWAY, THOUGH...
...REMRIN AND RAMCHI MUST BE STRUGGLING TO KEEP THIS PLACE RUNNING...
...SO PLEASE, LET ME WORK UNDER THEM!

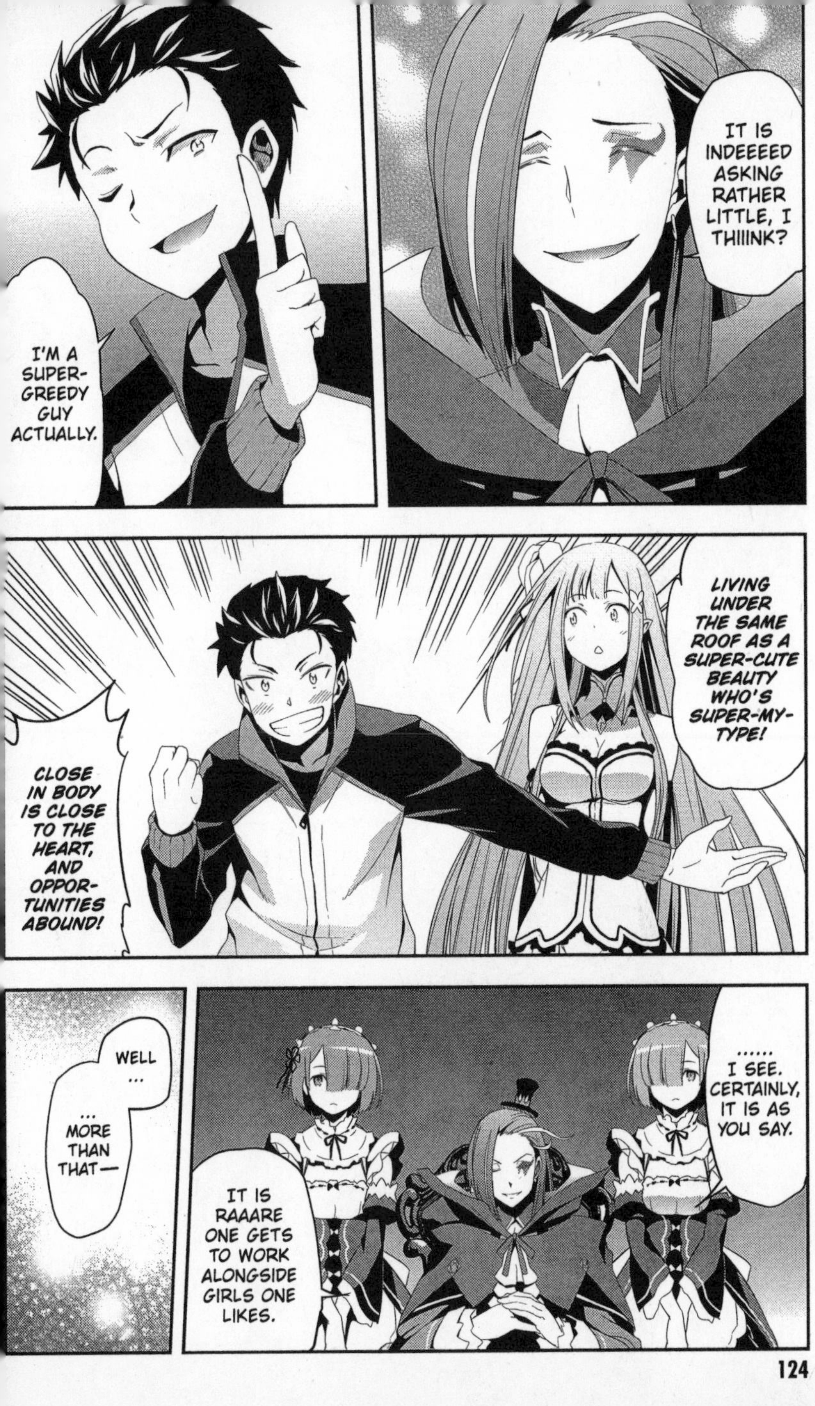
IT IS INDEEEED ASKING RATHER LITTLE, I THIIINK?
I'M A SUPER-GREEDY GUY ACTUALLY.
LIVING UNDER THE SAME ROOF AS A SUPER-CUTE BEAUTY WHO'S SUPER-MY-TYPE!
CLOSE IN BODY IS CLOSE TO THE HEART, AND OPPORTUNITIES ABOUND!
...... I SEE. CERTAINLY, IT IS AS YOU SAY.
IT IS RAAARE ONE GETS TO WORK ALONGSIDE GIRLS ONE LIKES.
WELL ... ... MORE THAN THAT—

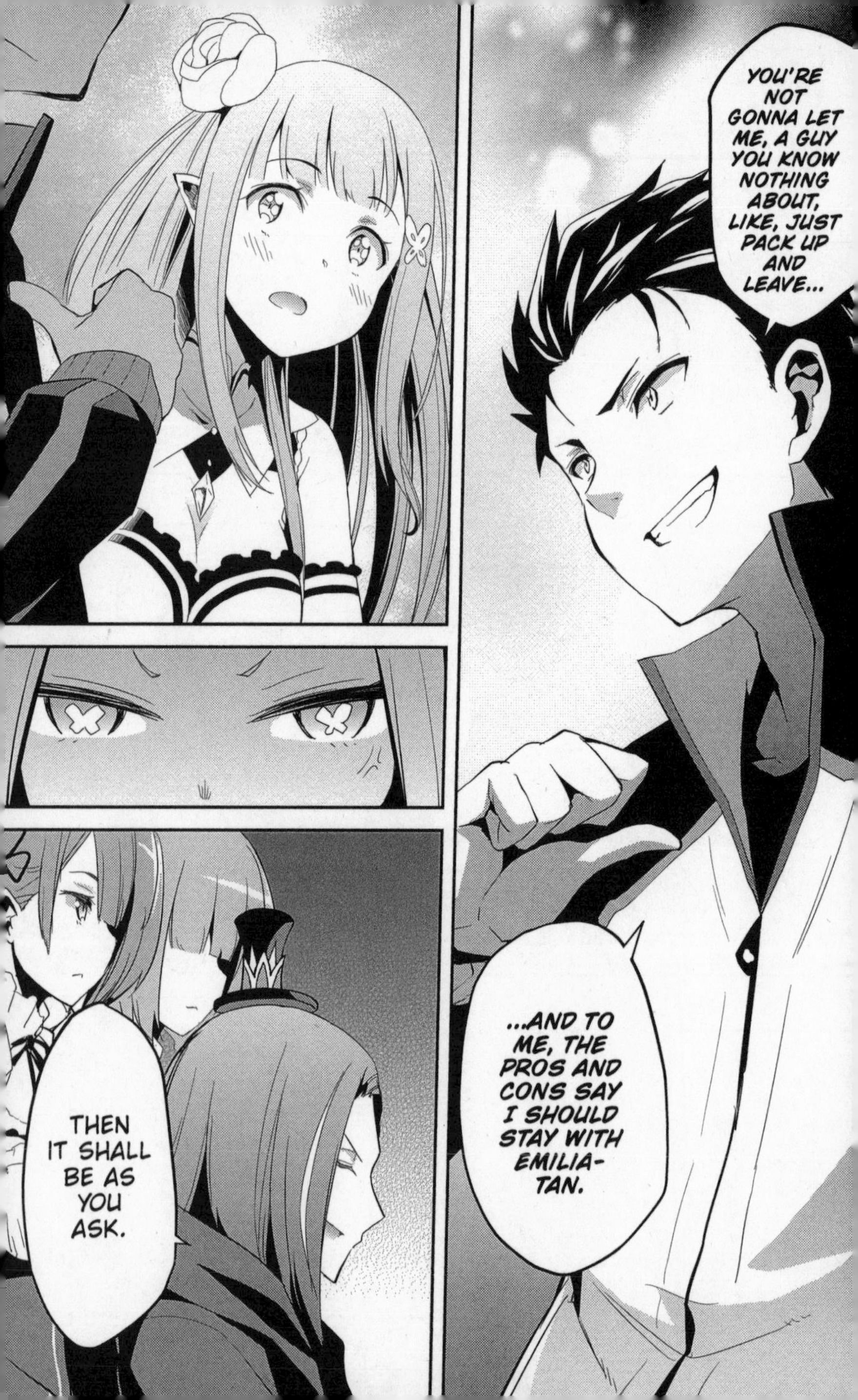
YOU'RE NOT GONNA LET ME, A GUY YOU KNOW NOTHING ABOUT, LIKE, JUST PACK UP AND LEAVE...
...AND TO ME, THE PROS AND CONS SAY I SHOULD STAY WITH EMILIA-TAN.
THEN IT SHALL BE AS YOU ASK.

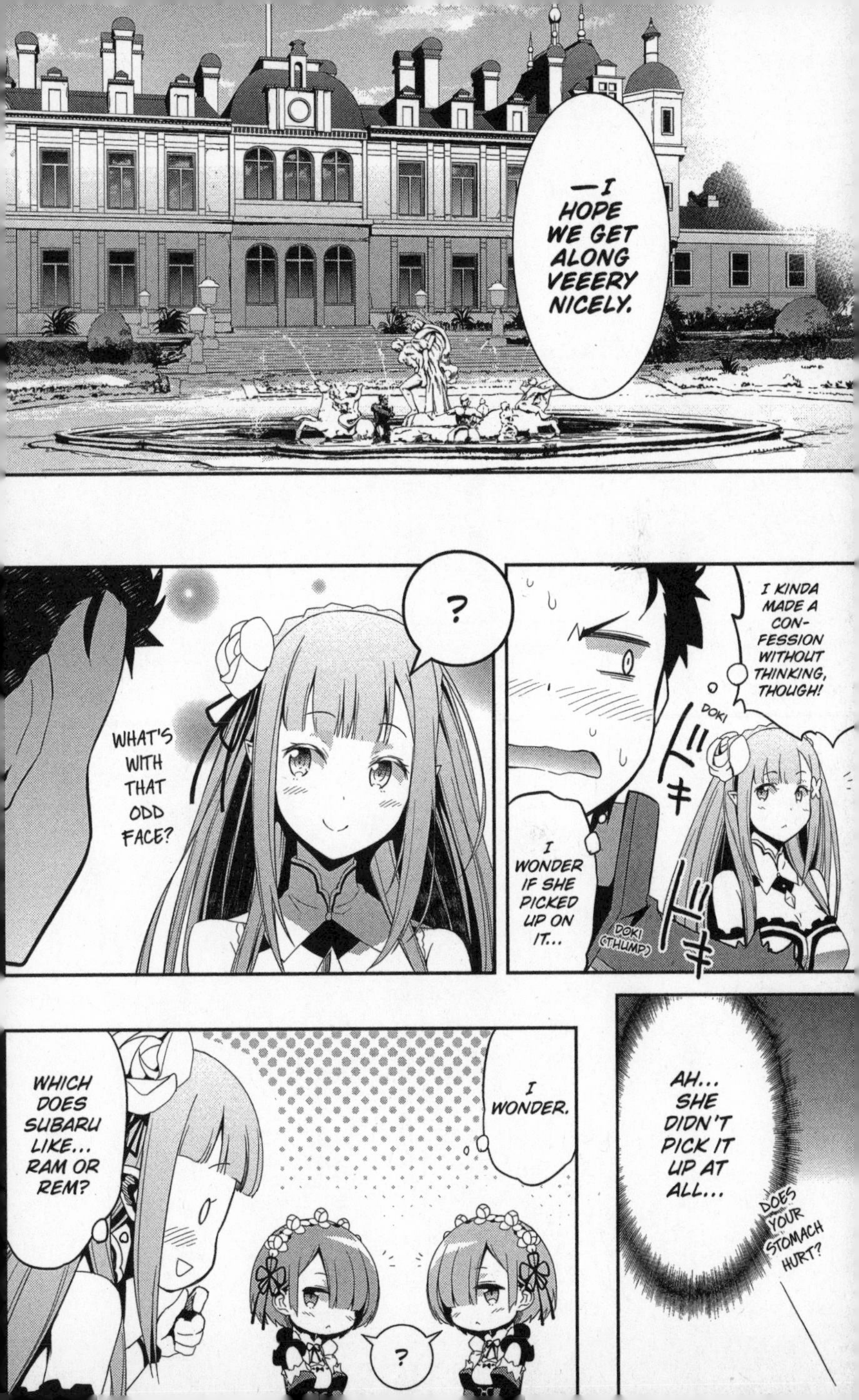
—I HOPE WE GET ALONG VEEERY NICELY.
I KINDA MADE A CON-FESSION WITHOUT THINKING, THOUGH!
DOKI
I WONDER IF SHE PICKED UP ON IT...
DOKI (THUMP)
?
WHAT'S WITH THAT ODD FACE?
AH... SHE DIDN'T PICK IT UP AT ALL...
DOES YOUR STOMACH HURT?
I WONDER.
WHICH DOES SUBARU LIKE... RAM OR REM?
?

Totally angelic Emilia!!
She is the underpinning of the uproar in the first chapter
and the tale to follow.
Now Subaru's life in another world begins.

Re:ZERO -Starting Life in Another World-

A Week at the Mansion

The only ability Subaru Natsuki gets when
he's summoned to another world is time
travel via his own death. But to save her,
he'll die as many times as it takes.

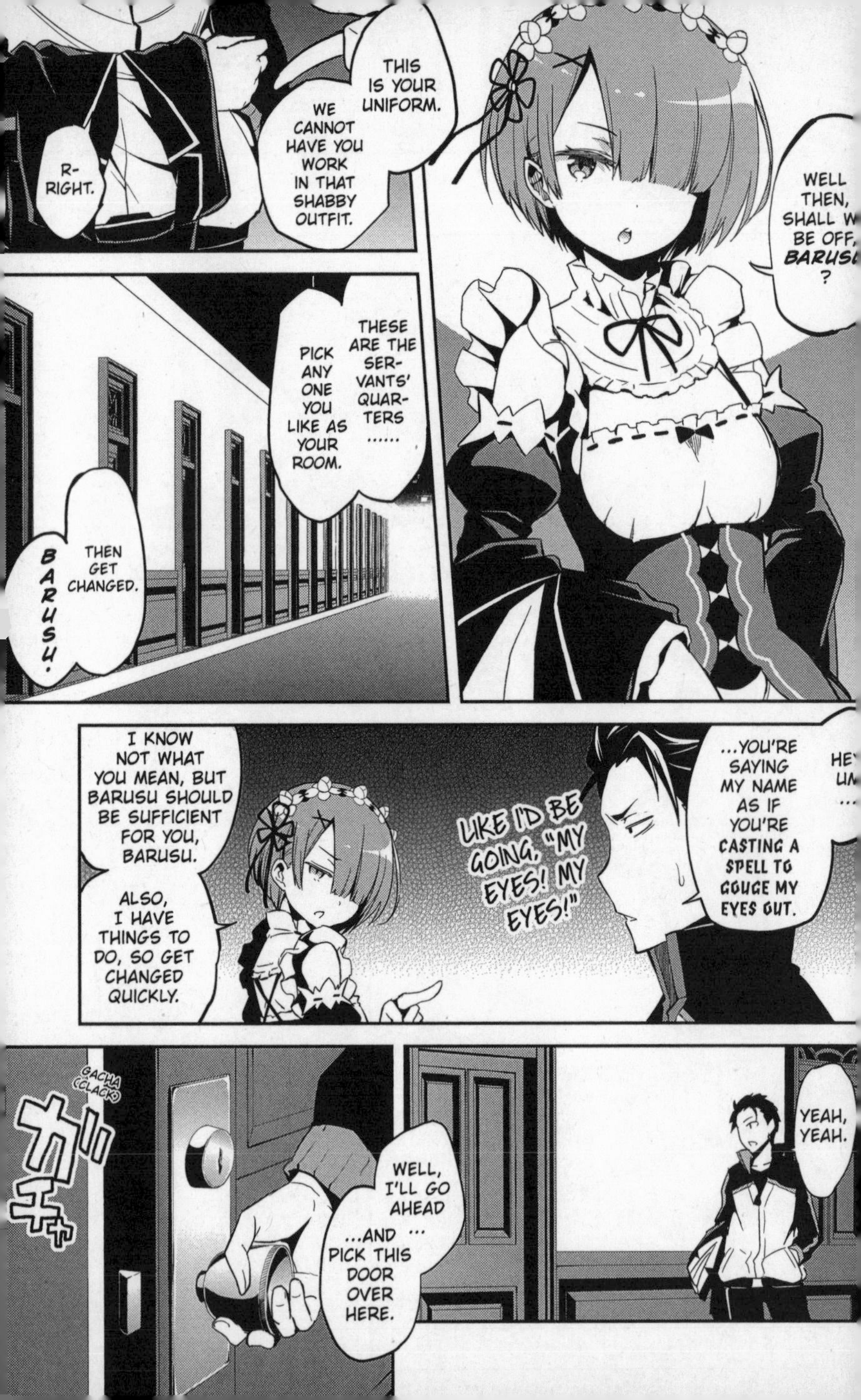
WELL THEN, SHALL W BE OFF, BARUS ?
THIS IS YOUR UNIFORM.
WE CANNOT HAVE YOU WORK IN THAT SHABBY OUTFIT.
R- RIGHT.
THESE ARE THE SER- VANTS' QUAR- TERS ......
PICK ANY ONE YOU LIKE AS YOUR ROOM.
THEN GET CHANGED.
BARUSU.
HE UM ...
...YOU'RE SAYING MY NAME AS IF YOU'RE CASTING A SPELL TO GOUGE MY EYES OUT.
LIKE I'D BE GOING, "MY EYES! MY EYES!"
I KNOW NOT WHAT YOU MEAN, BUT BARUSU SHOULD BE SUFFICIENT FOR YOU, BARUSU.
ALSO, I HAVE THINGS TO DO, SO GET CHANGED QUICKLY.
YEAH, YEAH.
WELL, I'LL GO AHEAD ...
...AND PICK THIS DOOR OVER HERE.
GACHA (CLACK)
ガチャ

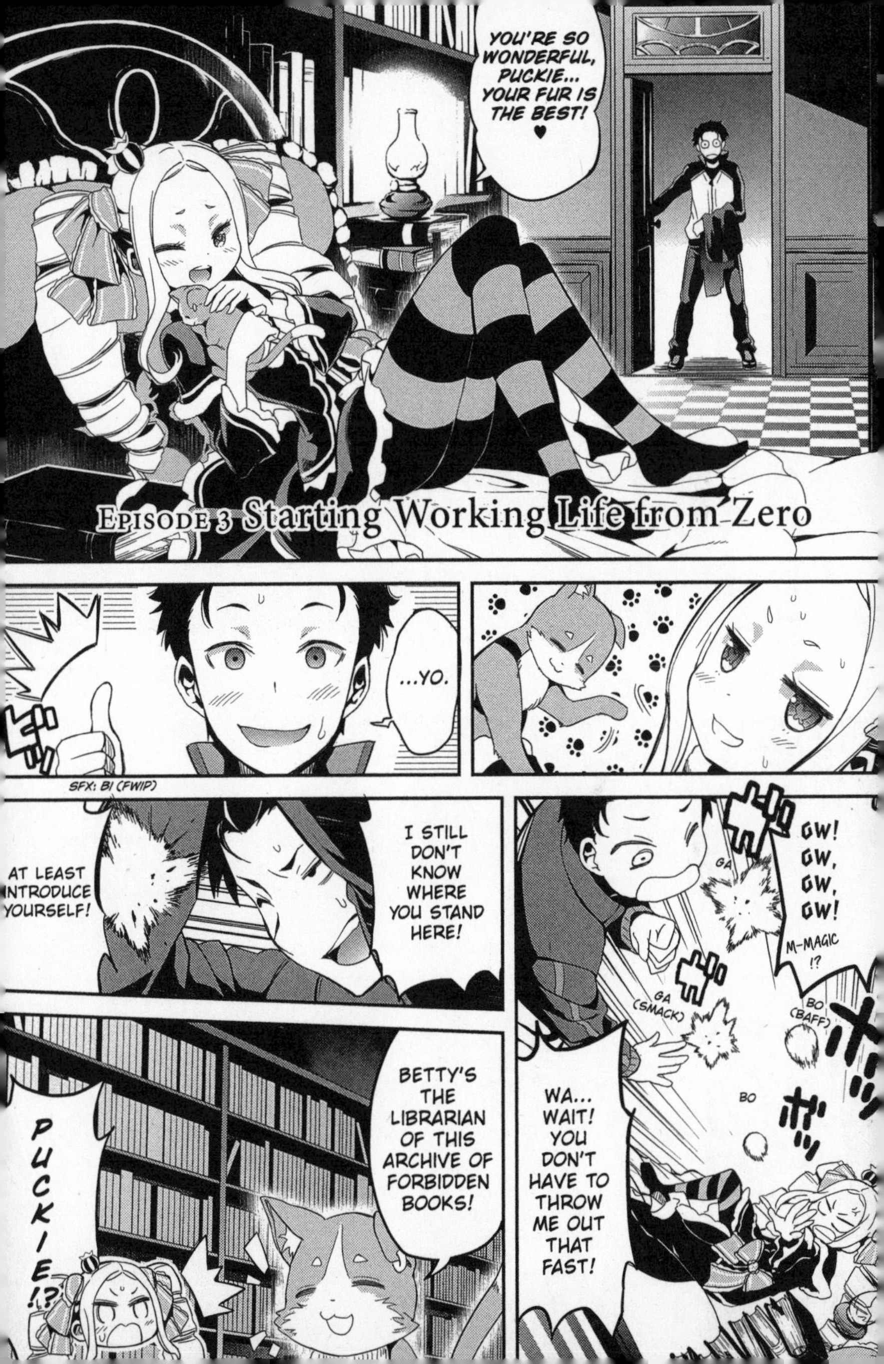
YOU'RE SO WONDERFUL, PUCKIE... YOUR FUR IS THE BEST! ♥
EPISODE 3 Starting Working Life from Zero
...YO.
SFX: BI (FWIP)
GW! GW, GW, GW!
GA
M-MAGIC !?
GA (SMACK)
BO (BAFF)
BO
WA... WAIT! YOU DON'T HAVE TO THROW ME OUT THAT FAST!
I STILL DON'T KNOW WHERE YOU STAND HERE!
AT LEAST INTRODUCE YOURSELF!
BETTY'S THE LIBRARIAN OF THIS ARCHIVE OF FORBIDDEN BOOKS!
PUCKIE!?

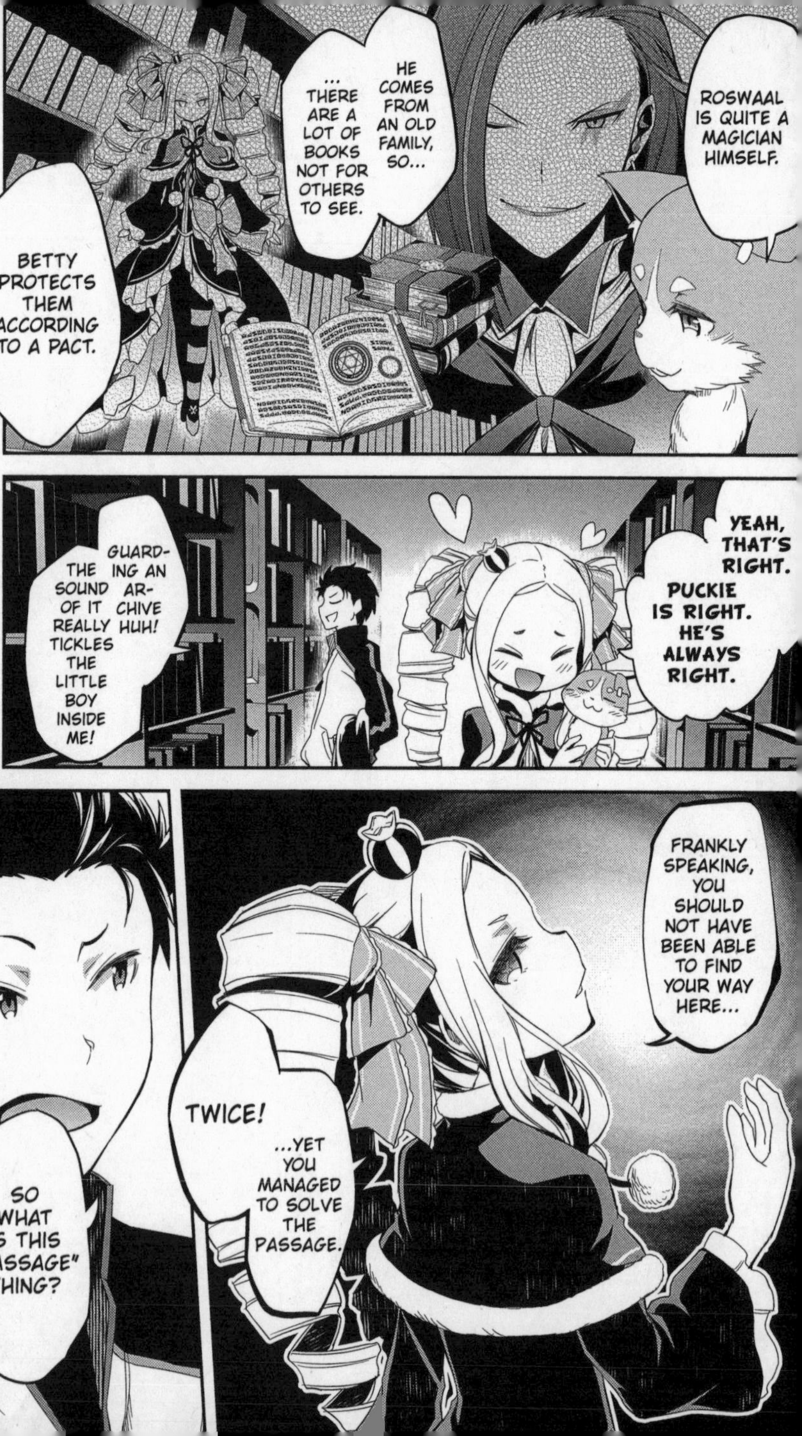
ROSWAAL IS QUITE A MAGICIAN HIMSELF.
HE COMES FROM AN OLD FAMILY, SO...
...THERE ARE A LOT OF BOOKS NOT FOR OTHERS TO SEE.
BETTY PROTECTS THEM ACCORDING TO A PACT.
YEAH, THAT'S RIGHT.
PUCKIE IS RIGHT. HE'S ALWAYS RIGHT.
GUARDING AN ARCHIVE HUH!
THE SOUND OF IT REALLY TICKLES THE LITTLE BOY INSIDE ME!
FRANKLY SPEAKING, YOU SHOULD NOT HAVE BEEN ABLE TO FIND YOUR WAY HERE...
...YET YOU MANAGED TO SOLVE THE PASSAGE.
TWICE!
SO WHAT IS THIS "PASSAGE" THING?

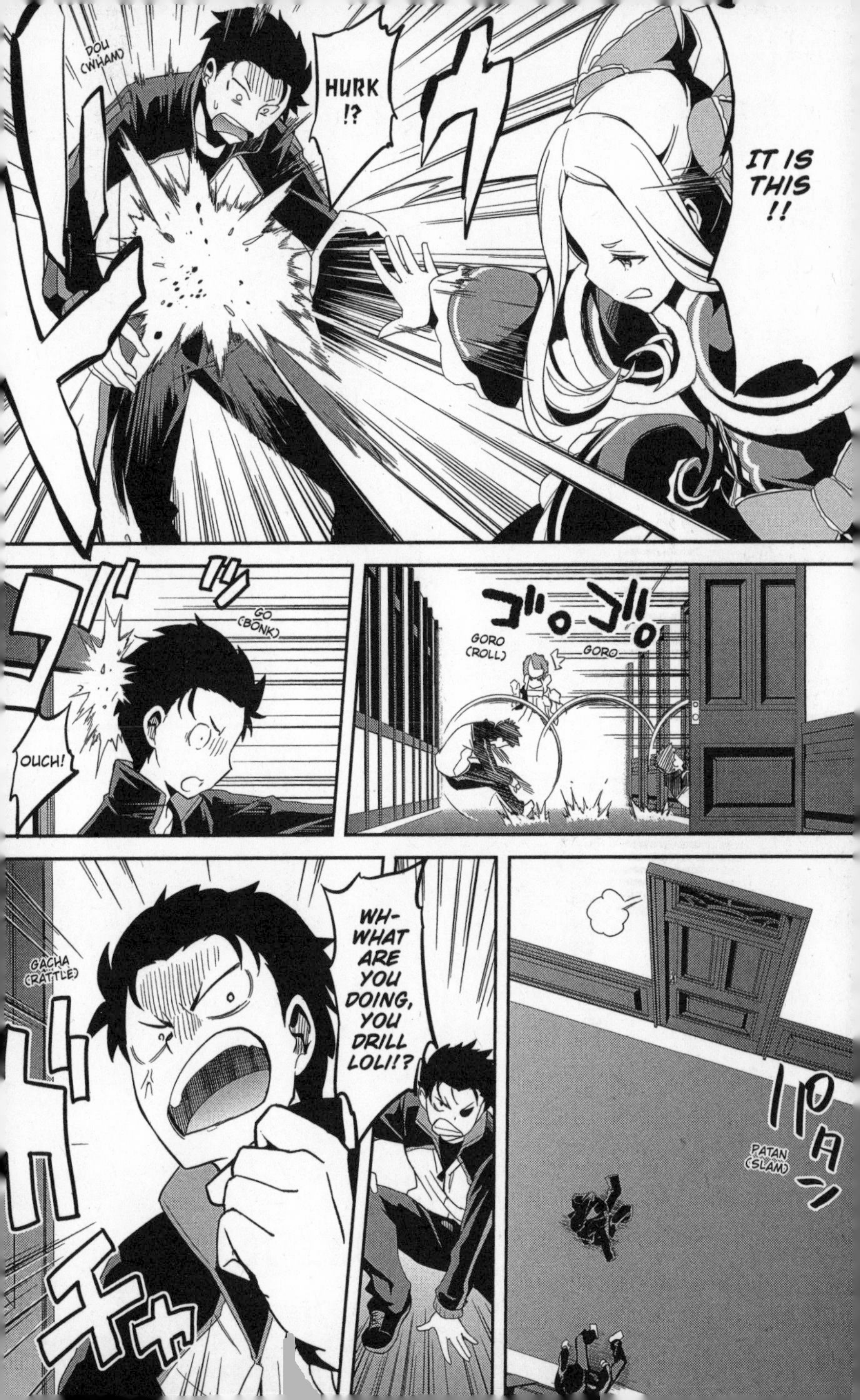
IT IS THIS!!
HURK!?
DOU (WHAM)
GORO (ROLL)
GORO
GO (BONK)
OUCH!
PATAN (SLAM)
WH-WHAT ARE YOU DOING, YOU DRILL LOLI!?
GACHA (RATTLE)

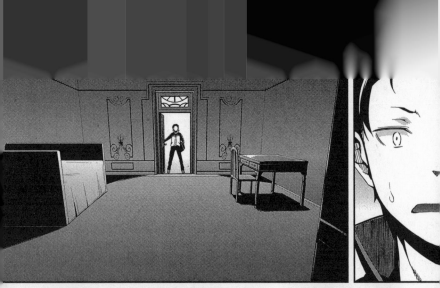

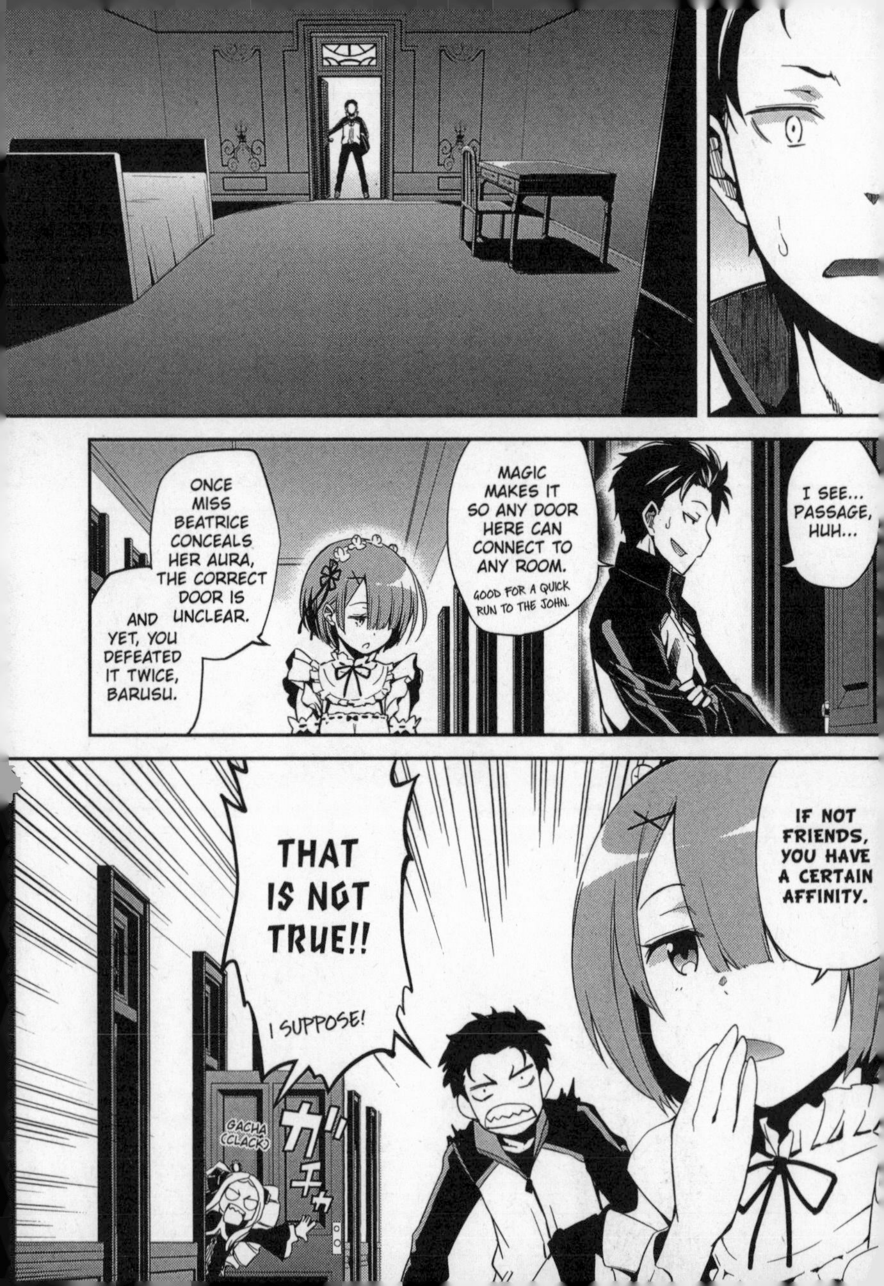
I SEE... PASSAGE, HUH...
MAGIC MAKES IT SO ANY DOOR HERE CAN CONNECT TO ANY ROOM.
GOOD FOR A QUICK RUN TO THE JOHN.
ONCE MISS BEATRICE CONCEALS HER AURA, THE CORRECT DOOR IS UNCLEAR.
AND YET, YOU DEFEATED IT TWICE, BARUSU.
IF NOT FRIENDS, YOU HAVE A CERTAIN AFFINITY.
THAT IS NOT TRUE!!
I SUPPOSE!
ガチャ
GACHA (CLACK)

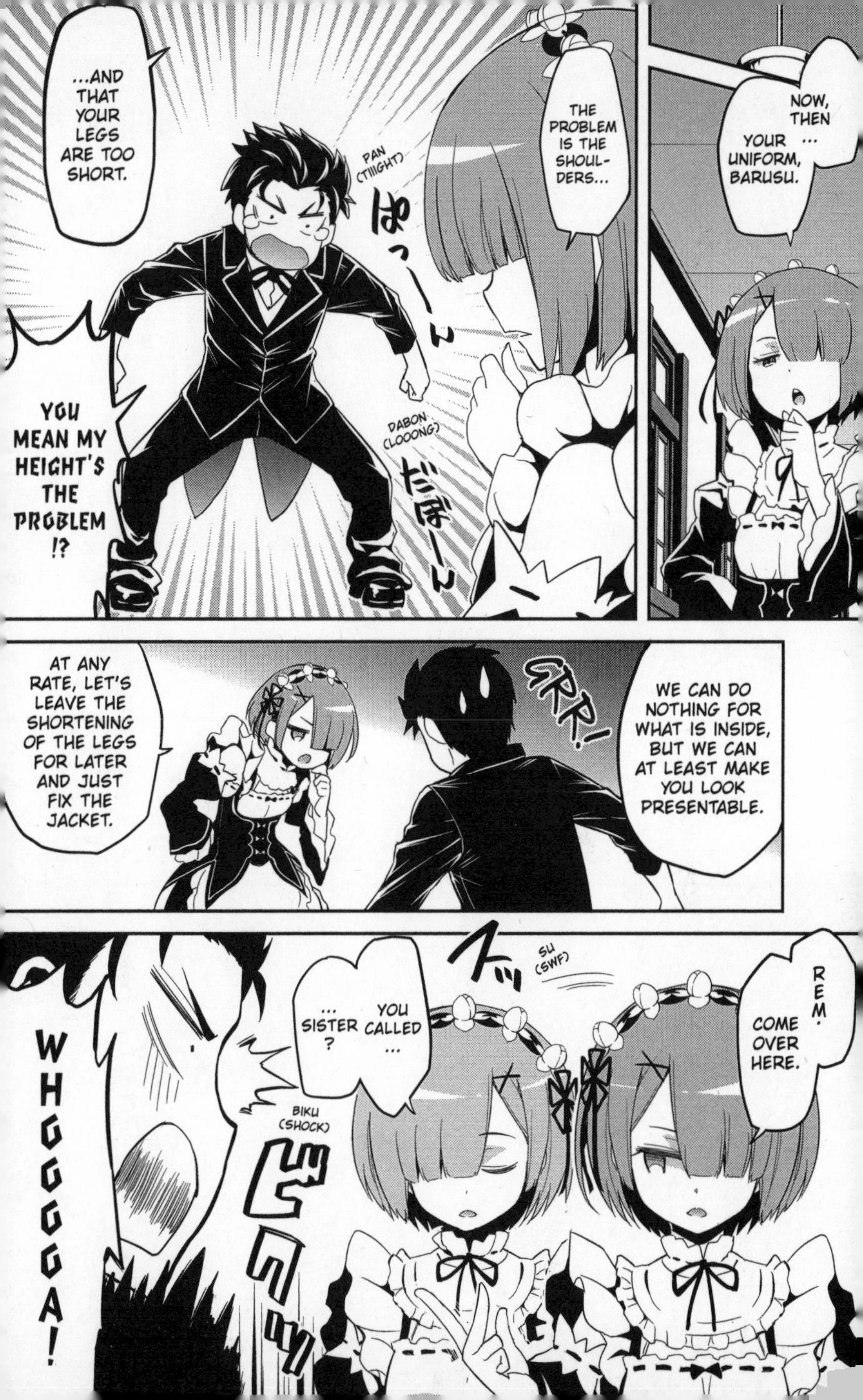
NOW, THEN ... YOUR UNIFORM, BARUSU.
THE PROBLEM IS THE SHOULDERS...
PAN (TIIIGHT)
ぱっつ〜ん
...AND THAT YOUR LEGS ARE TOO SHORT.
DABON (LOOOONG)
だぼ〜ん
YOU MEAN MY HEIGHT'S THE PROBLEM!?
WE CAN DO NOTHING FOR WHAT IS INSIDE, BUT WE CAN AT LEAST MAKE YOU LOOK PRESENTABLE.
GRR!
AT ANY RATE, LET'S LEAVE THE SHORTENING OF THE LEGS FOR LATER AND JUST FIX THE JACKET.
REM. COME OVER HERE.
SU (SWF)
スッ
YOU CALLED ...
... SISTER?
BIKU (SHOCK)
ビクッ
WHGGGGA!

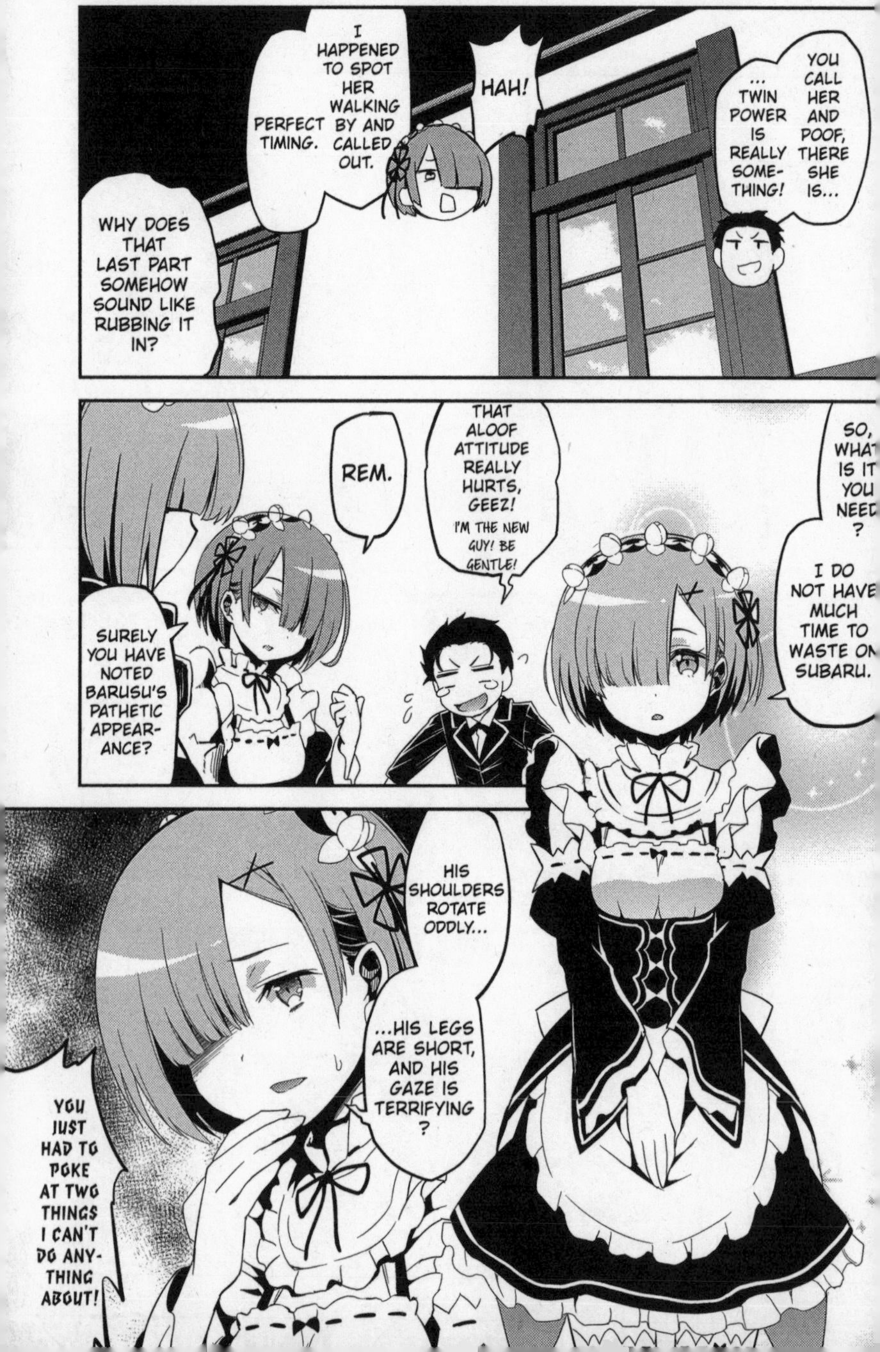
YOU CALL HER AND POOF, THERE SHE IS...
...TWIN POWER IS REALLY SOMETHING!
HAH!
I HAPPENED TO SPOT HER WALKING BY AND CALLED OUT.
PERFECT TIMING.
WHY DOES THAT LAST PART SOMEHOW SOUND LIKE RUBBING IT IN?
SO, WHAT IS IT YOU NEED?
I DO NOT HAVE MUCH TIME TO WASTE ON SUBARU.
THAT ALOOF ATTITUDE REALLY HURTS, GEEZ!
I'M THE NEW GUY! BE GENTLE!
REM.
SURELY YOU HAVE NOTED BARUSU'S PATHETIC APPEARANCE?
HIS SHOULDERS ROTATE ODDLY...
...HIS LEGS ARE SHORT, AND HIS GAZE IS TERRIFYING?
YOU JUST HAD TO POKE AT TWO THINGS I CAN'T DO ANYTHING ABOUT!

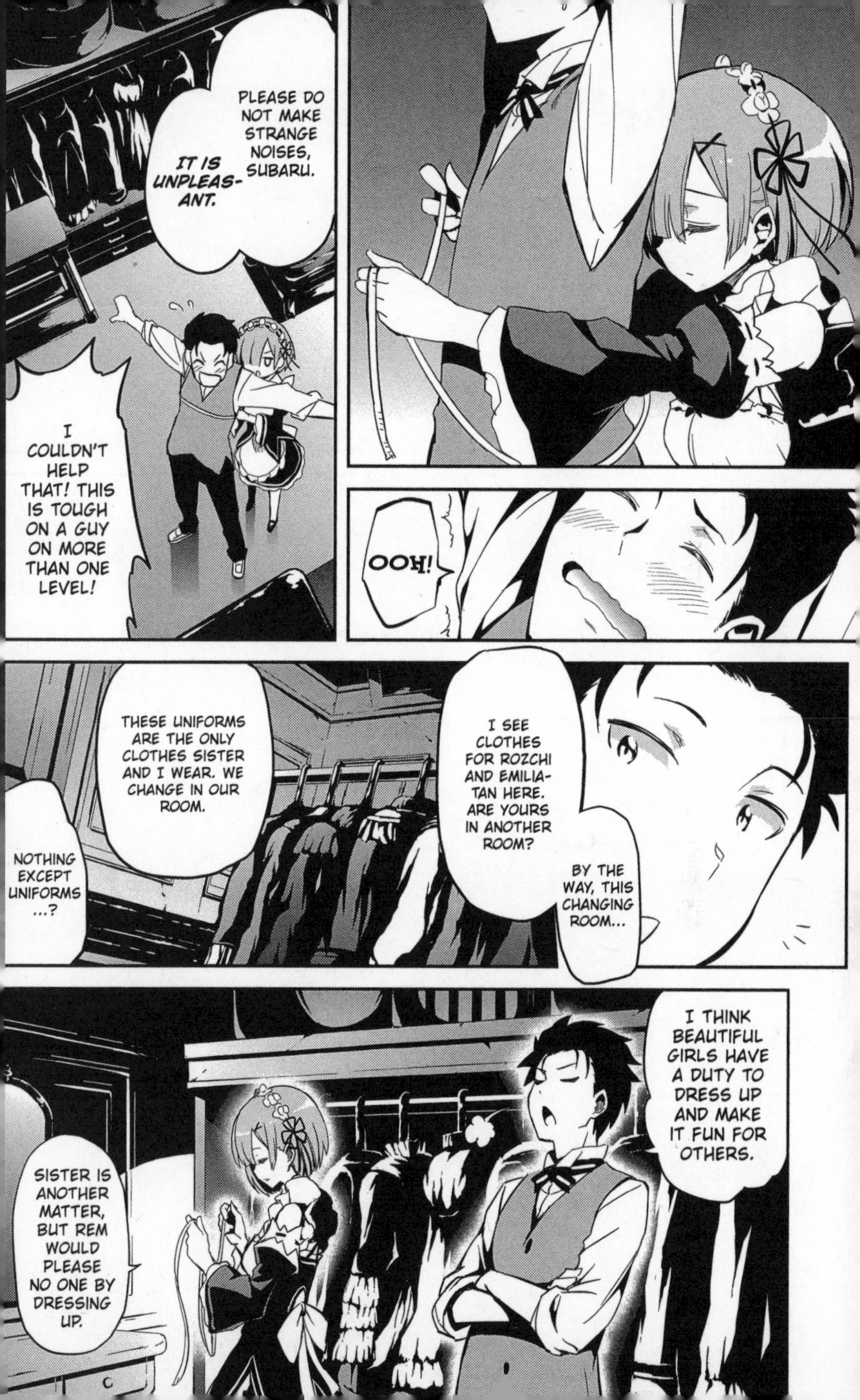
OOH!
PLEASE DO NOT MAKE STRANGE NOISES, SUBARU.
IT IS UNPLEASANT.
I COULDN'T HELP THAT! THIS IS TOUGH ON A GUY ON MORE THAN ONE LEVEL!
BY THE WAY, THIS CHANGING ROOM...
I SEE CLOTHES FOR ROZCHI AND EMILIA-TAN HERE. ARE YOURS IN ANOTHER ROOM?
THESE UNIFORMS ARE THE ONLY CLOTHES SISTER AND I WEAR. WE CHANGE IN OUR ROOM.
NOTHING EXCEPT UNIFORMS...?
I THINK BEAUTIFUL GIRLS HAVE A DUTY TO DRESS UP AND MAKE IT FUN FOR OTHERS.
SISTER IS ANOTHER MATTER, BUT REM WOULD PLEASE NO ONE BY DRESSING UP.

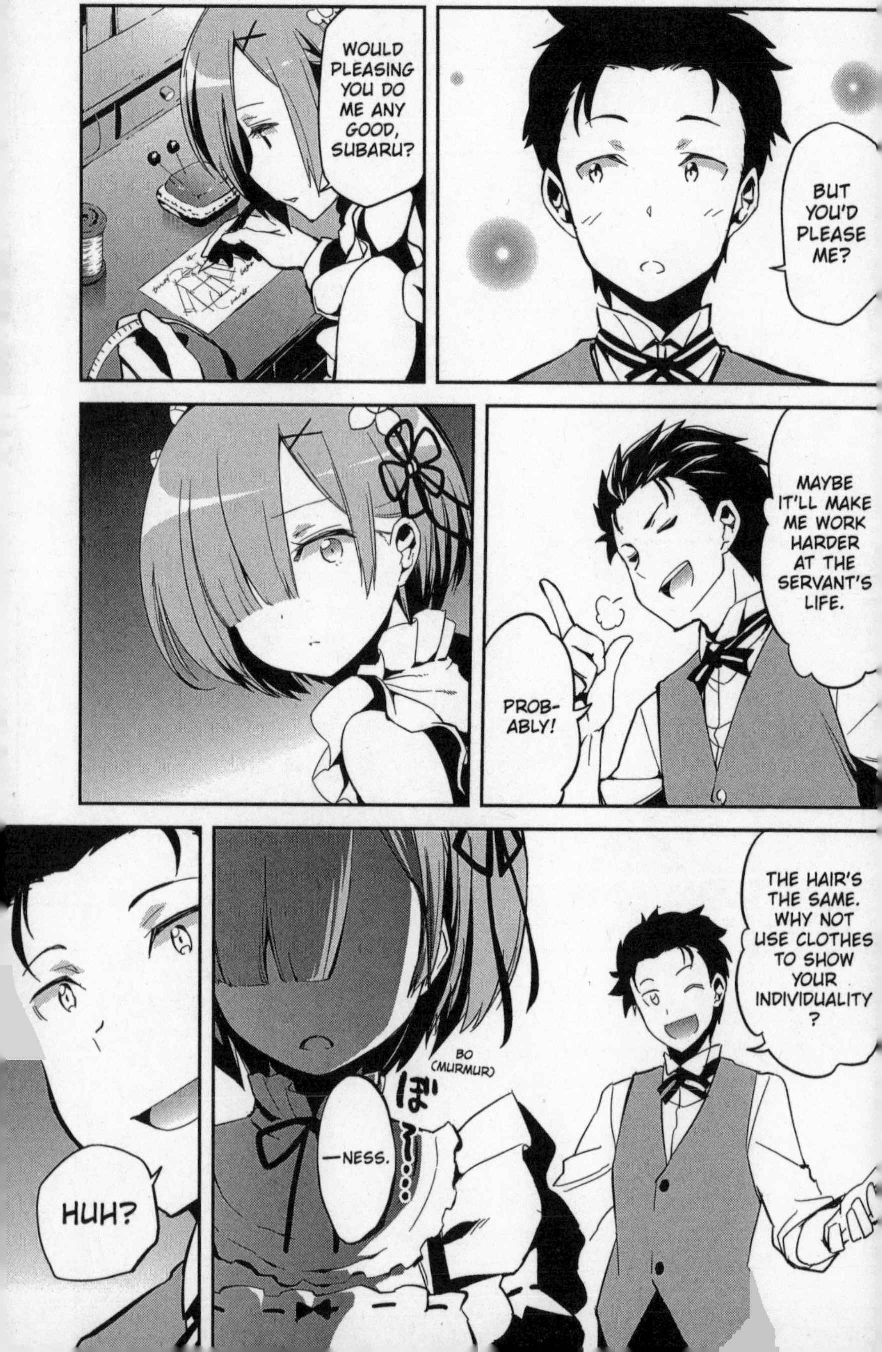
BUT YOU'D PLEASE ME?
WOULD PLEASING YOU DO ME ANY GOOD, SUBARU?
MAYBE IT'LL MAKE ME WORK HARDER AT THE SERVANT'S LIFE.
PROB-ABLY!
THE HAIR'S THE SAME. WHY NOT USE CLOTHES TO SHOW YOUR INDIVIDUALITY?
BO (MURMUR)
ぼ～…
—NESS.
HUH?

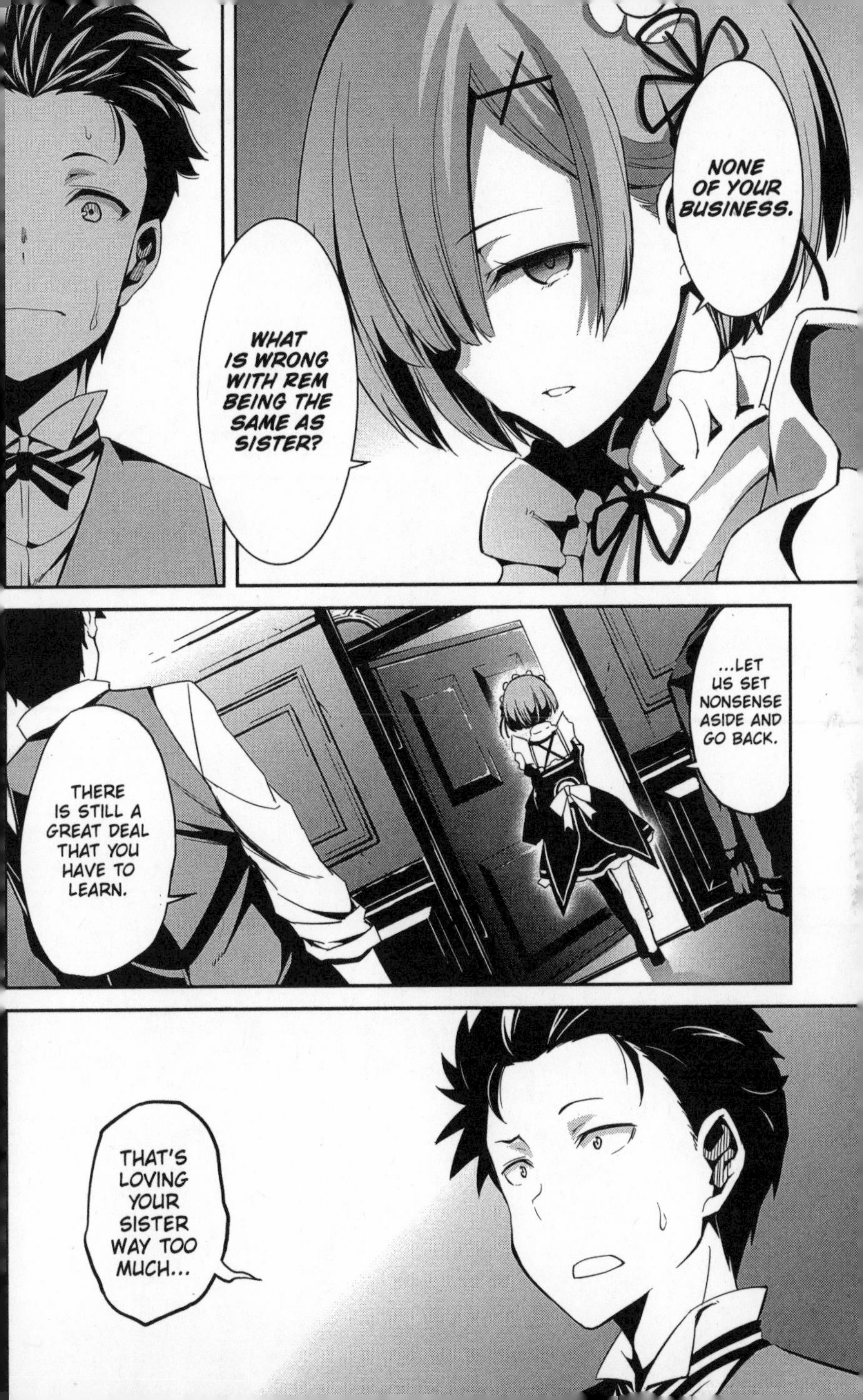
NONE OF YOUR BUSINESS.
WHAT IS WRONG WITH REM BEING THE SAME AS SISTER?
...LET US SET NONSENSE ASIDE AND GO BACK.
THERE IS STILL A GREAT DEAL THAT YOU HAVE TO LEARN.
THAT'S LOVING YOUR SISTER WAY TOO MUCH...

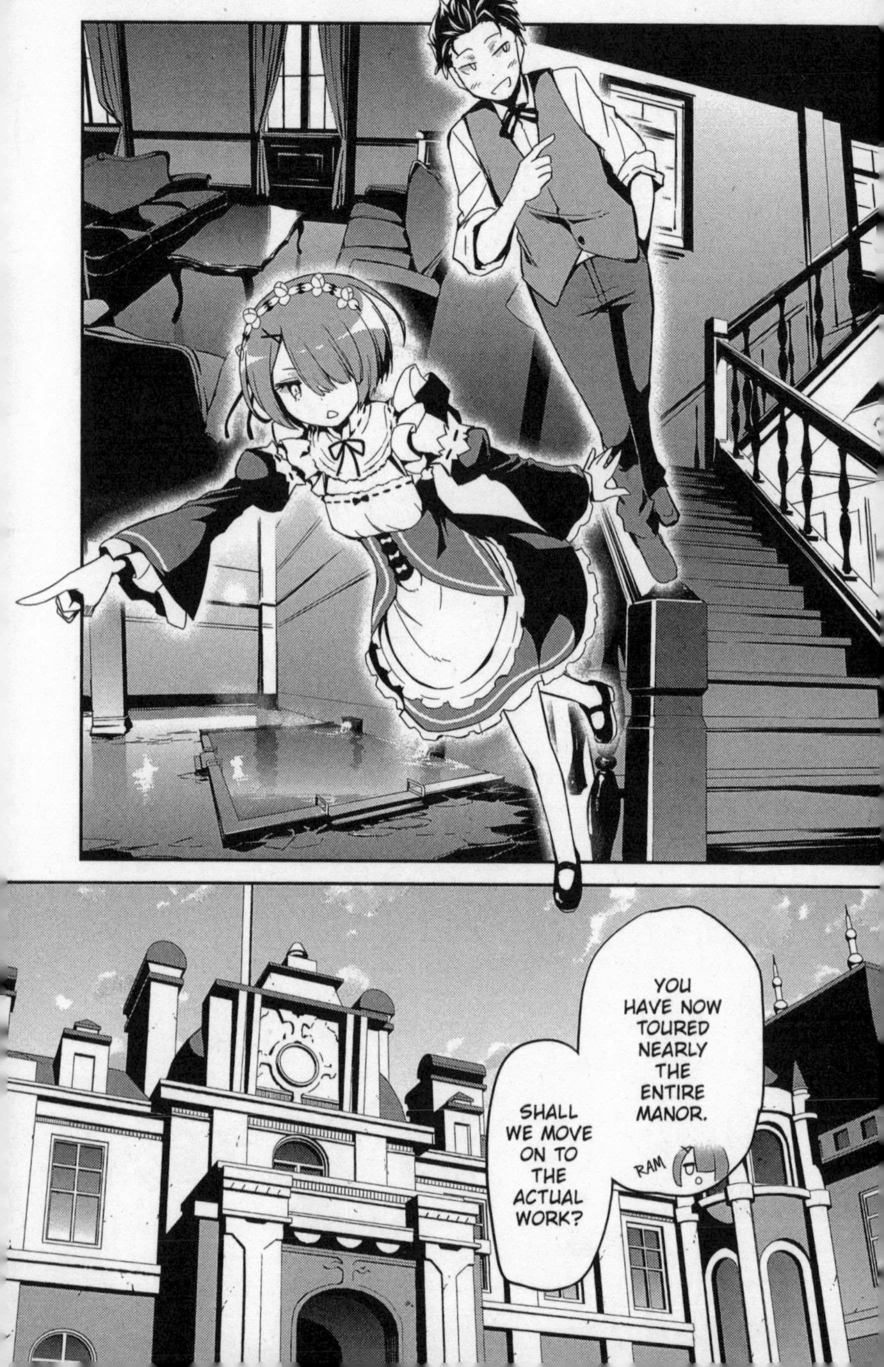
YOU HAVE NOW TOURED NEARLY THE ENTIRE MANOR.
SHALL WE MOVE ON TO THE ACTUAL WORK?
RAM

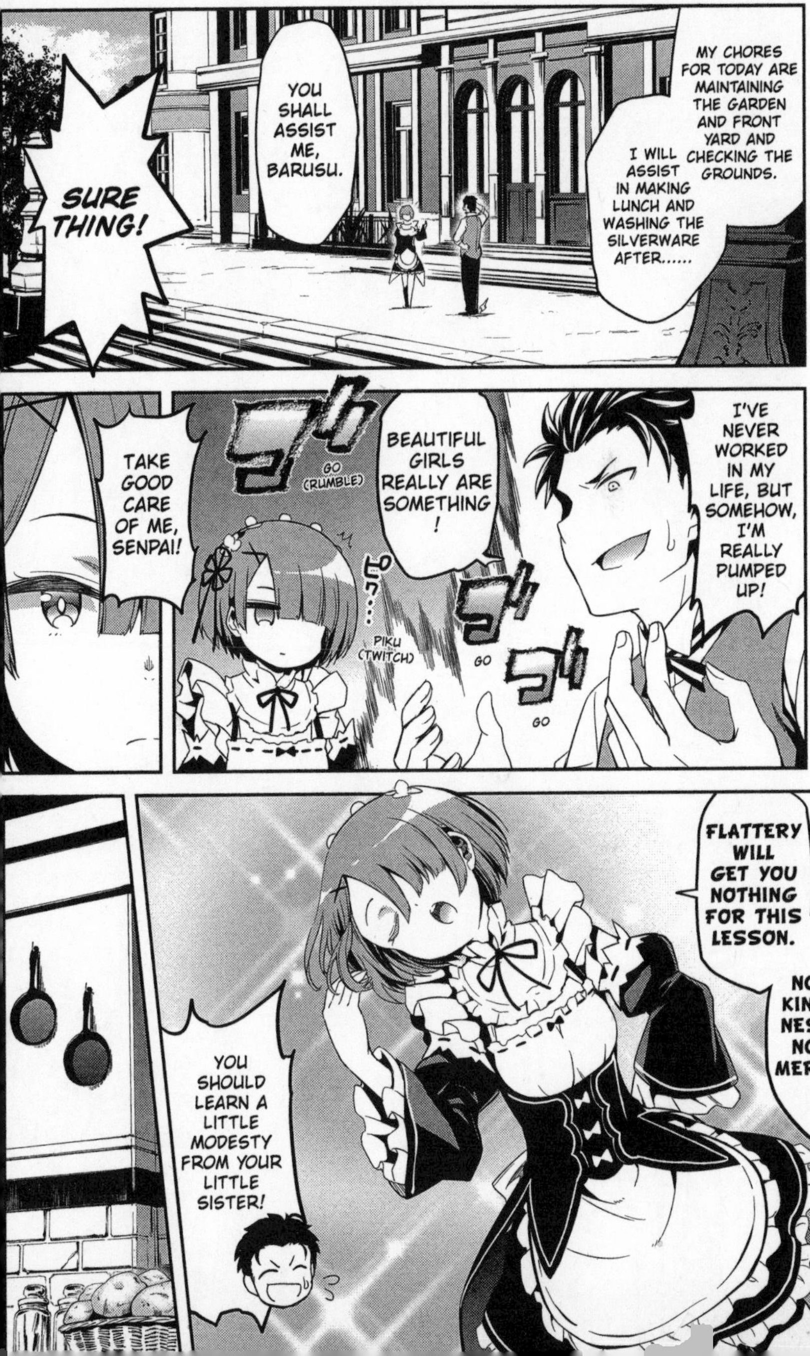
MY CHORES FOR TODAY ARE MAINTAINING THE GARDEN AND FRONT YARD AND CHECKING THE GROUNDS.
I WILL ASSIST IN MAKING LUNCH AND WASHING THE SILVERWARE AFTER......
YOU SHALL ASSIST ME, BARUSU.
SURE THING!
I'VE NEVER WORKED IN MY LIFE, BUT SOMEHOW, I'M REALLY PUMPED UP!
GO
GO
BEAUTIFUL GIRLS REALLY ARE SOMETHING!
PIKU (TWITCH)
GO (RUMBLE)
TAKE GOOD CARE OF ME, SENPAI!
FLATTERY WILL GET YOU NOTHING FOR THIS LESSON.
NOT KINDNESS, NOT MERCY.
YOU SHOULD LEARN A LITTLE MODESTY FROM YOUR LITTLE SISTER!

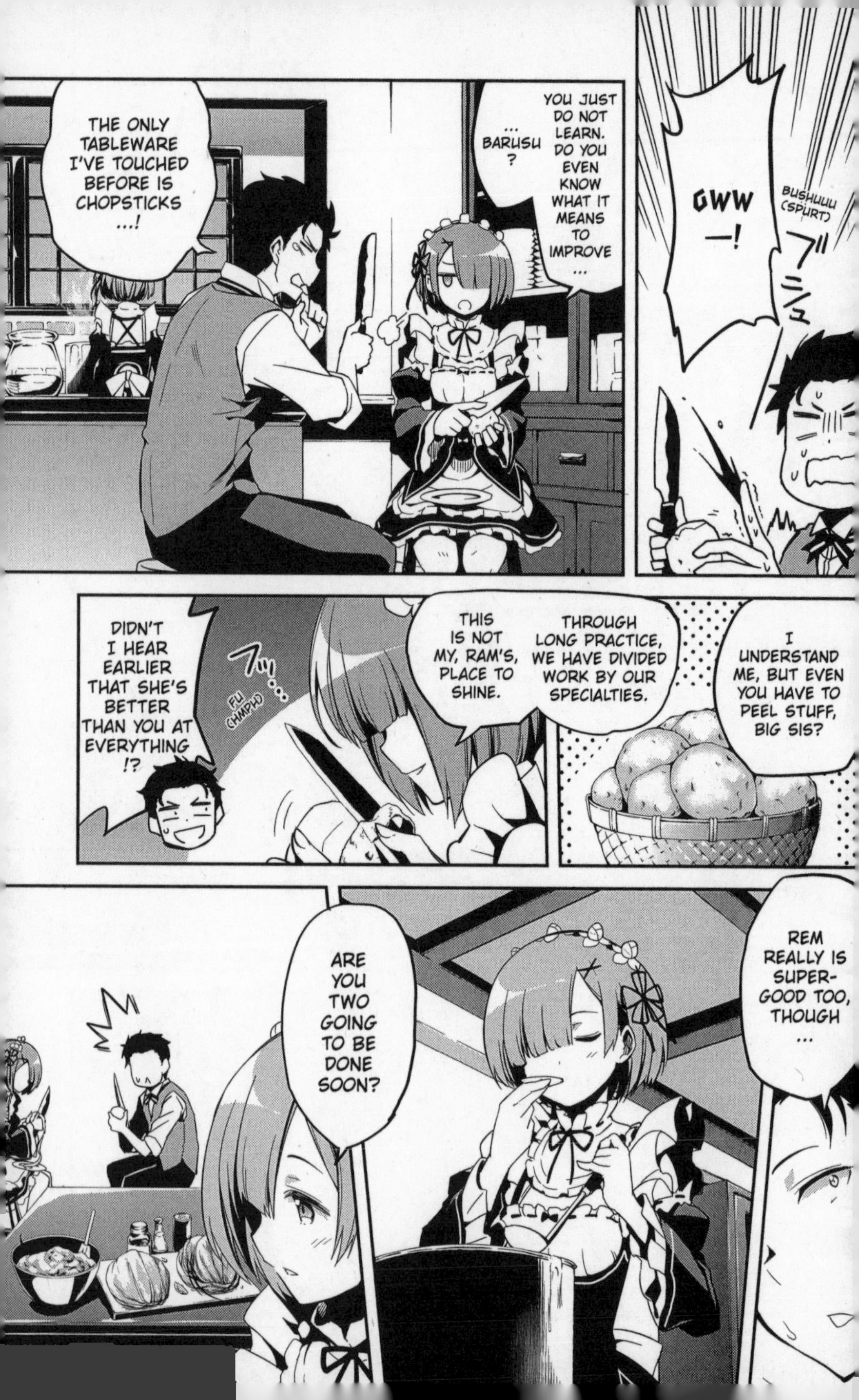
GWW —!
BUSHUUU (SPURT)
ブシュ
YOU JUST DO NOT LEARN. DO YOU EVEN KNOW WHAT IT MEANS TO IMPROVE ...
... BARUSU ?
THE ONLY TABLEWARE I'VE TOUCHED BEFORE IS CHOPSTICKS ...!
I UNDERSTAND ME, BUT EVEN YOU HAVE TO PEEL STUFF, BIG SIS?
THROUGH LONG PRACTICE, WE HAVE DIVIDED WORK BY OUR SPECIALTIES.
THIS IS NOT MY, RAM'S, PLACE TO SHINE.
フッ…
FU (HMPH)
DIDN'T I HEAR EARLIER THAT SHE'S BETTER THAN YOU AT EVERYTHING !?
REM REALLY IS SUPER-GOOD TOO, THOUGH ...
ARE YOU TWO GOING TO BE DONE SOON?

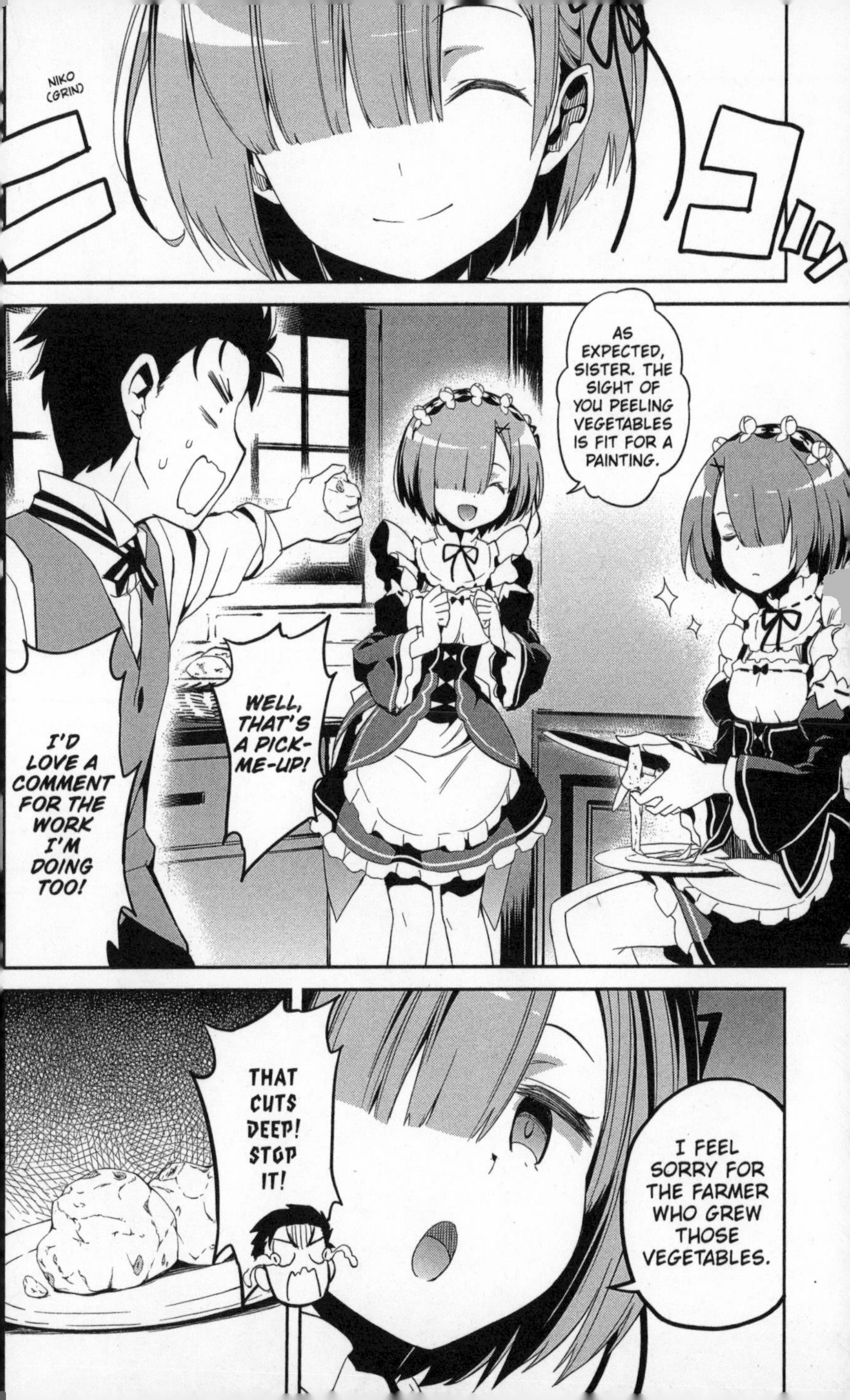
NIKO (GRIN)
AS EXPECTED, SISTER. THE SIGHT OF YOU PEELING VEGETABLES IS FIT FOR A PAINTING.
WELL, THAT'S A PICK-ME-UP!
I'D LOVE A COMMENT FOR THE WORK I'M DOING TOO!
I FEEL SORRY FOR THE FARMER WHO GREW THOSE VEGETABLES.
THAT CUTS DEEP! STOP IT!

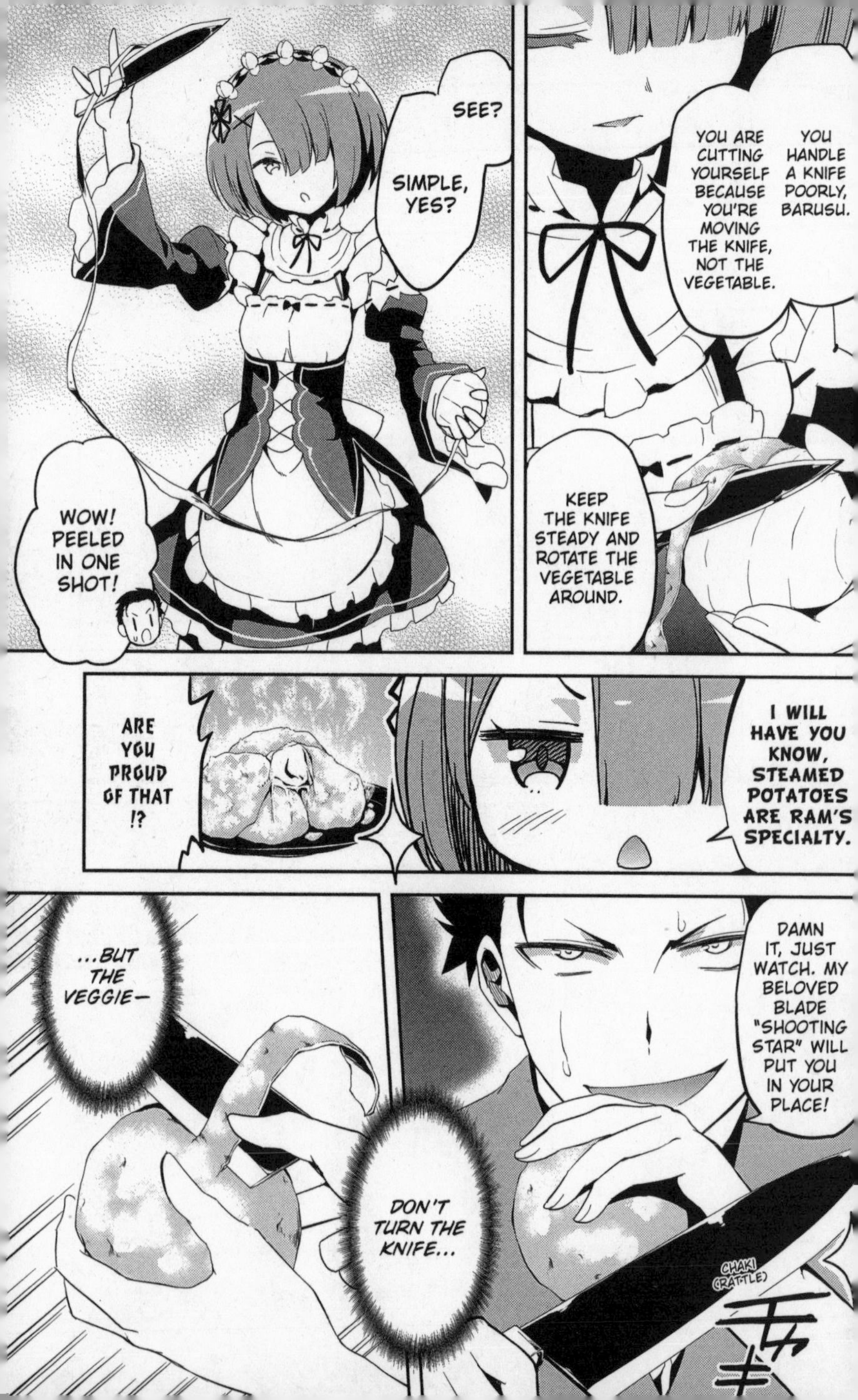
YOU HANDLE A KNIFE POORLY, BARUSU.
YOU ARE CUTTING YOURSELF BECAUSE YOU'RE MOVING THE KNIFE, NOT THE VEGETABLE.
KEEP THE KNIFE STEADY AND ROTATE THE VEGETABLE AROUND.
SEE?
SIMPLE, YES?
WOW! PEELED IN ONE SHOT!
I WILL HAVE YOU KNOW, STEAMED POTATOES ARE RAM'S SPECIALTY.
ARE YOU PROUD OF THAT!?
DAMN IT, JUST WATCH. MY BELOVED BLADE "SHOOTING STAR" WILL PUT YOU IN YOUR PLACE!
CHAKI (RATTLE)
DON'T TURN THE KNIFE...
...BUT THE VEGGIE—

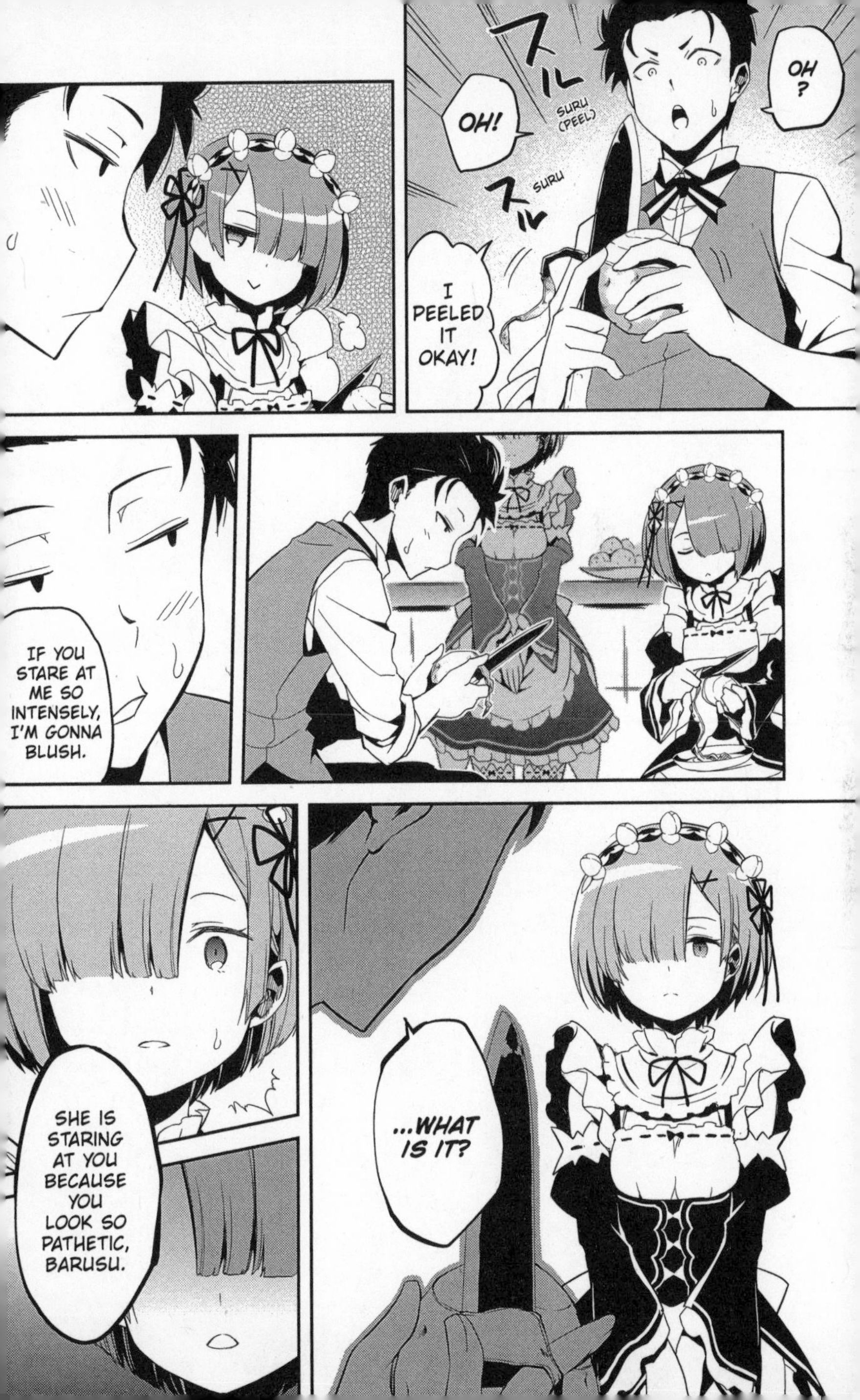
OH?
スル
SURU (PEEL)
OH!
スル
SURU
I PEELED IT OKAY!
IF YOU STARE AT ME SO INTENSELY, I'M GONNA BLUSH.
...WHAT IS IT?
SHE IS STARING AT YOU BECAUSE YOU LOOK SO PATHETIC, BARUSU.

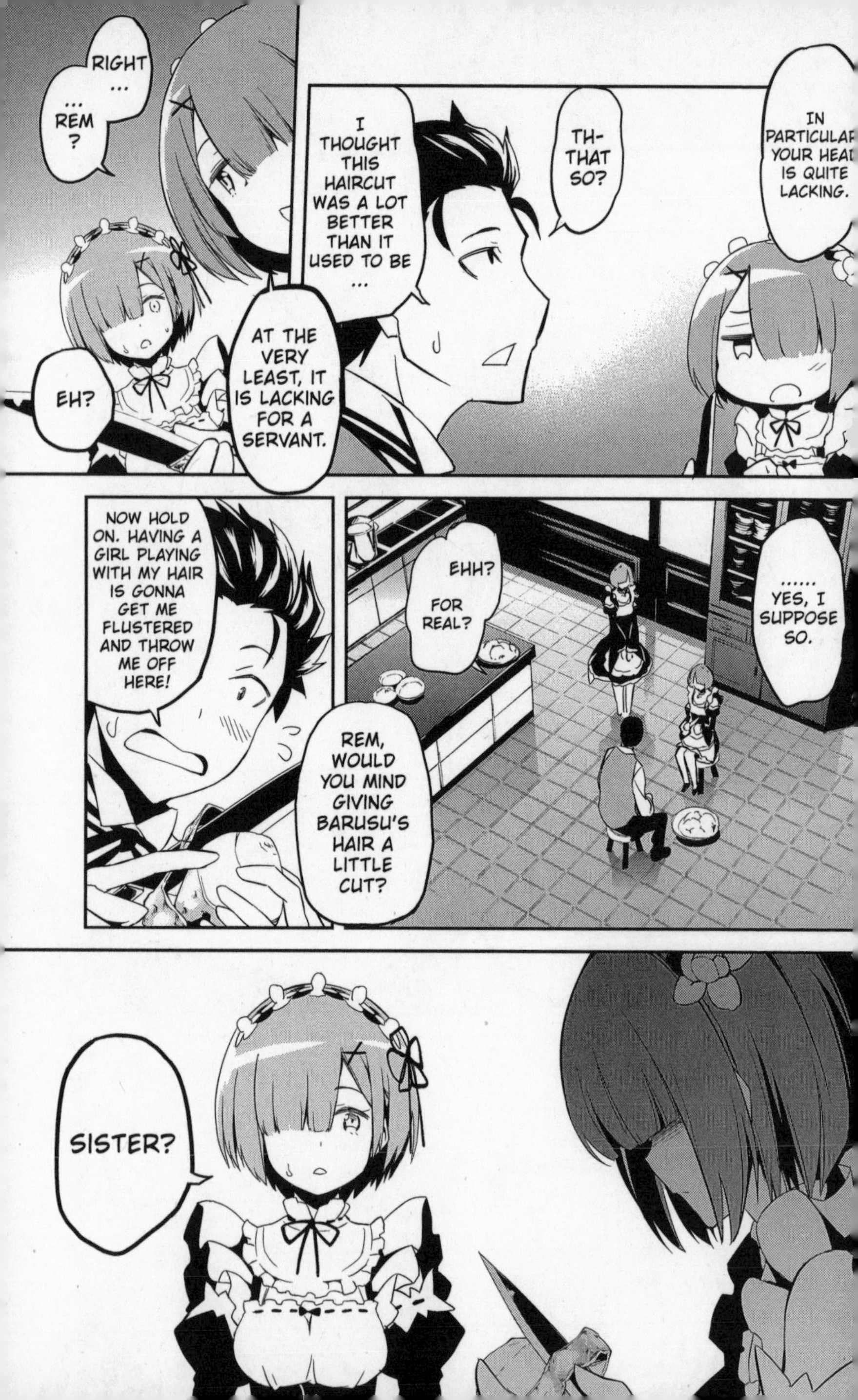
IN PARTICULAR YOUR HEAD IS QUITE LACKING.
TH- THAT SO?
I THOUGHT THIS HAIRCUT WAS A LOT BETTER THAN IT USED TO BE ...
AT THE VERY LEAST, IT IS LACKING FOR A SERVANT.
RIGHT ...
... REM ?
EH?
...... YES, I SUPPOSE SO.
EHH? FOR REAL?
REM, WOULD YOU MIND GIVING BARUSU'S HAIR A LITTLE CUT?
NOW HOLD ON. HAVING A GIRL PLAYING WITH MY HAIR IS GONNA GET ME FLUSTERED AND THROW ME OFF HERE!
SISTER?

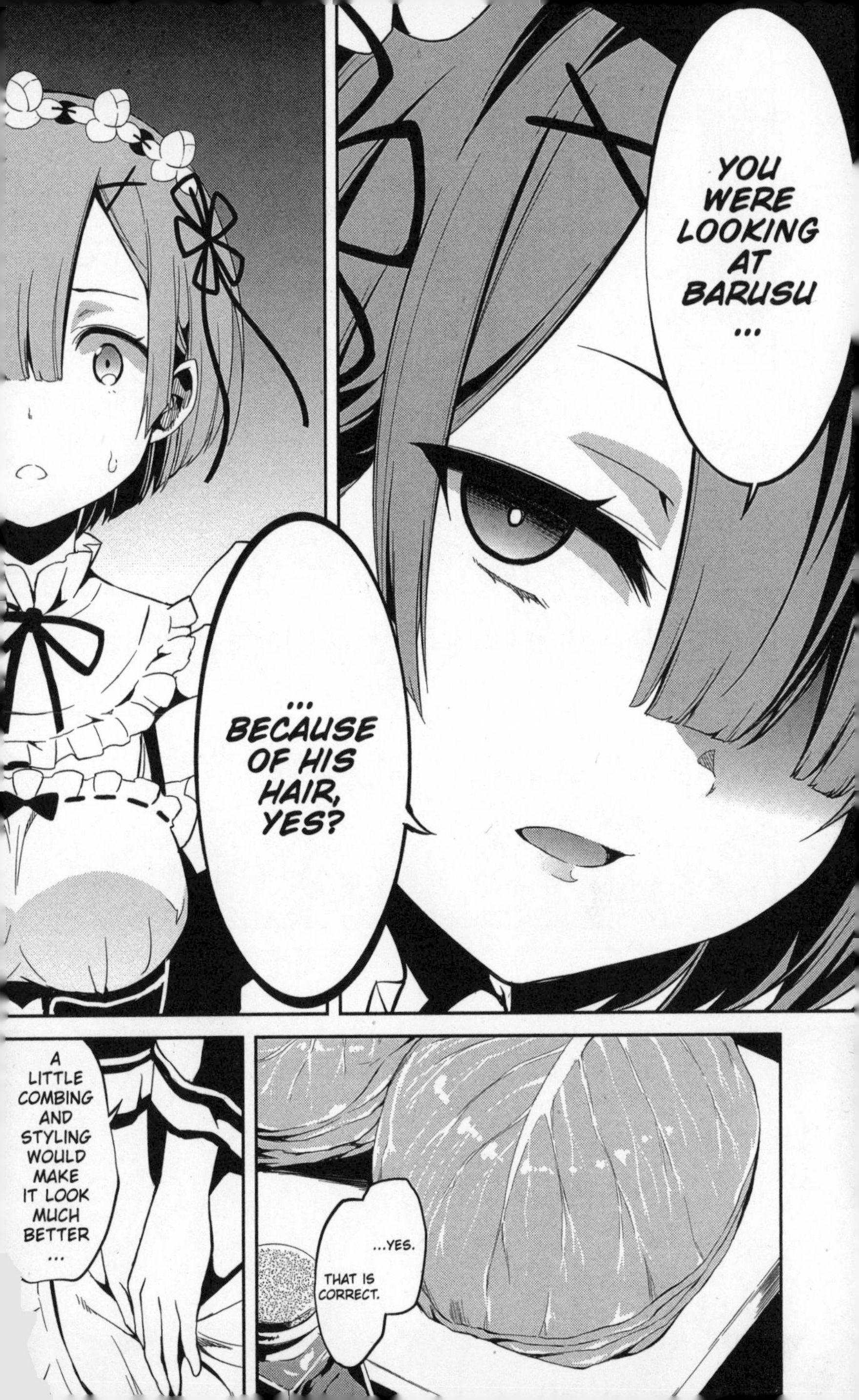
YOU WERE LOOKING AT BARUSU...
...BECAUSE OF HIS HAIR, YES?
...YES.
THAT IS CORRECT.
A LITTLE COMBING AND STYLING WOULD MAKE IT LOOK MUCH BETTER...

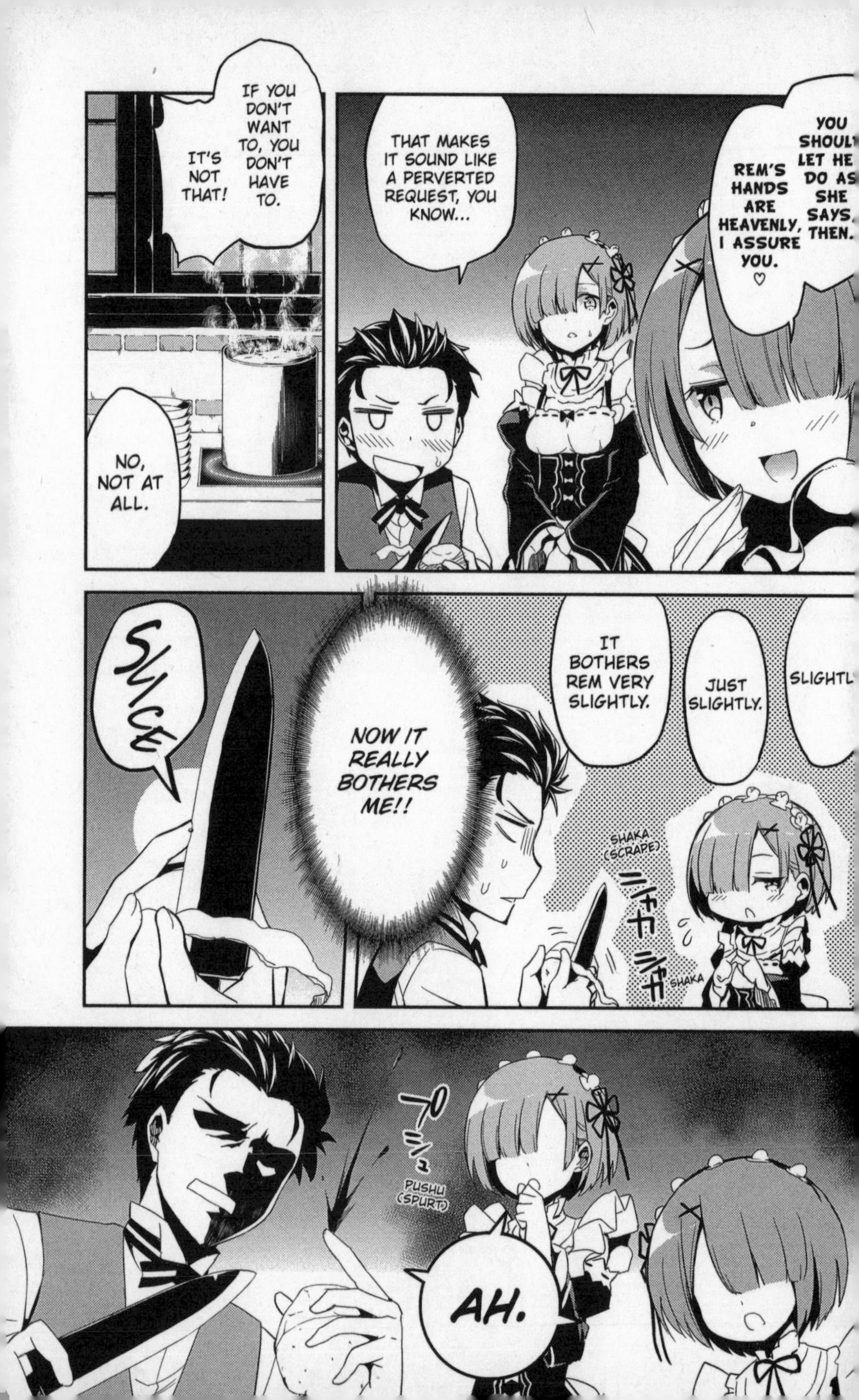
YOU SHOUL LET HE DO AS SHE SAYS, THEN.
REM'S HANDS ARE HEAVENLY, I ASSURE YOU. ♡
THAT MAKES IT SOUND LIKE A PERVERTED REQUEST, YOU KNOW...
IF YOU DON'T WANT TO, YOU DON'T HAVE TO.
IT'S NOT THAT!
NO, NOT AT ALL.
SLIGHTL
JUST SLIGHTLY.
IT BOTHERS REM VERY SLIGHTLY.
SHAKA (SCRAPE)
SHAKA
NOW IT REALLY BOTHERS ME!!
SLICE
PUSHU (SPURT)
AH.

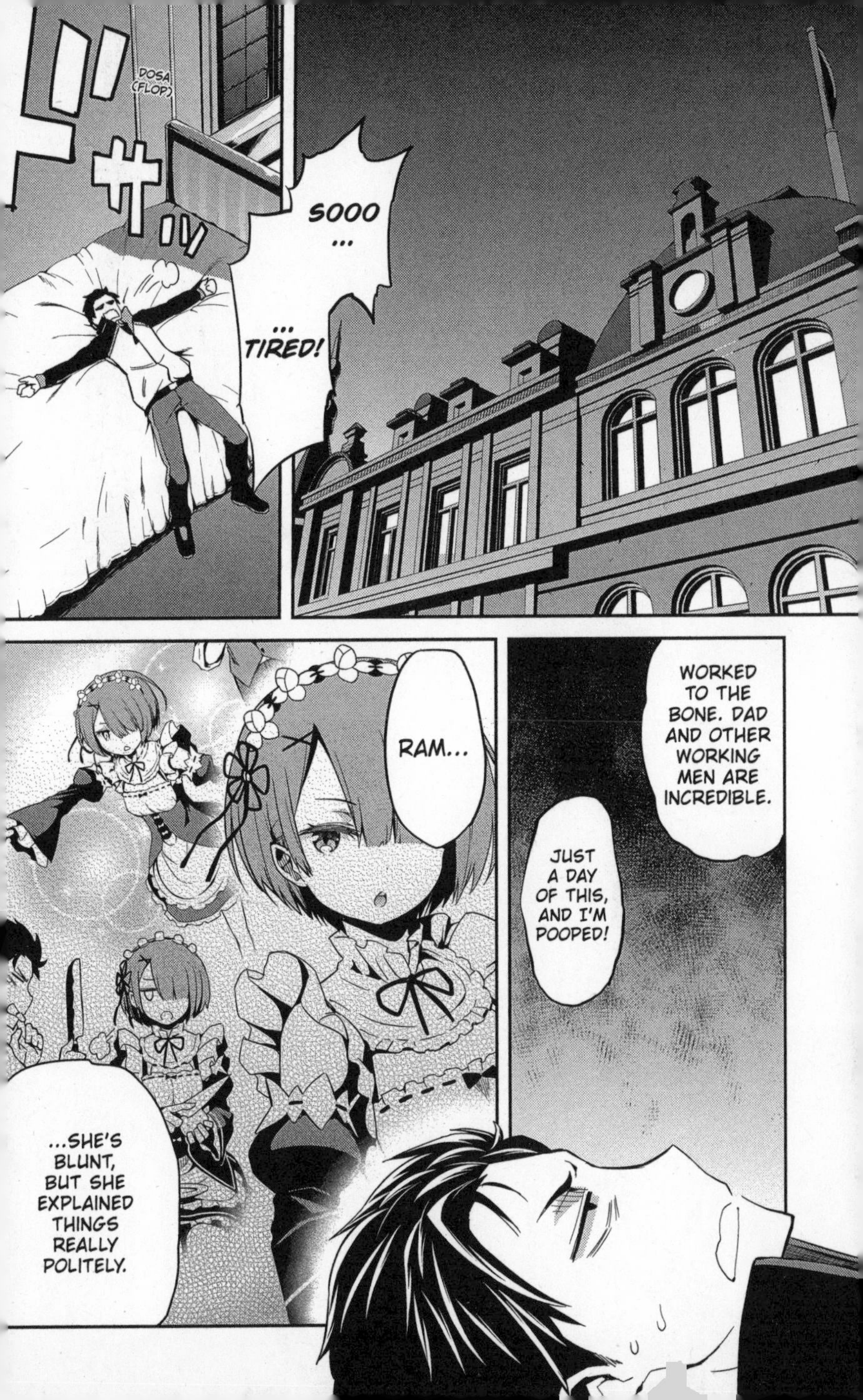
SOOO...
...TIRED!
DOSA (FLOP)
WORKED TO THE BONE. DAD AND OTHER WORKING MEN ARE INCREDIBLE.
JUST A DAY OF THIS, AND I'M POOPED!
RAM...
...SHE'S BLUNT, BUT SHE EXPLAINED THINGS REALLY POLITELY.

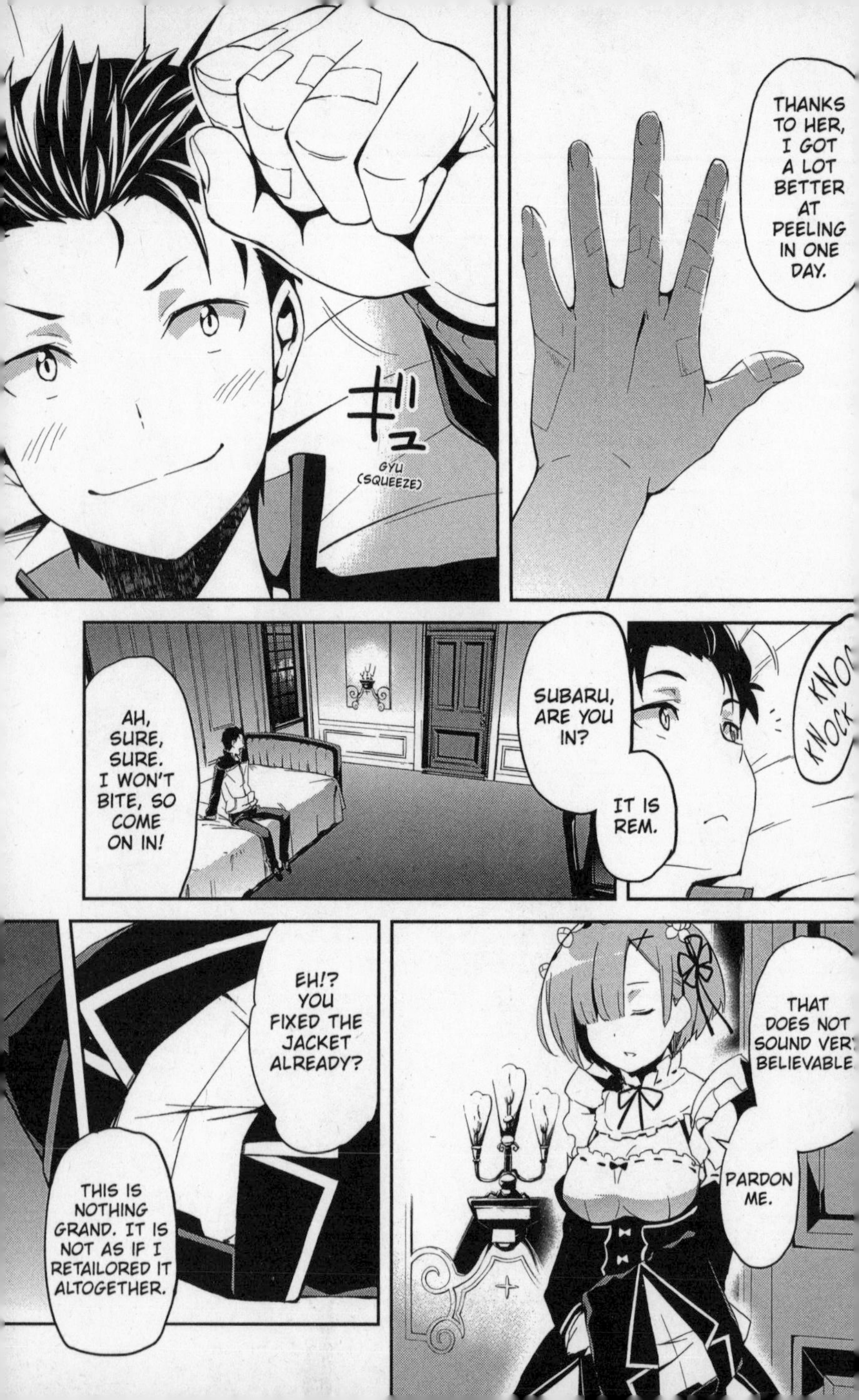
THANKS TO HER, I GOT A LOT BETTER AT PEELING IN ONE DAY.
ギュ
GYU (SQUEEZE)
KNOC
KNOCK
SUBARU, ARE YOU IN?
IT IS REM.
AH, SURE, SURE. I WON'T BITE, SO COME ON IN!
THAT DOES NOT SOUND VER BELIEVABLE
PARDON ME.
EH!? YOU FIXED THE JACKET ALREADY?
THIS IS NOTHING GRAND. IT IS NOT AS IF I RETAILORED IT ALTOGETHER.

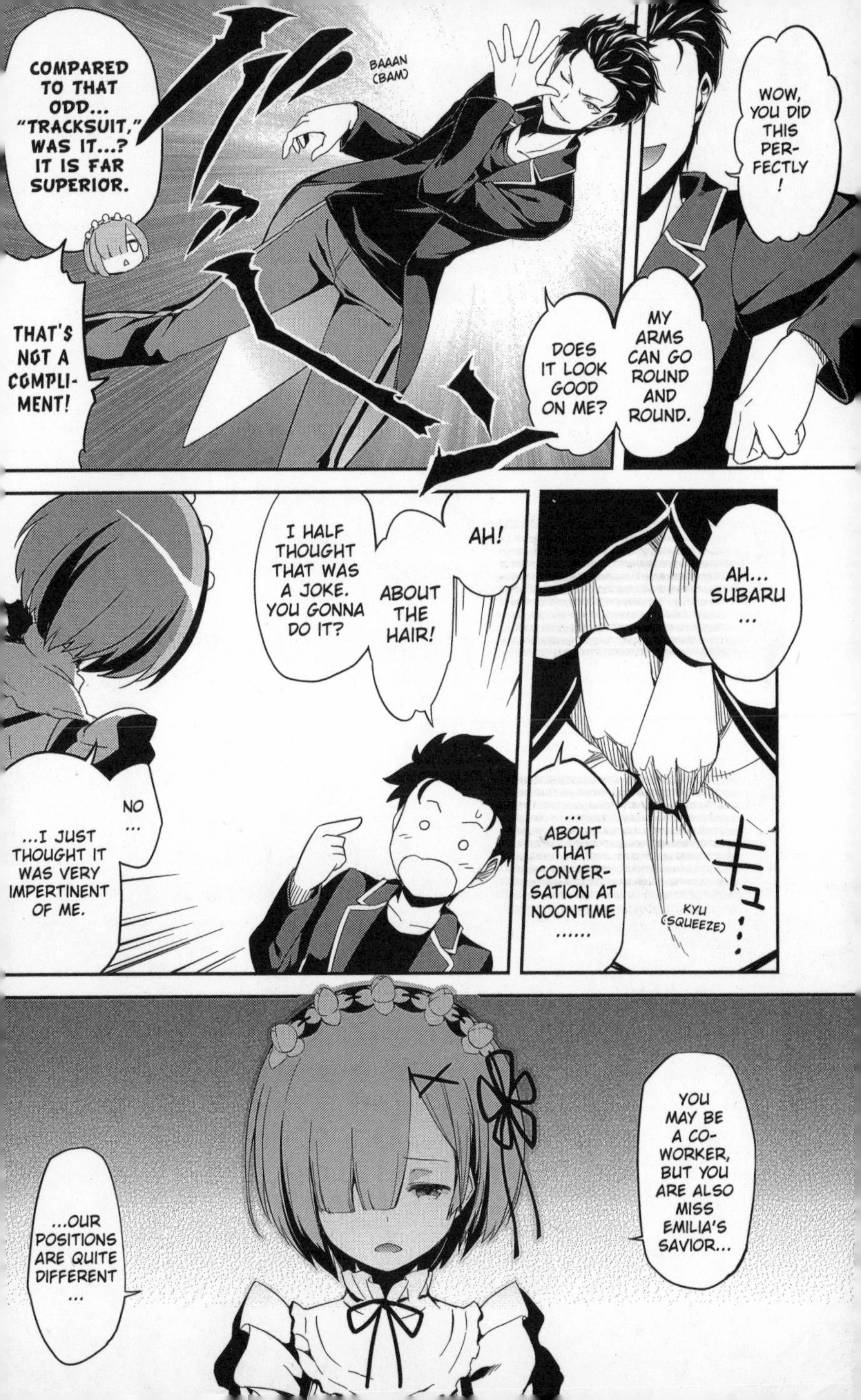
WOW, YOU DID THIS PERFECTLY!
MY ARMS CAN GO ROUND AND ROUND.
DOES IT LOOK GOOD ON ME?
BAAAN (BAM)
COMPARED TO THAT ODD... "TRACKSUIT," WAS IT...? IT IS FAR SUPERIOR.
THAT'S NOT A COMPLIMENT!
AH... SUBARU...
KYU (SQUEEZE)
...ABOUT THAT CONVERSATION AT NOONTIME ......
AH! ABOUT THE HAIR!
I HALF THOUGHT THAT WAS A JOKE. YOU GONNA DO IT?
NO...
...I JUST THOUGHT IT WAS VERY IMPERTINENT OF ME.
YOU MAY BE A CO-WORKER, BUT YOU ARE ALSO MISS EMILIA'S SAVIOR...
...OUR POSITIONS ARE QUITE DIFFERENT...

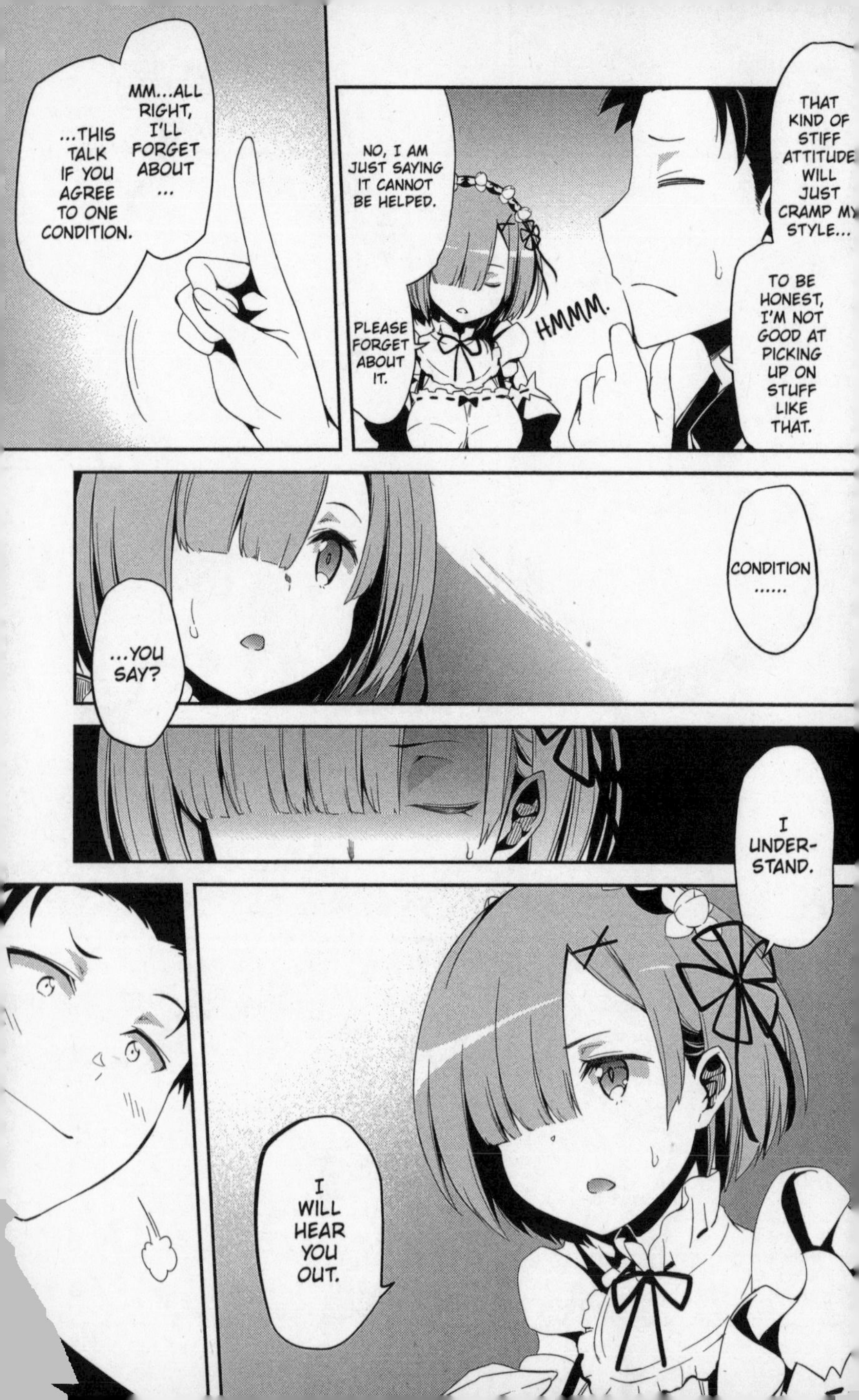
THAT KIND OF STIFF ATTITUDE WILL JUST CRAMP MY STYLE...
TO BE HONEST, I'M NOT GOOD AT PICKING UP ON STUFF LIKE THAT.
HMMM.
NO, I AM JUST SAYING IT CANNOT BE HELPED.
PLEASE FORGET ABOUT IT.
MM...ALL RIGHT, I'LL FORGET ABOUT ...
...THIS TALK IF YOU AGREE TO ONE CONDITION.
CONDITION ......
...YOU SAY?
I UNDER-STAND.
I WILL HEAR YOU OUT.

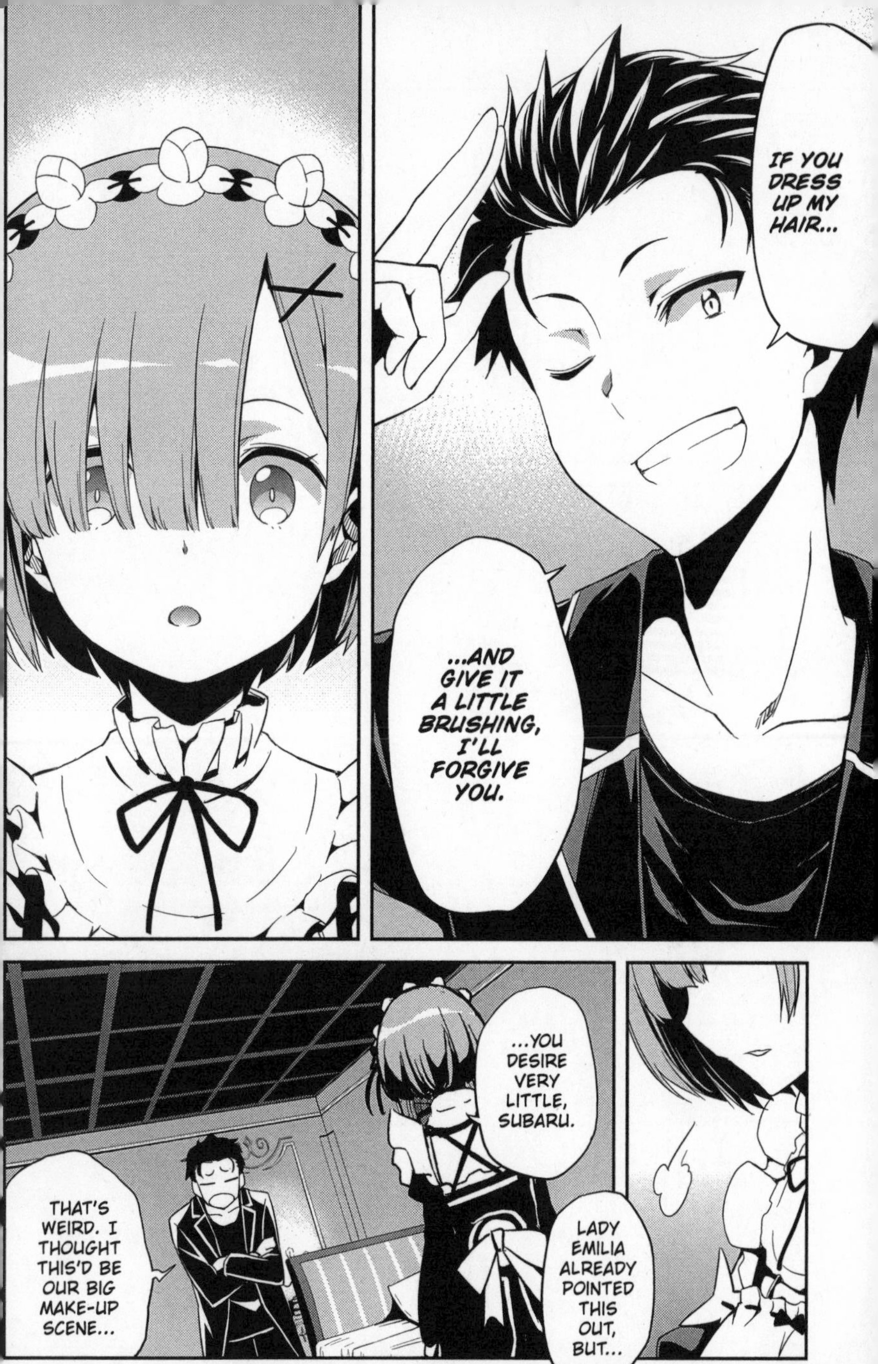
IF YOU DRESS UP MY HAIR...
...AND GIVE IT A LITTLE BRUSHING, I'LL FORGIVE YOU.
LADY EMILIA ALREADY POINTED THIS OUT, BUT...
...YOU DESIRE VERY LITTLE, SUBARU.
THAT'S WEIRD. I THOUGHT THIS'D BE OUR BIG MAKE-UP SCENE...

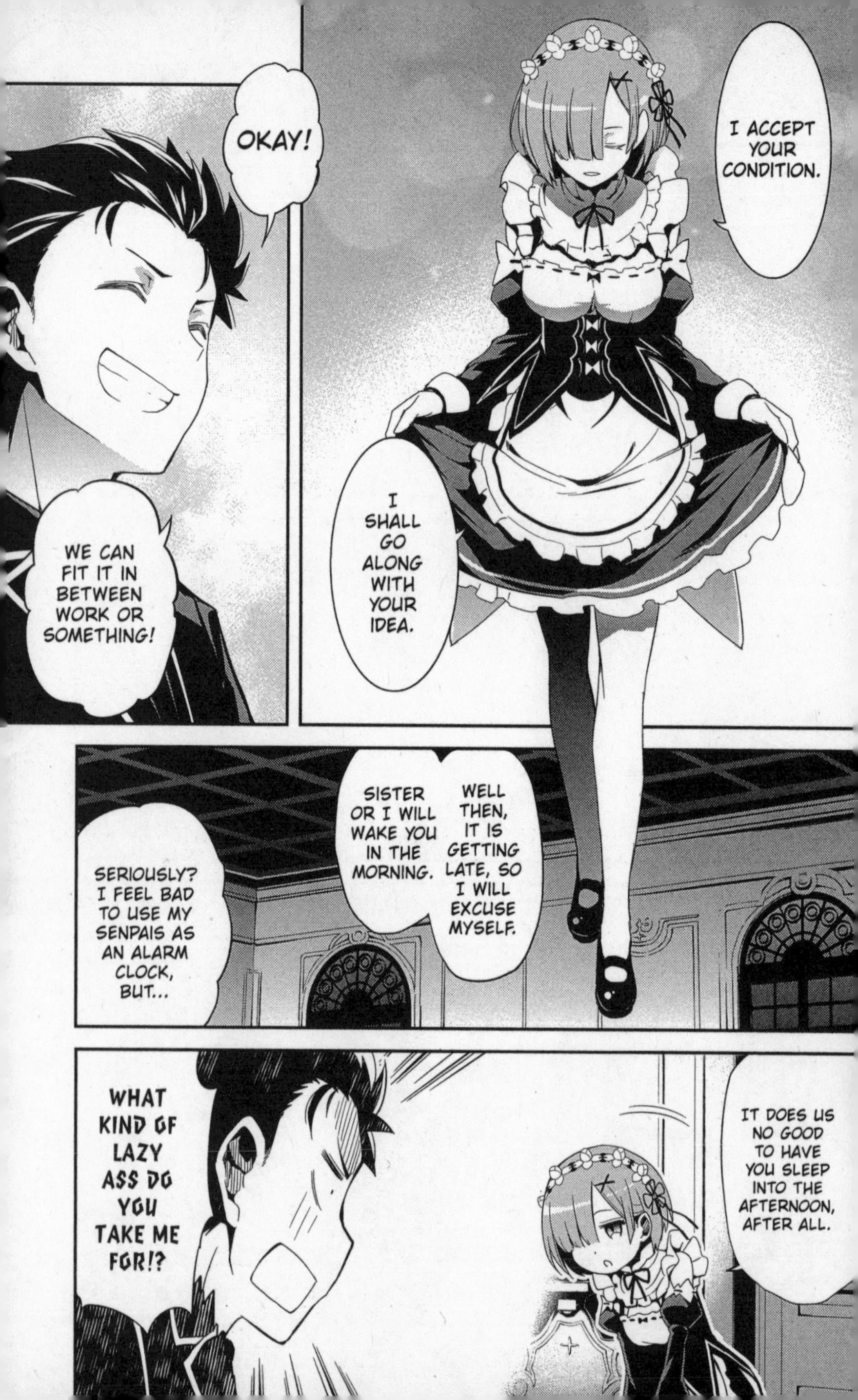
I ACCEPT YOUR CONDITION.
I SHALL GO ALONG WITH YOUR IDEA.
OKAY!
WE CAN FIT IT IN BETWEEN WORK OR SOMETHING!
WELL THEN, IT IS GETTING LATE, SO I WILL EXCUSE MYSELF.
SISTER OR I WILL WAKE YOU IN THE MORNING.
SERIOUSLY? I FEEL BAD TO USE MY SENPAIS AS AN ALARM CLOCK, BUT...
IT DOES US NO GOOD TO HAVE YOU SLEEP INTO THE AFTERNOON, AFTER ALL.
WHAT KIND OF LAZY ASS DO YOU TAKE ME FOR!?

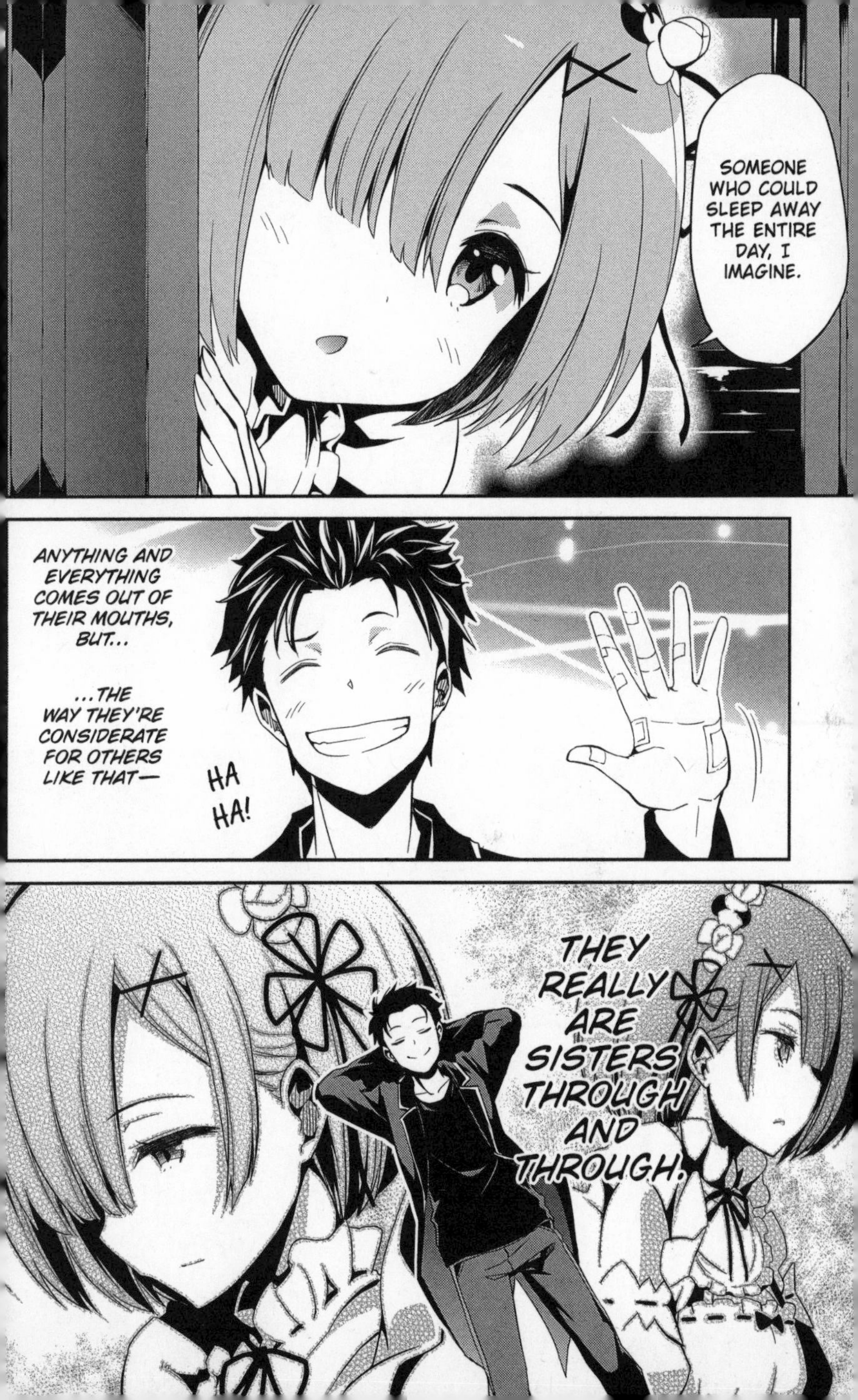
SOMEONE WHO COULD SLEEP AWAY THE ENTIRE DAY, I IMAGINE.
ANYTHING AND EVERYTHING COMES OUT OF THEIR MOUTHS, BUT...
...THE WAY THEY'RE CONSIDERATE FOR OTHERS LIKE THAT—
HA HA!
THEY REALLY ARE SISTERS THROUGH AND THROUGH.

Working life Subaru!
If only I could have Ram and Rem at my workplace...!

Re:ZeRo

-Starting Life in Another World-

A Week at the Mansion

The only ability Subaru Natsuki gets when he's summoned to another world is time travel via his own death. But to save her, he'll die as many times as it takes.

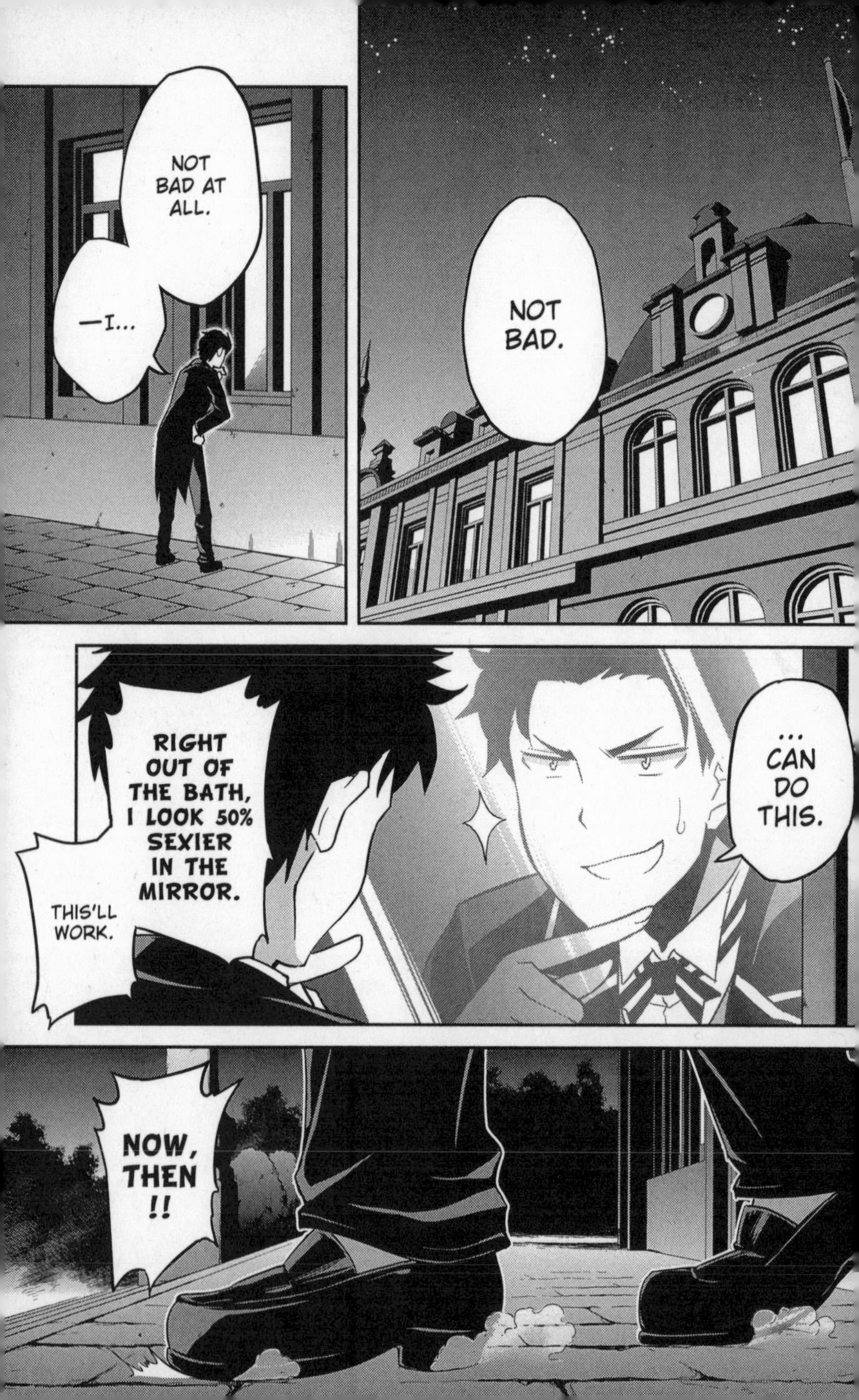
NOT BAD.
NOT BAD AT ALL.
—I...
...CAN DO THIS.
RIGHT OUT OF THE BATH, I LOOK 50% SEXIER IN THE MIRROR.
THIS'LL WORK.
NOW, THEN!!

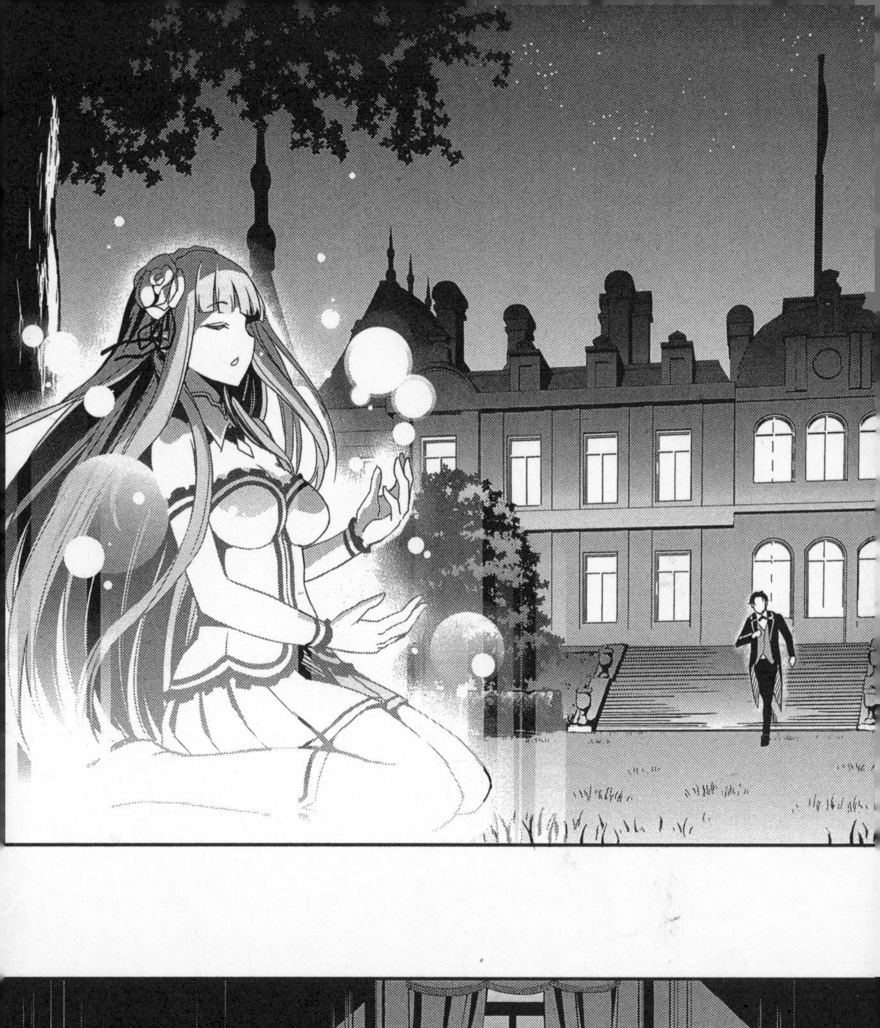
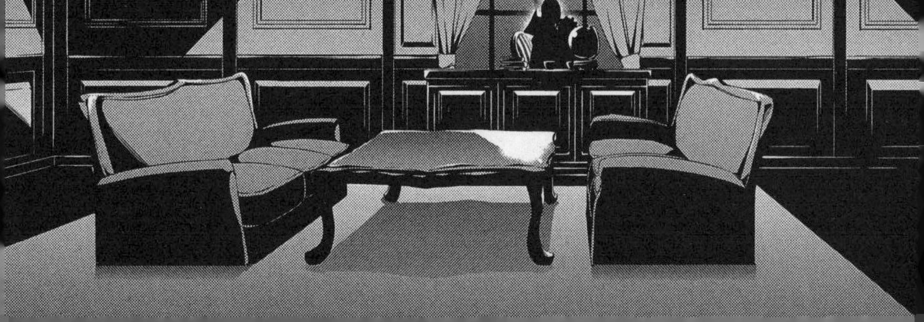

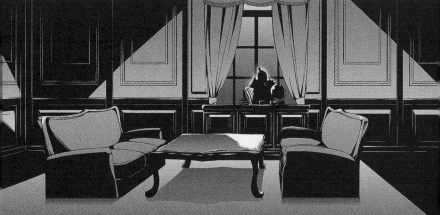

Episode 4 The Promised Morn Grows Distant

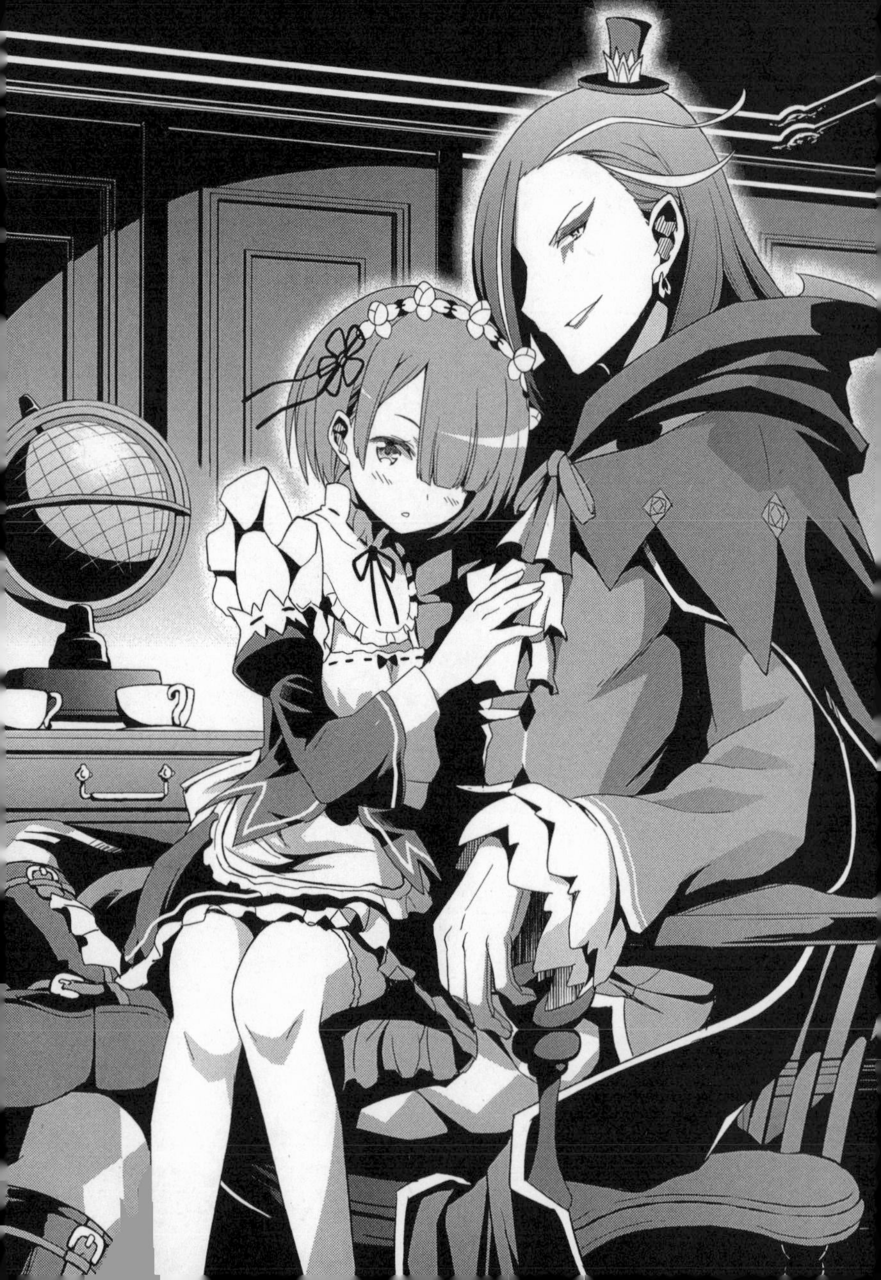

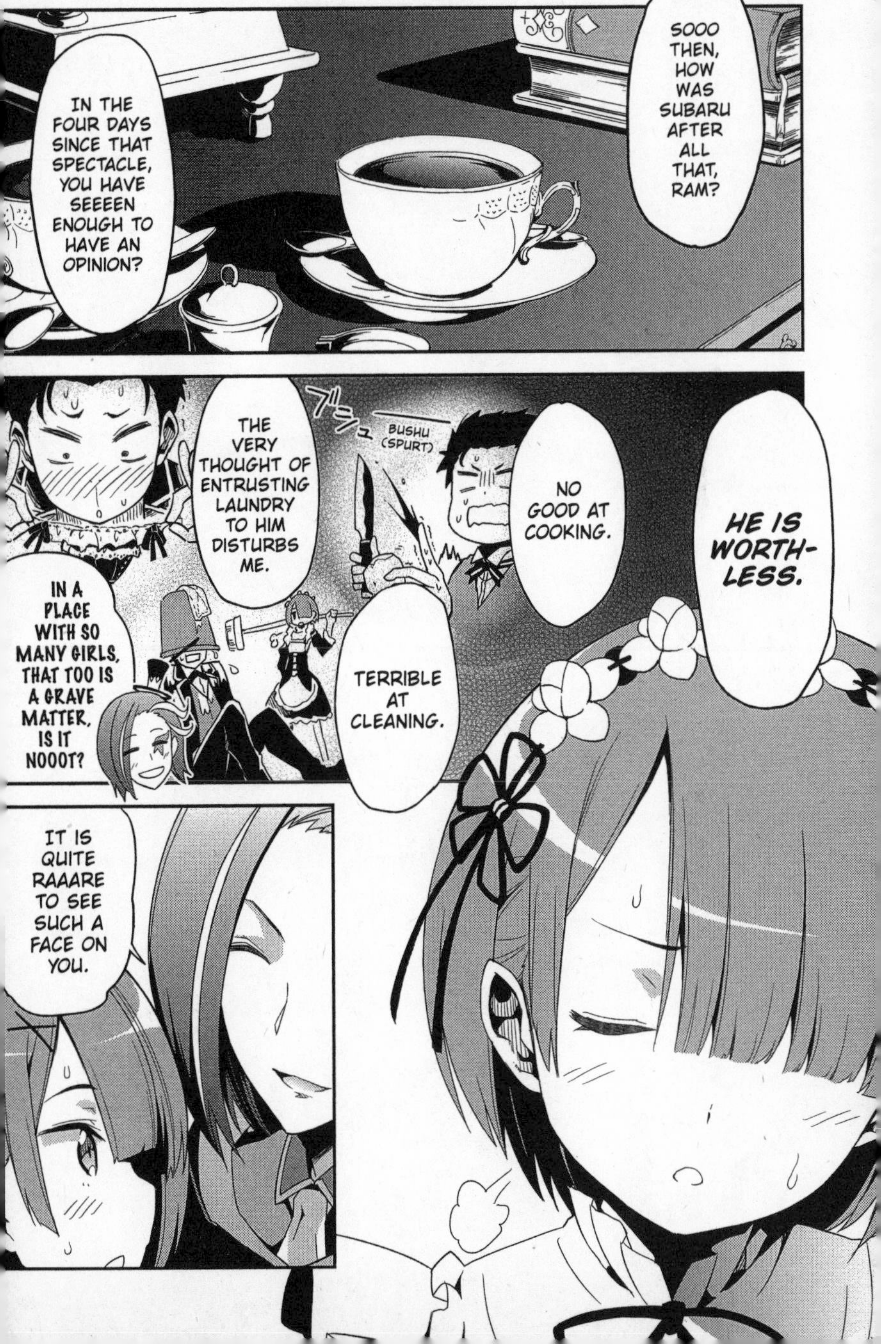
SOOO THEN, HOW WAS SUBARU AFTER ALL THAT, RAM?
IN THE FOUR DAYS SINCE THAT SPECTACLE, YOU HAVE SEEEEN ENOUGH TO HAVE AN OPINION?
HE IS WORTHLESS.
NO GOOD AT COOKING.
BUSHU (SPURT)
TERRIBLE AT CLEANING.
THE VERY THOUGHT OF ENTRUSTING LAUNDRY TO HIM DISTURBS ME.
IN A PLACE WITH SO MANY GIRLS, THAT TOO IS A GRAVE MATTER, IS IT NOOOT?
IT IS QUITE RAAARE TO SEE SUCH A FACE ON YOU.

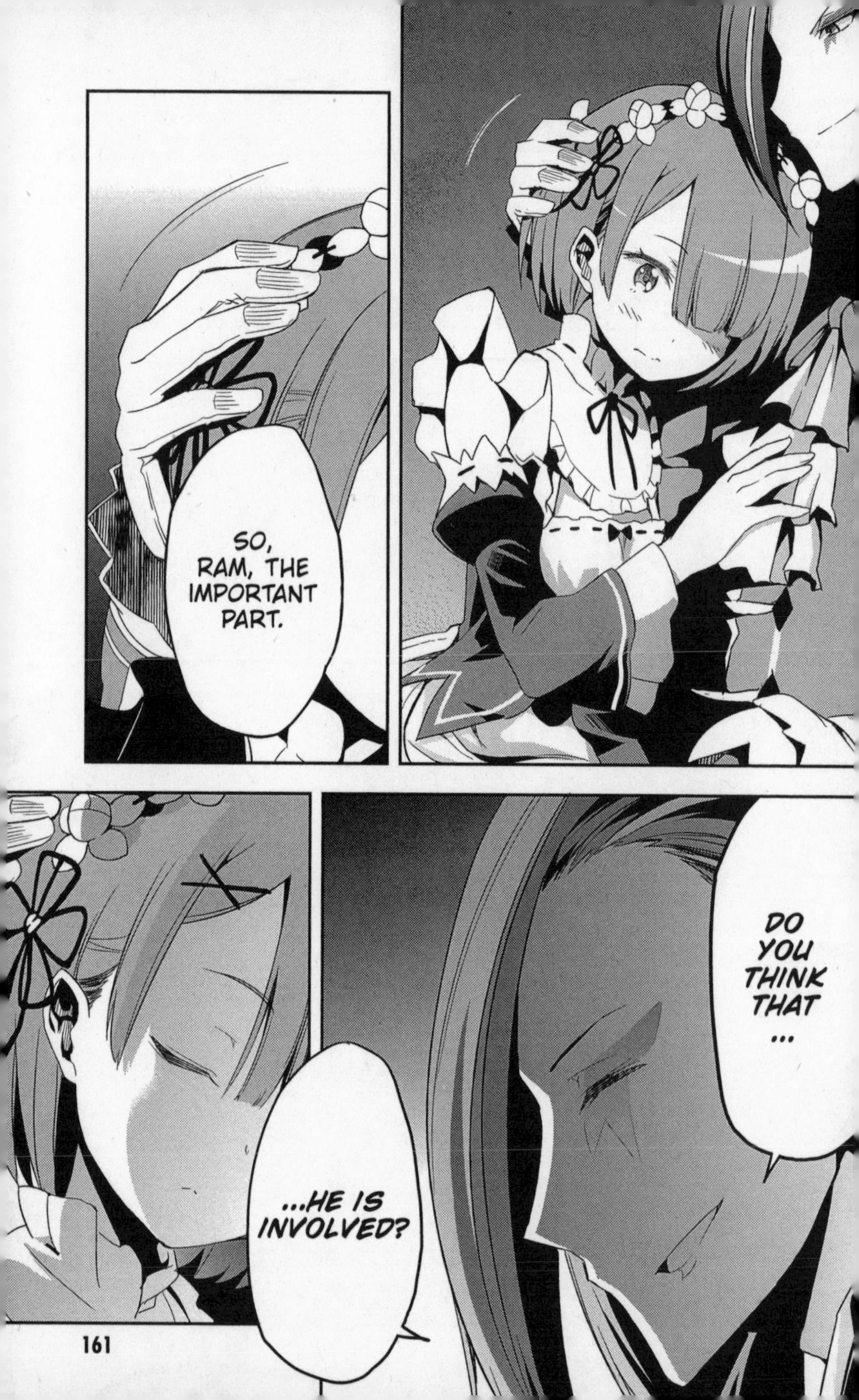
SO, RAM, THE IMPORTANT PART.
DO YOU THINK THAT ...
...HE IS INVOLVED?

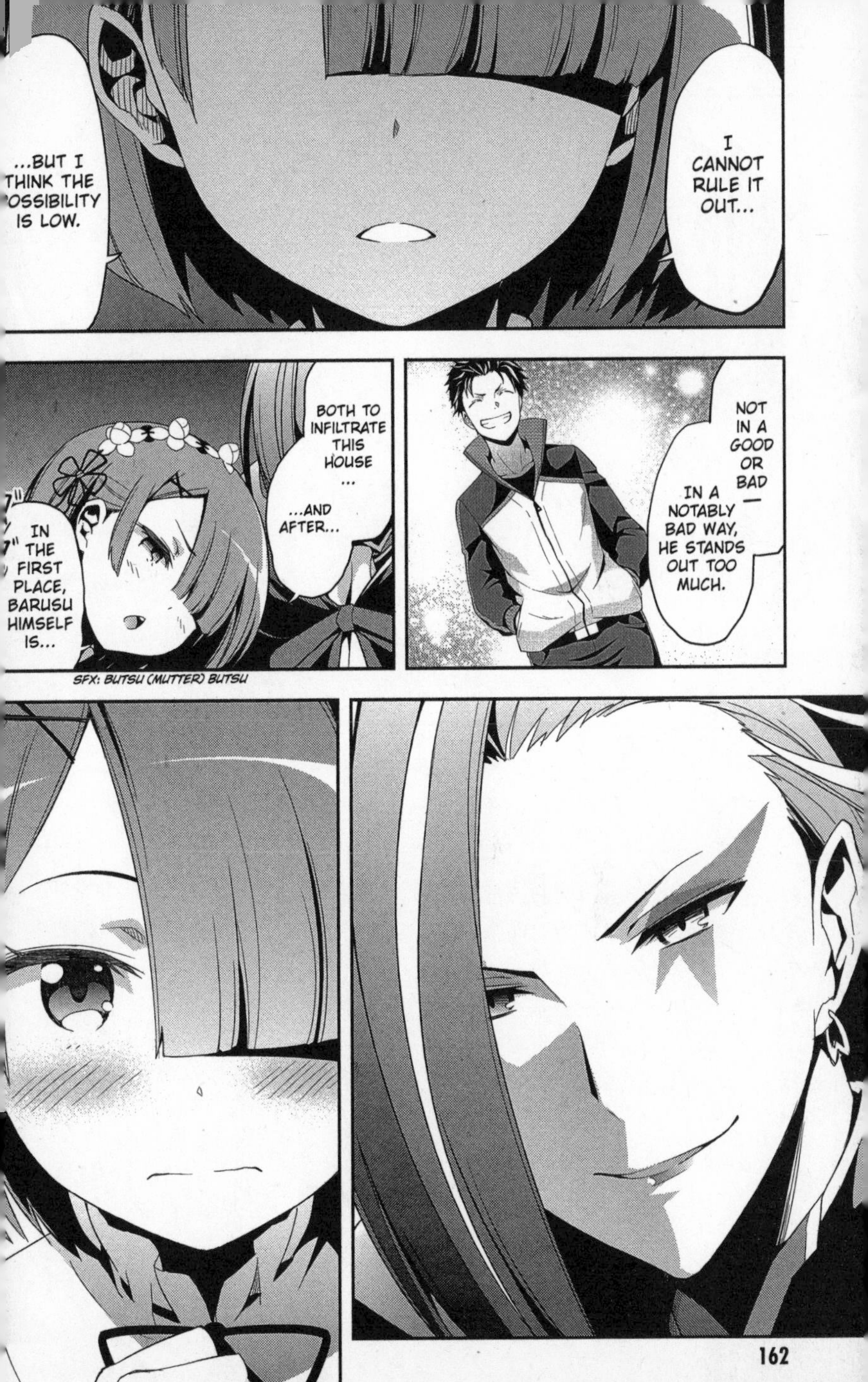
I CANNOT RULE IT OUT...
...BUT I THINK THE OSSIBILITY IS LOW.
NOT IN A GOOD OR BAD—
IN A NOTABLY BAD WAY, HE STANDS OUT TOO MUCH.
BOTH TO INFILTRATE THIS HOUSE ...
...AND AFTER...
IN THE FIRST PLACE, BARUSU HIMSELF IS...
SFX: BUTSU (MUTTER) BUTSU

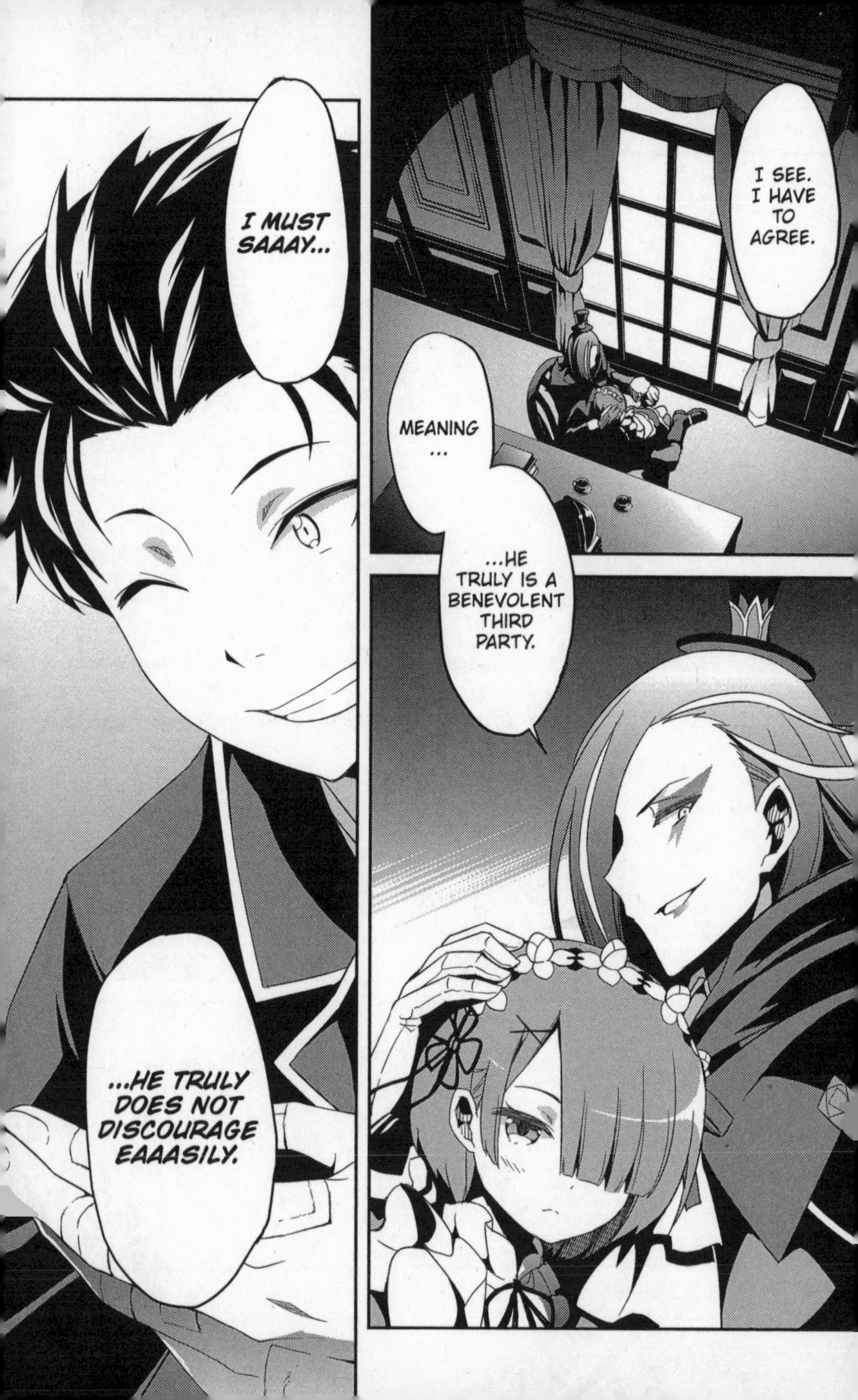
I SEE. I HAVE TO AGREE.
MEANING ...
...HE TRULY IS A BENEVOLENT THIRD PARTY.
I MUST SAAAY...
...HE TRULY DOES NOT DISCOURAGE EAAASILY.

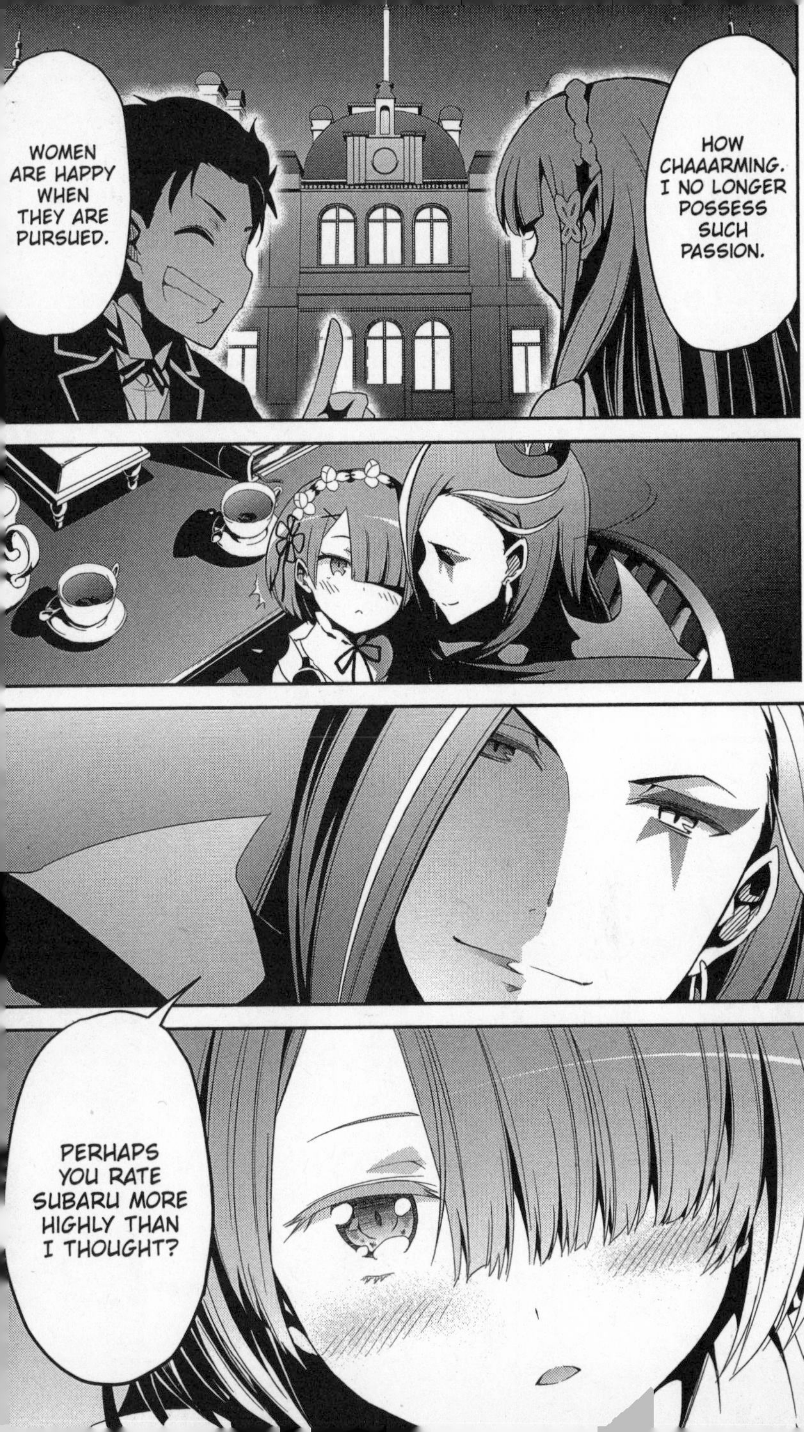
HOW CHAAARMING. I NO LONGER POSSESS SUCH PASSION.
WOMEN ARE HAPPY WHEN THEY ARE PURSUED.
PERHAPS YOU RATE SUBARU MORE HIGHLY THAN I THOUGHT?

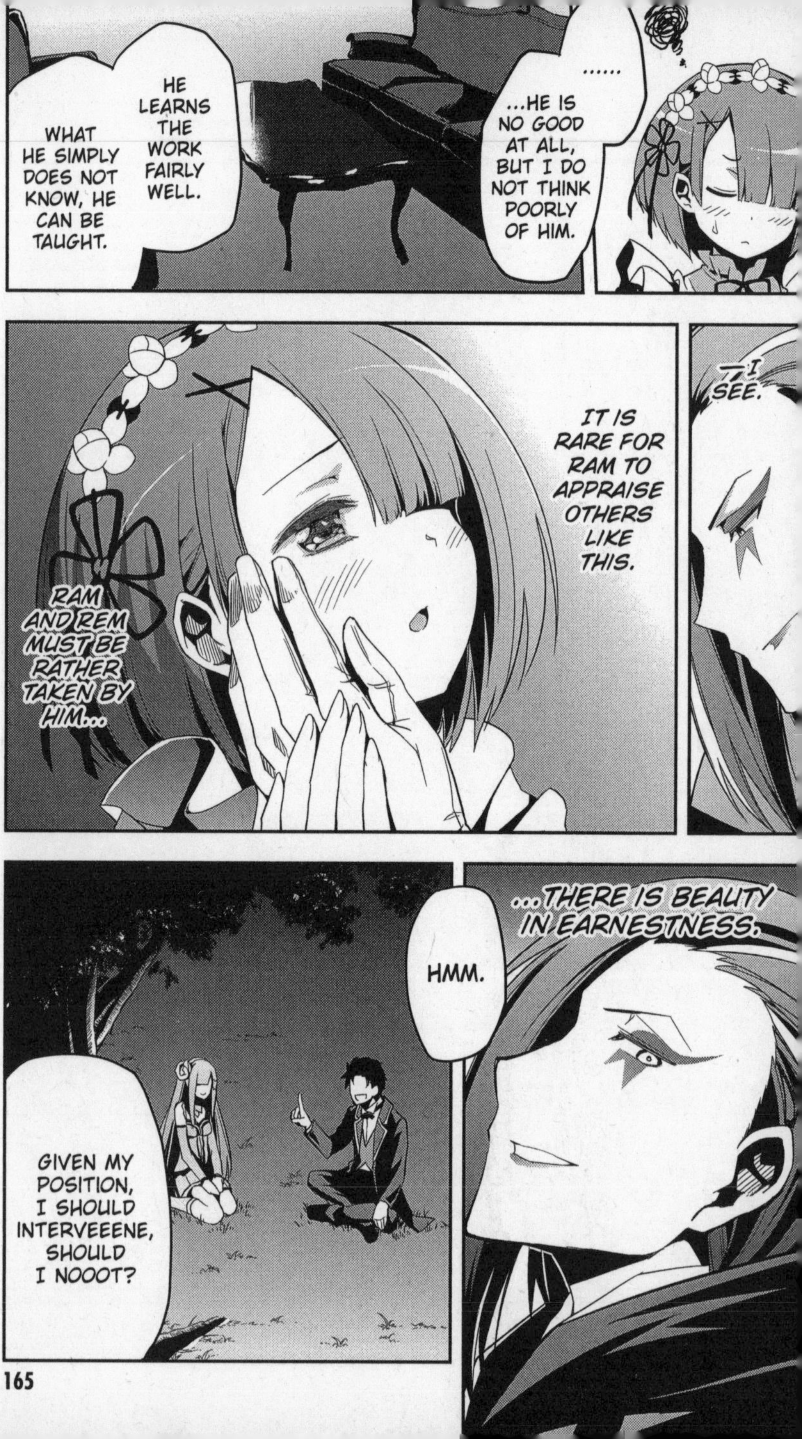
......
...HE IS NO GOOD AT ALL, BUT I DO NOT THINK POORLY OF HIM.
HE LEARNS THE WORK FAIRLY WELL.
WHAT HE SIMPLY DOES NOT KNOW, HE CAN BE TAUGHT.
—I SEE.
IT IS RARE FOR RAM TO APPRAISE OTHERS LIKE THIS.
RAM AND REM MUST BE RATHER TAKEN BY HIM...
...THERE IS BEAUTY IN EARNESTNESS.
HMM.
GIVEN MY POSITION, I SHOULD INTERVEEENE, SHOULD I NOOOT?

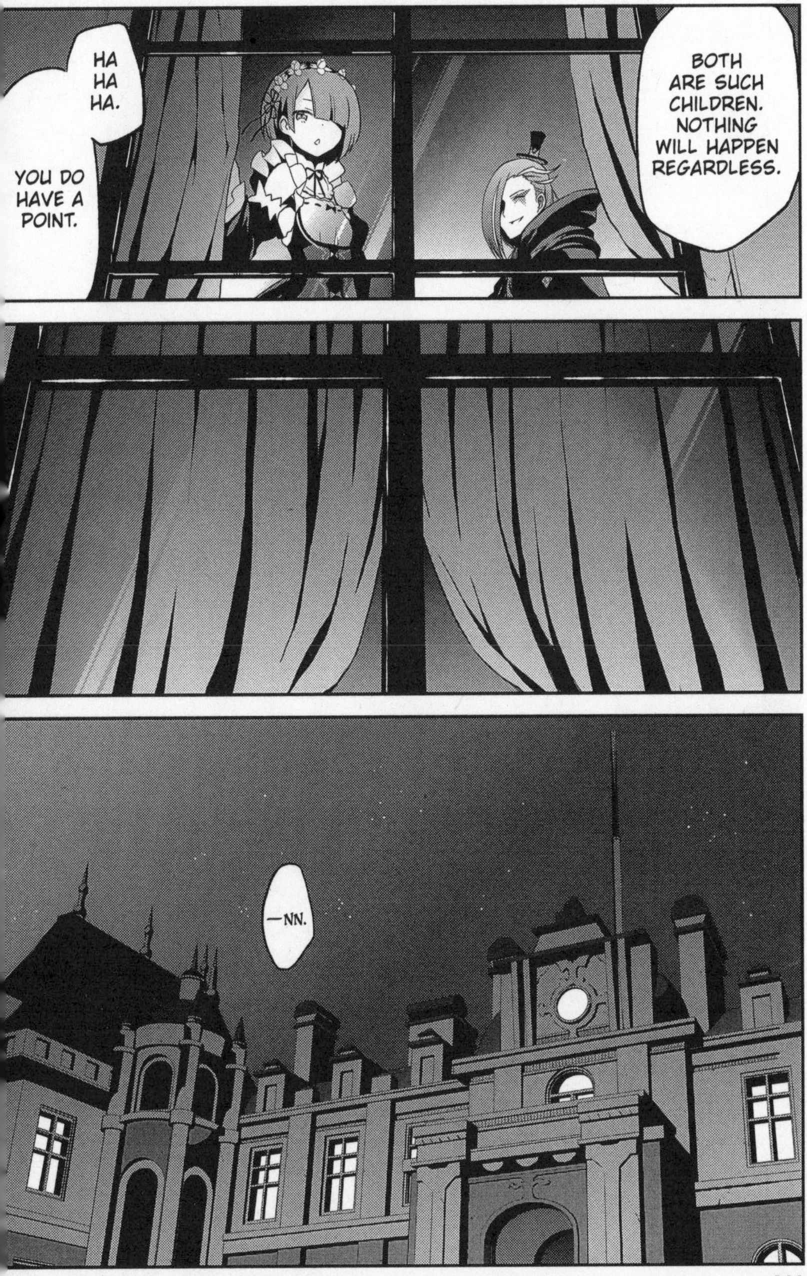
BOTH ARE SUCH CHILDREN. NOTHING WILL HAPPEN REGARDLESS.
HA HA HA.
YOU DO HAVE A POINT.
—NN.

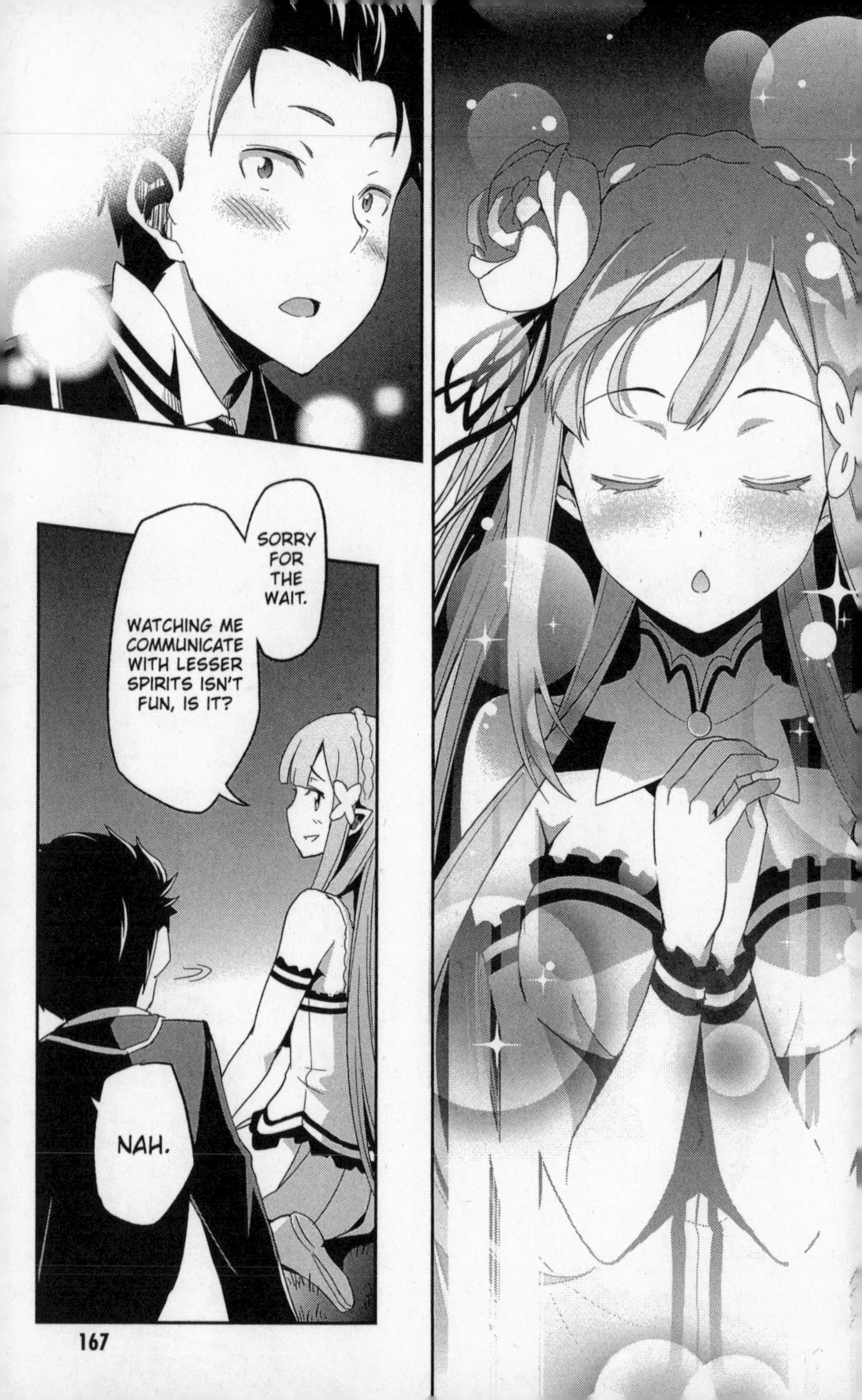
SORRY FOR THE WAIT.
WATCHING ME COMMUNICATE WITH LESSER SPIRITS ISN'T FUN, IS IT?
NAH.

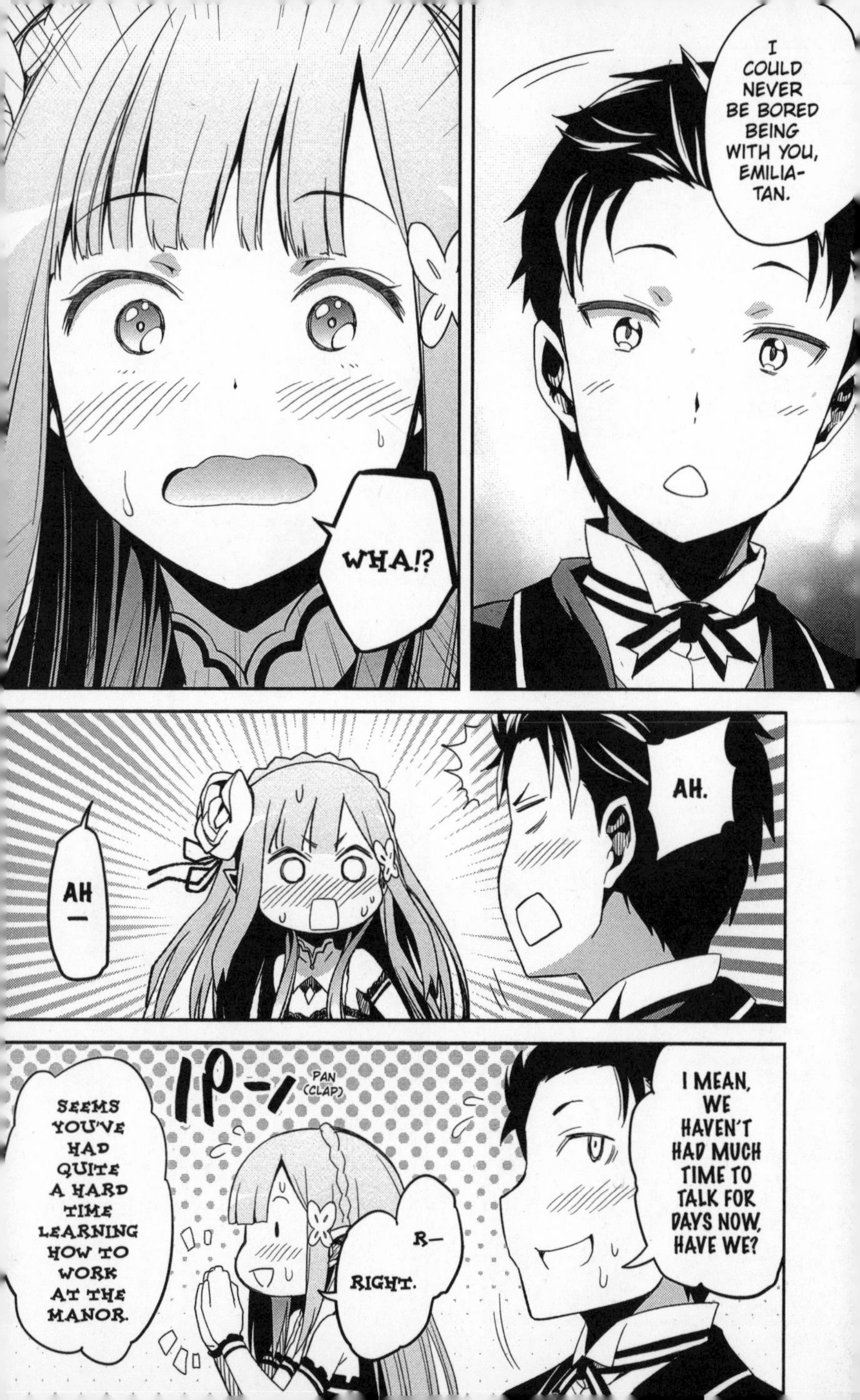

I COULD NEVER BE BORED BEING WITH YOU, EMILIA-TAN.
WHA!?
AH.
AH—
I MEAN, WE HAVEN'T HAD MUCH TIME TO TALK FOR DAYS NOW, HAVE WE?
PAN (CLAP)
R— RIGHT.
SEEMS YOU'VE HAD QUITE A HARD TIME LEARNING HOW TO WORK AT THE MANOR.

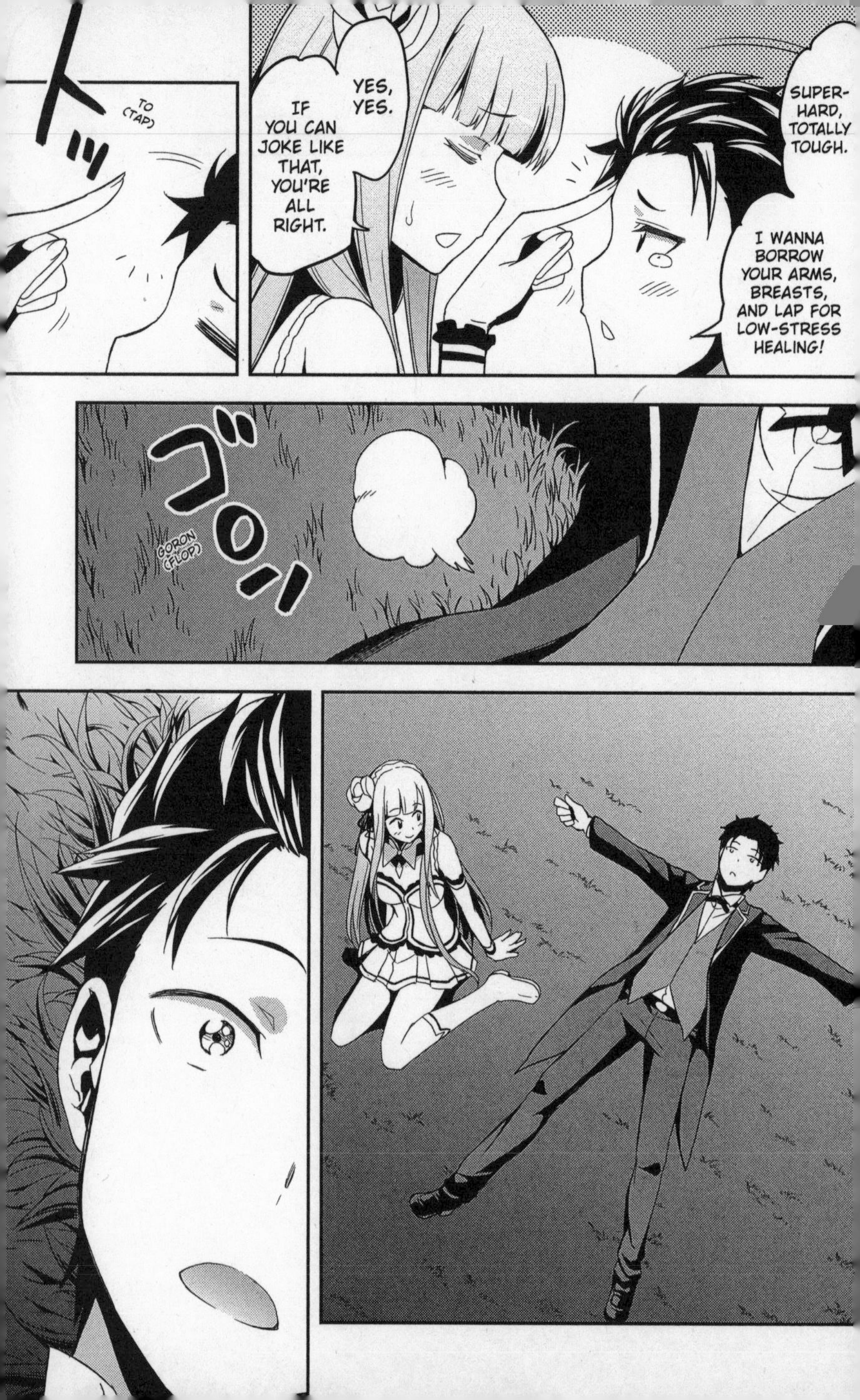
SUPER-HARD, TOTALLY TOUGH.
I WANNA BORROW YOUR ARMS, BREASTS, AND LAP FOR LOW-STRESS HEALING!
YES, YES.
IF YOU CAN JOKE LIKE THAT, YOU'RE ALL RIGHT.
トッ
TO (TAP)
ゴロッ
GORON (FLOP)

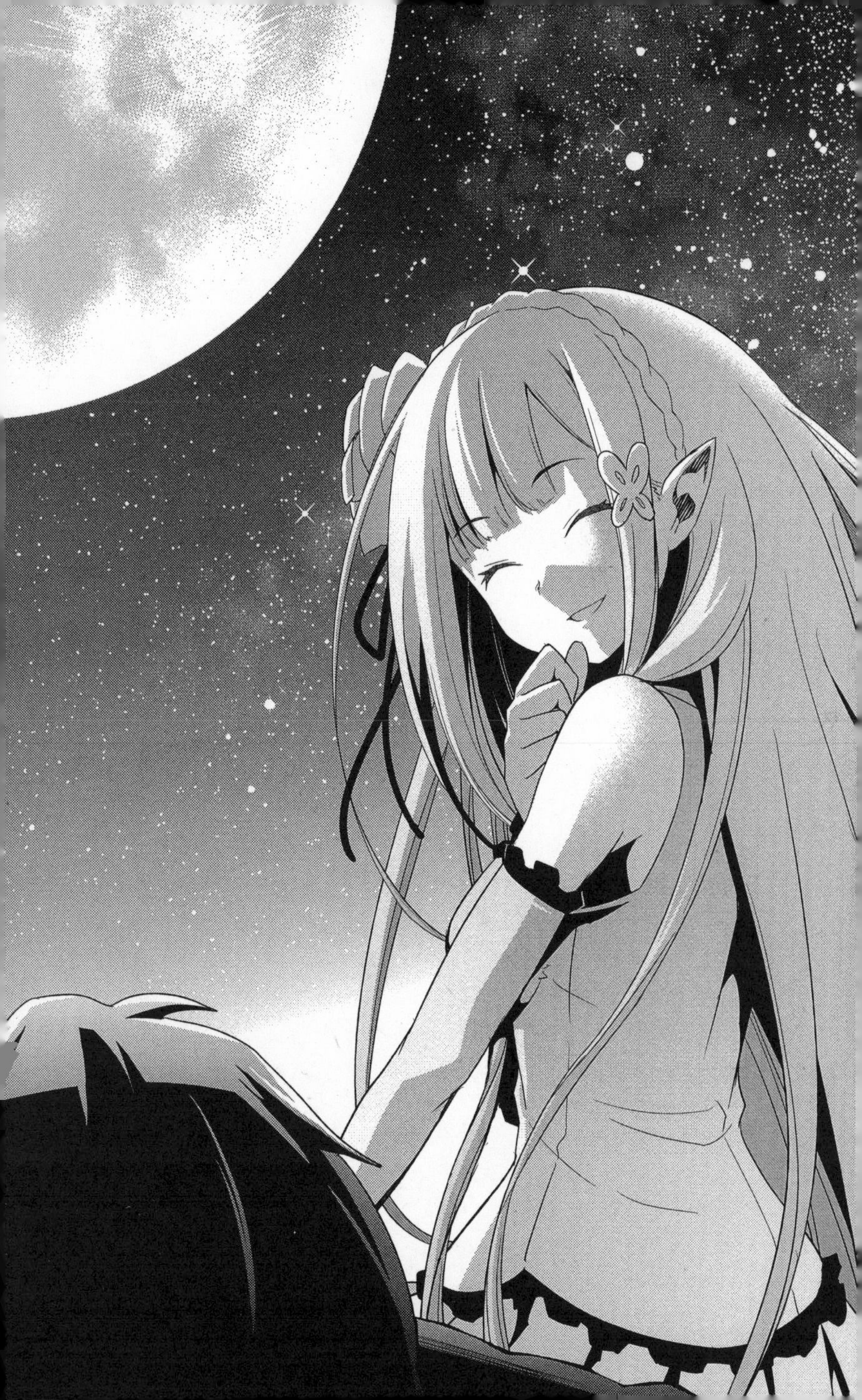

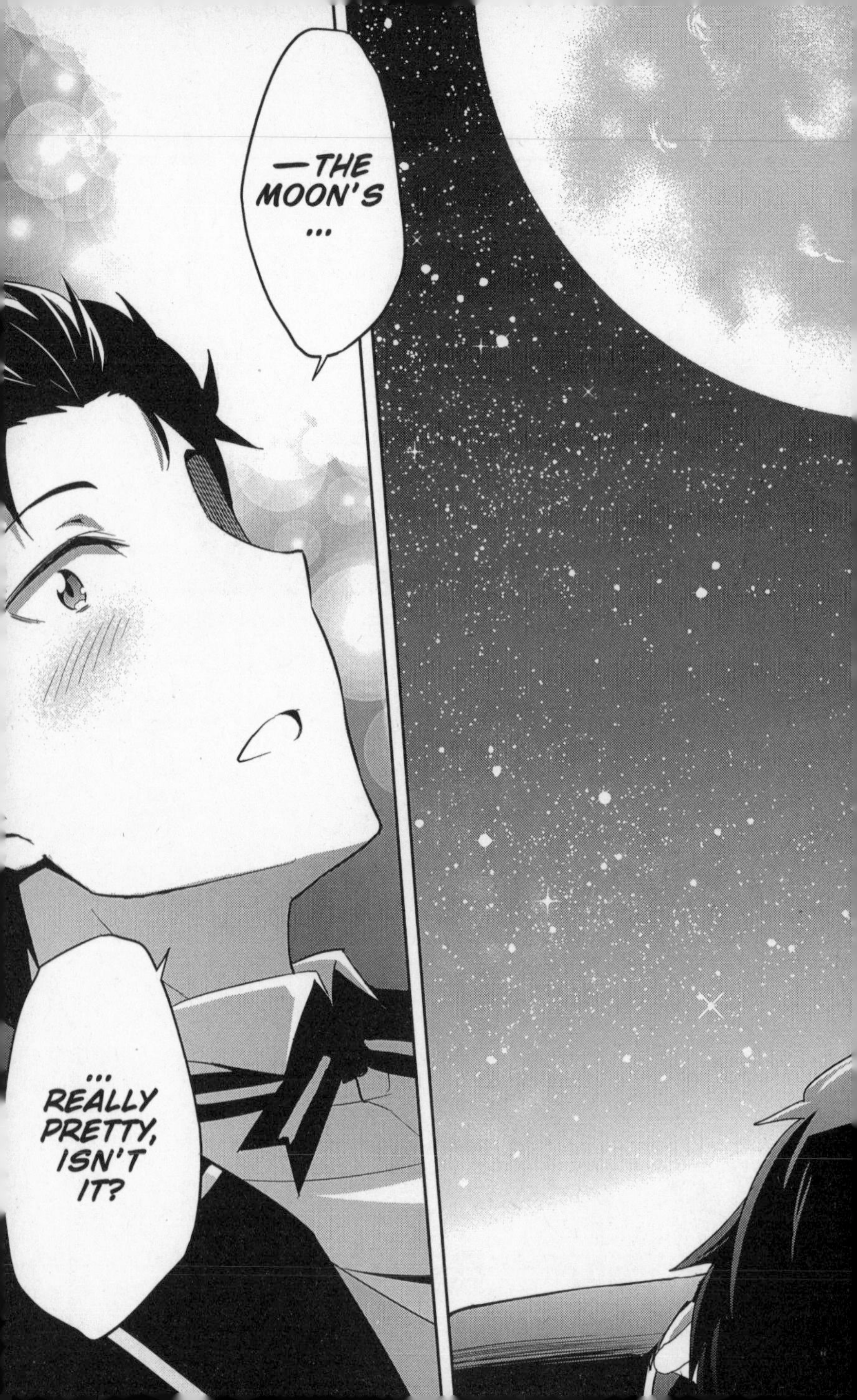
—THE MOON'S ...
... REALLY PRETTY, ISN'T IT?

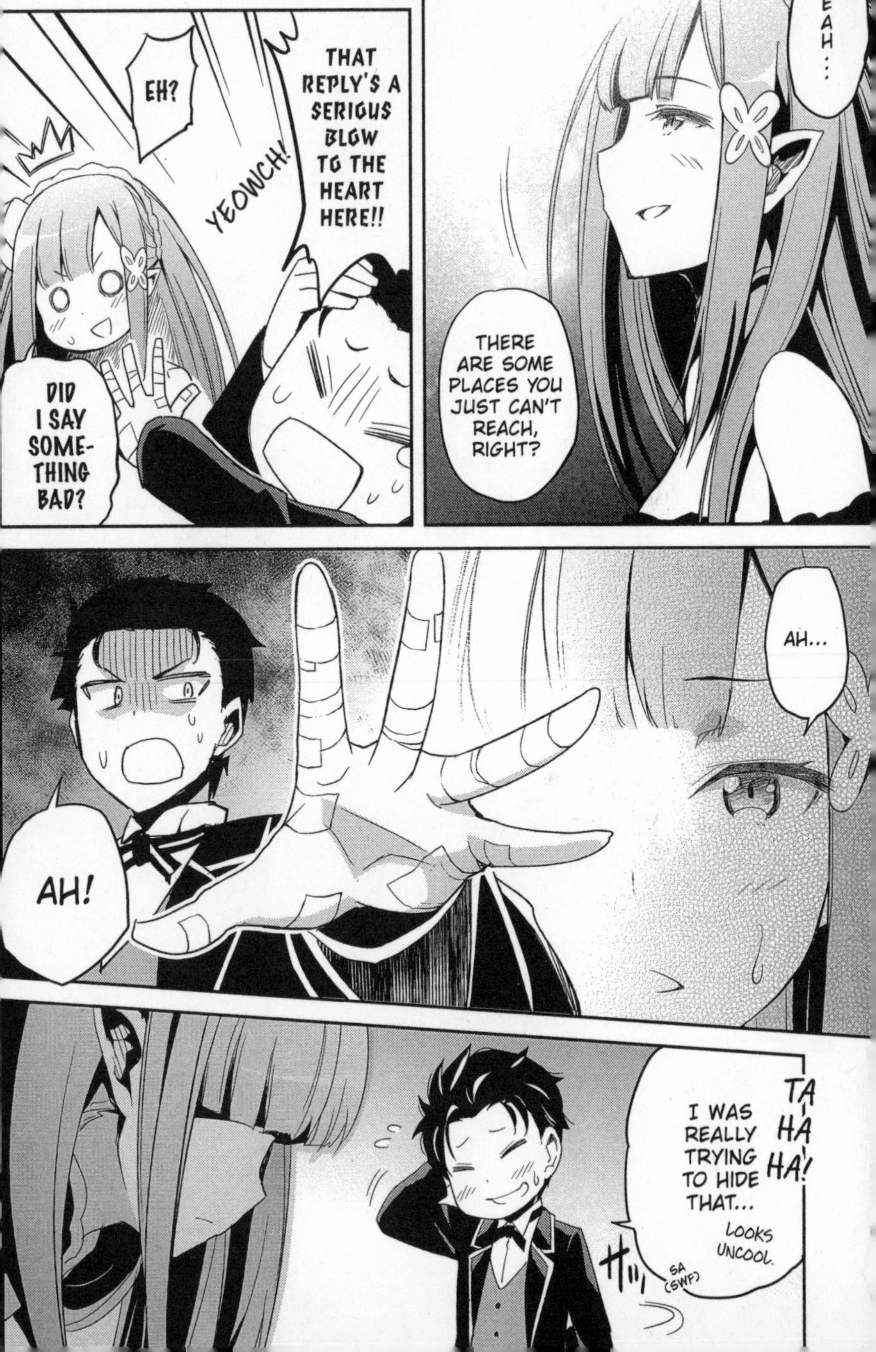
YEAH...
THERE ARE SOME PLACES YOU JUST CAN'T REACH, RIGHT?
THAT REPLY'S A SERIOUS BLOW TO THE HEART HERE!!
YEOWCH!
EH?
DID I SAY SOME-THING BAD?
AH...
AH!
TA HA HA!
I WAS REALLY TRYING TO HIDE THAT...
LOOKS UNCOOL.
SA (SWF)

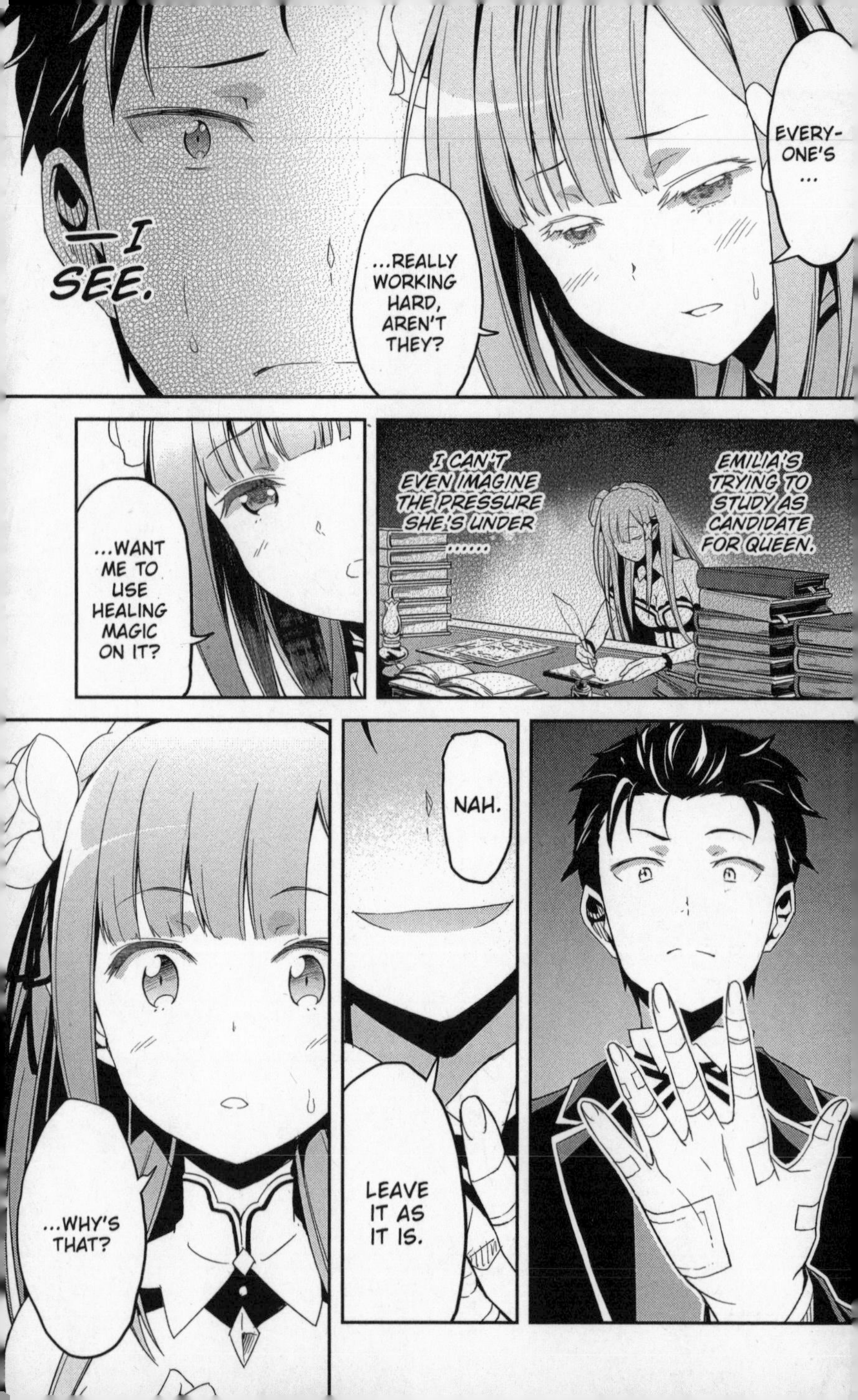
EVERY-ONE'S ...
...REALLY WORKING HARD, AREN'T THEY?
—I SEE.
EMILIA'S TRYING TO STUDY AS CANDIDATE FOR QUEEN.
I CAN'T EVEN IMAGINE THE PRESSURE SHE'S UNDER ......
...WANT ME TO USE HEALING MAGIC ON IT?
NAH.
LEAVE IT AS IT IS.
...WHY'S THAT?

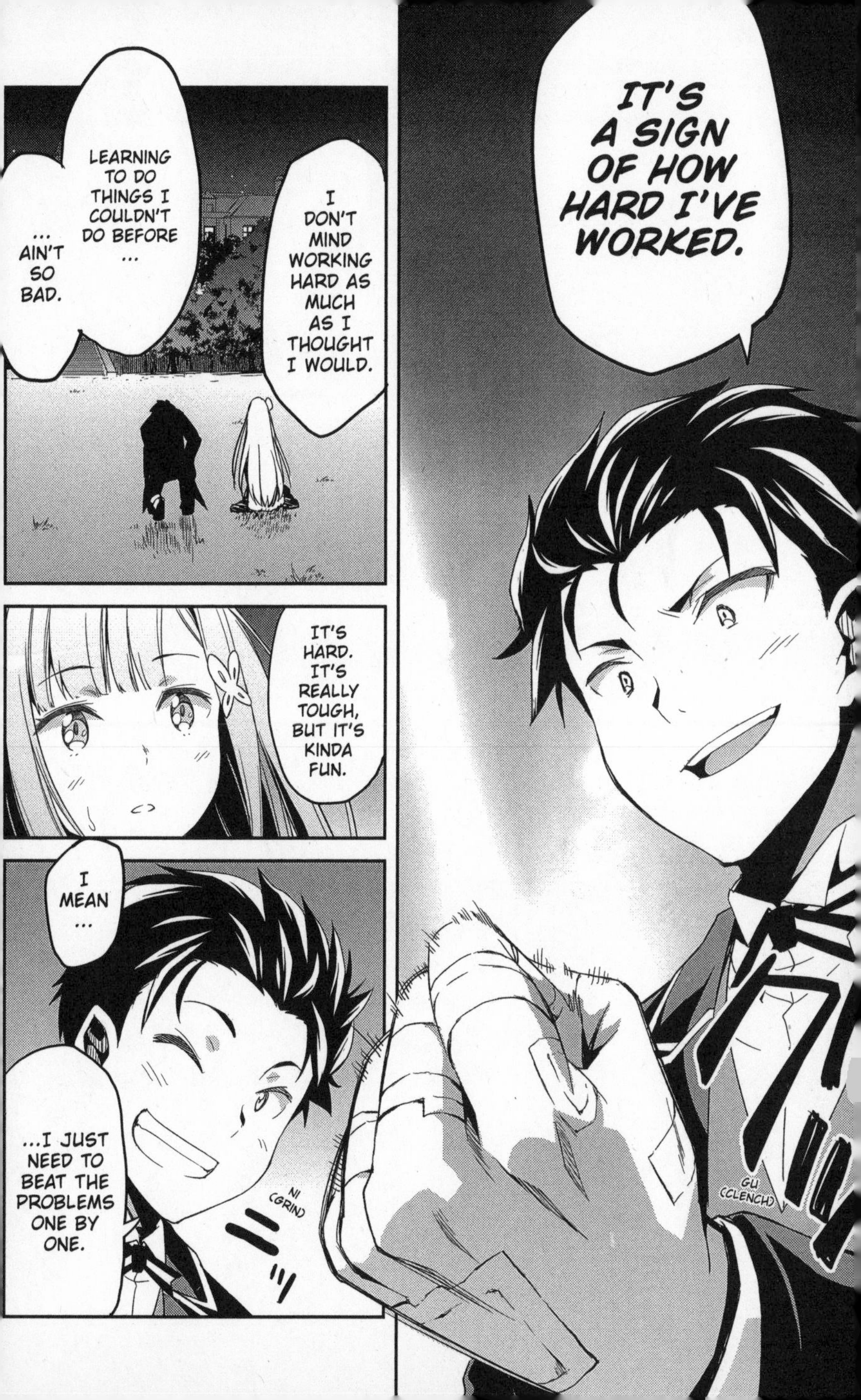
IT'S A SIGN OF HOW HARD I'VE WORKED.
GU (CLENCH)
I DON'T MIND WORKING HARD AS MUCH AS I THOUGHT I WOULD.
LEARNING TO DO THINGS I COULDN'T DO BEFORE ...
... AIN'T SO BAD.
IT'S HARD. IT'S REALLY TOUGH, BUT IT'S KINDA FUN.
I MEAN ...
NI (GRIN)
...I JUST NEED TO BEAT THE PROBLEMS ONE BY ONE.

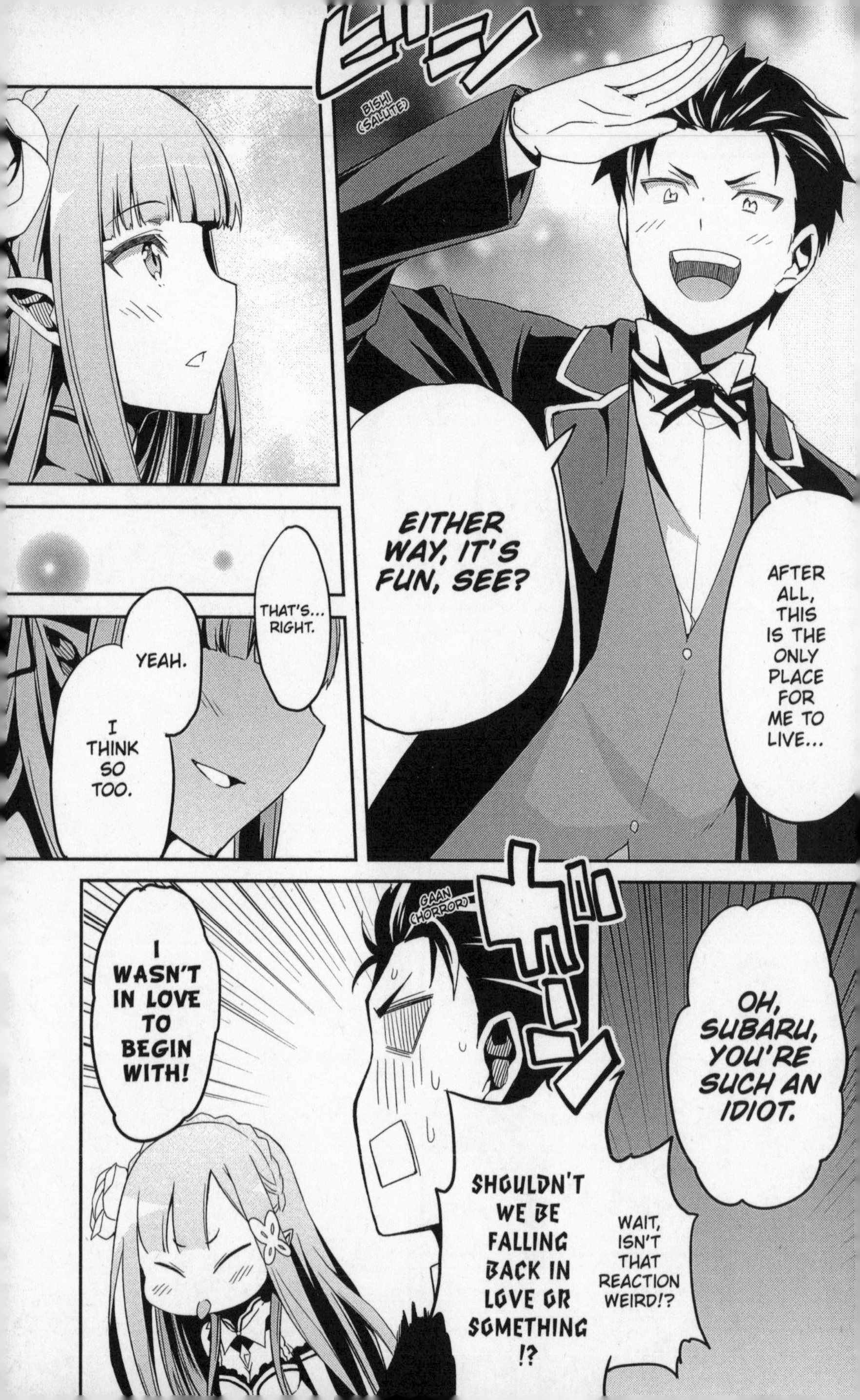
BISHI (SALUTE)
AFTER ALL, THIS IS THE ONLY PLACE FOR ME TO LIVE...
EITHER WAY, IT'S FUN, SEE?
THAT'S... RIGHT.
YEAH.
I THINK SO TOO.
OH, SUBARU, YOU'RE SUCH AN IDIOT.
GAAN (HORROR)
I WASN'T IN LOVE TO BEGIN WITH!
WAIT, ISN'T THAT REACTION WEIRD!?
SHOULDN'T WE BE FALLING BACK IN LOVE OR SOMETHING!?

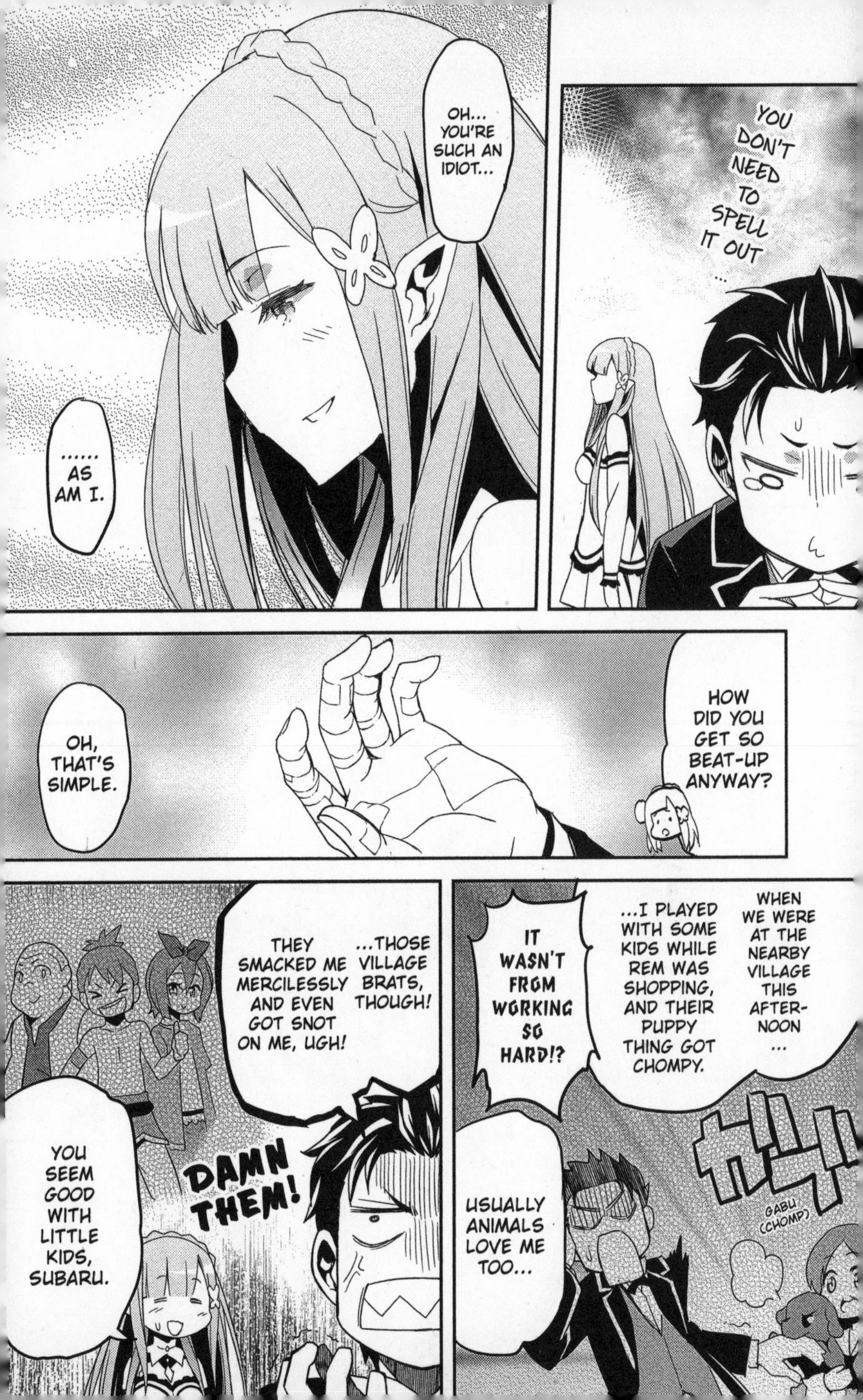

YOU DON'T NEED TO SPELL IT OUT...
OH... YOU'RE SUCH AN IDIOT...
...... AS AM I.
HOW DID YOU GET SO BEAT-UP ANYWAY?
OH, THAT'S SIMPLE.
WHEN WE WERE AT THE NEARBY VILLAGE THIS AFTER-NOON...
...I PLAYED WITH SOME KIDS WHILE REM WAS SHOPPING, AND THEIR PUPPY THING GOT CHOMPY.
IT WASN'T FROM WORKING SO HARD!?
GABU (CHOMP)
USUALLY ANIMALS LOVE ME TOO...
...THOSE VILLAGE BRATS, THOUGH!
THEY SMACKED ME MERCILESSLY AND EVEN GOT SNOT ON ME, UGH!
DAMN THEM!
YOU SEEM GOOD WITH LITTLE KIDS, SUBARU.

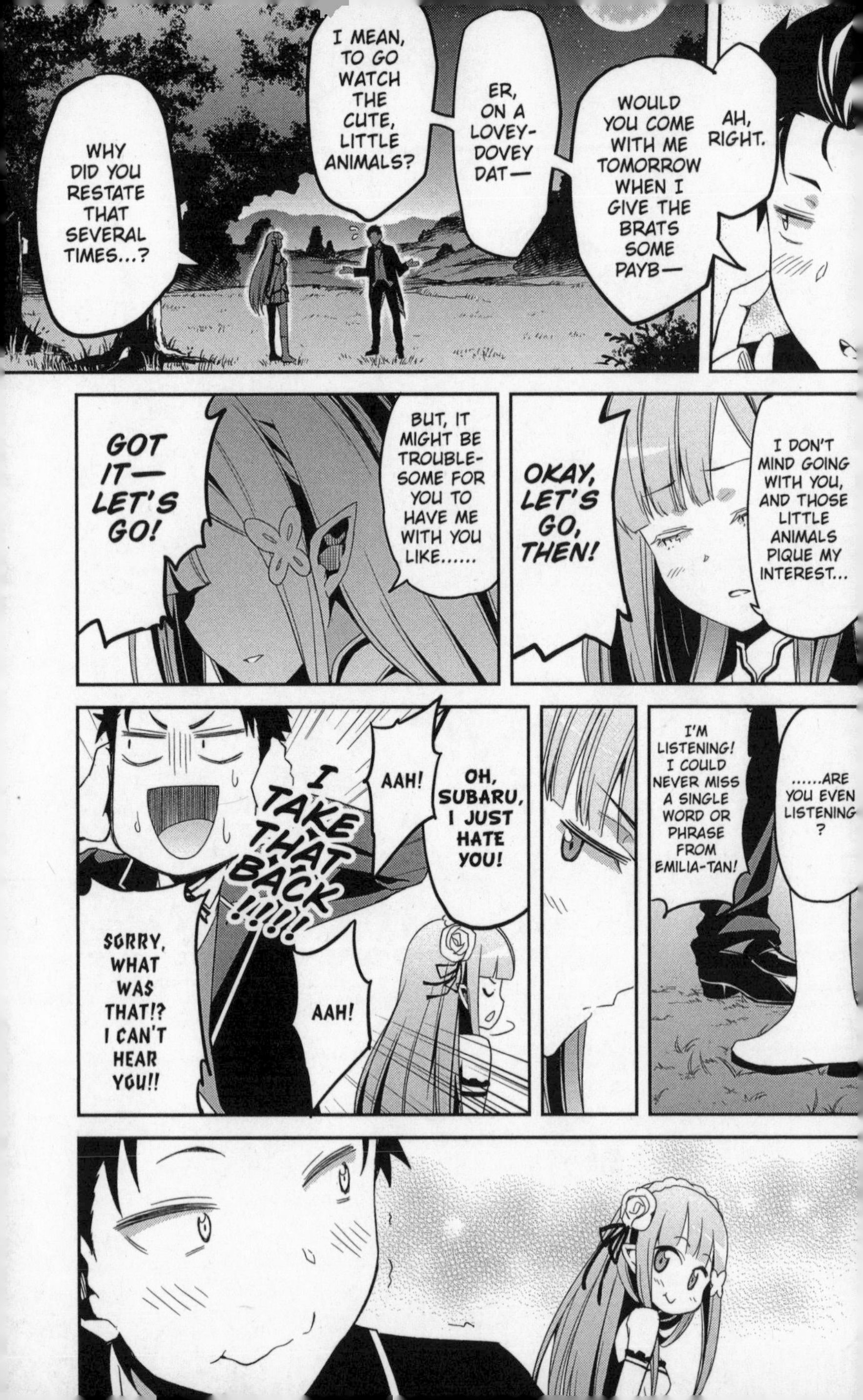
AH, RIGHT.
WOULD YOU COME WITH ME TOMORROW WHEN I GIVE THE BRATS SOME PAYB—
ER, ON A LOVEY-DOVEY DAT—
I MEAN, TO GO WATCH THE CUTE, LITTLE ANIMALS?
WHY DID YOU RESTATE THAT SEVERAL TIMES...?
I DON'T MIND GOING WITH YOU, AND THOSE LITTLE ANIMALS PIQUE MY INTEREST...
OKAY, LET'S GO, THEN!
BUT, IT MIGHT BE TROUBLE-SOME FOR YOU TO HAVE ME WITH YOU LIKE......
GOT IT— LET'S GO!
......ARE YOU EVEN LISTENING?
I'M LISTENING! I COULD NEVER MISS A SINGLE WORD OR PHRASE FROM EMILIA-TAN!
OH, SUBARU, I JUST HATE YOU!
AAH!
I TAKE THAT BACK!!!!!
AAH!
SORRY, WHAT WAS THAT!? I CAN'T HEAR YOU!!

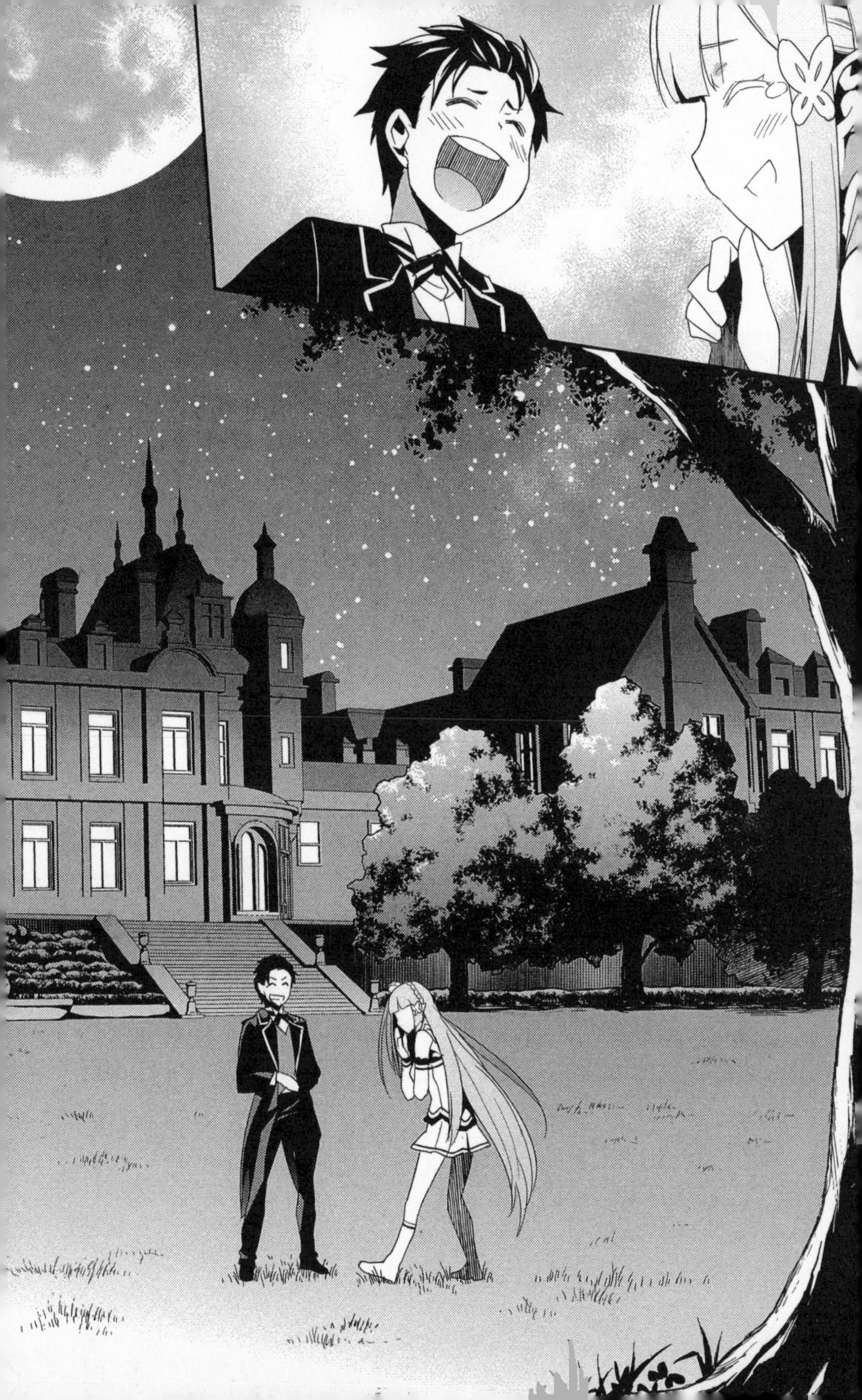

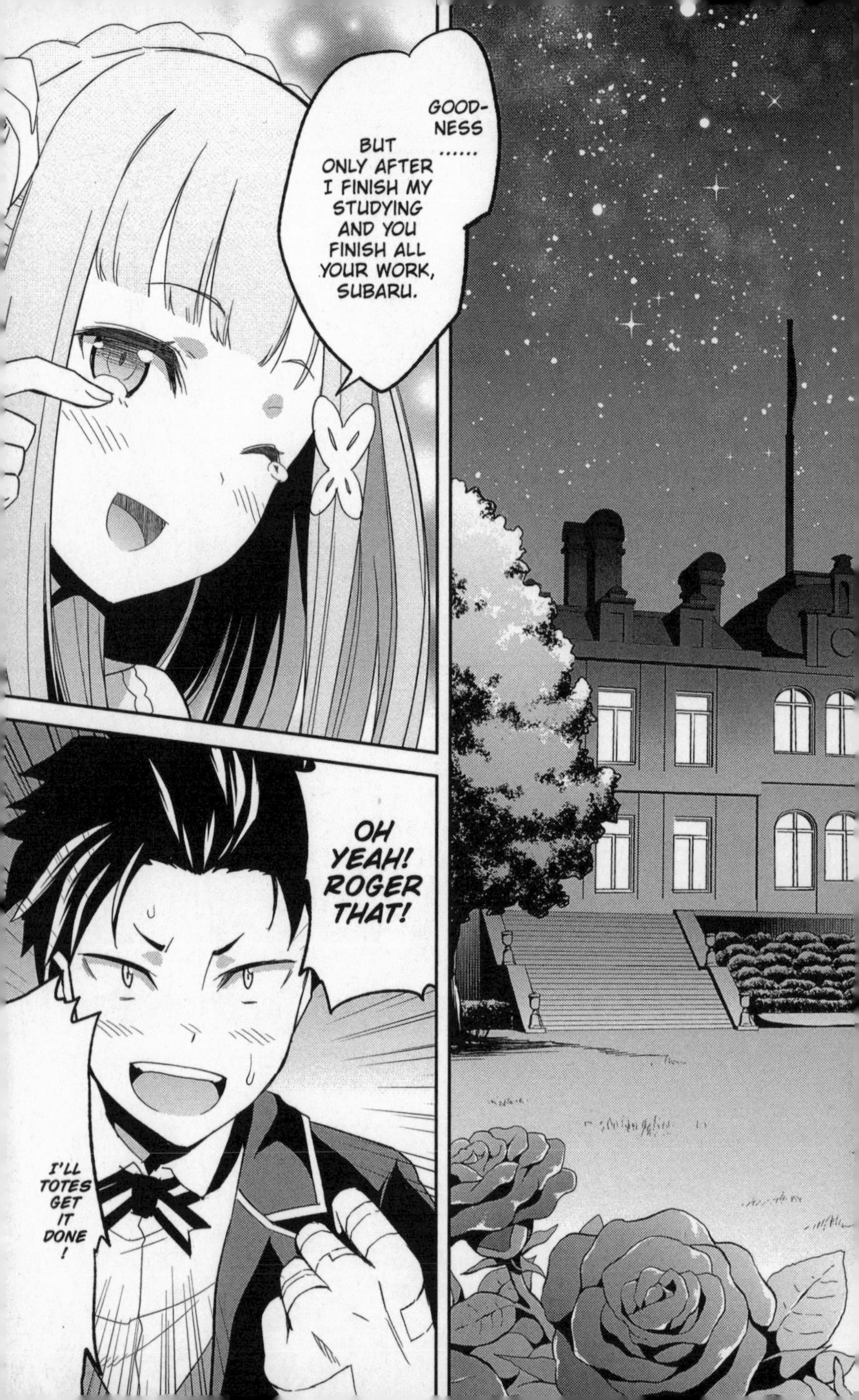
GOOD-NESS ...... BUT ONLY AFTER I FINISH MY STUDYING AND YOU FINISH ALL YOUR WORK, SUBARU.
OH YEAH! ROGER THAT!
I'LL TOTES GET IT DONE!

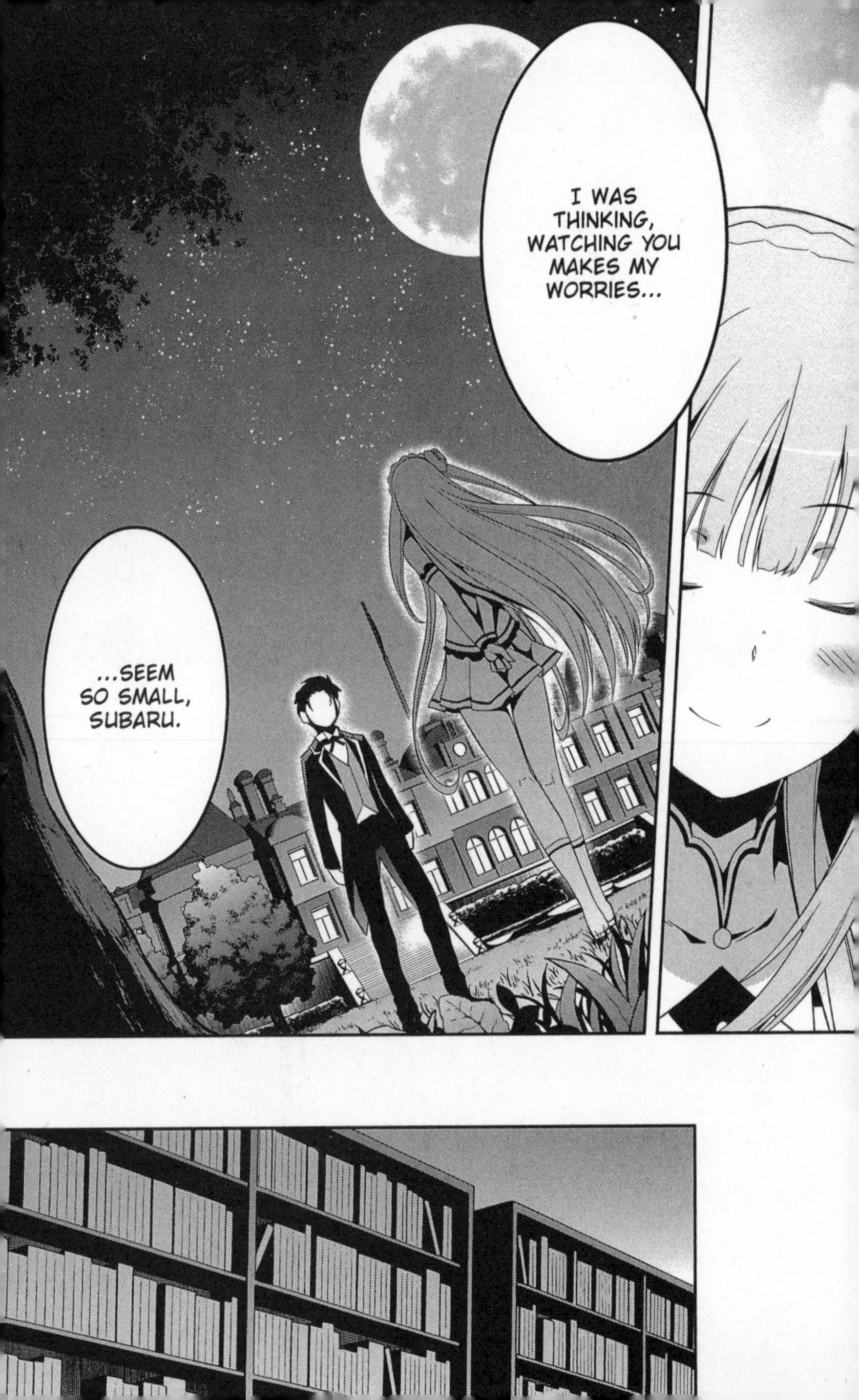
I WAS THINKING, WATCHING YOU MAKES MY WORRIES...
...SEEM SO SMALL, SUBARU.

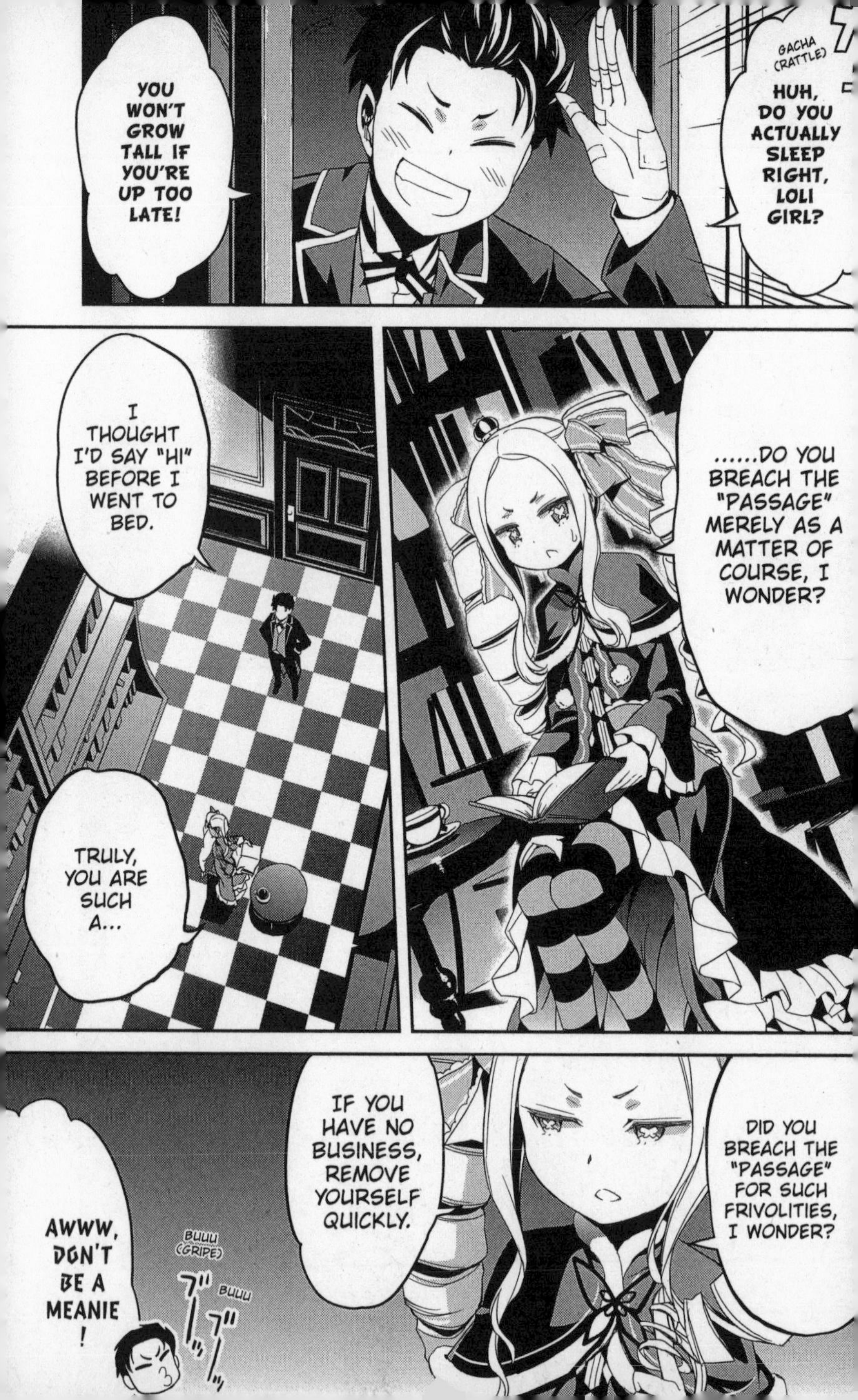
GACHA (RATTLE)
HUH, DO YOU ACTUALLY SLEEP RIGHT, LOLI GIRL?
YOU WON'T GROW TALL IF YOU'RE UP TOO LATE!
......DO YOU BREACH THE "PASSAGE" MERELY AS A MATTER OF COURSE, I WONDER?
I THOUGHT I'D SAY "HI" BEFORE I WENT TO BED.
TRULY, YOU ARE SUCH A...
DID YOU BREACH THE "PASSAGE" FOR SUCH FRIVOLITIES, I WONDER?
IF YOU HAVE NO BUSINESS, REMOVE YOURSELF QUICKLY.
BUUU (GRIPE)
BUUU
AWWW, DON'T BE A MEANIE!

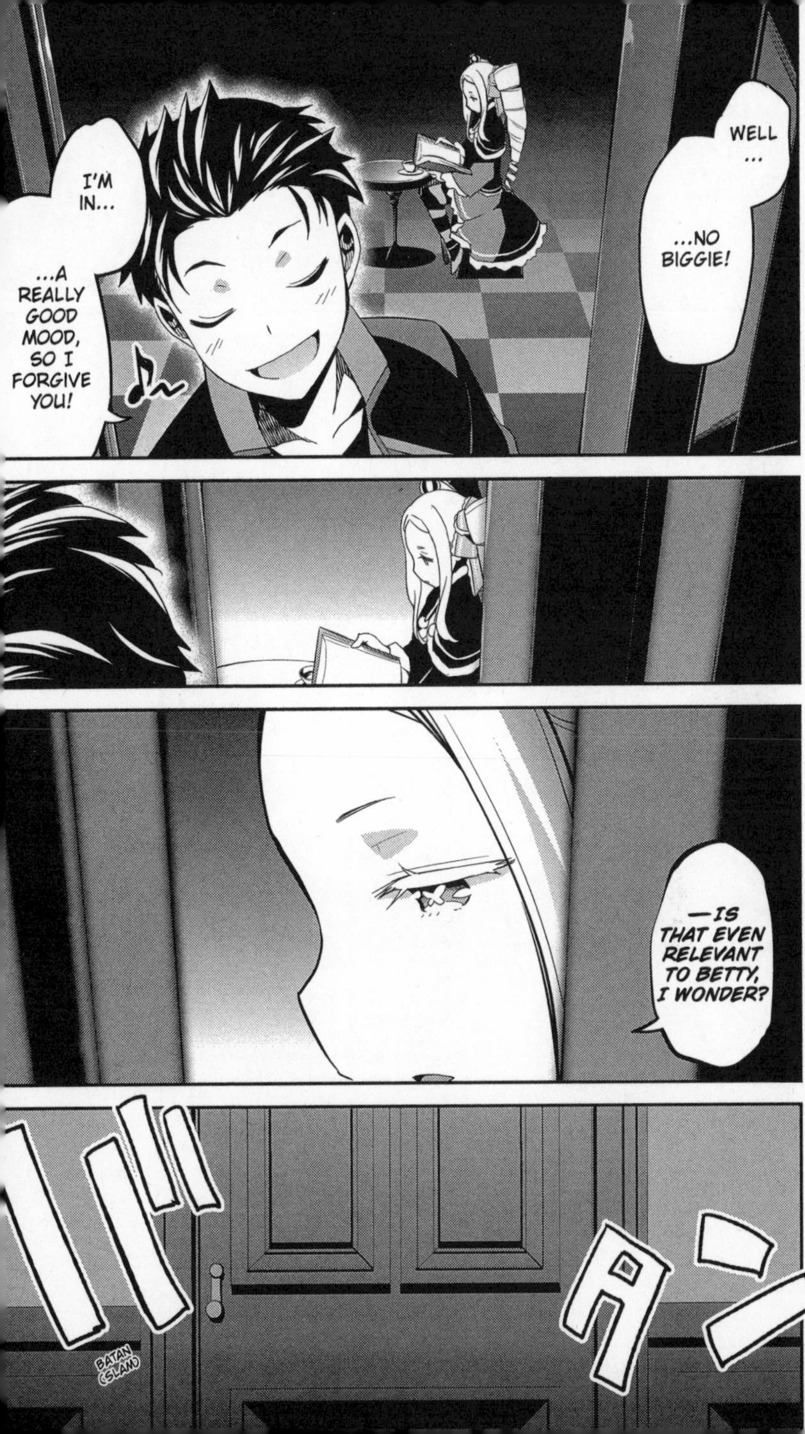
WELL ...
...NO BIGGIE!
I'M IN...
...A REALLY GOOD MOOD, SO I FORGIVE YOU!
—IS THAT EVEN RELEVANT TO BETTY, I WONDER?
BATAN (SLAM)

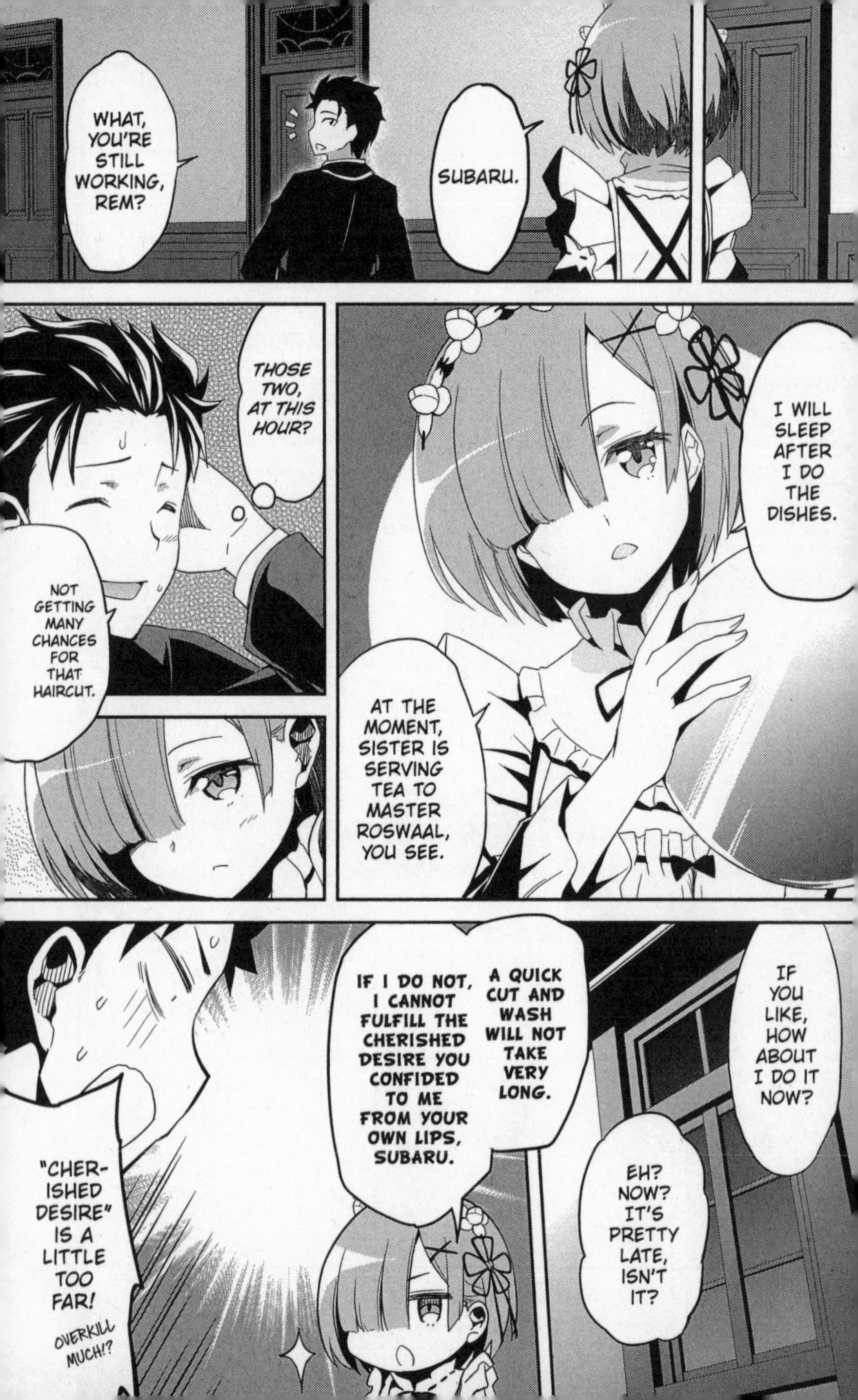
SUBARU.
WHAT, YOU'RE STILL WORKING, REM?
I WILL SLEEP AFTER I DO THE DISHES.
AT THE MOMENT, SISTER IS SERVING TEA TO MASTER ROSWAAL, YOU SEE.
THOSE TWO, AT THIS HOUR?
NOT GETTING MANY CHANCES FOR THAT HAIRCUT.
IF YOU LIKE, HOW ABOUT I DO IT NOW?
A QUICK CUT AND WASH WILL NOT TAKE VERY LONG.
IF I DO NOT, I CANNOT FULFILL THE CHERISHED DESIRE YOU CONFIDED TO ME FROM YOUR OWN LIPS, SUBARU.
EH? NOW? IT'S PRETTY LATE, ISN'T IT?
"CHER-ISHED DESIRE" IS A LITTLE TOO FAR!
OVERKILL MUCH!?

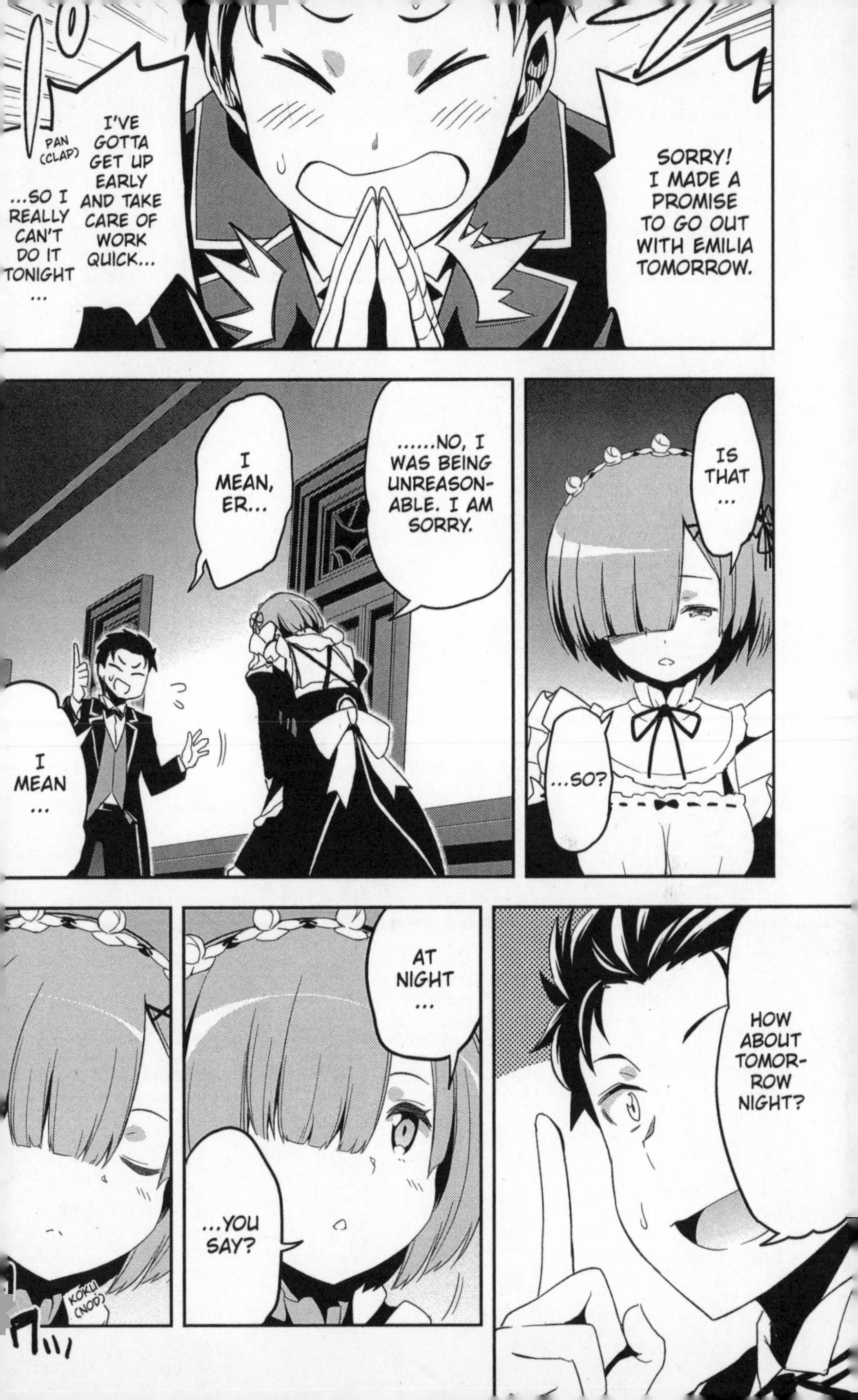
SORRY! I MADE A PROMISE TO GO OUT WITH EMILIA TOMORROW.
I'VE GOTTA GET UP EARLY AND TAKE CARE OF WORK QUICK...
PAN (CLAP)
...SO I REALLY CAN'T DO IT TONIGHT ...
IS THAT ...
...SO?
......NO, I WAS BEING UNREASON-ABLE. I AM SORRY.
I MEAN, ER...
I MEAN ...
HOW ABOUT TOMOR-ROW NIGHT?
AT NIGHT ...
...YOU SAY?
KOKU (NOD)

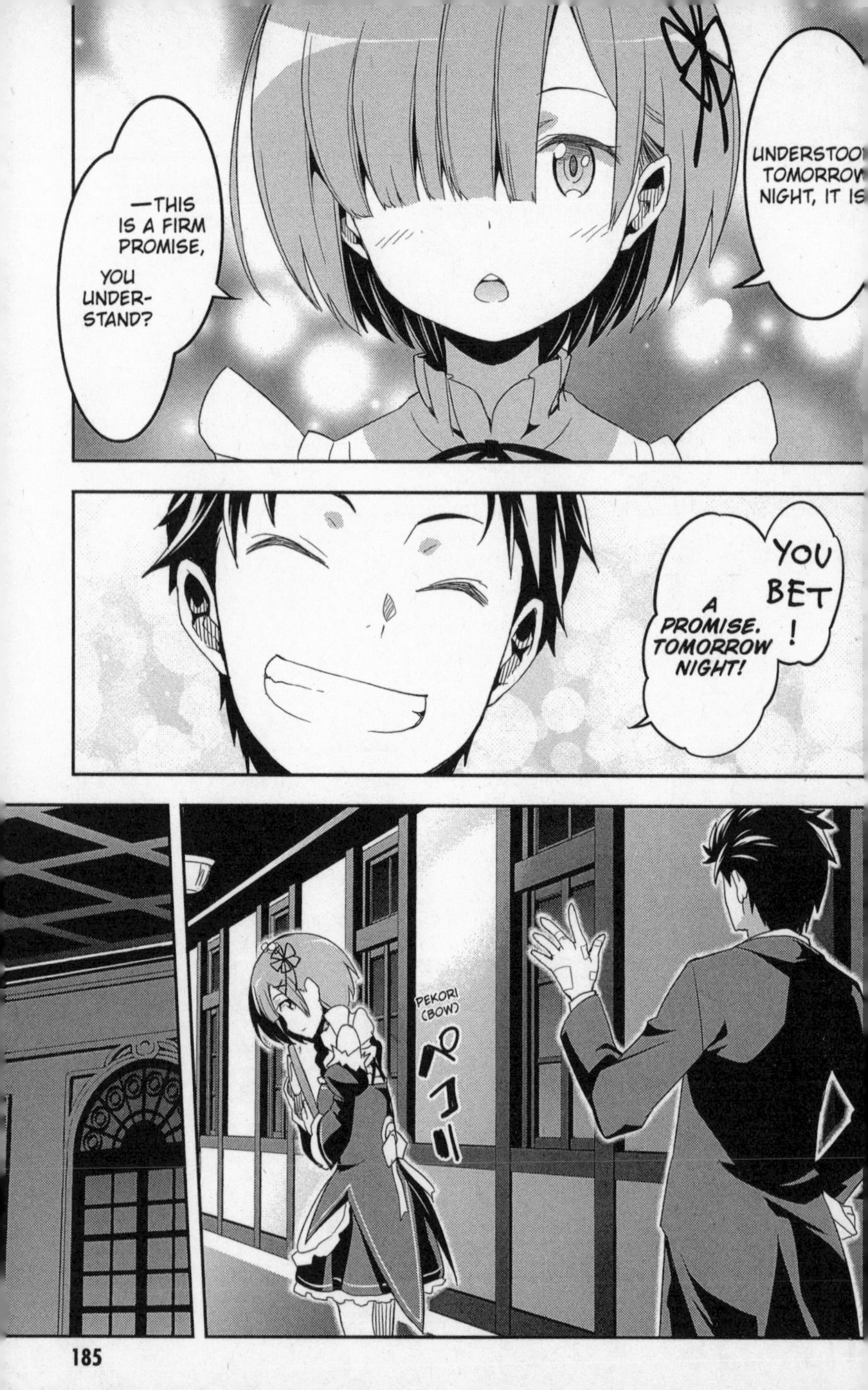
UNDERSTOO TOMORROW NIGHT, IT IS
—THIS IS A FIRM PROMISE, YOU UNDERSTAND?
YOU BET!
A PROMISE. TOMORROW NIGHT!
PEKORI (BOW)
ペコリ

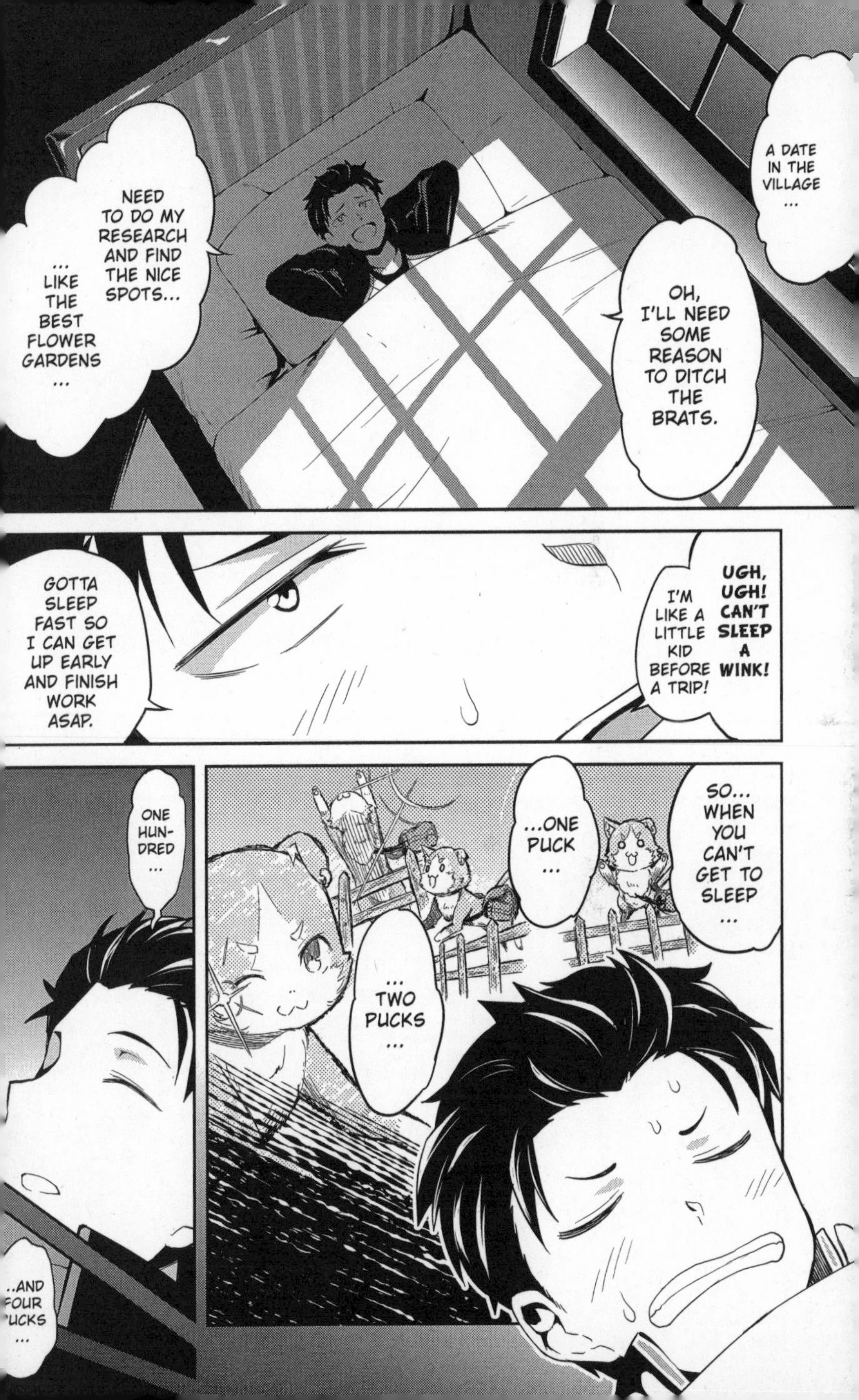

A DATE IN THE VILLAGE...
OH, I'LL NEED SOME REASON TO DITCH THE BRATS.
NEED TO DO MY RESEARCH AND FIND THE NICE SPOTS...
...LIKE THE BEST FLOWER GARDENS...
UGH, UGH! CAN'T SLEEP A WINK!
I'M LIKE A LITTLE KID BEFORE A TRIP!
GOTTA SLEEP FAST SO I CAN GET UP EARLY AND FINISH WORK ASAP.
SO... WHEN YOU CAN'T GET TO SLEEP...
...ONE PUCK...
...TWO PUCKS...
ONE HUNDRED...
..AND FOUR PUCKS...

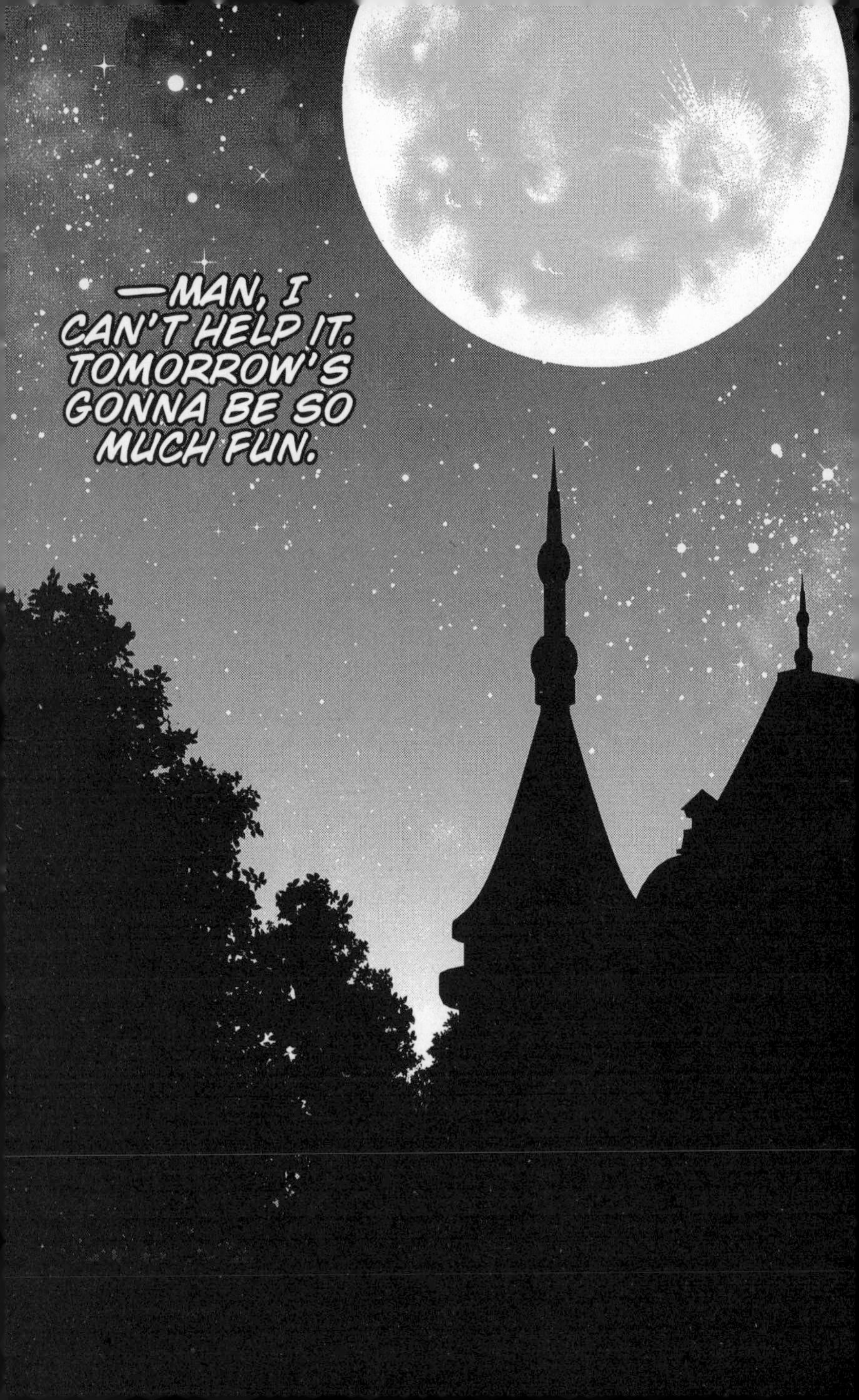
—MAN, I CAN'T HELP IT. TOMORROW'S GONNA BE SO MUCH FUN.

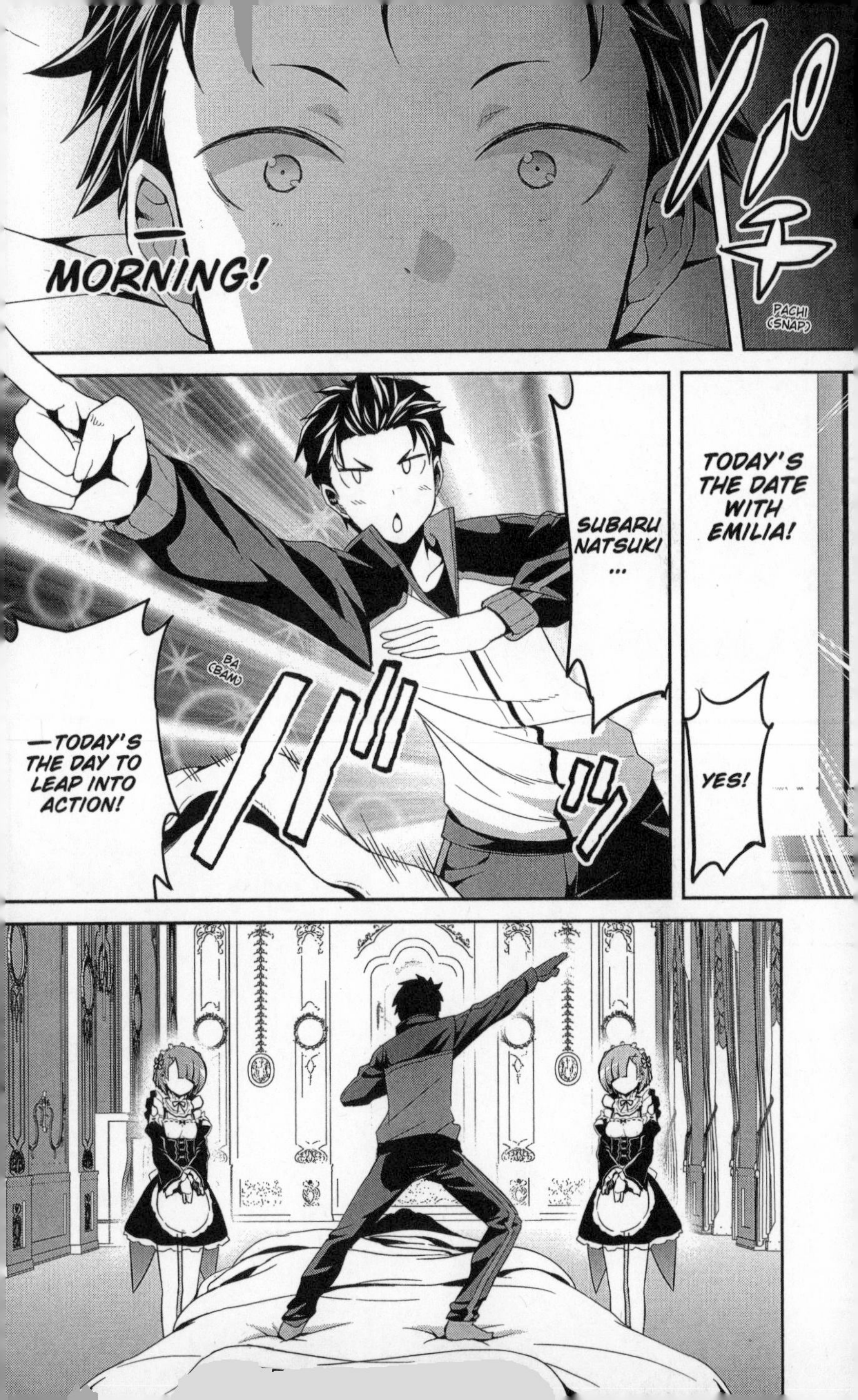
PACHI (SNAP)
MORNING!
TODAY'S THE DATE WITH EMILIA!
YES!
SUBARU NATSUKI ...
BA (BAM)
—TODAY'S THE DAY TO LEAP INTO ACTION!

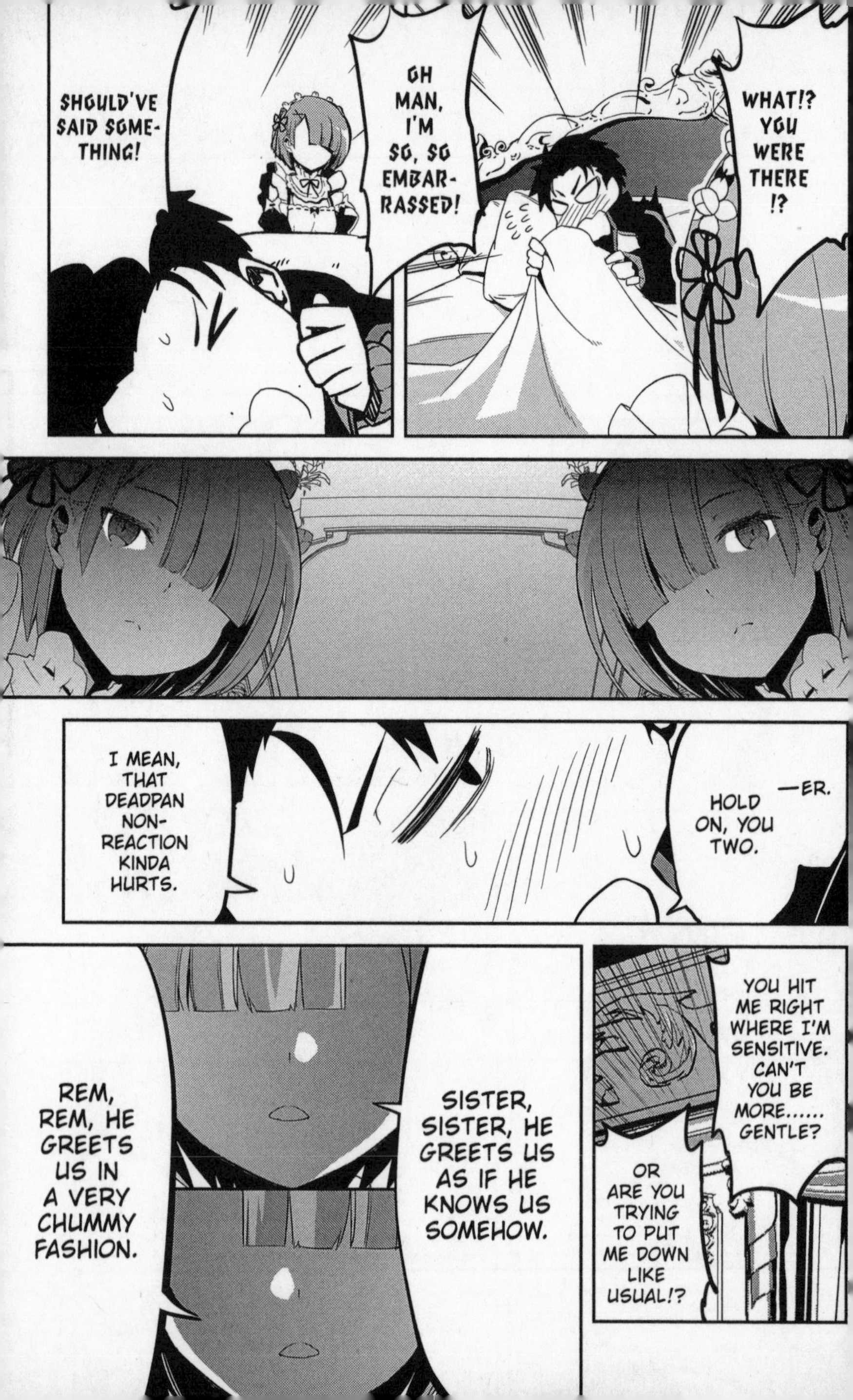
WHAT!? YOU WERE THERE !?
OH MAN, I'M SO, SO EMBARRASSED!
SHOULD'VE SAID SOMETHING!
—ER.
HOLD ON, YOU TWO.
I MEAN, THAT DEADPAN NON-REACTION KINDA HURTS.
YOU HIT ME RIGHT WHERE I'M SENSITIVE. CAN'T YOU BE MORE...... GENTLE?
OR ARE YOU TRYING TO PUT ME DOWN LIKE USUAL!?
SISTER, SISTER, HE GREETS US AS IF HE KNOWS US SOMEHOW.
REM, REM, HE GREETS US IN A VERY CHUMMY FASHION.

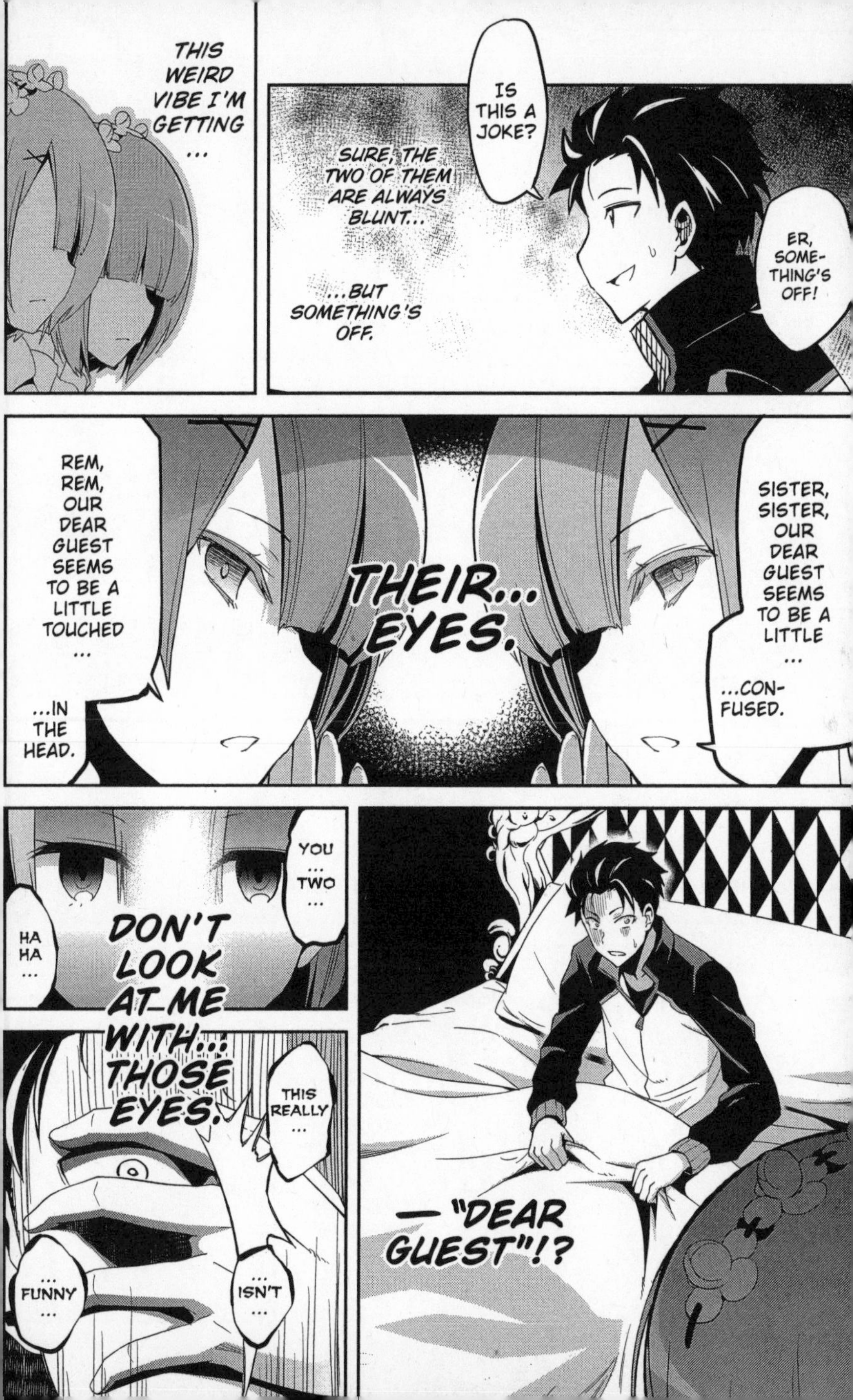
IS THIS A JOKE?
ER, SOME-THING'S OFF!
SURE, THE TWO OF THEM ARE ALWAYS BLUNT...
...BUT SOMETHING'S OFF.
THIS WEIRD VIBE I'M GETTING...
SISTER, SISTER, OUR DEAR GUEST SEEMS TO BE A LITTLE...
...CON-FUSED.
REM, REM, OUR DEAR GUEST SEEMS TO BE A LITTLE TOUCHED...
...IN THE HEAD.
THEIR... EYES.
—"DEAR GUEST"!?
YOU... TWO...
HA HA...
DON'T LOOK AT ME WITH... THOSE EYES.
THIS REALLY...
...ISN'T...
...FUNNY...

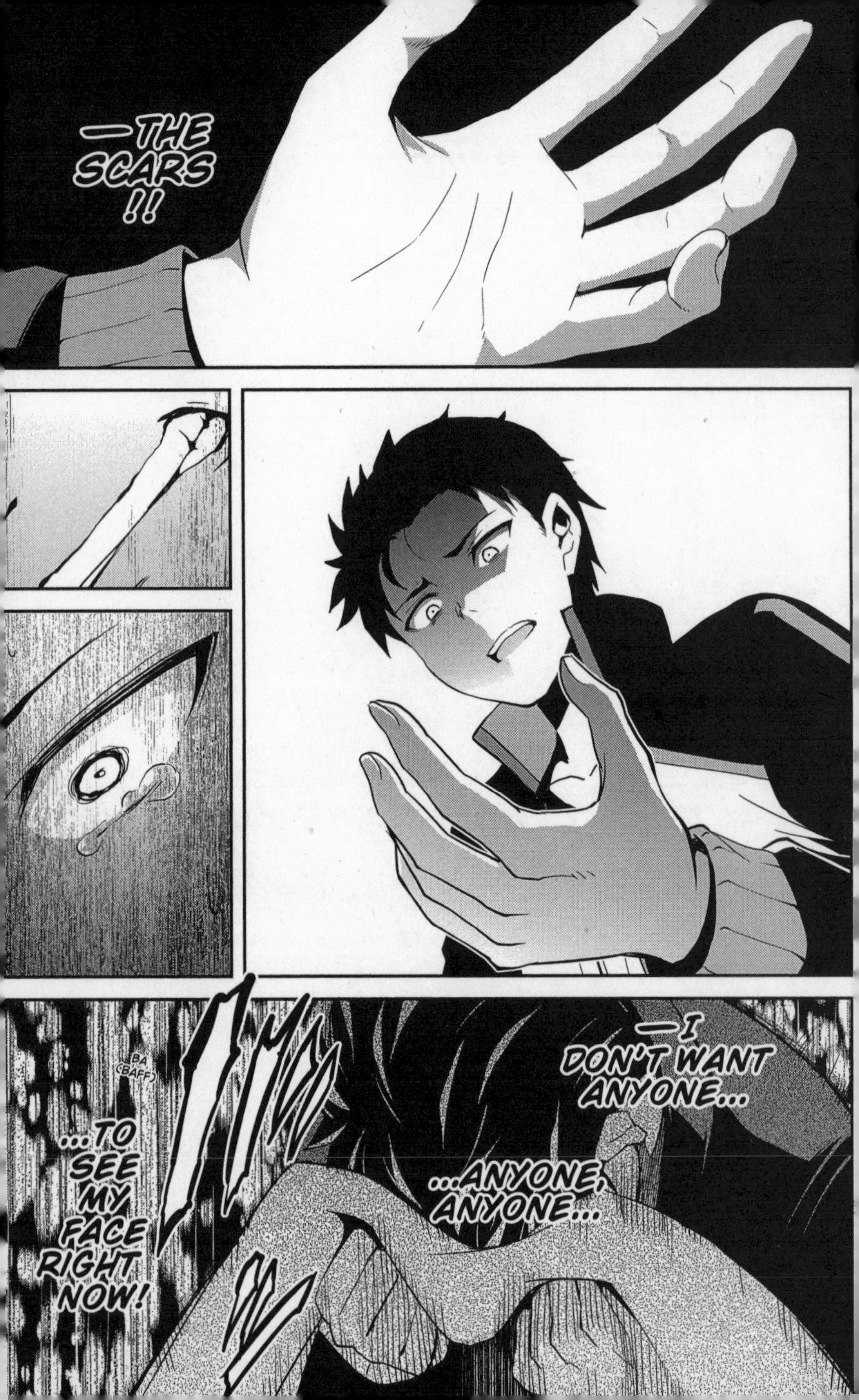
—THE SCARS!!
—I DON'T WANT ANYONE...
...ANYONE, ANYONE...
BA (BAFF)
...TO SEE MY FACE RIGHT NOW!

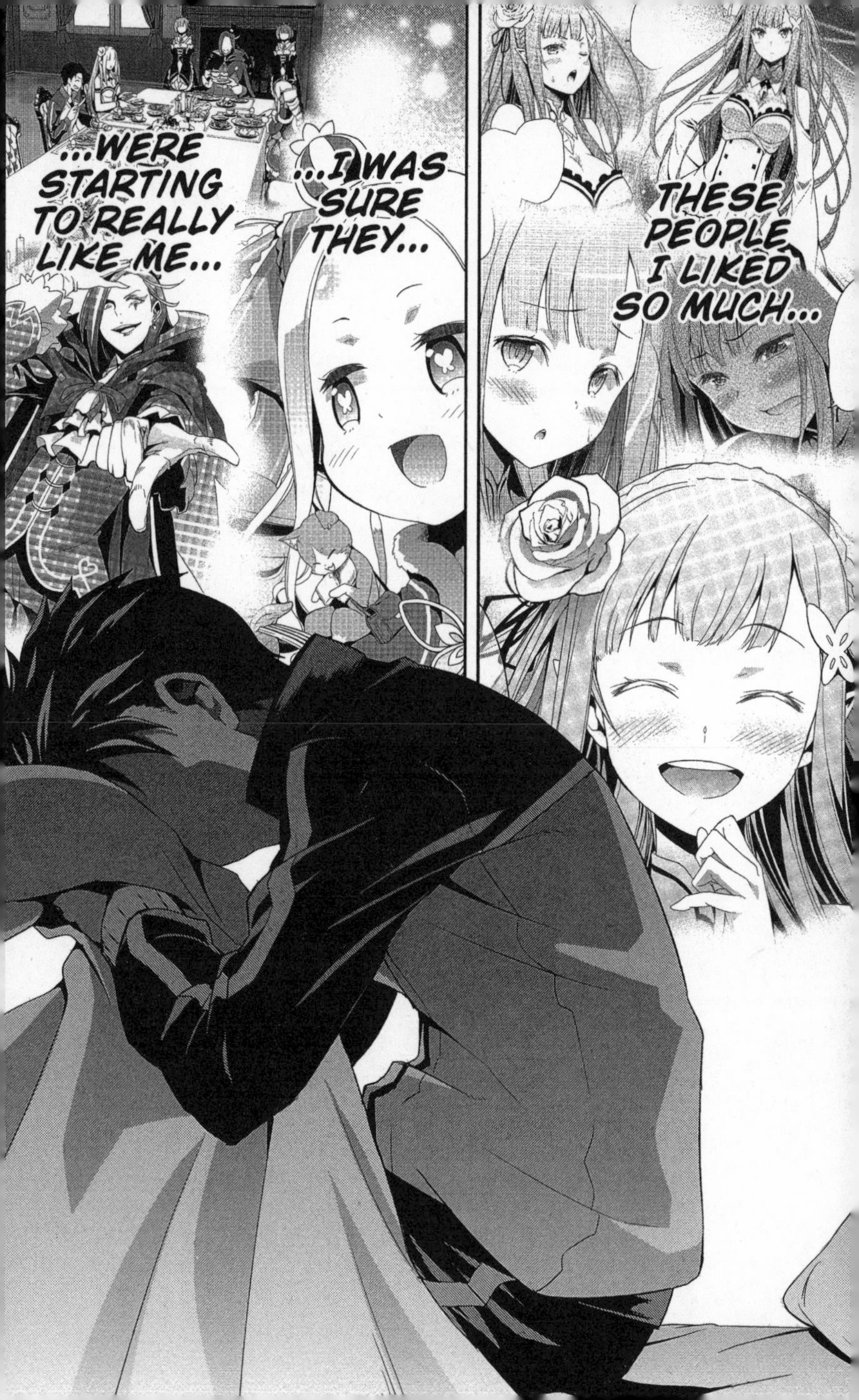
THESE PEOPLE I LIKED SO MUCH...
...I WAS SURE THEY...
...WERE STARTING TO REALLY LIKE ME...

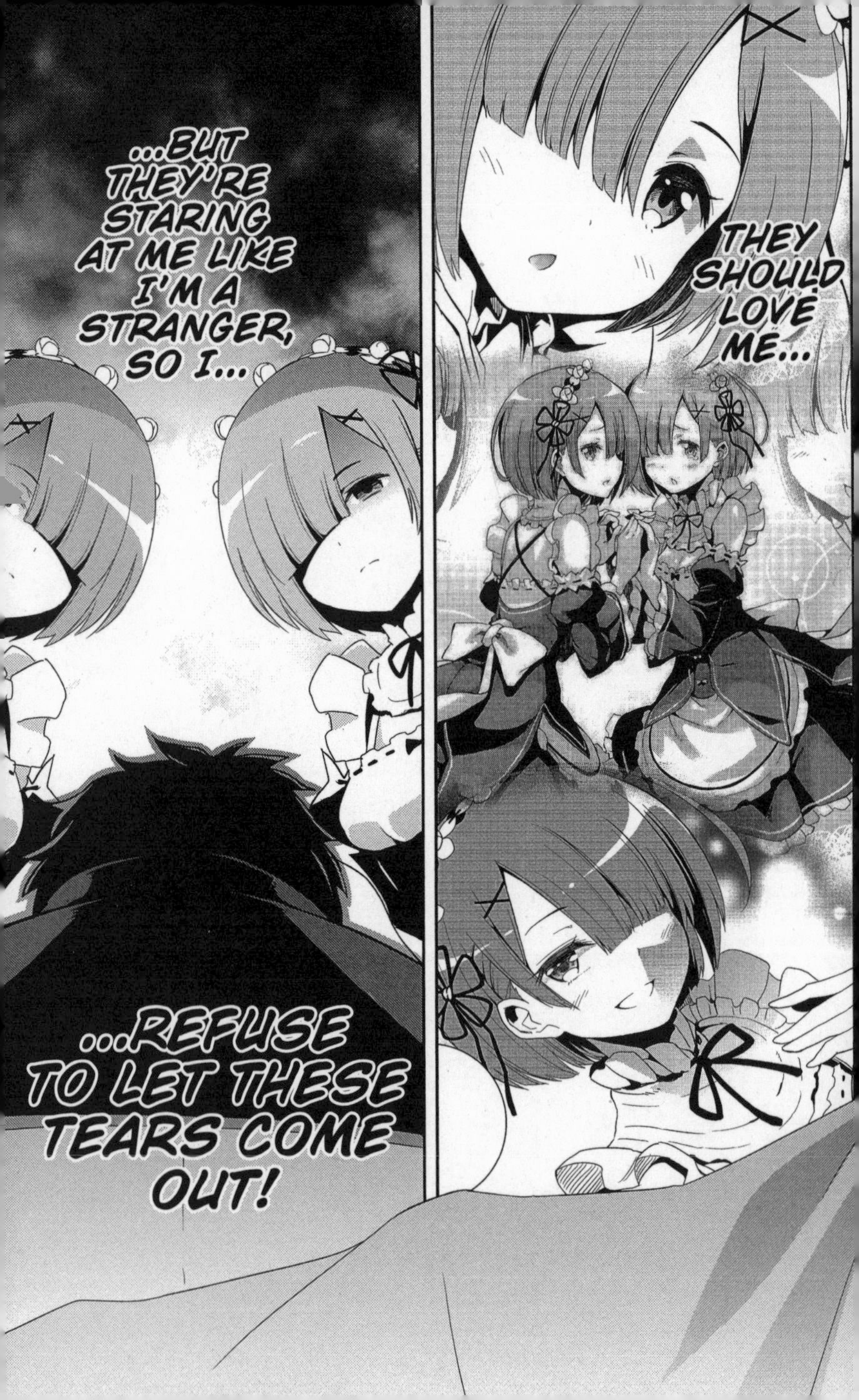
THEY SHOULD LOVE ME...
...BUT THEY'RE STARING AT ME LIKE I'M A STRANGER, SO I...
...REFUSE TO LET THESE TEARS COME OUT!

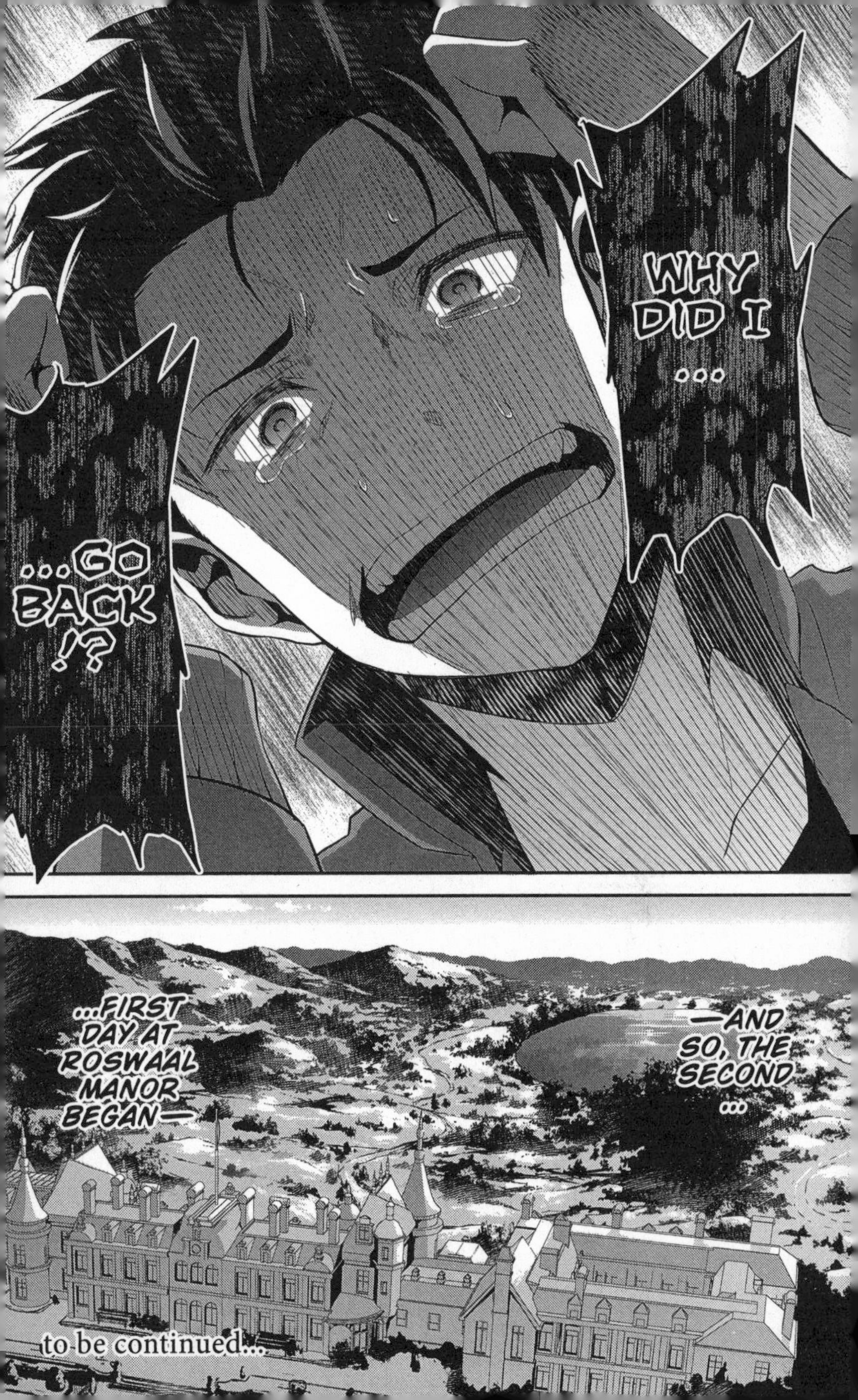
WHY DID I ...
...GO BACK!?
—AND SO, THE SECOND ...
...FIRST DAY AT ROSWAAL MANOR BEGAN—
to be continued...

Plant your feet upon the ground and gaze up to the sky.
For the first time, Subaru spent his time in everyday life in another world.
Ahh, what wonders will the new day bring!?

And then...

Re:ZERO -Starting Life in Another World-

A Week at the Mansion

The only ability Subaru Natsuki gets when he's summoned to another world is time travel via his own death. But to save her, he'll die as many times as it takes.

Turn to the end of the book for an original *Re:ZERO* short story from the light novel author, Tappei Nagatsuki!

Illustration by Shinichirou Otsuka (Character Designer)

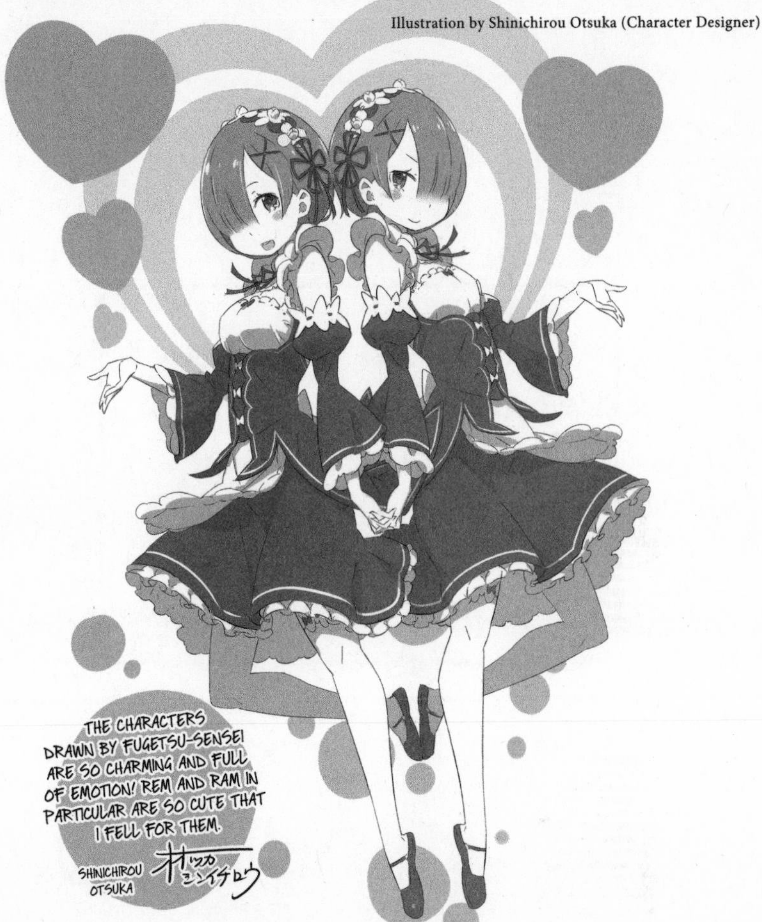
THE CHARACTERS DRAWN BY FUGETSU-SENSEI ARE SO CHARMING AND FULL OF EMOTION! REM AND RAM IN PARTICULAR ARE SO CUTE THAT I FELL FOR THEM.
SHINICHIROU OTSUKA

Re:ZERO -Starting Life in Another World-

Supporting Comments from the Author of the Original Work and the Character Designer

Makoto Fugetsu-sensei, congratulations on *Re: ZERO* Comic Vol. 1 going on sale!
It's a little unusual to start a serialization from the second volume of the original work, the Mansion Arc, but many thanks for having done it!
I imagine putting together Episode 0 and what followed after must have caused some anxiety. That being the case, let me say, it was perfect! No complaints whatsoever.
More than anything, I can't get over how adorable the heroines are! N-no, I haven't forgotten Subaru, our main character, or Rozchi. But, the girls are really cute.
You certainly made the opening image foreshadow the events yet to unfold and gave the nobleman's mansion an appropriate air. I'm extremely satisfied with the splendid, author-like way you set the stage!
As an author, I'm eagerly awaiting how Fugetsu-sensei will use his artistry to convey the nitty-gritty of this death-loop tale. I hope all of you readers are eagerly awaiting the next volume as well!

Author of the Original Work: Tappei Nagatsuki

CONGRATULATIONS ON CHAPTER 2, VOLUME 1 GOING ON SALE!

Re:ZERO -Starting Life in Another World-

Supporting Comments
from Daichi Matsuse

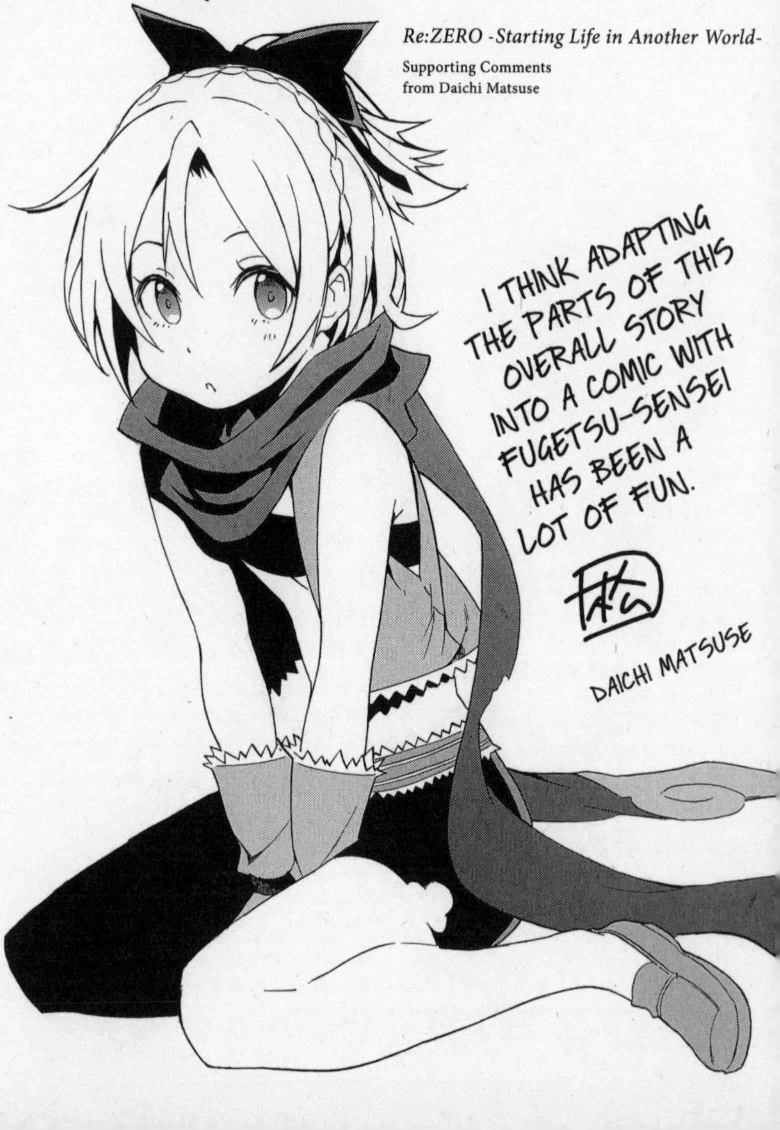
I THINK ADAPTING THE PARTS OF THIS OVERALL STORY INTO A COMIC WITH FUGETSU-SENSEI HAS BEEN A LOT OF FUN.
DAICHI MATSUSE

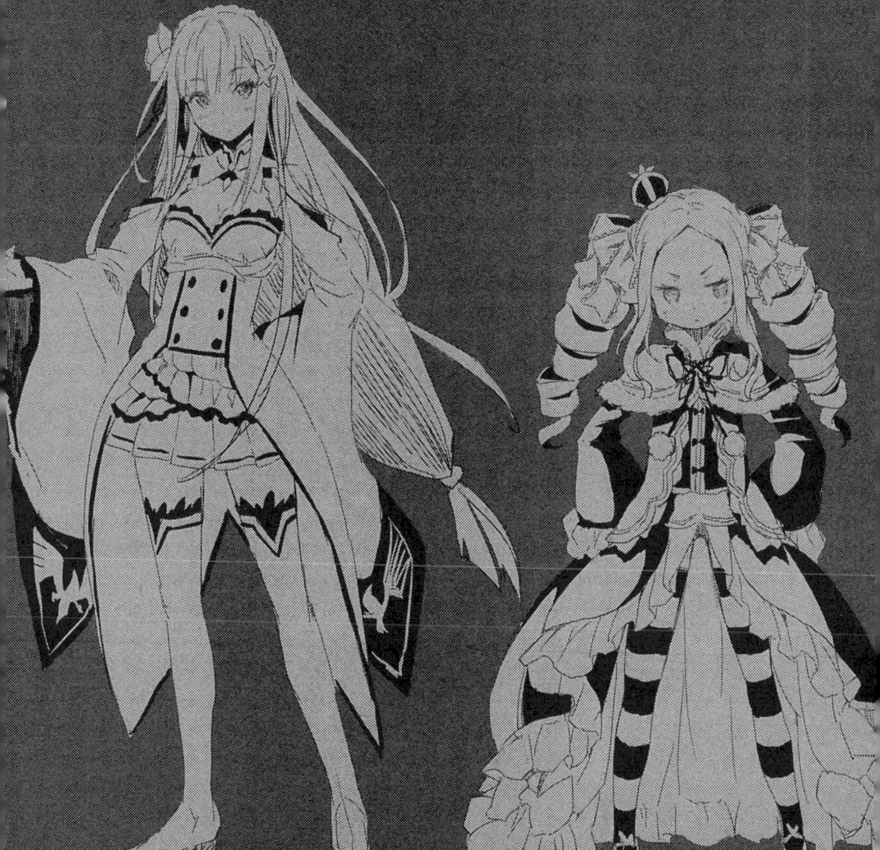

Re:ZeRo

-Starting Life in Another World-

Chapter 2: A Week at the Mansion

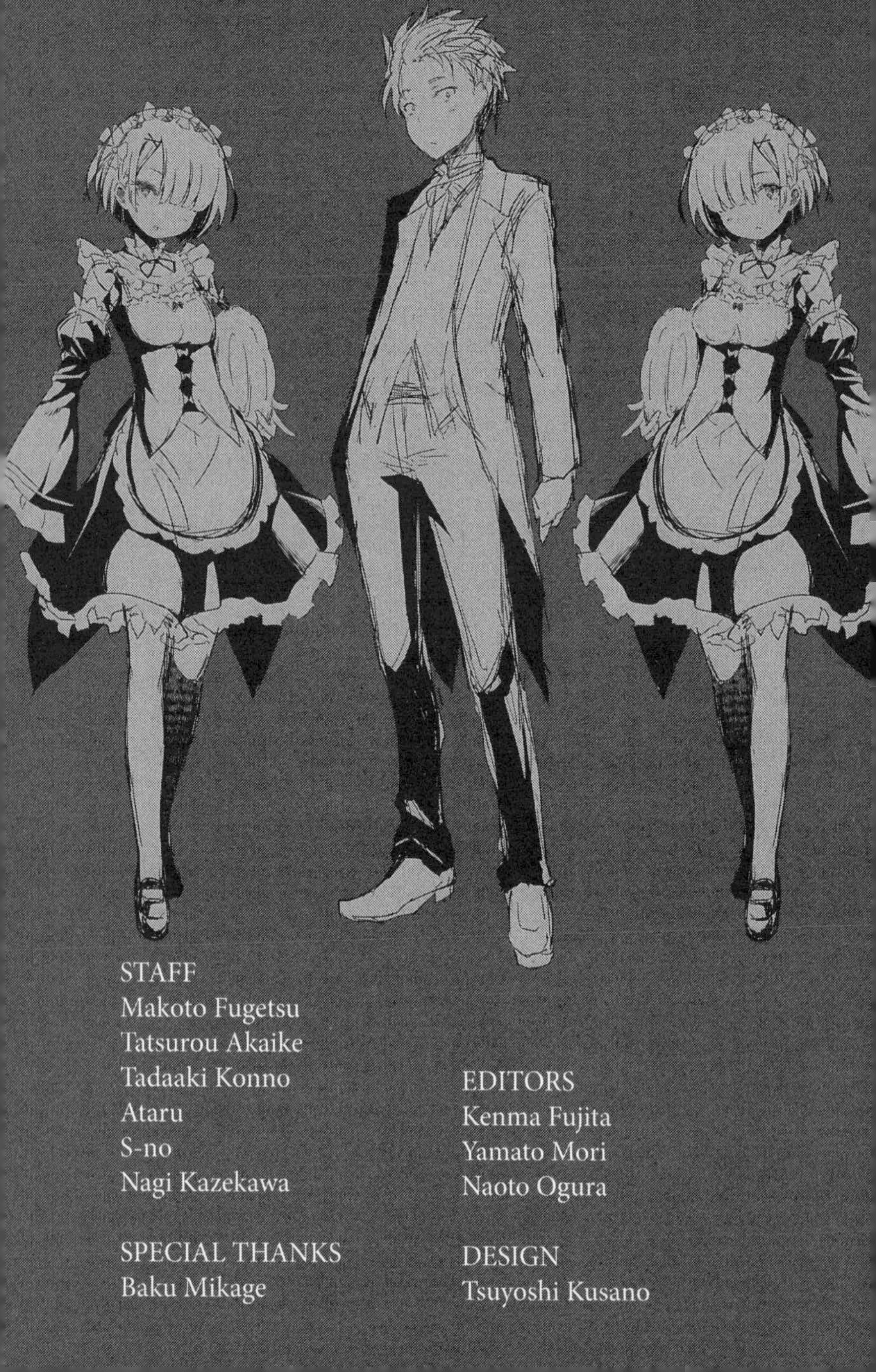

STAFF
Makoto Fugetsu
Tatsurou Akaike
Tadaaki Konno
Ataru
S-no
Nagi Kazekawa

SPECIAL THANKS
Baku Mikage

EDITORS
Kenma Fujita
Yamato Mori
Naoto Ogura

DESIGN
Tsuyoshi Kusano

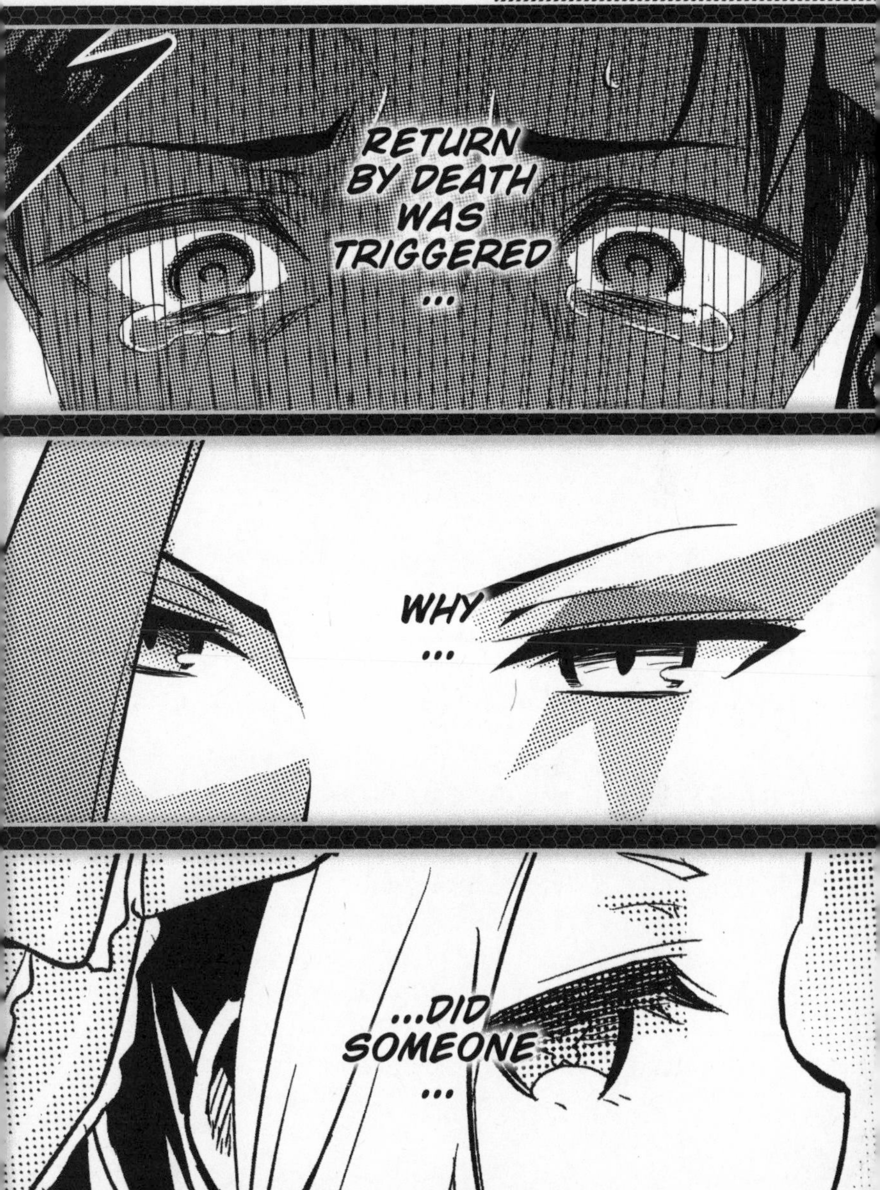
RETURN BY DEATH WAS TRIGGERED ...
WHY ...
...DID SOMEONE ...

NEXT

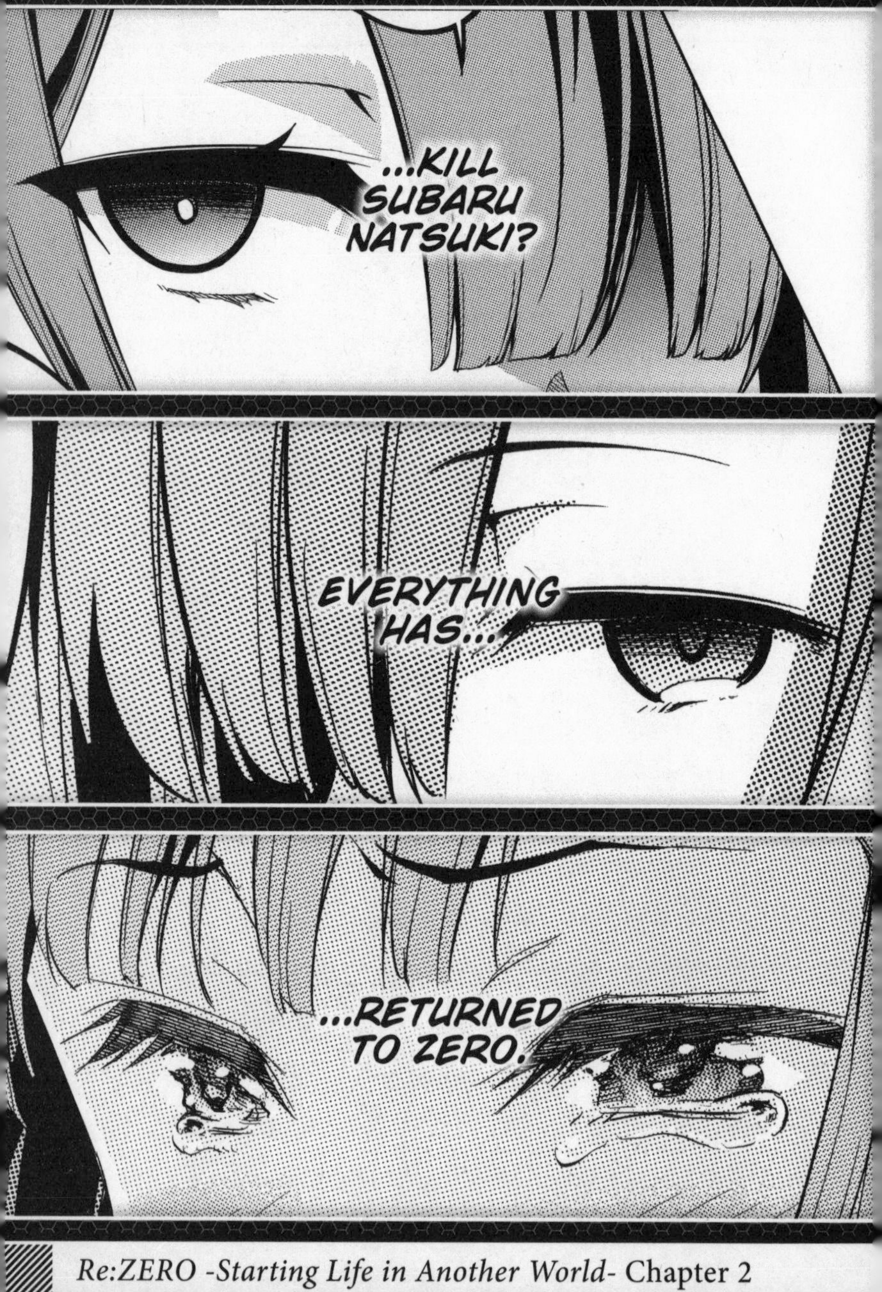
...KILL SUBARU NATSUKI?
EVERYTHING HAS...
...RETURNED TO ZERO.

Re:ZERO -Starting Life in Another World- Chapter 2